FREE Test Taking Tips DVD Offer

To help us better serve you, we have developed a Test Taking Tips DVD that we would like to give you for FREE. **This DVD covers world-class test taking tips that you can use to be even more successful when you are taking your test.**

All that we ask is that you email us your feedback about your study guide. Please let us know what you thought about it – whether that is good, bad or indifferent.

To get your **FREE Test Taking Tips DVD**, email freedvd@studyguideteam.com with "FREE DVD" in the subject line and the following information in the body of the email:

a. The title of your study guide.

b. Your product rating on a scale of 1-5, with 5 being the highest rating.

c. Your feedback about the study guide. What did you think of it?

d. Your full name and shipping address to send your free DVD.

If you have any questions or concerns, please don't hesitate to contact us at freedvd@studyguideteam.com.

Thanks again!

MTEL General Curriculum 03 Study Guide
MTEL General Curriculum Math Subtest & Multi Subject Subtest Test Prep & Practice Test Questions

Test Prep Books Teaching Team

Table of Contents

Quick Overview

As you draw closer to taking your exam, effective preparation becomes more and more important. Thankfully, you have this study guide to help you get ready. Use this guide to help keep your studying on track and refer to it often.

This study guide contains several key sections that will help you be successful on your exam. The guide contains tips for what you should do the night before and the day of the test. Also included are test-taking tips. Knowing the right information is not always enough. Many well-prepared test takers struggle with exams. These tips will help equip you to accurately read, assess, and answer test questions.

A large part of the guide is devoted to showing you what content to expect on the exam and to helping you better understand that content. Near the end of this guide is a practice test so that you can see how well you have grasped the content. Then, answer explanations are provided so that you can understand why you missed certain questions.

Don't try to cram the night before you take your exam. This is not a wise strategy for a few reasons. First, your retention of the information will be low. Your time would be better used by reviewing information you already know rather than trying to learn a lot of new information. Second, you will likely become stressed as you try to gain a large amount of knowledge in a short amount of time. Third, you will be depriving yourself of sleep. So be sure to go to bed at a reasonable time the night before. Being well-rested helps you focus and remain calm.

Be sure to eat a substantial breakfast the morning of the exam. If you are taking the exam in the afternoon, be sure to have a good lunch as well. Being hungry is distracting and can make it difficult to focus. You have hopefully spent lots of time preparing for the exam. Don't let an empty stomach get in the way of success!

When travelling to the testing center, leave earlier than needed. That way, you have a buffer in case you experience any delays. This will help you remain calm and will keep you from missing your appointment time at the testing center.

Be sure to pace yourself during the exam. Don't try to rush through the exam. There is no need to risk performing poorly on the exam just so you can leave the testing center early. Allow yourself to use all of the allotted time if needed.

Remain positive while taking the exam even if you feel like you are performing poorly. Thinking about the content you should have mastered will not help you perform better on the exam.

Once the exam is complete, take some time to relax. Even if you feel that you need to take the exam again, you will be well served by some down time before you begin studying again. It's often easier to convince yourself to study if you know that it will come with a reward!

Test-Taking Strategies

1. Predicting the Answer

When you feel confident in your preparation for a multiple-choice test, try predicting the answer before reading the answer choices. This is especially useful on questions that test objective factual knowledge or that ask you to fill in a blank. By predicting the answer before reading the available choices, you eliminate the possibility that you will be distracted or led astray by an incorrect answer choice. You will feel more confident in your selection if you read the question, predict the answer, and then find your prediction among the answer choices. After using this strategy, be sure to still read all of the answer choices carefully and completely. If you feel unprepared, you should not attempt to predict the answers. This would be a waste of time and an opportunity for your mind to wander in the wrong direction.

2. Reading the Whole Question

Too often, test takers scan a multiple-choice question, recognize a few familiar words, and immediately jump to the answer choices. Test authors are aware of this common impatience, and they will sometimes prey upon it. For instance, a test author might subtly turn the question into a negative, or he or she might redirect the focus of the question right at the end. The only way to avoid falling into these traps is to read the entirety of the question carefully before reading the answer choices.

3. Looking for Wrong Answers

Long and complicated multiple-choice questions can be intimidating. One way to simplify a difficult multiple-choice question is to eliminate all of the answer choices that are clearly wrong. In most sets of answers, there will be at least one selection that can be dismissed right away. If the test is administered on paper, the test taker could draw a line through it to indicate that it may be ignored; otherwise, the test taker will have to perform this operation mentally or on scratch paper. In either case, once the obviously incorrect answers have been eliminated, the remaining choices may be considered. Sometimes identifying the clearly wrong answers will give the test taker some information about the correct answer. For instance, if one of the remaining answer choices is a direct opposite of one of the eliminated answer choices, it may well be the correct answer. The opposite of obviously wrong is obviously right! Of course, this is not always the case. Some answers are obviously incorrect simply because they are irrelevant to the question being asked. Still, identifying and eliminating some incorrect answer choices is a good way to simplify a multiple-choice question.

4. Don't Overanalyze

Anxious test takers often overanalyze questions. When you are nervous, your brain will often run wild, causing you to make associations and discover clues that don't actually exist. If you feel that this may be a problem for you, do whatever you can to slow down during the test. Try taking a deep breath or counting to ten. As you read and consider the question, restrict yourself to the particular words used by the author. Avoid thought tangents about what the author *really* meant, or what he or she was *trying* to say. The only things that matter on a multiple-choice test are the words that are actually in the question. You must avoid reading too much into a multiple-choice question, or supposing that the writer meant something other than what he or she wrote.

5. No Need for Panic

It is wise to learn as many strategies as possible before taking a multiple-choice test, but it is likely that you will come across a few questions for which you simply don't know the answer. In this situation, avoid panicking. Because most multiple-choice tests include dozens of questions, the relative value of a single wrong answer is small. Moreover, your failure on one question has no effect on your success elsewhere on the test. As much as possible, you should compartmentalize each question on a multiple-choice test. In other words, you should not allow your feelings about one question to affect your success on the others. When you find a question that you either don't understand or don't know how to answer, just take a deep breath and do your best. Read the entire question slowly and carefully. Try rephrasing the question a couple of different ways. Then, read all of the answer choices carefully. After eliminating obviously wrong answers, make a selection and move on to the next question.

6. Confusing Answer Choices

When working on a difficult multiple-choice question, there may be a tendency to focus on the answer choices that are the easiest to understand. Many people, whether consciously or not, gravitate to the answer choices that require the least concentration, knowledge, and memory. This is a mistake. When you come across an answer choice that is confusing, you should give it extra attention. A question might be confusing because you do not know the subject matter to which it refers. If this is the case, don't eliminate the answer before you have affirmatively settled on another. When you come across an answer choice of this type, set it aside as you look at the remaining choices. If you can confidently assert that one of the other choices is correct, you can leave the confusing answer aside. Otherwise, you will need to take a moment to try to better understand the confusing answer choice. Rephrasing is one way to tease out the sense of a confusing answer choice.

7. Your First Instinct

Many people struggle with multiple-choice tests because they overthink the questions. If you have studied sufficiently for the test, you should be prepared to trust your first instinct once you have carefully and completely read the question and all of the answer choices. There is a great deal of research suggesting that the mind can come to the correct conclusion very quickly once it has obtained all of the relevant information. At times, it may seem to you as if your intuition is working faster even than your reasoning mind. This may in fact be true. The knowledge you obtain while studying may be retrieved from your subconscious before you have a chance to work out the associations that support it. Verify your instinct by working out the reasons that it should be trusted.

8. Key Words

Many test takers struggle with multiple-choice questions because they have poor reading comprehension skills. Quickly reading and understanding a multiple-choice question requires a mixture of skill and experience. To help with this, try jotting down a few key words and phrases on a piece of scrap paper. Doing this concentrates the process of reading and forces the mind to weigh the relative importance of the question's parts. In selecting words and phrases to write down, the test taker thinks about the question more deeply and carefully. This is especially true for multiple-choice questions that are preceded by a long prompt.

9. Subtle Negatives

One of the oldest tricks in the multiple-choice test writer's book is to subtly reverse the meaning of a question with a word like *not* or *except*. If you are not paying attention to each word in the question, you can easily be led astray by this trick. For instance, a common question format is, "Which of the following is...?" Obviously, if the question instead is, "Which of the following is not...?," then the answer will be quite different. Even worse, the test makers are aware of the potential for this mistake and will include one answer choice that would be correct if the question were not negated or reversed. A test taker who misses the reversal will find what he or she believes to be a correct answer and will be so confident that he or she will fail to reread the question and discover the original error. The only way to avoid this is to practice a wide variety of multiple-choice questions and to pay close attention to each and every word.

10. Reading Every Answer Choice

It may seem obvious, but you should always read every one of the answer choices! Too many test takers fall into the habit of scanning the question and assuming that they understand the question because they recognize a few key words. From there, they pick the first answer choice that answers the question they believe they have read. Test takers who read all of the answer choices might discover that one of the latter answer choices is actually *more* correct. Moreover, reading all of the answer choices can remind you of facts related to the question that can help you arrive at the correct answer. Sometimes, a misstatement or incorrect detail in one of the latter answer choices will trigger your memory of the subject and will enable you to find the right answer. Failing to read all of the answer choices is like not reading all of the items on a restaurant menu: you might miss out on the perfect choice.

11. Spot the Hedges

One of the keys to success on multiple-choice tests is paying close attention to every word. This is never more true than with words like *almost*, *most*, *some*, and *sometimes*. These words are called "hedges" because they indicate that a statement is not totally true or not true in every place and time. An absolute statement will contain no hedges, but in many subjects, like literature and history, the answers are not always straightforward or absolute. There are always exceptions to the rules in these subjects. For this reason, you should favor those multiple-choice questions that contain hedging language. The presence of qualifying words indicates that the author is taking special care with his or her words, which is certainly important when composing the right answer. After all, there are many ways to be wrong, but there is only one way to be right! For this reason, it is wise to avoid answers that are absolute when taking a multiple-choice test. An absolute answer is one that says things are either all one way or all another. They often include words like *every*, *always*, *best*, and *never*. If you are taking a multiple-choice test in a subject that doesn't lend itself to absolute answers, be on your guard if you see any of these words.

12. Long Answers

In many subject areas, the answers are not simple. As already mentioned, the right answer often requires hedges. Another common feature of the answers to a complex or subjective question are qualifying clauses, which are groups of words that subtly modify the meaning of the sentence. If the question or answer choice describes a rule to which there are exceptions or the subject matter is complicated, ambiguous, or confusing, the correct answer will require many words in order to be expressed clearly and accurately. In essence, you should not be deterred by answer choices that seem excessively long. Oftentimes, the author of the text will not be able to write the correct answer without offering some qualifications and modifications. Your job is to read the answer choices thoroughly and completely and to select the one that most accurately and precisely answers the question.

13. Restating to Understand

Sometimes, a question on a multiple-choice test is difficult not because of what it asks but because of how it is written. If this is the case, restate the question or answer choice in different words. This process serves a couple of important purposes. First, it forces you to concentrate on the core of the question. In order to rephrase the question accurately, you have to understand it well. Rephrasing the question will concentrate your mind on the key words and ideas. Second, it will present the information to your mind in a fresh way. This process may trigger your memory and render some useful scrap of information picked up while studying.

14. True Statements

Sometimes an answer choice will be true in itself, but it does not answer the question. This is one of the main reasons why it is essential to read the question carefully and completely before proceeding to the answer choices. Too often, test takers skip ahead to the answer choices and look for true statements. Having found one of these, they are content to select it without reference to the question above. Obviously, this provides an easy way for test makers to play tricks. The savvy test taker will always read the entire question before turning to the answer choices. Then, having settled on a correct answer choice, he or she will refer to the original question and ensure that the selected answer is relevant. The mistake of choosing a correct-but-irrelevant answer choice is especially common on questions related to specific pieces of objective knowledge, like historical or scientific facts. A prepared test taker will have a wealth of factual knowledge at his or her disposal, and should not be careless in its application.

15. No Patterns

One of the more dangerous ideas that circulates about multiple-choice tests is that the correct answers tend to fall into patterns. These erroneous ideas range from a belief that B and C are the most common right answers, to the idea that an unprepared test-taker should answer "A-B-A-C-A-D-A-B-A." It cannot be emphasized enough that pattern-seeking of this type is exactly the WRONG way to approach a multiple-choice test. To begin with, it is highly unlikely that the test maker will plot the correct answers according to some predetermined pattern. The questions are scrambled and delivered in a random order. Furthermore, even if the test maker was following a pattern in the assignation of correct answers, there is no reason why the test taker would know which pattern he or she was using. Any attempt to discern a pattern in the answer choices is a waste of time and a distraction from the real work of taking the test. A test taker would be much better served by extra preparation before the test than by reliance on a pattern in the answers.

FREE DVD OFFER

Don't forget that doing well on your exam includes both understanding the test content and understanding how to use what you know to do well on the test. We offer a completely FREE Test Taking Tips DVD that covers world class test taking tips that you can use to be even more successful when you are taking your test.

All that we ask is that you email us your feedback about your study guide. To get your **FREE Test Taking Tips DVD**, email freedvd@studyguideteam.com with "FREE DVD" in the subject line and the following information in the body of the email:

- The title of your study guide.
- Your product rating on a scale of 1-5, with 5 being the highest rating.
- Your feedback about the study guide. What did you think of it?
- Your full name and shipping address to send your free DVD.

Introduction to the MTEL General Curriculum (03)

Function of the Test

The MTEL (Massachusetts Tests for Educator Licensure) program includes an array of forty tests that can be taken by candidates interested in teaching grades Pre-Kindergarten through 12 in the state of Massachusetts. In 2004, the program was expanded to include tests for vocational technical and adult basic education. The purpose of this program is to confirm that candidates interested in becoming an educator in Massachusetts have the ability to effectively communicate with students, parents and guardians, as well as other educators. They must have reading comprehension and clear writing skills. The test also ensures that they are competent within the subject area they wish to teach.

The General Curriculum test (03) consists of two subtests; candidates must achieve a passing score on both subtests to satisfy the passing requirements for this test. Both tests can be attempted at the same testing appointment or they may be taken on different dates. The Mathematics subtest and the Multi-subject subtest are both administered via computer. Between the two subtests, the content of the General Curriculum test addresses a wide variety of subareas that prospective educators must understand. This test is part of the certification process for those teachers seeking the following licenses: Elementary Education, Teacher of Students with Moderate and Severe Disabilities, American Sign Language/Total Communication, Oral/Aural, and Teacher of the Visually Impaired.

Test Administration

Tests are offered via computer at testing centers throughout the state of Massachusetts. The General Curriculum test is offered year-round, Monday through Saturday, by appointment; appointments are not offered on some holidays. Candidates can take one or both subtests at one testing appointment. The fee to take both subtests in one testing appointment offers candidates a cost savings over separate registrations and administrations. If a candidate does not pass a subtest successfully, there is no limit on the number of times the test can be retaken. However, candidates must wait at least forty-five days before retaking the test.

Students with disabilities should fill out and submit an Alternative Testing Arrangement Request Form with documentation to support the request for appropriate accommodations. They can also call MTEL Customer Service at (866) 565-4894 with questions. Candidates needing accommodations are encouraged to submit their requests as early as possible in case a special version of the test needs to be produced, an example being a test written in Braille. Requests are reviewed and determined on a case-by-case basis.

Test Format

Both subtests in the General Curriculum test consist of multiple-choice and one open-response question. The Mathematics subtest has 45 multiple-choice questions, while the Multi-subject subtest has 55. Calculators are not permitted on the Mathematics subtest. Candidates have four hours to complete the test, regardless as to whether they take one or both tests in a testing appointment. Prior to the start of the test, candidates have an additional fifteen minutes to review a computer-based testing tutorial and a non-disclosure agreement. The format for each of the two subtests can be found in the table below:

Mathematics Subtest	
Subarea	**Number of Questions**
Numbers and Operations	19-21 multiple-choice questions
Fractions and Algebra	10-12 multiple-choice questions
Geometry and Measurement	8-10 multiple-choice questions
Statistics and Probability	4-6 multiple-choice questions
Integration of Knowledge and Understanding	1 open-response assignment

Multi-Subject Subtest	
Subarea	Number of Questions
Language Arts	18-20 multiple-choice questions
History and Social Science	17-19 multiple-choice questions
Science and Technology/Engineering	17-19 multiple-choice questions
Integration of Knowledge and Understanding	1 open-response assignment

Scoring

Each test has a scaled score range of 100 to 300. The qualifying score for passing the General Curriculum test is 240, which must be achieved for each subtest. Open-response assignments are scored from 1 to 4 and this score factors into the total scaled score and required passing score, contributing ten percent to each subtest score. There is no penalty for guessing on the multiple-choice questions. Score reports for each subtest include the candidate's passing or non-passing status, the score achieved if the candidate did not obtain the minimum passing score, and his or her general performance on each of the subtest's subareas. Score reports can be emailed, if the option is selected during registration, or can be downloaded from the candidates MTEL account. The date they are released is roughly two to six weeks after administration; the exact date for a given testing window is available online.

MTEL General Curriculum Exam Open Responses

Both sections of the MTEL General Curriculum exam—the Mathematics subtest and the Multi-Subject subtest—include one open-response assignment. Test takers are provided with a prompt and must prepare and produce a 150-300 word (1-2 pages) written response that addresses the assignment tasked in the prompt.

The primary goal of the open-response assignments is for test takers to demonstrate their ability to integrate their knowledge of different concepts and communicate their understanding of the subject matter in a concise and coherent manner. Test takers are expected to connect concepts, analyze ideas, and otherwise use the written response assignment to demonstrate a deep understanding of the applicable concepts in the subject area.

The open-response assignments are evaluated using a rubric that helps assign a point value of 1-4 based on the following four criteria:

1. **Purpose:** how well the response fulfills the assignment's intent

2. **Subject Knowledge:** the degree to which the test taker has correctly and appropriately applied his or her knowledge and understanding of subject knowledge

3. **Support:** the effectiveness, correctness, and relevance of the supporting evidence the test taker has included to substantiate his or her ideas and claims

4. **Rationale:** the extent to which the test taker's argument and ideas are sound and demonstrate an understanding of the subject area

For example, a score of 1 indicates a weak response to the assignment. Responses earning this poor score do not achieve the purpose of the assignment; contain inaccurate or little appropriate knowledge of the subject matter; include little, if any, relevant, effective supportive evidence and examples; and demonstrate little or no understanding or rationale for the test taker's ideas regarding the topic. On the other hand, a score of 4 indicates a strong written response that fully achieves the purpose of the assignment; demonstrates accurate, comprehensive, and effective use of subject knowledge; includes high-quality, sound supportive evidence and useful examples; and compiles a reasonable and thorough rationale for ideas and points regarding the topic. A complete scoring rubric is available on the MTEL website: http://www.mtel.nesinc.com.

Although it is recommended that test takers take time after carefully and fully reading the assignment to brainstorm and outline content and organization ideas using the provided erasable booklet, the final response must be either typed into the computer's on-screen response box, written on an official response sheet and scanned in via the workstation's scanner, or a combination of both. For example, if text is accompanied with calculations and sketches, it is acceptable to type the text portion into the on-screen response box and then hand-create and scan in the accompanying graphics using the paper response sheet and scanner.

Writing should be clear, formal, and conform to the standard American English conventions. All work must be written in the test taker's own words, pertain to the assigned topic, and be developed and created without the use of any reference materials. It is strongly encouraged that test takers read through, edit, and revise their final response before submitting it for scoring. This will help ensure the response is as organized, sound, complete, and polished as possible.

It is important to note that responses must be fully scanned in or submitted via the on-screen box prior to the conclusion of the testing session. For that reason, it is crucial for test takers to monitor the amount of time remaining in the testing session so that ample time is left to ensure the written response is submitted before time runs out. Any time spent planning, organizing, drafting, revising, and scanning response sheets counts towards the test taker's testing time. Materials written, typed, or created that are not scanned in during the testing time will not be reviewed or scored. Any hand-written content must be neat and legible, or it will not be scored.

The open-response assignment in the multi-subject subtest, will call upon test takers to create a written analysis on a Science and Technology/Engineering topic or a History and Social Sciences one. For example, test takers may need to compare and contrast two different types of government or discuss the process of genetic inheritance and the ramifications of recombination.

For the Mathematics subtest, the open-response assignment will require reasoning, understanding, and the ability to integrate at least two different math domains from the following list of four domains: Numbers and Operations, Functions and Algebra, Statistics and Probability, and Geometry and Measurement. Oftentimes, test takers will be provided a sample math problem and an example of a fictitious student's answer and work. The test taker must write a response that considers and analyzes the student's work, explains any mistakes or flawed reasoning, and provides a thorough written and mathematical demonstration of how to arrive at the correct answer. The test taker should explain their methodology thoroughly so that the fictitious student would be able to learn the appropriate steps to arrive at the answer and replicate finding the solution to a similar problem on their own.

In order to best prepare for the two open-response assignments, test takers should try and attain a thorough understanding of the topics in all content areas on the exam. In addition, test takers should practice generating 150-300 word responses on different topics under similar time constraints. The following sections provide advice and helpful tips to consider when planning, organizing, and writing essay-type responses, such as the two open-response assignments on the MTEL General Curriculum exam:

Brainstorming

One of the most important steps in writing an essay is prewriting. Before drafting an essay, it's helpful to think about the topic for a moment or two, in order to gain a more solid understanding of what the task is. Then, spending about five minutes jotting down the immediate ideas that could work for the essay is recommended. It is a way to get some words on the page and offer a reference for ideas when drafting. Scratch paper is provided for writers to use any prewriting techniques such as webbing, free writing, or listing. The goal is to get ideas out of the mind and onto the page.

Considering Opposing Viewpoints

In the planning stage, it's important to consider all aspects of the topic, including different viewpoints on the subject. There are more than two ways to look at a topic, and a strong argument considers those opposing viewpoints. Considering opposing viewpoints can help writers present a fair, balanced, and informed essay that shows consideration for all readers. This approach can also strengthen an argument by recognizing and potentially refuting the opposing viewpoint(s).

Drawing from personal experience may help to support ideas. For example, if the goal for writing is a personal narrative, then the story should be from the writer's own life. Many writers find it helpful to draw from personal experience, even in an essay that is not strictly narrative. Personal anecdotes or short stories can help to illustrate a point in other types of essays as well.

Moving from Brainstorming to Planning

Once the ideas are on the page, it's time to turn them into a solid plan for the essay. The best ideas from the brainstorming results can then be developed into a more formal outline. An outline typically has one main point (the thesis) and at least three sub-points that support the main point. Here's an example:

Main Idea

- Point #1
- Point #2
- Point #3

Of course, there will be details under each point, but this approach is the best for dealing with timed writing.

Staying on Track

Basing the essay on the outline aids in both organization and coherence. The goal is to ensure that there is enough time to develop each sub-point in the essay, roughly spending an equal amount of time on each idea. Keeping an eye on the time will help. If there are fifteen minutes left to draft the essay, then it makes sense to spend about 5 minutes on each of the ideas. Staying on task is critical to success, and timing out the parts of the essay can help writers avoid feeling overwhelmed.

Parts of the Essay

The introduction has to do a few important things:

- Establish the topic of the essay in original wording (i.e., not just repeating the prompt)

- Clarify the significance/importance of the topic or purpose for writing (not too many details, a brief overview)

- Offer a thesis statement that identifies the writer's own viewpoint on the topic (typically one-two brief sentences as a clear, concise explanation of the main point on the topic)

Body paragraphs reflect the ideas developed in the outline. Three-four points is probably sufficient for a short essay, and they should include the following:

- A topic sentence that identifies the sub-point (e.g., a reason why, a way how, a cause or effect)

- A detailed explanation of the point, explaining why the writer thinks this point is valid

- Illustrative examples, such as personal examples or real world examples, that support and validate the point (i.e., "prove" the point)

- A concluding sentence that connects the examples, reasoning, and analysis to the point being made

The conclusion, or final paragraph, should be brief and should reiterate the focus, clarifying why the discussion is significant or important. It is important to avoid adding specific details or new ideas to this paragraph. The purpose of the conclusion is to sum up what has been said to bring the discussion to a close.

Don't Panic!

Writing an essay can be overwhelming, and performance panic is a natural response. The outline serves as a basis for the writing and helps writers keep focused. Getting stuck can also happen, and it's helpful to remember that brainstorming can be done at any time during the writing process. Following the steps of the writing process is the best defense against writer's block.

Timed essays can be particularly stressful, but assessors are trained to recognize the necessary planning and thinking for these timed efforts. Using the plan above and sticking to it helps with time management. Timing each part of the process helps writers stay on track. Sometimes writers try to cover too much in their essays. If time seems to be running out, this is an opportunity to determine whether all of the ideas in the outline are necessary. Three body paragraphs are sufficient, and more than that is probably too much to cover in a short essay.

More isn't always better in writing. A strong essay will be clear and concise. It will avoid unnecessary or repetitive details. It is better to have a concise, five-paragraph essay that makes a clear point, than a ten-paragraph essay that doesn't. The goal is to write one to two pages of quality writing. Paragraphs should also reflect balance; if the introduction goes to the bottom of the first page, the writing may be going off-track or be repetitive. It's best to fall into the one-two page range, but a complete, well-developed essay is the ultimate goal.

The Final Steps

Leaving a few minutes at the end to revise and proofread offers an opportunity for writers to polish things up. Putting one's self in the reader's shoes and focusing on what the essay actually says helps writers identify problems—it's a movement from the mindset of writer to the mindset of editor. The goal is to have a clean, clear copy of the essay. The following areas should be considered when proofreading:

- Sentence fragments
- Awkward sentence structure
- Run-on sentences
- Incorrect word choice
- Grammatical agreement errors
- Spelling errors
- Punctuation errors
- Capitalization errors

The Short Overview

The essay may seem challenging, but following these steps can help writers focus:

1. Take one or two minutes to think about the topic.
2. Generate some ideas through brainstorming (three-four minutes).

3. Organize ideas into a brief outline, selecting just three-four main points to cover in the essay (eventually the body paragraphs).
4. Develop essay in parts:
    a. Introduction paragraph, with intro to topic and main points
        i. Viewpoint on the subject at the end of the introduction
    b. Body paragraphs, based on outline
        i. Each paragraph: makes a main point, explains the viewpoint, uses examples to support the point
    c. Brief conclusion highlighting the main points and closing
5. Read over the essay (last five minutes).
    a. Look for any obvious errors, making sure that the writing makes sense.

Language Arts

Developments of the English Language

The English language originated between the fifth and seventh centuries by Germanic tribes that invaded Britain. The English language transcends time beginning with Old English, transforming to Middle English, then Early Modern English, and finally adapting into the most current, Late Modern English. Throughout the history of the English language, there have been many developments, including the invention of the printing press, standardization of written language, and development of the dictionary. Review the history of each below.

Invention of the Printing Press

In 1450, Johannes Gutenberg decided to use existing technologies to create movable print, otherwise known as the printing press. As opposed to using block letters and ink to create pages one at a time, Gutenberg had an idea to use preexisting technology and small metal pieces to rapidly print page upon page. The printing press could print thousands of pages per day versus forty to fifty pages with the dated printing method.

Gutenberg's invention of the printing press had a huge impact on the English language. Information was printed at a faster, more efficient pace, and in high volume. The ability to print a ton of information quickly led to literacy and knowledge expansion among different socioeconomic classes. Below is a model of one of the first printing presses.

Standardization of Written Language

The invention of the printing press provided people with the opportunity to have access to more books, documents, and news. Readers now had the ability to obtain written language for their own use. The printing press initially prompted a need to standardize written language so that there could be a universal language used.

In the late 1600s, the English alphabet, spelling, and the use of punctuation marks became more prevalent. At this point in history, there was an assortment of languages among the nation. Now that the printing press allowed print and distribution of written language, the need for a guide providing word meanings and uses was clear.

Development of the Dictionary

There have been many dictionaries created throughout history. Review the timeline below demonstrating the development of the dictionary.

- 1582: Mulcaster's Elementarie was a compilation of 8,000 words produced in 1582. Although this text did not have word definitions, this was one of the first attempts to organize the English language.

- 1604: In the early seventeenth century, Robert Cawdrey published one of the first single-word dictionaries called *A Table Alphabeticall*. This dictionary included definitions and was directed toward people who were less educated. This dictionary included approximately 2,500 words.

- 1755: After Cawdrey's idea to publish his single-word dictionary, Samuel Johnson published a list of approximately 40,000 words and definitions often called "The first great English dictionary." This is considered one of the first dictionaries to standardize spelling.

- 1798: In 1798, Samuel Johnson Jr. published one of the first American dictionaries. The one eight years before, *A School Dictionary: Being a Compendium of the Latest and Most Improved Dictionaries*, was published by Samuel Johnson (no relation to Samuel Johnson Jr.).

- 1806: The *Compendious Dictionary of the English Language* was published by Noah Webster in 1806. In 1828, Webster also published *American Dictionary of the English Language*. The term "Webster's Dictionary" is a generic trademark for dictionaries used in English and may refer to any one of a line of dictionaries published by Webster in the early nineteenth century.

- 1884: The *Oxford English Dictionary* was created in response to the outdated words and definitions found in other dictionaries. The committee behind the creation of this dictionary spent thirty years compiling a team of philologists and editors in order to create one of the most popular dictionaries in history.

Origins of the English Language

The English language has had many influences over time. It was brought to Britain by Germanic invaders between the fifth and seventh century; however, the language has adopted many dialects, inflections, and elements as time passed. In this section, three major linguistic origin influences will be explored. These include Anglo-Saxon roots, Celtic influences, and Greek and Roman elements.

Anglo-Saxon Roots

In the *Anglo-Saxon* period, also known as the Old English era, a new culture was formed when three Germanic tribes (the Angles, the Saxons, and the Jutes) merged. Anglo-Saxon was first written using the Runic alphabet but was later replaced with the Latin alphabet. For over seven hundred years, Anglo-Saxon roots influenced many dialects throughout kingdoms and regions. There are four main dialects of Old English:

- Northumbrian
- Mercia
- Kentish
- West-Saxon

Changes in dialect during this time period occurred for two main reasons. When Britain converted to Christianity, new words and connotations were borrowed from Old French or Latin languages, which in turn increased Anglo-Saxon's vocabulary. Another event that influenced Old English dialect was when the Viking invaders and Norse settlers merged. In the late 700s, England and Denmark united after the Norse invasions. Instead of being enemies, the two cultures merged and produced a mixture of Anglo-Saxon and Norse languages. The integration of languages produced synonyms and simplified ending sounds of words and inflections.

Celtic Influences

When the Anglo-Saxons arrived in Britain, the Celtic population spoke Latin and Celtic languages. Once the Anglo-Saxons integrated with the Celts, Old English became the primary language. The Celtic language was viewed as mediocre, and therefore many words did not endure the transition. The Celtic language survived in a few regions and split into two main groups, Goidelic (Gaelic) and Brythonic (British). Despite the fact that the Celtic language did not have a drastic influence on many English language words, the Celtic language is apparent in location names. Names of rivers (such as the Yare and

Thames) and towns (such as York and London) are just a couple of the lasting language from the Celtic period.

Greek and Roman Influences

When the Romans invaded Britain, Latin became the dominant language of the region and was commonly used for religious purposes. Latin was thought to have been a language of upper class and educated citizens, as opposed to the Celtic language that was disregarded as "ordinary." Much of the Latin language stems from Greek origins.

Many of the Greek morphemes and word patterns that were modified into the Latin language over fifteen hundred years have carried over into the English language today. Words using the *ph* pattern, such as *photograph, philosophy, physical,* and *physician,* derive from the Greek origin. Other word patterns such as *th* (words such as *path, clothe,* and *theory*), *ch* (words such as *churn* and *chart*), *y* (words such as *myth, sky,* and *my*), and *z* (words such as *zebra* and *zeta*) also originate from the Greek origin.

Derivatives and Borrowings

Derivatives are words that are formed from other words, otherwise known as *root words*. Word derivatives add morphemes, or affixes, to the beginning or ending of root words to create new words with new meanings. Below are some of the commonly used derivatives in the English language:

English Language Derivatives:

Root Word	Affix	Derivative
favor	-able	favorable
bare	-ness	bareness
child	-like	childlike
boast	-ful	boastful
whole	-some	wholesome
seven	-th	seventh
west	-ward	westward
north	-ern	northern
health	-y	healthy

Remember, sometimes the spelling of the root word changes once the affix is added to form the derivative. For example, by adding the affix *-iation* to the root word *affiliate,* first drop the *e,* and then add the *-iation,* to form *affiliation*.

Borrowings, otherwise referred to as *loanwords,* are words that are borrowed and incorporated into one's own language originating from a different language. It is not as though the borrowed words are returned like a library book; however, these words tend to relate strongly to the language loaning the words as opposed to the language borrowing the words. For example, the English word *music* is a borrowed word from the French word *musique.* The Spanish word *chofer* is borrowed from the French word *chauffeur.* On the following page, review some of the borrowed words from the Germanic Period, Old English Period, Middle English Period, Early Modern English Period, and the Modern English Period.

English Language Borrowings

Germanic Period

Language	Borrowed Word Examples
Latin	butere (butter), sacc (sack), win (wine)

Old English Period

Language	Borrowed Word Examples
Latin	cest (chest), maegester (master), tigle (tile), circul (circle)
Celtic	brocc (badger), cumb (combe, valley)

Middle English Period

Language	Borrowed Word Examples
French	attorney, baron, boil, crime, question, special
Scandinavian	cake, lump, skirt, ugly, want

Early Modern English Period

Language	Borrowed Word Examples
Arabic	alcove, algebra, orange, sugar, zero
Greek	critic, data, pneumonia, tragedy
Latin	area, compensate, dexterity, vindicate

Modern English Period

Language	Borrowed Word Examples
Dutch	booze, bow, scum, uproar
French	ballet, cabernet, brigade, battalion
German	dunk, hamburger, pretzel, strudel
Italian	balcony, grotto, regatta, zucchini
Russian	icon, vodka
Scandinavian	ski, slalom, smorgasbord
Spanish	alligator, coyote, ranch, tornado
Yiddish	bagel, kosher, oy vey

Word borrowing occurred frequently throughout history. Historical events and trends influence which languages influence one another.

Formality and Dialect

Identifying Variation in Dialect and Diction

Language arts educators often seem to be in the position of teaching the "right" way to use English, particularly in lessons about grammar and vocabulary. However, all it takes is back-to-back viewings of speeches by the queen of England and the president of the United States or side-by-side readings of a contemporary poem and one written in the 1600s to come to the conclusion that there is no single, fixed, correct form of spoken or written English. Instead, language varies and evolves across different regions and time periods. It also varies between cultural groups depending on factors such as race, ethnicity, age, and socioeconomic status. Students should come away from a language arts class with more than a strictly prescriptive view of language; they should have an appreciation for its rich diversity.

It is important to understand some key terms in discussing linguistic variety.

Language is a tool for communication. It may be spoken, unspoken—as with body language—written, or codified in other ways. Language is symbolic in the sense that it can describe objects, ideas, and events that are not actually present, have not actually occurred, or only exist in the mind of the speaker. All languages are governed by systematic rules of grammar and semantics. These rules allow speakers to manipulate a finite number of elements, such as sounds or written symbols, to create an infinite number of meanings.

A *dialect* is a distinct variety of a language in terms of patterns of grammar, vocabulary, and/or *phonology*—the sounds used by its speakers—that distinguish it from other forms of that language. Two dialects are not considered separate languages if they are *mutually intelligible*—if speakers of each dialect are able to understand one another. A dialect is not a subordinate version of a language. Examples of English dialects include Scottish English and American Southern English.

By definition, *Standard English* is a dialect. It is one variety of English with its own usage of grammar, vocabulary, and pronunciation. Given that Standard English is taught in schools and used in places like government, journalism, and other professional workplaces, it is often elevated above other English dialects. Linguistically, though, there is nothing that makes Standard English more correct or advanced than other dialects.

A *pidgin* is formed when speakers of different languages begin utilizing a simplified mixture of elements from both languages to communicate with each other. In North America, pidgins occurred when Africans were brought to European colonies as slaves, leading to a mixture of African and European languages. Historically, pidgins also sprung up in areas of international trade. A pidgin is communication born of necessity and lacks the full complexity or standardized rules that govern a language.

When a pidgin becomes widely used and is taught to children as their native language, it becomes a *Creole*. An example is Haitian Creole, a language based on French and including elements of West African languages.

An *accent* is a unique speech pattern, particularly in terms of tone or intonation. Speakers from different regions tend to have different accents, as do learners of English from different native languages. In some cases, accents are mutually intelligible, but in other cases, speakers with different accents might have some difficulty in understanding one another.

Colloquial language is language that is used conversationally or familiarly—e.g., "What's up?"—in contrast to formal, professional, or academic language—"How are you this evening?"

Vernacular refers to the native, everyday language of a place. Historically, for instance, Bibles and religious services across Europe were primarily offered in Latin, even centuries after the fall of the Roman Empire. After the revolution of the printing press and the widespread availability of vernacular translations of the Bible in the fifteenth and sixteenth centuries, everyday citizens were able to study from Bibles in their own language without needing specialized training in Latin.

A *regionalism* is a word or expression used in a particular region. In the United States, for instance, examples of regionalisms might be *soda, pop,* or *Coke*—terms that vary in popularity according to region.

Jargon is vocabulary used within a specialized field, such as computer programming or mechanics. Jargon may consist of specialized words or of everyday words that have a different meaning in this specialized context.

Slang refers to non-standard expressions that are not used in elevated speech and writing. Slang creates linguistic in-groups and out-groups of people, those who can understand the slang terms and those who can't. Slang is often tied to a specific time period. For example, "groovy" and "far out" are connected to the 1970s, and "as if!" and "4-1-1-" are connected to the 1990s.

A language arts classroom should demonstrate the history and evolution of language, rather than presenting fixed, unchangeable linguistic regulations. Particularly for students who feel intimidated or excluded by Standard English, instructors can make lessons more relatable or inclusive by allowing students to share or explore their own patterns of language. Students can be encouraged to act as linguists or anthropologists by getting involved in projects. Some examples include asking them to identify and compare slang in their generation to slang from their parents' generation, to exchange information about their dialect with students who come from different cultural backgrounds, or to conduct a linguistic survey of their friends, family, or neighbors. Language arts class can also be integrated with history topics by having students research unfamiliar slang or words that have shifted in meaning from the past until now—a type of study particularly useful when reading a text from a past era.

Understanding Dialect and its Appropriateness
While students should come away from class feeling supported in their linguistic diversity, the reality is that certain forms of language are viewed differently depending on the context. Lessons learned in the classroom have a real-life application to a student's future, so he or she should know where, when, and how to utilize different forms of language.

For students preparing for college, knowledge of the conventions of Standard English is essential. The same is true for students who plan to enter professional job fields. Without necessarily having a word for it, many students are already familiar with the concept of *code-switching*—altering speech patterns depending upon context. For example, a person might use a different accent or slang with neighborhood friends than with coworkers or pick up new vocabulary and speech patterns after moving to a new region, either unconsciously or consciously. In this way, speakers have an innate understanding of how their language use helps them fit into any given situation.

Instructors can design activities that help students pay attention to their language use in a given context. When discussing a novel in class, students might be encouraged to spend a few minutes freewriting in a journal to generate ideas and express their unedited thoughts. Later, though, students will then be asked to present those thoughts in a formal writing assignment that requires adherence to Standard English grammar, employing academic vocabulary and expressions appropriate to literary discussions. Alternatively, students might design an advertisement that appeals to teenagers and another one that appeals to adults, utilizing different language in each. In this way, students can learn how to reformulate their thoughts using the language appropriate to the task at hand.

Awareness of dialect can also help students as readers, too. Many writers of literary fiction and nonfiction utilize dialect and colloquialisms to add verisimilitude to their writing. This is especially true for authors who focus on a particular region or cultural group in their works, also known as *regionalism* or *local color literature*. Examples include Zora Neale Hurston's *Their Eyes Were Watching God* and the short stories of Kate Chopin. Students can be asked to consider how the speech patterns in a text affect a reader's understanding of the characters—how the pattern reflects a character's background and place in society. They might consider a reader's impression of the region—how similar or different it is from the reader's region or what can be inferred about the region based on how people speak. In some cases, unfamiliar dialect may be very difficult for readers to understand on the page but becomes much more intelligible when read aloud—as in the reading of Shakespeare.

Reading passages together in class and then finding recordings or videos of the dialect presented in the text can help familiarize students with different speech patterns. And of course, students should also consider how use of dialect affects the audience or if it is directed to a specific audience. Who was the intended audience for *Their Eyes Were Watching God*, a novel that recreates the speech patterns of African Americans in early 1900s Florida? How might the novel be understood differently by readers who recognize that dialect than by readers who are encountering it for the first time? What would be lost if the characters didn't converse in their local dialect? Being alert to these questions creates students who are attuned to the nuances of language use in everyday life.

Fundamental Language Structures

Among all languages, it is important to have fundamental structure to clearly communicate. There needs to be a logical way to organize words within a sentence so that people can read, speak, and listen in a meaningful way. There are four components of language structure:

- Morphology
- Semantics
- Syntax
- Phonology

Let's review each independently.

<u>Morphology</u>
Morphology is the study of words. It explores how words are formed using morphemes (words or parts of words that contain their own meanings), as well as their relationship with other words within a language. For example, look at the word *cupcake*. The beginning and ending sounds *c* and *silent e* do not have meaning on their own. However, when combined with other morphemes, this compound word takes on a whole new meaning. Each word, *cup* and *cake,* has independent meanings. When you combine them, a new word, *cupcake,* takes on a completely independent definition.

Morphology examines root words, affixes (prefixes and suffixes), and stems. Not only does it analyze each part of words, morphology also looks at how words are used. Morphology can often answer how words are pronounced or the context in which words are used.

<u>Semantics</u>
Semantics studies the meanings of words, phrases, sentences, and texts. Semantics can be divided into two major categories: lexical semantics and phrasal semantics.

Lexical semantics not only studies individual words, but it also analyzes affixes, compound words, and phrases, whereas phrasal semantics studies the meaning of phrases and words. It looks at word meanings as opposed to how words are used. Lexical semantics compares and contrasts linguistic semantics structures across languages.

Syntax

Generally, sentences are formed using a very simple pattern: Subject + Verb + Object. For example, in "The boy ran down the street," the subject is "The boy," the verb is "ran," and the object is "the street." Syntax provides a set structure to sentences in a language. It provides an order to this sentence to make its meaning clear to the reader. Syntax can create a mood for a reader or express an author's purpose.

Phonology

Phonology is the study of how speech sounds in a language are organized to make words. These patterns of sounds also include the study of phonemes (single units of sounds), syllables (vowel sounds heard within a word), stress or accent (emphasis on a sound or syllable within a word), and intonation (variation of tone or pitch in words). Despite their differences, phonology and phonetics (the study of isolated sounds in words) are often confused. Remember, phonology studies how sounds change in syllables, words, and sentences, as opposed to phonetics, where the focus is on a single speech sound.

Identifying Parts of Speech

Nouns

A noun is a person, place, thing ,or idea. All nouns fit into one of two types, common or proper.

A *common noun* is a word that identifies any of a class of people, places, or things. Examples include numbers, objects, animals, feelings, concepts, qualities, and actions. *A, an,* or *the* usually precedes the common noun. These parts of speech are called *articles*. Here are some examples of sentences using nouns preceded by articles.

> *A* building is under construction.
> *The* girl would like to move to *the* city.

A *proper noun* (also called a *proper name*) is used for the specific name of an individual person, place, or organization. The first letter in a proper noun is capitalized. "My name is *Mary*." "I work for *Walmart*."

Nouns sometimes serve as adjectives (which themselves describe nouns), such as "hockey player" and "state government."

An abstract noun is an idea, state, or quality. It is something that can't be touched, such as happiness, courage, evil, or humor.

A concrete noun is something that can be experienced through the senses (touch, taste, hear, smell, see). Examples of concrete nouns are birds, skateboard, pie, and car.

A collective noun refers to a collection of people, places, or things that act as one. Examples of collective nouns are as follows: team, class, jury, family, audience, and flock.

Pronouns

A word used in place of a noun is known as a *pronoun*. Pronouns are words like *I, mine, hers,* and *us*.

Pronouns can be split into different classifications (seen below) which make them easier to learn; however, it's not important to memorize the classifications.

- Personal pronouns: refer to people
- First person: we, I, our, mine
- Second person: you, yours
- Third person: he, them
- Possessive pronouns: demonstrate ownership (mine, my, his, yours)
- Interrogative pronouns: ask questions (what, which, who, whom, whose)
- Relative pronouns: include the five interrogative pronouns and others that are relative (whoever, whomever, that, when, where)
- Demonstrative pronouns: replace something specific (this, that, those, these)
- Reciprocal pronouns: indicate something was done or given in return (each other, one another)
- Indefinite pronouns: have a nonspecific status (anybody, whoever, someone, everybody, somebody)

Indefinite pronouns such as *anybody, whoever, someone, everybody*, and *somebody* command a singular verb form, but others such as *all, none,* and *some* could require a singular or plural verb form.

Antecedents

An *antecedent* is the noun to which a pronoun refers; it needs to be written or spoken before the pronoun is used. For many pronouns, antecedents are imperative for clarity. In particular, many of the personal, possessive, and demonstrative pronouns need antecedents. Otherwise, it would be unclear who or what someone is referring to when they use a pronoun like *he* or *this*.

Pronoun reference means that the pronoun should refer clearly to one, clear, unmistakable noun (the antecedent).

Pronoun-antecedent agreement refers to the need for the antecedent and the corresponding pronoun to agree in gender, person, and number. Here are some examples:

The *kidneys* (plural antecedent) are part of the urinary system. *They* (plural pronoun) serve several roles."

The kidneys are part of the *urinary system* (singular antecedent). *It* (singular pronoun) is also known as the renal system.

Pronoun Cases

The subjective pronouns —*I, you, he/she/it, we, they,* and *who*—are the subjects of the sentence.

Example: *They* have a new house.

The objective pronouns—*me, you (singular), him/her, us, them,* and *whom*—are used when something is being done for or given to someone; they are objects of the action.

Example: The teacher has an apple for *us*.

The possessive pronouns—*mine, my, your, yours, his, hers, its, their, theirs, our,* and *ours*—are used to denote that something (or someone) belongs to someone (or something).

> Example: It's *their* chocolate cake.
> Even Better Example: It's *my* chocolate cake!

One of the greatest challenges and worst abuses of pronouns concerns *who* and *whom*. Just knowing the following rule can eliminate confusion. *Who* is a subjective-case pronoun used only as a subject or subject complement. *Whom* is only objective-case and, therefore, the object of the verb or preposition.

> *Who* is going to the concert?

> You are going to the concert with *whom*?

Hint: When using *who* or *whom*, think of whether someone would say *he* or *him*. If the answer is *he*, use *who*. If the answer is *him*, use *whom*. This trick is easy to remember because *he* and *who* both end in vowels, and *him* and *whom* both end in the letter *M*.

Verbs

The *verb* is the part of speech that describes an action, state of being, or occurrence.

A *verb* forms the main part of a predicate of a sentence. This means that the verb explains what the noun (which will be discussed shortly) is doing. A simple example is *time flies*. The verb *flies* explains what the action of the noun, *time*, is doing. This example is a *main* verb.

Helping (auxiliary) verbs are words like *have, do, be, can, may, should, must,* and *will*. "I *should* go to the store." Helping verbs assist main verbs in expressing tense, ability, possibility, permission, or obligation.

Particles are minor function words like *not, in, out, up,* or *down* that become part of the verb itself. "I might *not*."

Participles are words formed from verbs that are often used to modify a noun, noun phrase, verb, or verb phrase.

> The *running* teenager collided with the cyclist.

Participles can also create compound verb forms.

> He is *speaking*.

Verbs have five basic forms: the *base* form, the *-s* form, the *-ing* form, the *past* form, and the *past participle* form.

The *past* forms are either *regular* (*love/loved; hate/hated*) or *irregular* because they don't end by adding the common past tense suffix "-ed" (*go/went; fall/fell; set/set*).

Verb Forms

Shifting verb forms entails *conjugation*, which is used to indicate *tense, voice,* or *mood*.

Verb tense is used to show when the action in the sentence took place. There are several different verb tenses, and it is important to know how and when to use them. Some verb tenses can be achieved by changing the form of the verb, while others require the use of helping verbs (e.g., *is, was,* or *has*).

Present tense shows the action is happening currently or is ongoing:

> I walk to work every morning.

> She is stressed about the deadline.

Past tense shows that the action happened in the past or that the state of being is in the past:

> I walked to work yesterday morning.

> She was stressed about the deadline.

Future tense shows that the action will happen in the future or is a future state of being:

> I will walk to work tomorrow morning.

> She will be stressed about the deadline.

Present perfect tense shows action that began in the past, but continues into the present:

> I have walked to work all week.

> She has been stressed about the deadline.

Past perfect tense shows an action was finished before another took place:

> I had walked all week until I sprained my ankle.

> She had been stressed about the deadline until we talked about it.

Future perfect tense shows an action that will be completed at some point in the future:

> By the time the bus arrives, I will have walked to work already.

Voice

Verbs can be in the active or passive voice. When the subject completes the action, the verb is in *active voice*. When the subject receives the action of the sentence, the verb is in *passive voice*.

> Active: Jamie ate the ice cream.

> Passive: The ice cream was eaten by Jamie.

In active voice, the subject (*Jamie*) is the "do-er" of the action (*ate*). In passive voice, the subject *ice cream* receives the action of being eaten.

While passive voice can add variety to writing, active voice is the generally preferred sentence structure.

Mood

Mood is used to show the speaker's feelings about the subject matter. In English, there is *indicative mood, imperative mood,* and *subjective mood.*

Indicative mood is used to state facts, ask questions, or state opinions:

> Bob will make the trip next week.

> When can Bob make the trip?

Imperative mood is used to state a command or make a request:

> Wait in the lobby.

> Please call me next week.

Subjunctive mood is used to express a wish, an opinion, or a hope that is contrary to fact:

> If I were in charge, none of this would have happened.

> Allison wished she could take the exam over again when she saw her score.

Adjectives

Adjectives are words used to modify nouns and pronouns. They can be used alone or in a series and are used to further define or describe the nouns they modify.

> Mark made us a delicious, four-course meal.

The words *delicious* and *four-course* are adjectives that describe the kind of meal Mark made.

Articles are also considered adjectives because they help to describe nouns. Articles can be general or specific. The three articles in English are: a, an, and the.

Indefinite articles (a, an) are used to refer to nonspecific nouns. The article *a* proceeds words beginning with consonant sounds, and the article *an* proceeds words beginning with vowel sounds.

> A car drove by our house.

> An alligator was loose at the zoo.

> He has always wanted a ukulele. (The first *u* makes a *y* sound.)

Note that *a* and *an* should only proceed nonspecific nouns that are also singular. If a nonspecific noun is plural, it does not need a preceding article.

> Alligators were loose at the zoo.

The *definite article (the)* is used to refer to specific nouns:

> The car pulled into our driveway.

Note that *the* should proceed all specific nouns regardless of whether they are singular or plural.

> The cars pulled into our driveway.

Comparative adjectives are used to compare nouns. When they are used in this way, they take on positive, comparative, or superlative form.

The *positive* form is the normal form of the adjective:

Alicia is tall.

The *comparative* form shows a comparison between two things:

Alicia is taller than Maria.

Superlative form shows comparison between more than two things:

Alicia is the tallest girl in her class.

Usually, the comparative and superlative can be made by adding *–er* and *–est* to the positive form, but some verbs call for the helping verbs *more* or *most*. Other exceptions to the rule include adjectives like *bad*, which uses the comparative *worse* and the superlative *worst*.

An adjective phrase is not a bunch of adjectives strung together, but a group of words that describes a noun or pronoun and, thus, functions as an adjective. *Very ugly* is an adjective phrase; so are *way too fat* and *faster than a speeding bullet.*

Adverbs

Adverbs have more functions than adjectives because they modify or qualify verbs, adjectives, or other adverbs as well as word groups that express a relation of place, time, circumstance, or cause. Therefore, adverbs answer any of the following questions: *How, when, where, why, in what way, how often, how much, in what condition,* and/or *to what degree. How good looking is he? He is <u>very</u> handsome.*

Here are some examples of adverbs for different situations:

- how: quickly
- when: daily
- where: there
- in what way: easily
- how often: often
- how much: much
- in what condition: badly
- what degree: hardly

As one can see, for some reason, many adverbs end in *-ly.*

Adverbs do things like emphasize (*really, simply,* and *so*), amplify (*heartily, completely,* and *positively*), and tone down (*almost, somewhat,* and *mildly*).

Adverbs also come in phrases.

The dog ran as <u>though his life depended on it.</u>

Prepositions

Prepositions are connecting words and, while there are only about 150 of them, they are used more often than any other individual groups of words. They describe relationships between other words. They are placed before a noun or pronoun, forming a phrase that modifies another word in the sentence. *Prepositional phrases* begin with a preposition and end with a noun or pronoun, the *object of the preposition*. A pristine lake is <u>near the store</u> and <u>behind the bank</u>.

Some commonly used prepositions are *about, after, anti, around, as, at, behind, beside, by, for, from, in, into, of, off, on, to,* and *with.*

Complex prepositions, which also come before a noun or pronoun, consist of two or three words such as *according to, in regards to,* and *because of.*

Conjunctions

Conjunctions are vital words that connect words, phrases, thoughts, and ideas. Conjunctions show relationships between components. There are two types:

Coordinating conjunctions are the primary class of conjunctions placed between words, phrases, clauses, and sentences that are of equal grammatical rank; the coordinating conjunctions are for, and, nor, but, or, yes, and so. A useful memorization trick is to remember that the first letter of these conjunctions collectively spell the word *fanboys*.

> I need to go shopping, *but* I must be careful to leave enough money in the bank.
> She wore a black, red, *and* white shirt.

Subordinating conjunctions are the secondary class of conjunctions. They connect two unequal parts, one *main* (or *independent*) and the other *subordinate* (or *dependent*). I must go to the store *even though* I do not have enough money in the bank.

> *Because* I read the review, I do not want to go to the movie.

Notice that the presence of subordinating conjunctions makes clauses dependent. *I read the review* is an independent clause, but *because* makes the clause dependent. Thus, it needs an independent clause to complete the sentence.

Interjections

Interjections are words used to express emotion. Examples include *wow, ouch,* and *hooray.* Interjections are often separate from sentences; in those cases, the interjection is directly followed by an exclamation point. In other cases, the interjection is included in a sentence and followed by a comma. The punctuation plays a big role in the intensity of the emotion that the interjection is expressing. Using a comma or semicolon indicates less excitement than using an exclamation mark..

Sentence Types and Purposes

Sentence Types

There are four ways in which we can structure sentences: simple, compound, complex, and compound-complex. Sentences can be composed of just one clause or many clauses joined together.

When a sentence is composed of just one clause (an independent clause), we call it a simple sentence. Simple sentences do not necessarily have to be short sentences. They just require one independent clause with a subject and a predicate. For example:

> Thomas marched over to Andrew's house.

> Jonah and Mary constructed a simplified version of the Eiffel Tower with Legos.

When a sentence has two or more independent clauses we call it a compound sentence. The clauses are connected by a comma and a coordinating conjunction—*and, but, or, nor, for*—or by a semicolon. Compound sentences do not have dependent clauses. For example:

> We went to the fireworks stand, and we bought enough fireworks to last all night.

> The children sat on the grass, and then we lit the fireworks one at a time.

When a sentence has just one independent clause and includes one or more dependent clauses, we call it a complex sentence:

> Because she slept well and drank coffee, Sarah was quite productive at work.

> Although Will had coffee, he made mistakes while using the photocopier.

When a sentence has two or more independent clauses and at least one dependent clause, we call it a compound-complex sentence:

> It may come as a surprise, but I found the tickets, and you can go to the show.

> Jade is the girl who dove from the high-dive, and she stunned the audience silent.

Sentence Purposes

There isn't an overabundance of absolutes in grammar, but here is one: every sentence in the English language falls into one of four categories.

- Declarative: a simple statement that ends with a period

  > The price of milk per gallon is the same as the price of gasoline.

- Imperative: a command, instruction, or request that ends with a period

  > Buy milk when you stop to fill up your car with gas.

- Interrogative: a question that ends with a question mark

  > Will you buy the milk?

- Exclamatory: a statement or command that expresses emotions like anger, urgency, or surprise and ends with an exclamation mark

  > Buy the milk now!

Declarative sentences are the most common type, probably because they are comprised of the most general content, without any of the bells and whistles that the other three types contain. They are, simply, declarations or statements of any degree of seriousness, importance, or information.

Imperative sentences often seem to be missing a subject. The subject is there, though; it is just not visible or audible because it is *implied*. Look at the imperative example sentence.

> Buy the milk when you fill up your car with gas.

You is the implied subject, the one to whom the command is issued. This is sometimes called *the understood you* because it is understood that *you* is the subject of the sentence.

Interrogative sentences—those that ask questions—are defined as such from the idea of the word *interrogation*, the action of questions being asked of suspects by investigators. Although that is serious business, interrogative sentences apply to all kinds of questions.

To exclaim is at the root of *exclamatory* sentences. These are made with strong emotions behind them. The only technical difference between a declarative or imperative sentence and an exclamatory one is the exclamation mark at the end. The example declarative and imperative sentences can both become an exclamatory one simply by putting an exclamation mark at the end of the sentences.

> The price of milk per gallon is the same as the price of gasoline!
> Buy milk when you stop to fill up your car with gas!

After all, someone might be really excited by the price of gas or milk, or they could be mad at the person that will be buying the milk! However, as stated before, exclamation marks in abundance defeat their own purpose! After a while, they begin to cause fatigue! When used only for their intended purpose, they can have their expected and desired effect.

Conventions of Edited American English

<u>Errors in Standard English Grammar, Usage, Syntax, and Mechanics</u>

Sentence Fragments
A *complete sentence* requires a verb and a subject that expresses a complete thought. Sometimes, the subject is omitted in the case of the implied *you*, used in sentences that are the command or imperative form—e.g., "Look!" or "Give me that." It is understood that the subject of the command is *you*, the listener or reader, so it is possible to have a structure without an explicit subject. Without these elements, though, the sentence is incomplete—it is a *sentence fragment*. While sentence fragments often occur in conversational English or creative writing, they are generally not appropriate in academic writing. Sentence fragments often occur when dependent clauses are not joined to an independent clause:

> *Sentence fragment*: Because the airline overbooked the flight.

The sentence above is a dependent clause that does not express a complete thought. What happened as a result of this cause? With the addition of an independent clause, this now becomes a complete sentence:

> *Complete sentence*: Because the airline overbooked the flight, several passengers were unable to board.

Sentences fragments may also occur through improper use of conjunctions:

I'm going to the Bahamas for spring break. And to New York City for New Year's Eve.

While the first sentence above is a complete sentence, the second one is not because it is a prepositional phrase that lacks a subject [I] and a verb [am going]. Joining the two together with the coordinating conjunction forms one grammatically-correct sentence:

I'm going to the Bahamas for spring break and to New York City for New Year's Eve.

Run-ons

A *run-on* is a sentence with too many independent clauses that are improperly connected to each other:

This winter has been very cold some farmers have suffered damage to their crops.

The sentence above has two subject-verb combinations. The first is "this winter has been"; the second is "some farmers have suffered." However, they are simply stuck next to each other without any punctuation or conjunction. Therefore, the sentence is a run-on.

Another type of run-on occurs when writers use inappropriate punctuation:

This winter has been very cold, some farmers have suffered damage to their crops.

Though a comma has been added, this sentence is still not correct. When a comma alone is used to join two independent clauses, it is known as a **comma splice**. Without an appropriate conjunction, a comma cannot join two independent clauses by itself.

Run-on sentences can be corrected by either dividing the independent clauses into two or more separate sentences or inserting appropriate conjunctions and/or punctuation. The run-on sentence can be amended by separating each subject-verb pair into its own sentence:

This winter has been very cold. Some farmers have suffered damage to their crops.

The run-on can also be fixed by adding a comma and conjunction to join the two independent clauses with each other:

This winter has been very cold, so some farmers have suffered damage to their crops.

Parallelism

Parallel structure occurs when phrases or clauses within a sentence contain the same structure. Parallelism increases readability and comprehensibility because it is easy to tell which sentence elements are paired with each other in meaning.

Jennifer enjoys cooking, knitting, and to spend time with her cat.

This sentence is not parallel because the items in the list appear in two different forms. Some are *gerunds*, which is the verb + ing: *cooking, knitting*. The other item uses the *infinitive* form, which is to + verb: *to spend*. To create parallelism, all items in the list may reflect the same form:

Jennifer enjoys cooking, knitting, and spending time with her cat.

All of the items in the list are now in gerund forms, so this sentence exhibits parallel structure. Here's another example:

> The company is looking for employees who are responsible and with a lot of experience.

Again, the items that are listed in this sentence are not parallel. "Responsible" is an adjective, yet "with a lot of experience" is a prepositional phrase. The sentence elements do not utilize parallel parts of speech.

> The company is looking for employees who are responsible and experienced.

"Responsible" and "experienced" are both adjectives, so this sentence now has parallel structure.

Dangling and Misplaced Modifiers
Modifiers enhance meaning by clarifying or giving greater detail about another part of a sentence. However, incorrectly-placed modifiers have the opposite effect and can cause confusion. A *misplaced modifier* is a modifier that is not located appropriately in relation to the word or phrase that it modifies:

> Because he was one of the greatest thinkers of Renaissance Italy, John idolized Leonardo da Vinci.

In this sentence, the modifier is "because he was one of the greatest thinkers of Renaissance Italy," and the noun it is intended to modify is "Leonardo da Vinci." However, due to the placement of the modifier next to the subject, John, it seems as if the sentence is stating that John was a Renaissance genius, not Da Vinci.

> John idolized Leonard da Vinci because he was one of the greatest thinkers of Renaissance Italy.

The modifier is now adjacent to the appropriate noun, clarifying which of the two men in this sentence is the greatest thinker.

Dangling modifiers modify a word or phrase that is not readily apparent in the sentence. That is, they "dangle" because they are not clearly attached to anything:

> After getting accepted to college, Amir's parents were proud.

The modifier here, "after getting accepted to college," should modify who got accepted. The noun immediately following the modifier is "Amir's parents"—but they are probably not the ones who are going to college.

> After getting accepted to college, Amir made his parents proud.

The subject of the sentence has been changed to Amir himself, and now the subject and its modifier are appropriately matched.

Inconsistent Verb Tense
Verb tense reflects when an action occurred or a state existed. For example, the tense known as *simple present* expresses something that is happening right now or that happens regularly:

> She *works* in a hospital.

Present continuous tense expresses something in progress. It is formed by to be + verb + -ing.

> Sorry, I can't go out right now. I *am doing* my homework.

Past tense is used to describe events that previously occurred. However, in conversational English, speakers often use present tense or a mix of past and present tense when relating past events because it gives the narrative a sense of immediacy. In formal written English, though, consistency in verb tense is necessary to avoid reader confusion.

> I traveled to Europe last summer. As soon as I stepped off the plane, I feel like I'm in a movie! I'm surrounded by quaint cafes and impressive architecture.

The passage above abruptly switches from past tense—*traveled, stepped*—to present tense—*feel, am surrounded.*

> I *traveled* to Europe last summer. As soon as I *stepped* off the plane, I *felt* like I was in a movie! I *was surrounded* by quaint cafes and impressive architecture.

All verbs are in past tense, so this passage now has consistent verb tense.

Split Infinitives

The *infinitive form* of a verb consists of "to + base verb"—e.g., to walk, to sleep, to approve. A *split infinitive* occurs when another word, usually an adverb, is placed between *to* and the verb:

> I decided *to simply walk* to work to get more exercise every day.

The infinitive *to walk* is split by the adverb *simply.*

> It was a mistake *to hastily approve* the project before conducting further preliminary research.

The infinitive *to approve* is split by *hastily.*

Although some grammarians still advise against split infinitives, this syntactic structure is common in both spoken and written English and is widely accepted in standard usage.

Subject-Verb Agreement

In English, verbs must agree with the subject. The form of a verb may change depending on whether the subject is singular or plural, or whether it is first, second, or third person. For example, the verb *to be* has various forms:

> I <u>am</u> a student.

> You <u>are</u> a student.

> She <u>is</u> a student.

> We <u>are</u> students.

> They <u>are</u> students.

Errors occur when a verb does not agree with its subject. Sometimes, the error is readily apparent:

> We is hungry.

Is is not the appropriate form of *to be* when used with the third person plural *we*.

> We are hungry.

This sentence now has correct subject-verb agreement.

However, some cases are trickier, particularly when the subject consists of a lengthy noun phrase with many modifiers:

> Students who are hoping to accompany the anthropology department on its annual summer trip to Ecuador needs to sign up by March 31st.

The verb in this sentence is *needs*. However, its subject is not the noun adjacent to it—Ecuador. The subject is the noun at the beginning of the sentence—students. Because *students* is plural, *needs* is the incorrect verb form.

> *Students* who are hoping to accompany the anthropology department on its annual summer trip to Ecuador *need* to sign up by March 31st.

This sentence now uses correct agreement between *students* and *need*.

Another case to be aware of is a *collective noun*. A collective noun refers to a group of many things or people but can be singular in itself—e.g., family, committee, army, pair team, council, jury. Whether or not a collective noun uses a singular or plural verb depends on how the noun is being used. If the noun refers to the group performing a collective action as one unit, it should use a singular verb conjugation:

> The family is moving to a new neighborhood.

The whole family is moving together in unison, so the singular verb form *is* is appropriate here.

> The committee has made its decision.

The verb *has* and the possessive pronoun *its* both reflect the word *committee* as a singular noun in the sentence above; however, when a collective noun refers to the group as individuals, it can take a plural verb:

> The newlywed pair spend every moment together.

This sentence emphasizes the love between two people in a pair, so it can use the plural verb *spend*.

> The council are all newly elected members.

The sentence refers to the council in terms of its individual members and uses the plural verb *are*.

Overall though, American English is more likely to pair a collective noun with a singular verb, while British English is more likely to pair a collective noun with a plural verb.

Grammar, Usage, Syntax, and Mechanics Choices

Colons and Semicolons

In a sentence, *colons* are used before a list, a summary or elaboration, or an explanation related to the preceding information in the sentence:

> There are two ways to reserve tickets for the performance: by phone or in person.

> One thing is clear: students are spending more on tuition than ever before.

As these examples show, a colon must be preceded by an independent clause. However, the information after the colon may be in the form of an independent clause or in the form of a list.

Semicolons can be used in two different ways—to join ideas or to separate them. In some cases, semicolons can be used to connect what would otherwise be stand-alone sentences. Each part of the sentence joined by a semicolon must be an independent clause. The use of a semicolon indicates that these two independent clauses are closely related to each other:

> The rising cost of childcare is one major stressor for parents; healthcare expenses are another source of anxiety.

> Classes have been canceled due to the snowstorm; check the school website for updates.

Semicolons can also be used to divide elements of a sentence in a more distinct way than simply using a comma. This usage is particularly useful when the items in a list are especially long and complex and contain other internal punctuation.

> Retirees have many modes of income: some survive solely off their retirement checks; others supplement their income through part time jobs, like working in a supermarket or substitute teaching; and others are financially dependent on the support of family members, friends, and spouses.

Its and It's

These pronouns are some of the most confused in the English language as most possessives contain the suffix –'s. However, for *it*, it is the opposite. *Its* is a possessive pronoun:

> The government is reassessing *its* spending plan.

It's is a contraction of the words *it is*:

> *It's* snowing outside.

Saw and Seen

Saw and *seen* are both conjugations of the verb *to see*, but they express different verb tenses. *Saw* is used in the simple past tense. *Seen* is the past participle form of *to see* and can be used in all perfect tenses.

> I seen her yesterday.

This sentence is incorrect. Because it expresses a completed event from a specified point in time in the past, it should use simple past tense:

> I *saw* her yesterday.

This sentence uses the correct verb tense. Here's how the past participle is used correctly:

I *have seen* her before.

The meaning in this sentence is slightly changed to indicate an event from an unspecific time in the past. In this case, present perfect is the appropriate verb tense to indicate an unspecified past experience. Present perfect conjugation is created by combining *to have* + past participle.

Then and Than
Then is generally used as an adverb indicating something that happened next in a sequence or as the result of a conditional situation:

We parked the car and *then* walked to the restaurant.

If enough people register for the event, *then* we can begin planning.

Than is a conjunction indicating comparison:

This watch is more expensive *than* that one.

The bus departed later *than* I expected.

They're, Their, and There
They're is a contraction of the words *they are*:

They're moving to Ohio next week.

Their is a possessive pronoun:

The baseball players are training for *their* upcoming season.

There can function as multiple parts of speech, but it is most commonly used as an adverb indicating a location:

Let's go to the concert! Some great bands are playing *there*.

Insure and Ensure
These terms are both verbs. *Insure* means to guarantee something against loss, harm, or damage, usually through an insurance policy that offers monetary compensation:

The robbers made off with her prized diamond necklace, but luckily it was *insured* for one million dollars.

Ensure means to make sure, to confirm, or to be certain:

Ensure that you have your passport before entering the security checkpoint.

Accept and Except
Accept is a verb meaning to take or agree to something:

I would like to *accept* your offer of employment.

Except is a preposition that indicates exclusion:

I've been to every state in America *except* Hawaii.

Affect and Effect
Affect is a verb meaning to influence or to have an impact on something:

The amount of rainfall during the growing season *affects* the flavor of wine produced from these grapes.

Effect can be used as either a noun or a verb. As a noun, *effect* is synonymous with a result:

If we implement the changes, what will the *effect* be on our profits?

As a verb, *effect* means to bring about or to make happen:

In just a few short months, the healthy committee has *effected* real change in school nutrition.

Major Literary Works of U.S. Literature

Literature refers to a collection of written works that are the distinctive voices of peoples, time periods, and cultures. The world has gained great insight into human thought, vices, virtues, and desires through the written word. As the work pertains to the author's approach to these insights, literature can be classified as fiction or non-fiction.

The MTEL test assumes test takers will have a familiarity with a wide range of American, British, World, and Young Adult literary works. In most cases, the test taker will be presented with a quoted literary passage and be required to answer one or more questions about it. This may involve having to identify the literary work presented from a list of options.

The ability of the test taker to demonstrate familiarity of major literary works is key in success when taking this exam. The following chart offers some examples of major works in addition to those listed elsewhere in this guide, but the list not exhaustive.

American
Fictional Prose
- Harriet Beecher Stowe | *Uncle Tom's Cabin*
- Ernest Hemingway | *For Whom the Bell Tolls*
- Jack London | *The Call of the Wild*
- Toni Morrison | *Beloved*
- N. Scott Momaday | *The Way to Rainy Mountain*
- J.D. Salinger | *Catcher in the Rye*
- John Steinbeck | *Grapes of Wrath*
- Alice Walker | *The Color Purple*

Drama
- Edward Albee | *Who's Afraid of Virginia Woolf?*
- Lorraine Hansberry | *A Raisin in the Sun*
- Amiri Baraka | *Dutchman*
- Eugene O'Neill |*Long Day's Journey into Night*
- Sam Shephard | *Buried Child*

- Thornton Wilder I *Our Town*
- Tennessee Williams | *A Streetcar Named Desire*

Poetry
- Anne Bradstreet | "In Reference to her Children, 23 June 1659"
- Emily Dickinson | "Because I could not stop for Death"
- Sylvia Plath | "Mirror"
- Langston Hughes | "Harlem"
- Edgar Allen Poe | "The Raven"
- Phillis Wheatley | "On Being Brought from Africa to America"
- Walt Whitman | "Song of Myself"

Literary Non-fiction
- Maya Angelou | *I Know Why the Caged Bird Sings*
- Truman | *Capote In Cold Blood*
- Frederick Douglass | *My Bondage and My Freedom*
- Archie Fire | *Lame Deer The Gift of Power: The Life and Teachings of a Lakota Medicine Man*
- Helen Keller | *The Story of My Life*
- Dave Pelzer | *A Child Called "It"*

Literature from Classical and Contemporary Periods

<u>British</u>
Fictional Prose
- John Bunyan | *The Pilgrim's Progress*
- Joseph Conrad | *Heart of Darkness*
- Charles Dickens | *Tale of Two Cities*
- George Eliot | *Middlemarch*
- George Orwell | *1984*
- Mary Shelley | *Frankenstein*

Drama
- Samuel Beckett |*Waiting for Godot*
- Caryl Churchill | *Top Girls*
- William Congreve | *The Way of the World*
- Michael Frayn | *Noises Off*
- William Shakespeare | *Macbeth*
- Oscar Wilde | *The Importance of Being Earnest*

Poetry
- Elizabeth Barrett Browning | "How Do I Love Thee? (Sonnet 43)"
- Robert Burns | "A Red, Red Rose"
- Samuel Taylor Coleridge | "Rime of the Ancient Mariner"
- T.S. Eliot | "Love Song of J. Alfred Prufrock"
- John Milton | "Paradise Lost"

Literary Non-fiction
- Vera Brittain | *Testament of Youth*
- T. E. Lawrence | *Seven Pillars of Wisdom*
- Doris Lessing | *Going Home*
- Brian Blessed | *Absolute Pandemonium: The Autobiography*
- Virginia Woolf | *A Room of One's Own*

World
Fictional Prose
- Anonymous | *The Epic of Gilgamesh*
- Chinua Achebe | *Things Fall Apart*
- Margaret Atwood | *The Handmaid's Tale*
- Pearl S. Buck | *The Good Earth*
- Miguel de Cervantes | *Don Quixote*
- Fyodor Dostoyevsky | *Crime and Punishment*
- Gabriel Garcia Marquez | *One Hundred Years of Solitude*
- James Joyce | *Ulysses*
- Nikos Kazantzakis | *Zorba the Greek*
- Boris Pasternak | *Dr. Zhivago*
- Amy Tan | *The Joy Luck Club*
- Voltaire | *Candide*

Drama
- Bertolt Brecht | *Mother Courage and her Children*
- Anton Chekhov | *The Seagull*
- Lady Gregory | *Workhouse Ward*
- Henrik Ibsen | *A Doll's House*
- Luigi Pirandello | *Six Characters in Search of an Author*
- Molière | *Tartuffe*
- Sophocles | *Antigone*
- August Strindberg | *Miss Julie*
- Vyasa | *The Bhagavad Gita*
- Johann Wolfgang von Goethe | *Faust*

Poetry
- Anonymous | *Beowulf*
- Anonymous | *The Ramayana*
- Dante Alighieri | *The Divine Comedy*
- Federico García Lorca | *Gypsy Ballads*
- Omar Khayyám | *The Rubaiyat*
- Kahlil Gibran | *The Prophet*
- Andrew Barton "Banjo" Paterson | *"Waltzing Matilda"*
- Taslima Nasrin | *"Character"*
- Kostis Palamas | *"Ancient Eternal And Immortal Spirit"*
- Maria Elena Cruz Varela | *"Kaleidoscope"*
- Unknown | The 23rd Psalm, the Judeo-Christian bible

Literary Non-fiction

- Pavel Basinsky | *Flight from Paradise*
- Jung Chang | *Wild Swans*
- Confucius | *The Analects of Confucius*
- Viktor Frankl | *Man's Search for Meaning*
- Mahatma Gandhi | *India of my Dreams*
- Nelson Mandela | *Long Walk to Freedom*
- Fatema Mernissi | *Beyond the Veil*
- Jonathan Swift | "A Modest Proposal"

Recognizing Literature of Other Cultures

Literature from other cultures can vary based on an author's purpose. Stories can be passed down from one generation to the next through different types of literature. Fables, folktales, poetry, drama, fiction, and nonfiction texts often represent cultural themes from country to country. Readers may use literature from other cultures to compare and contrast cultural groups or time periods or even educate themselves on their own heritage.

In the tables below, review various types of literature from both Western and Eastern cultures. All literature listed has been published within the past one hundred years.

Western Culture:

Title	Author	Country	Genre	Year
The Hobbit	J.R.R. Tolkien	England	Fantasy	1937
Animal Farm	George Orwell	England	Political allegory/satire	1945
1984	George Orwell	England	Dystopia novel/fiction	1949
The Catcher in the Rye	J.D. Salinger	United States	Fiction	1951
The Old Man and the Sea	Ernest Hemingway	United States	Fiction	1952
Lolita	Vladimir Nabokov	Russia	Fiction	1955
To Kill a Mockingbird	Harper Lee	United States	Southern Gothic/fiction	1960
White Teeth	Zadie Smith	England	Fiction	2000
Atonement	Ian McEwan	England	Metafiction	2001
Half a Yellow Sun	Chimamanda Ngozi Adichie	Nigeria	Historical fiction	2006
Wolf Hall	Hilary Mantel	England	Biographical fiction	2010

Eastern Culture:

Title	Author	Country	Genre	Year
The Home and the World	Rabindranath Tagore	India	Historical fiction	1916
Rickshaw Boy	Lao She	China	Fiction	1937
An Insular Possession	Timothy Mo	Hong Kong	Historical fiction	1986
Wild Swans: Three Daughters of China	Jung Chang	China	Biography	1991
To Live	Yu Hua	China	Novel	1993
A Fine Balance	Rohinton Mistry	Canada	Historical novel	1995
The God of Small Things	Arundhati Roy	India	Fiction/coming of age	1997
Frog	Mo Yan	China	Fiction	2009

Elements of Literary Analysis

Literary texts also employ rhetorical devices. Figurative language like simile and metaphor is a type of rhetorical device commonly found in literature. In addition to rhetorical devices that play on the *meanings* of words, there are also rhetorical devices that use the *sounds* of words. These devices are most often found in poetry but may also be found in other types of literature and in non-fiction writing like speech texts.

Alliteration and *assonance* are both varieties of sound repetition. Other types of sound repetition include: anaphora, repetition that occurs at the beginning of the sentences; epiphora, repetition occurring at the end of phrases; antimetabole, repetition of words in reverse order; and antiphrasis, a form of denial of an assertion in a text.

Alliteration refers to the repetition of the first sound of each word. Recall Robert Burns' opening line:

My love is like a red, red rose

This line includes two instances of alliteration: "love" and "like" (repeated *L* sound), as well as "red" and "rose" (repeated *R* sound). Next, assonance refers to the repetition of vowel sounds, and can occur anywhere within a word (not just the opening sound). Here is the opening of a poem by John Keats:

When I have fears that I may cease to be

Before my pen has glean'd my teeming brain

Assonance can be found in the words "fears," "cease," "be," "glean'd," and "teeming," all of which stress the long *E* sound. Both alliteration and assonance create a harmony that unifies the writer's language.

Another sound device is *onomatopoeia*, or words whose spelling mimics the sound they describe. Words like "crash," "bang," and "sizzle" are all examples of onomatopoeia. Use of onomatopoetic language adds auditory imagery to the text.

Readers are probably most familiar with the technique of *pun*. A pun is a play on words, taking advantage of two words that have the same or similar pronunciation. Puns can be found throughout Shakespeare's plays, for instance:

> Now is the winter of our discontent
> Made glorious summer by this son of York

These lines from *Richard III* contain a play on words. Richard III refers to his brother, the newly crowned King Edward IV, as the "son of York," referencing their family heritage from the house of York. However, while drawing a comparison between the political climate and the weather (times of political trouble were the "winter," but now the new king brings "glorious summer"), Richard's use of the word "son" also implies another word with the same pronunciation, "sun"—so Edward IV is also like the sun, bringing light, warmth, and hope to England. Puns are a clever way for writers to suggest two meanings at once.

Some examples of figurative language are included in the following graphic.

	Definition	Example
Simile	Compares two things using "like" or "as"	Her hair was like gold.
Metaphor	Compares two things as if they are the same	He was a giant teddy bear.
Idiom	Using words with predictable meanings to create a phrase with a different meaning	The world is your oyster.
Alliteration	Repeating the same beginning sound or letter in a phrase for emphasis	The busy baby babbled.
Personification	Attributing human characteristics to an object or an animal	The house glowered menacingly with a dark smile.
Symbolism	Using symbols to represent ideas and provide a different meaning	The ring represented the bond between us.
Onomatopoeia	Using words that imitate sound	The tire went off with a bang and a crunch.
Imagery	Appealing to the senses by using descriptive language	The sky was painted with red and pink and streaked with orange.
Hyperbole	Using exaggeration not meant to be taken literally	The girl weighed less than a feather.

Focuses of Literary Criticism

A *literary theory* can be considered a methodology for understanding literature. It asks, "What is literature?" and offers readers a working set of principles to understand common themes, ideas, and intent. Classifications of literary theory are often referred to as *schools of thought*. These schools are based on subdivisions in historical perspective and in philosophical thinking across literary analysts and critics.

Romanticism/Aestheticism

Romanticism/Aestheticism spanned the 19th century and developed in response to the idea that enlightenment and reason were the source of all truth and authority in philosophy. Romanticism and Aestheticism embraced the tenet that *aesthetics*—all that is beautiful and natural—in art and literature should be considered the highest-held principle, overriding all others. Popular authors include Oscar Wilde, Edgar Allan Poe, Mary Shelley, and John Keats.

Marxism

Marxism as a literary theory developed in the early twentieth century after the Russian October Revolution of 1917. It loosely embraced the idea that social realism was the highest form of literature and that the social classes' struggle for progress was the most important concept literature could emphasize. Examples of authors include Simone de Beauvoir and Bertolt Brecht.

Structuralism

Structuralism included all aspects of philosophy, linguistics, anthropology, and literary theory. Beginning in the early 1900s, this school of thought focused on ideas surrounding how human culture is understood within its larger structures and how those structures influence people's thoughts and actions. Specifically, structuralism examines how literature is interconnected through structure. It examines common elements in the stories and the myths that contribute to literature as a whole. Popular theorists and writers include Claude Levi-Strauss, Umberto Eco, and Roland Barthes.

Post-Structuralism and Deconstruction

Post-Structuralism and *deconstruction* developed out of structuralism in the twentieth century. It expanded on the idea of overall structure in literature, but both theories argue varying analytical concepts of how that structure should be examined and utilized. For example, while structuralism acknowledges oppositional relationships in literature—e.g., male/female, beginning/end, rational/emotional—post-structuralism and deconstruction began de-emphasizing the idea that one idea is always dominant over another. Both also assert that studying text also means studying the knowledge that produced the text. Popular theorists and writers include Roland Barthes and Michel Foucault.

New Criticism

New Criticism dominated American culture in the mid-twentieth century. It purports that close, critical reading was necessary to understanding literary works, especially poetry. Popular theory also focused on the inherent beauty of text itself. New Criticism rejected the previous critical focus of how history, use of language, and the author's experience influence literature, asserting those ideas as being too loosely interpretive in examining literature. As a movement, it tended to separate literature from historical context and an author's intent. It embraced the idea that formal study of structure and text should not be separated. Theorists of note include Stephen Greenblatt and Jonathan Goldberg.

Feminist and Queer Theory

Feminist and *Queer Theory* are more recent schools of thought that critically examine the roles of gender identity, sexuality, and the feminist movement in literature. Feminist theory uses the principles of feminism as a framework, examining the language of the literature and the ways that literature portrays male domination. Queer Theory examines works through the lens of a lesbian/gay readers as well as the concept of homosexuality, socially-constructed nature of sex, and identity. Theorists of note include Judith Butler and Eve Sedgwick.

Basic Literary Terminology

- Foreshadowing: Giving an indication that something is going to happen later in the story
- Flashback: A moment where one of the characters experiences a memory of a previous event
- Allegory: A story that is told as a larger metaphor, usually with a moral purpose
- Parody: A parody is a humorous narrative meant to mimic a more serious work
- Protagonist: The main character of a narrative
- Antagonist: The character pitted against the protagonist in a narrative
- Archetype: An archetype is a character that is consistent across all genres, such as the hero, villain, evil stepmother, etc.
- Allusion: A reference to an earlier person, work, or idea in history
- Hyperbole: An exaggeration
- Juxtaposition: When two different things are held up side-by-side in order to make a comparison
- Motif: A recurring symbol
- Personification: When an animal or object is given human characteristics

Characteristics of Literary Genres

Fictional Prose
Fiction written in prose can be further broken down into **fiction genres**—types of fiction. Some of the more common genres of fiction are as follows:

- **Classical fiction**: a work of fiction considered timeless in its message or theme, remaining noteworthy and meaningful over decades or centuries—e.g., Charlotte Brontë's *Jane Eyre*, Mark Twain's *Adventures of Huckleberry Finn*

- **Fables**: short fiction that generally features animals, fantastic creatures, or other forces within nature that assume human-like characters and has a moral lesson for the reader—e.g., *Aesop's Fables*

- **Fairy tales**: children's stories with magical characters in imaginary, enchanted lands, usually depicting a struggle between good and evil, a sub-genre of folklore—e.g., Hans Christian Anderson's *The Little Mermaid*, *Cinderella* by the Brothers Grimm

- **Fantasy**: fiction with magic or supernatural elements that cannot occur in the real world, sometimes involving medieval elements in language, usually includes some form of sorcery or witchcraft and sometimes set on a different world—e.g., J.R.R. Tolkien's *The Hobbit*, J.K. Rowling's *Harry Potter and the Sorcerer's Stone*, George R.R. Martin's *A Game of Thrones*

- **Folklore**: types of fiction passed down from oral tradition, stories indigenous to a particular region or culture, with a local flavor in tone, designed to help humans cope with their condition in life and validate cultural traditions, beliefs, and customs—e.g., William Laughead's *Paul Bunyan and The Blue Ox*, the Buddhist story of "The Banyan Deer"

- **Mythology**: closely related to folklore but more widespread, features mystical, otherworldly characters and addresses the basic question of why and how humans exist, relies heavily on allegory and features gods or heroes captured in some sort of struggle—e.g., Greek myths, Genesis I and II in the Bible, Arthurian legends

- **Science fiction**: fiction that uses the principle of extrapolation—loosely defined as a form of prediction—to imagine future realities and problems of the human experience—e.g., Robert Heinlein's *Stranger in a Strange Land*, Ayn Rand's *Anthem*, Isaac Asimov's *I, Robot*, Philip K. Dick's *Do Androids Dream of Electric Sheep?*

- **Short stories**: short works of prose fiction with fully-developed themes and characters, focused on mood, generally developed with a single plot, with a short period of time for settings—e.g., Edgar Allan Poe's "Fall of the House of Usher," Shirley Jackson's "The Lottery," Isaac Bashevis Singer's "Gimpel the Fool"

Drama

Drama is fiction that is written to be performed in a variety of media, intended to be performed for an audience, and structured for that purpose. It might be composed using poetry or prose, often straddling the elements of both in what actors are expected to present. Action and dialogue are the tools used in drama to tell the story. Please see the section called "Types of Drama" to see a more comprehensive list.

Poetry

Poetry is fiction in verse that has a unique focus on the rhythm of language and focuses on intensity of feeling. It is not an entire story, though it may tell one; it is compact in form and in function. Poetry can be considered as a poet's brief word picture for a reader. Poetic structure is primarily composed of lines and stanzas. Together, poetic structure and devices are the methods that poets use to lead readers to feeling an effect and, ultimately, to the interpretive message. Please see the section called "Types of Poetry" for a more comprehensive list, and the section "Poetry Techniques" for more information on the genre of poetry.

Nonfiction

Nonfiction is prose writing that is based on facts. It can be about real-life events, people, places, or things. Biographies, autobiographies, "how-to" books, memoirs, and essays are examples of nonfiction writing. There are many common features of nonfiction writing, including the use of chronological order, compare and contrast, illustration, captions, and keys. Review some of these features below:

Types of Nonfiction
Biography
A *biography* is a work written about a real person (historical or currently living). It involves factual accounts of the person's life, often in a re-telling of those events based on available, researched factual information. The re-telling and dialogue, especially if related within quotes, must be accurate and reflect reliable sources. A biography reflects the time and place in which the person lived, with the goal of creating an understanding of the person and his/her human experience. Examples of well-known biographies include *The Life of Samuel Johnson* by James Boswell and *Steve Jobs* by Walter Isaacson.

Autobiography
An *autobiography* is a factual account of a person's life written by that person. It may contain some or all of the same elements as a biography, but the author is the subject matter. An autobiography will be told in first person narrative. Examples of well-known autobiographies in literature include *Night* by Elie Wiesel and *Margaret Thatcher: The Autobiography* by Margaret Thatcher.

Memoir
A *memoir* is a historical account of a person's life and experiences written by one who has personal, intimate knowledge of the information. The line between memoir, autobiography, and biography is

often muddled, but generally speaking, a memoir covers a specific timeline of events as opposed to the other forms of nonfiction. A memoir is less all-encompassing. It is also less formal in tone and tends to focus on the emotional aspect of the presented timeline of events. Some examples of memoirs in literature include *Angela's Ashes* by Frank McCourt and *All Creatures Great and Small* by James Herriot.

Journalism
Some forms of *journalism* can fall into the category of literary non-fiction—e.g., travel writing, nature writing, sports writing, the interview, and sometimes, the essay. Some examples include Elizabeth Kolbert's "The Lost World, in the Annals of Extinction series for *The New Yorker* and Gary Smith's "Ali and His Entourage" for *Sports Illustrated*.

Organizational Features of Nonfiction
Chronological Order
Nonfiction texts tend to place events in chronological order, in other words, arrange events based on what happened first, second, third, and so on. Chronological order provides a timeline of events for readers to easily follow. For example, review the childhood poem "Jack and Jill":

"Jack and Jill went up the hill to fetch a pail of water. Jack fell down, and broke his crown, and Jill came tumbling after."

This children's poem provides a very clear order of events. First, Jack and Jill went up the hill to fetch a pail of water. Next, Jack fell down. Then, he broke his crown. Finally, Jill came tumbling after.

Compare and Contrast
Another feature of nonfiction text is the use of compare and contrast. This feature takes two or more objects and studies their similarities (comparisons) and differences (contrasts). A Venn diagram is commonly used to compare and contrast objects in nonfiction texts.

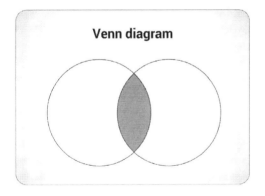

Venn diagram

Illustrations
Illustrations are drawings, photographs, or artwork that provide a visual image to readers. In nonfiction texts, illustrations can be used to give readers a true sense of time periods, locations, events, people, or things.

Captions
Nonfiction texts often use diagrams or illustrations. Captions use words to describe what the illustrations or diagrams are about.

Keys or Legends
Keys are often used to help navigate maps in nonfiction texts. Map keys identify what symbols or colors mean on a map. A map key is also known as a *legend*.

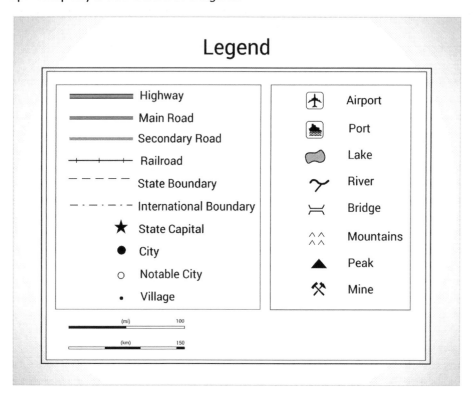

Elements in Fiction

There is no one, final definition of what literary elements are. They can be considered features or characteristics of fiction, but they are really more of a way that readers can unpack a text for the purpose of analysis and understanding the meaning. The elements contribute to a reader's literary interpretation of a passage as to how they function to convey the central message of a work. The most common literary elements used for analysis are the presented below.

Point of View
The *point of view* is the position the narrator takes when telling the story in prose. If a narrator is incorporated in a drama, the point of view may vary; in poetry, point of view refers to the position the speaker in a poem takes.

First Person
The first person point of view is when the writer uses the word "I" in the text. Poetry often uses first person, e.g., William Wordsworth's "I Wandered Lonely as a Cloud." Two examples of prose written in first person are Suzanne Collins' *The Hunger Games* and Anthony Burgess's *A Clockwork Orange*.

Second Person
The second person point of view is when the writer uses the pronoun "you." It is not widely used in prose fiction, but as a technique, it has been used by writers such as William Faulkner in *Absalom, Absalom!* and Albert Camus in *The Fall*. It is more common in poetry—e.g., Pablo Neruda's "If You Forget Me."

Third Person

Third person point of view is when the writer utilizes pronouns such as him, her, or them. It may be the most utilized point of view in prose as it provides flexibility to an author and is the one with which readers are most familiar. There are two main types of third person used in fiction. *Third person omniscient* uses a narrator that is all-knowing, relating the story by conveying and interpreting thoughts/feelings of all characters. In *third person limited,* the narrator relates the story through the perspective of one character's thoughts/feelings, usually the main character.

Plot

The *plot* is what happens in the story. Plots may be singular, containing one problem, or they may be very complex, with many sub-plots. All plots have exposition, a conflict, a climax, and a resolution. The *conflict* drives the plot and is something that the reader expects to be resolved. The plot carries those events along until there is a resolution to the conflict.

Tone

The *tone* of a story reflects the author's attitude and opinion about the subject matter of the story or text. Tone can be expressed through word choice, imagery, figurative language, syntax, and other details. The emotion or mood the reader experiences relates back to the tone of the story. Some examples of possible tones are humorous, somber, sentimental, and ironic.

Setting

The *setting* is the time, place, or set of surroundings in which the story occurs. It includes time or time span, place(s), climates, geography—man-made or natural—or cultural environments. Emily Dickinson's poem "Because I could not stop for Death" has a simple setting—the narrator's symbolic ride with Death through town towards the local graveyard. Conversely, Leo Tolstoy's *War and Peace* encompasses numerous settings within settings in the areas affected by the Napoleonic Wars, spanning 1805 to 1812.

Characters

Characters are the story's figures that assume primary, secondary, or minor roles. *Central* or *major* characters are those integral to the story—the plot cannot be resolved without them. A central character can be a *protagonist* or hero. There may be more than one protagonist, and he/she doesn't always have to possess good characteristics. A character can also be an *antagonist*—the force against a protagonist.

Dynamic characters change over the course of the plot time. *Static* characters do not change. A *symbolic* character is one that represents an author's idea about society in general—e.g., Napoleon in Orwell's *Animal Farm*. *Stock* characters are those that appear across genres and embrace stereotypes—e.g., the cowboy of the Wild West or the blonde bombshell in a detective novel. A *flat* character is one that does not present a lot of complexity or depth, while a *rounded* character does. Sometimes, the *narrator* of a story or the *speaker* in a poem can be a character—e.g., Nick Carraway in F. Scott Fitzgerald's *The Great Gatsby* or the speaker in Robert Browning's "My Last Duchess." The narrator might also function as a character in prose, though not be part of the story—e.g., Charles Dickens' narrator of *A Christmas Carol*.

Types of Poetry

Different poetic structures and devices are used to create the various major forms of poetry. Some of the most common forms are discussed in the following chart.

Type	Poetic Structure	Example
Ballad	A poem or song passed down orally which tells a story and in English tradition usually uses an ABAB or ABCB rhyme scheme	William Butler Yeats' "The Ballad Of Father O'Hart"
Epic	A long poem from ancient oral tradition which narrates the story of a legendary or heroic protagonist	Homer's The Odyssey Virgil's The Aeneid
Haiku	A Japanese poem of three unrhymed lines with five, seven, and five syllables (in English) with nature as a common subject matter	Matsuo Bashō An old silent pond... A frog jumps into the pond, splash! Silence again.
Limerick	A five-line poem written in an AABBA rhyme scheme, with a witty focus	From Edward Lear's Book of Nonsense— "There was a Young Person of Smyrna Whose grandmother threatened to burn her..."
Ode	A formal lyric poem that addresses and praises a person, place, thing, or idea	Edna St. Vincent Millay's "Ode To Silence"
Sonnet	A fourteen-line poem written in iambic pentameter	Shakespeare's Sonnets 18 and 130
Lyric	A lyric poem expresses the personal and emotional feelings of the author	Emily Dickinson "I Felt a Funeral in my Brain"
Narrative	A narrative poem tells a story	Edgar Allan Poe "The Raven"
Dramatic Monologue	A dramatic monologue is a poem where a character speaks to an auditor for the entire poem	Robert Browning "My Last Duchess"

Poetic Techniques

Poetic Devices

Rhyme is the poet's use of corresponding word sounds in order to create an effect. Most rhyme occurs at the ends of a poem's lines, which is how readers arrive at the *rhyme scheme*. Each line that has a corresponding rhyming sound is assigned a letter—A, B, C, and so on. When using a rhyme scheme, poets will often follow lettered patterns. Robert Frost's *"The Road Not Taken"* uses the ABAAB rhyme scheme:

Two roads diverged in a yellow wood,	A
And sorry I could not travel both	B
And be one traveler, long I stood	A
And looked down one as far as I could	A
To where it bent in the undergrowth;	B

Another important poetic device is *rhythm*—metered patterns within poetry verses. When a poet develops rhythm through *meter,* he or she is using a combination of stressed and unstressed syllables to create a sound effect for the reader.

Rhythm is created by the use of *poetic feet*—individual rhythmic units made up of the combination of stressed and unstressed syllables. A line of poetry is made up of one or more poetic feet. There are five standard types in English poetry, as depicted in the chart below.

Foot Type	Rhythm	Pattern
Iamb	buh Buh	Unstressed/stressed
Trochee	Buh buh	Stressed/unstressed
Spondee	Buh Buh	Stressed/stressed
Anapest	buh buh Buh	Unstressed/unstressed/stressed
Dactyl	Buh buh buh	Stressed/unstressed/unstressed

Structure

Poetry is most easily recognized by its structure, which varies greatly. For example, a structure may be strict in the number of lines it uses. It may use rhyming patterns or may not rhyme at all. There are three main types of poetic structures:

- *Verse*—poetry with a consistent meter and rhyme scheme
- *Blank verse*—poetry with consistent meter but an inconsistent rhyme scheme
- *Free verse*—poetry with inconsistent meter or rhyme

Verse poetry is most often developed in the form of *stanzas*—groups of word lines. Stanzas can also be considered *verses*. The structure is usually formulaic and adheres to the protocols for the form. For example, the English *sonnet* form uses a structure of fourteen lines and a variety of different rhyming patterns. The English *ode* typically uses three ten-line stanzas and has a particular rhyming pattern.

Poets choose poetic structure based on the effect they want to create. Some structures—such as the ballad and haiku—developed out of cultural influences and common artistic practice in history, but in more modern poetry, authors choose their structure to best fit their intended effect.

Types of Drama

Drama refers to a form of literature written for the purpose of performance for an audience. Like prose fiction, drama has several genres. The following are the most common ones:

- *Comedy*—a humorous play designed to amuse and entertain, often with an emphasis on the common person's experience, generally resolved in a positive way—e.g., Richard Sheridan's *School for Scandal*, Shakespeare's *Taming of the Shrew*, Neil Simon's *The Odd Couple*

- *History*—a play based on recorded history where the fate of a nation or kingdom is at the core of the conflict—e.g., Christopher Marlowe's *Edward II*, Shakespeare's *King Richard III*, Arthur Miller's *The Crucible*

- *Tragedy*—a serious play that often involves the downfall of the protagonist, in modern tragedies, the protagonist is not necessarily in a position of power or authority—e.g., Jean Racine's *Phèdre*, Arthur Miller's *Death of a Salesman*, John Steinbeck's *Of Mice and Men*

- *Melodrama*—a play that is emphasizes heightened emotion and sensationalism, generally with stereotypical characters in exaggerated or realistic situations and with moral polarization—e.g., Jean-Jacques Rousseau's *Pygmalion*

- *Tragi-comedy*—a play that has elements of both tragedy—a character experiencing a tragic loss—and comedy—the resolution is often positive with no clear distinctive mood for either—e.g., Shakespeare's *The Merchant of Venice*, Anton Chekhov's *The Cherry Orchard*

Major Works in Children's Literature

<u>Young Adult</u>
Fictional Prose
Jodi Lynn Anderson | *Tiger Lily*
Lois Lowry | *The Giver*
Scott O'Dell | *Island of the Blue Dolphins*
Katherine Paterson Jacob | *Have I Loved*
Antoine de Saint-Exupéry | *The Little Prince*
Ellen Raskin | *The Westing Game*
P. L. Travers | *Mary Poppins*
Marcus Zusak | *The Book Thief*

Drama
Peter Dee | *Voices from the High School*
William Gibson | *The Miracle Worker*

Poetry
Sandra Cisneros | "Eleven"
Eamon Grennan | "Cat Scat"
Tom Junod | "My Mother Couldn't Cook"
Tupac Shakur | "The Rose that Grew from Concrete"

Literary Non-fiction
Sherman Alexie | *The Absolutely True Diary of a Part-Time Indian*
Anne Frank | *The Diary of Anne Frank*
Philip Hoose | *The Boys who Challenged Hitler*
Cynthia Levinson | *We've Got a Job*
Malala Yousafzai and Christina Lamb | *I am Malala*

Genres of Children's Literature

There are seven main genres of children's literature. The genres include fiction (realistic, historical, and science fiction), nonfiction (biography, autobiography, and informational texts), poetry, fantasy, mystery or suspense, folklore and fairy tales, and myths. Review each genre independently:

Fiction
Fiction is a type of literature based on imaginary events, people, or places. Fiction texts are not real, although they can appear to be real. Realistic fiction is a make-believe story about someone or something in an authentic setting. Fiction texts may also be based on historical events or science; however, details may be fabricated.

Nonfiction
Nonfiction texts are fact based. They represent real-life events, people, places, and things. Nonfiction texts include biography (a story about a person written by another person), autobiography (a story about someone written by themselves), and informational text (a text written to educate readers about a topic).

Poetry
Poetry is a piece of literary work meant to express feelings and ideas through rhythm and rhyme; however, not all poems rhyme. There are seven poetry forms: sonnet (short rhyming poem with 14 lines), limerick (5-line poem with rhythm), haiku (3-line poem following line-by-line syllable patterns), narrative (poem that tells a short story), epic (long poem usually featuring a hero or adventure), couplet (2-line rhyming poem), and finally, free verse (poem that does not follow any poetry rules).

Fantasy
In the fantasy genre, characters, places, and events are completely fictional. In no way, shape, or form could these things exist in real life.

Mystery or Suspense
The mystery or suspense genre is a fictional story involving some sort of crime or suspenseful event that needs to be solved. It can take place in a novel or a series of short stories.

Folklore and Fairy Tales
Folklore and fairy tales are stories that are told and passed down among generations. This genre usually includes animals, songs, cultural myths, and jokes. Fairy tales are also folkloric texts that may include magical creatures like dragons, giants, witches, or fairies.

Myths
Myths are fictional legendary stories incorporating heroic characters.

Major Themes Associated with Children's Literature

Children's literature tends to have overlapping themes throughout different genres. A theme is the overall subject or message in a story. Common themes in children's literature are family, friendship, growing up, self-esteem, and morality.

Family
Family tends to be a common theme in children's literature. Authors provide readers with examples of relationships such as father/son, mother/daughter, grandparent/grandchild, and cousin/cousin. These relationships may display positive or negative feelings of love, joy, pain, or sadness. They can also find

strengths or weaknesses in family communication or togetherness. One popular children's book centered on family is *A Chair for My Mother* by Vera B. Williams. In this story, a family works hard to save money to buy their mother a special chair after all of her furniture is lost in a fire. The tale of hard work, sacrifice, and love teaches many lessons to students of all ages.

Friendship

Another common theme in children's literature is friendship. Children are greatly influenced by friends. Texts may portray positive or negative choices among friends leading to a great or poor outcome. Throughout friendship-themed literature, children learn all sorts of valuable lessons like compromise, coping skills, togetherness, caring for others, inclusion, and adversity. One popular children's book centered on friendship is *Charlotte's Web* by E.B. White. In this story, unlikely friendships occur in many forms. A young girl and a pig, a pig and a spider, and a goose and a horse all celebrate one another's differences and support each other's decisions through this children's tale.

Growing Up

Growing up is another common theme in children's literature. Children's literature has countless texts of kids going through different scenarios as they get older. Overlapping themes include friendship, puberty, judgment calls, overcoming challenges, and accepting responsibilities. For example, the children's book, *Alice in Wonderland,* by Lewis Carroll, demonstrates concepts such as the challenges of being big and small, as well as decision-making.

Self-Esteem

Self-esteem is the emotional feelings one has about himself or herself. Self-esteem–themed children's literature tries to demonstrate positive feelings and emotions to build self-esteem. Acceptance, love, learning opportunities, goal setting, pride, and trying new things are common subjects in self-esteem–themed texts. For example, the children's book, *I Like Myself,* by Karen Beaumont, discusses how to be proud and confident regardless of physical appearances.

Morality

Morality is the judgment of right from wrong. Children always have choices. Morality-themed children's books share the principles and outcomes of good and poor choices. Themes such as honesty, friend choices, respect, and sharing are common in morality-themed children's texts. For example, the children's book series, *The Berenstain Bears,* by Stan and Jan Berenstain, always reveals a predicament where the kids or adults need to use problem-solving skills to solve the issue. One of the books in the series, *The Berenstain Bears and the Truth,* discusses how to feel proud of telling the truth and how important truth telling is.

Rhetorical and Literary Devices in Children's Literature

Rhetorical devices are techniques and language used by authors to influence readers' perspectives of texts. *Literary devices* are methods that authors use to create special effects in literature. Both devices are commonly used in children's literature to create visual representations and examples for young readers. Four commonly used devices are analogies, similes, metaphors, and symbolism. Review each device individually below.

Analogies

Analogies compare two objects that are different yet share similar characteristics. When comparing two objects, the goal is to demonstrate how the objects relate to one another. Analogies often use similes and metaphors to compare objects. For example, in the simile "Her hands were as cold as ice," "her hands" are clearly not made of ice; however, the reference to "ice" tells the reader that her hands were extremely cold. Let's review the differences between similes and metaphors below.

Similes

A simile compares two objects using the words "like" or "as." For example, in the sentence, "The muffin was as hard as a rock," "the muffin" is clearly not a rock; however, the word "rock" creates a visual image for the reader that the muffin was very hard.

Metaphors

Metaphors compare two unlike objects by replacing one word with another word. For example, in the sentence, "The students were angels for the substitute teacher," "the students" are not actually angels; however, the term "angels" portrays good behavior, leading the reader to understand that the students were well behaved for the substitute teacher.

Symbolism

Metaphors use symbolism. Symbolism uses symbolic images, people, places, or things to represent them as something completely different. It provides a deeper meaning to literary works. For example, in the fairy tale, "Beauty and the Beast," a curse was cast on a prince, turning him into a beast. The prince needed to find true love and acceptance despite his new appearance as a beast. A single rose symbolized the amount of time the beast had to find true love, acceptance, and beauty in all things (including an ugly beast). As the rose wilted, the beast had less time and may have indefinitely remained a beast. Fortunately, the beast found true love, acceptance, and beauty in all things before the final rose petal fell, and the spell was broken.

Different Styles and Communicative Purposes in Children's Literature

Children's literature is an important teaching tool both inside and outside the classroom. No child has the same experience as another. Children are from different cultures, socioeconomic status, and families, yet they may all be in the same classroom expected to read and learn the same material. For this reason, it is important to expose all readers to a variety of texts to gain, or relate to, different outlooks and experiences. It is also vital to allow readers time to respond to what they have read and form their own opinions or summaries of texts in order to gain complete understanding.

Children's texts allow young readers to use their imaginations to build visual maps of stories in their heads or out loud in group settings. Children's literature also allows students to deal with personal situations by learning and relating to characters, settings, or problem-solving solutions. Review the chart below examining suggested book categories according to age groups. Remember, every child is different and may read above or below the suggested styles.

Suggested Age-Based Literature Categories:

Age	Category	Definition
Zero to 5 (Pre-readers)	Picture books	Combinations of visual images and short narratives to convey a message
5 to 7	Early readers	Short stories intended to help build reading skills
7 to 12	Chapter books: short (ages 7 to 9), long (ages 9 to 12)	Longer books with multiple chapters that build a story line
12 to 18	Young adult fiction	Story lines requiring critical thinking or focus on overcoming challenges

Each category has a variety of texts to communicate varying purposes. From picture books to chapter books, authors intend to strengthen language, fluency, and critical thinking skills. The exposure to new vocabulary words, phrases, tone, and dilemmas provides students with opportunities to activate their prior knowledge on topics as well as expand their thoughts further. One way teachers and parents can help young readers interpret text meaning is by doing a "picture walk." A picture walk is when students review the text's pictures to determine the meaning of the story. It is a great way to introduce stories or unfamiliar context to young readers. Picture walking also allows young readers to think about what may happen next or as a result of a previous action. Engaging students in the story, whether by interpreting pictures or recapping chapters, is key to successfully understanding literature. Simply put, any style of children's literature sparks discussions of all kinds.

Criteria for Evaluating Children's Literature

Children learn in different ways. What may interest one student may be a complete bore to another. Educationally, students are on all different levels. It is important for teachers and parents to expose students to a variety of texts to properly evaluate the type of literature they should be reading. Remember, students should be engaged while reading. Therefore, they need literature that they take interest in, or on their own level. If the content of the text is over their heads or uninteresting, what will the students learn or take away from the text? When evaluating children's literature, parents and teachers should consider reading level, literary quality, richness in vocabulary, student interests, illustrations, and gender and cultural bias. Below, review each evaluation topic individually.

Reading Level
Reading levels evaluate the difficulty of texts for students. Teachers and parents can assess students' reading levels by simply assessing their reading skills. There are four major reading-level assessment tests:

- The Lexile Framework for Reading
- Fountas and Pinnell
- Reading Recovery
- Developmental Reading Assessment (DRA)

Each of these assessments focuses on phonemic awareness, word blends, segmenting, syllabication, fluency, and comprehension to help target students' reading level. Once students' reading levels are determined, parents and teachers can guide students to books they will understand yet remained challenged.

Literary Quality
Another thing to consider when evaluating children's literature is the text quality. Is the story written well? Is the text engaging for the intended audience? Does the story use proper grammar and syntax to make the story readable for the age in which the story was written? Literary quality should represent a variety of perspectives; however, texts should also be well written and easy to understand. Poorly written or vague texts are confusing to readers. It is important for parents and teachers to properly evaluate the literary quality of texts to ensure that they are suitable for their students.

Richness in Vocabulary
Texts are word rich. Students learn new words and meanings through exposure. It is important for teachers and parents to provide text-rich literature to help children's vocabulary grow. If students read the same words over and over, their vocabulary will not expand. Exposing students to word meanings, synonyms, and antonyms will increase their overall literacy skills.

Student Interests
Teachers and parents must consider their audience when selecting literature for students. Children have different interests. Allowing students to choose their own texts is one option, as long as parents and/or teachers review the texts to ensure other aspects such as reading level and text quality are on target. Teachers or parents may also provide a variety of topics in their library. This allows students to find an interesting topic to read about. Teachers and parents may want to consider the use of "book bags." Book bags are designed for each student. Every individual bag contains books that are interesting to the intended reader and on the reader's level.

When evaluating student interests in children's literature, it is also important to make sure parents and teachers choose texts that are not embarrassing. Remember, the point of properly evaluating children's literature is to encourage reading, not to embarrass readers.

Illustrations
Illustrations are pictures used in a book to clarify text. Illustrations should tell stories of their own. Before teachers or parents read a children's book to students, they often ask, "What do you see on the cover? What do you think this story is about?" Pictures help students form thoughts and opinions on what the text is, or might be, about. Illustrations engage readers further into texts and make stories more understandable.

Evaluating illustrations in children's literature is important because teachers and parents should make sure that the illustrations help build story lines and critical thinking skills, not just make the cover or pages look pretty.

Gender and Cultural Bias
Finally, when evaluating children's literature, it is important to consider and assess gender and cultural bias in texts. Teachers and parents should check the story lines to make sure there is not any implicit or explicit race, gender, or cultural bias, unless that is the specific study topic. Character portrayal, settings, and language used in children's literature should be authentic, not generic.

Children's Literature in Relation to Style, Theme, or Voice

Style, theme, and voice are three influential factors on a reader's perspective of text. The way a reader interprets language, settings, characters, and plots is subjective to the author's purpose. If an author's style, theme, or voice is inconsistent in a text, what they are reading may confuse readers. Review each of the terms below.

Style

In literature, style is the way in which an author writes. It influences how readers understand the story line and perceive the text itself. Authors must decide if they are going to write in the first or third person to portray the story line, the role(s) each character will play throughout the story's development, the key focus per page or chapter, and the setting of the story (including past or present tense as well as location(s)). All of these factors affect the clarity of the text. As long as authors are consistent with their style, readers should be able to unambiguously follow the plot.

Theme

Theme is the centralized topic of a text. Common themes in children's literature include friendship, family, growing up, acceptance, morality, and self-esteem. Each theme attempts to educate and influence readers and keeps the story line fluid. Some authors carry a theme through a series of texts with prequels and sequels.

Voice

Voice is the way in which the narrator conveys his or her message of a given text. The voice in a text grabs a reader's attention. It makes the text relatable and expressive. There are two main types of voices: author's voice and character's voice. When using an author's voice, the author uses his or her own language style and flow to influence how the text is interpreted. When the author uses a character's voice, he or she uses the main character of the text to portray a message. First- and third-person perspectives are commonly used in a character's voice.

Uses of Children's Literature

Children's literature is mainly used to model reading and writing skills. Beyond its basic purpose, children's literature opens the eyes and minds of young readers to the world much bigger than they know it. It is a way for children to learn about experiences that they may have yet to encounter but may cross paths with in the future. Children's literature allows young readers to engage and visualize word meanings through rich and deep language and illustrations.

Teachers and parents can use children's literature to help children "connect the dots" between varieties of subject matter. In classrooms, teachers can utilize children's literature to enhance other areas of the curriculum. In classrooms and homes, teachers and parents can use children's literature to foster cross-cultural understanding. Review ways in which teachers and parents use children's literature inside and outside classrooms and homes.

Other Areas of the Curriculum

Children's literature has a wide range of themes and topics for all ages. All major curricula subjects can utilize children's literature to reinforce material being taught in classrooms or in homes. For example, young learners begin their literacy and mathematical adventures with the alphabet and numbers. Teachers and parents can teach letters and numbers one way and then present a fun and engaging children's book reiterating the same concepts.

Using children's literature is not just for pre-readers or young readers. Social studies and science teachers often use informational children's literature to recap or introduce content. Nonfiction texts, including biographies, autobiographies, how-to books, and journal articles, are commonly used across social studies and science curricula.

Cross-Cultural Understanding
Children's literature celebrates how people, places, and things are different. Stories that range in topics addressing gender, race, and socioeconomic status are presented in a way that is easy for children to understand. Children's literature teaches moral lessons such as acceptance, perseverance, and kindness, often through relatable words and imagery.

Cross-cultural children's books help students understand their own cultures and discover information about their peers' cultures as well. It is important for teachers and parents to provide texts that are representative of the classroom population. Children come from all different backgrounds and experiences. Therefore, cross-cultural understanding should be fostered through multicultural books.

Prewriting Strategies

Recognizing Research-Based Strategies for Teaching the Writing Process
Current trends in education have recognized the need to cultivate writing skills that prepare students for higher education and professional careers. To this end, writing skills are being integrated into other subjects beyond the language arts classroom. The skills and strategies used in language arts class, then, should be adaptable for other learning tasks. In this way, students can achieve greater proficiency by incorporating writing strategies into every aspect of learning.

To teach writing, it is important that writers know the writing process. Students should be familiar with the five components of the writing process:

1. *Pre-writing*: The drafting, planning, researching, and brainstorming of ideas
2. *Writing*: The part of the project in which the actual, physical writing takes place
3. *Revising*: Adding to, removing, rearranging, or re-writing sections of the piece
4. *Editing*: Analyzing and correcting mistakes in grammar, spelling, punctuation, formatting, and word choice
5. *Publishing*: Distributing the finished product to the teacher, employer, or other students

The *writing workshop* is possibly the most common approach to teaching writing. It is an organized approach in which the student is guided by the teacher and usually contains the following components:

- *Short lesson* (~10 min) in which the teacher focuses on a particular aspect of the writing process—e.g., strategies, organization, technique, processes, craft—and gives explicit instructions for the task at hand

- *Independent writing time* (~30 min) in which the student engages in the writing activity and works through the process while receiving help from the teacher, writing in his/her own style on either a chosen topic or one assigned, and engaging with other students

- *Sharing* (~10 min) in which the student shares a piece of his or her work, either in a small group or as a class, and gains insight by listening to the work of other students

Another common strategy is *teacher modeling*, in which the student views the teacher as a writer and is therefore more apt to believe the teacher's instruction on the subject. To be a good writing teacher, the teacher must be a good writer. Therefore, it is important that the teacher practice his or her own writing on a somewhat regular basis through blogging, journaling, or creative writing, in order to keep his or her skills sharp. The following are some strategies for teacher writing:

- *Sharing written work*: This strategy is a good audio and/or visual learning technique. The teacher should frequently share personal writing with students so that the student recognizes the instructor as having authority on the subject. Many teachers also encourage feedback from the students to stimulate critical thinking skills.

- *Writing in front of students*: This strategy is very effective as a visual learning technique as the students watch as the teacher works through the writing process. This could include asking the students to provide a question or topic on which to write and then writing on blackboard or projector.

- *Encouraging real-world writing*: This is a kinesthetic teaching strategy in which the teacher urges students to write as frequently as possible and to share their written work with other students or an authentic audience. Teachers may also find it beneficial to show students their own blogs and other online media to demonstrate exactly how it's done. Students may also choose to model their writing after a published author, imitating his or her style, sentence structure, and word choices to become comfortable with the writing process.

Finally, a good thing for a student to have is a *writer's notebook*, which contains all the student's written work over the course of the curriculum, including warm-up assignments, drafts, brainstorming templates, and completed works. This allows the student to review previous writing assignment, learn from their mistakes, and see concrete evidence for improvement. Depending on the age group, many of the assignments could be performed on a word processor to encourage computer literacy.

Formal Elements of Writing

Organizational Structure within Informational Text
Informational text is specifically designed to relate factual information, and although it is open to a reader's interpretation and application of the facts, the structure of the presentation is carefully designed to lead the reader to a particular conclusion or central idea. When reading informational text, it is important that readers are able to understand its organizational structure as the structure often directly relates to an author's intent to inform and/or persuade the reader.

The first step in identifying the text's structure is to determine the thesis or main idea. The thesis statement and organization of a work are closely intertwined. *A thesis statement* indicates the writer's purpose and may include the scope and direction of the text. It may be presented at the beginning of a text or at the end, and it may be explicit or implicit.

Once a reader has a grasp of the thesis or main idea of the text, he or she can better determine its organizational structure. Test takers are advised to read informational text passages more than once in order to comprehend the material fully. It is also helpful to examine any text features present in the text including the table of contents, index, glossary, headings, footnotes, and visuals. The analysis of these features and the information presented within them, can offer additional clues about the central idea and structure of a text.

The following questions should be asked when considering structure:

- How does the author assemble the parts to make an effective whole argument?
- Is the passage linear in nature and if so, what is the timeline or thread of logic?
- What is the presented order of events, facts, or arguments? Are these effective in contributing to the author's thesis?
- How can the passage be divided into sections? How are they related to each other and to the main idea or thesis?
- What key terms are used to indicate the organization?

Next, test takers should skim the passage, noting the first line or two of each body paragraph—the *topic sentences*—and the conclusion. Key *transitional terms*, such as *on the other hand, also, because, however, therefore, most importantly*, and *first*, within the text can also signal organizational structure. Based on these clues, readers should then be able to identify what type of organizational structure is being used. The following organizational structures are most common:

- *Problem/solution*—organized by an analysis/overview of a problem, followed by potential solution(s)

- *Cause/effect*—organized by the effects resulting from a cause or the cause(s) of a particular effect

- *Spatial order*—organized by points that suggest location or direction—e.g., top to bottom, right to left, outside to inside

- *Chronological/sequence order*—organized by points presented to indicate a passage of time or through purposeful steps/stages

- *Comparison/Contrast*—organized by points that indicate similarities and/or differences between two things or concepts

- *Order of importance*—organized by priority of points, often most significant to least significant or vice versa

Using Varied and Effective Transitions

Transitions are the glue that holds the writing together. They function to purposefully incorporate new topics and supporting details in a smooth and coherent way. Usually, transitions are found at the beginnings of sentences, but they can also be located in the middle as a way to link clauses together. There are two types of clauses: independent and dependent as discussed in the language use and vocabulary section.

Transition words connect clauses within and between sentences for smoother writing. "I dislike apples. They taste like garbage." is choppier than "I dislike apples because they taste like garbage." Transitions demonstrate the relationship between ideas, allow for more complex sentence structures, and can alert the reader to which type of organizational format the author is using. For example, the above selection on human evolution uses the words *first, another*, and *finally* to indicate that the writer will be listing the reasons why humans and apes are evolutionarily different.

Transition words can be categorized based on the relationships they create between ideas:

- *General order*: signaling elaboration of an idea to emphasize a point—e.g., *for example, for instance, to demonstrate, including, such as, in other words, that is, in fact, also, furthermore, likewise, and, truly, so, surely, certainly, obviously, doubtless*

- *Chronological order*: referencing the time frame in which main event or idea occurs—e.g., *before, after, first, while, soon, shortly thereafter, meanwhile*

- *Numerical order/order of importance*: indicating that related ideas, supporting details, or events will be described in a sequence, possibly in order of importance—e.g., *first, second, also, finally, another, in addition, equally important, less importantly, most significantly, the main reason, last but not least*

- *Spatial order*: referring to the space and location of something or where things are located in relation to each other—e.g., *inside, outside, above, below, within, close, under, over, far, next to, adjacent to*

- *Cause and effect order*: signaling a causal relationship between events or ideas—e.g., *thus, therefore, since, resulted in, for this reason, as a result, consequently, hence, for, so*

- *Compare and contrast order*: identifying the similarities and differences between two or more objects, ideas, or lines of thought—e.g., *like, as, similarly, equally, just as, unlike, however, but, although, conversely, on the other hand, on the contrary*

- *Summary order*: indicating that a particular idea is coming to a close—e.g., *in conclusion, to sum up, in other words, ultimately, above all*

Sophisticated writing also aims to avoid overuse of transitions and ensure that those used are meaningful. Using a variety of transitions makes the writing appear more lively and informed and helps readers follow the progression of ideas.

Revisions of Written Text

Organization
Good writing is not merely a random collection of sentences. No matter how well written, sentences must relate and coordinate appropriately with one another. If not, the writing seems random, haphazard, and disorganized. Therefore, good writing must be organized, where each sentence fits a larger context and relates to the sentences around it.

Transition Words
The writer should act as a guide, showing the reader how all the sentences fit together. Consider the seat belt example again:

> Seat belts save more lives than any other automobile safety feature. Many studies show that airbags save lives as well. Not all cars have airbags. Many older cars don't. Air bags aren't entirely reliable. Studies show that in 15% of accidents, airbags don't deploy as designed. Seat belt malfunctions are extremely rare.

There's nothing wrong with any of these sentences individually, but together they're disjointed and difficult to follow. The best way for the writer to communicate information is through the use of transition words. Here are examples of transition words and phrases that tie sentences together, enabling a more natural flow:

- To show causality: *as a result*, *therefore*, and *consequently*
- To compare and contrast: *however*, *but*, and *on the other hand*
- To introduce examples: *for instance*, *namely*, and *including*
- To show order of importance: *foremost*, *primarily*, *secondly*, and *lastly*

NOTE: This is not a complete list of transitions. There are many more that can be used; however, most fit into these or similar categories. The important point is that the words should clearly show the relationship between sentences, supporting information, and the main idea.

Here is an update to the previous example using transition words. These changes make it easier to read and bring clarity to the writer's points:

Seat belts save more lives than any other automobile safety feature. Many studies show that airbags save lives as well; however, not all cars have airbags. For instance, some older cars don't. Furthermore, air bags aren't entirely reliable. For example, studies show that in 15% of accidents, airbags don't deploy as designed, but, on the other hand, seat belt malfunctions are extremely rare.

Also be prepared to analyze whether the writer is using the best transition word or phrase for the situation. Take this sentence for example: "As a result, seat belt malfunctions are extremely rare." This sentence doesn't make sense in the context above because the writer is trying to show the contrast between seat belts and airbags, not the causality.

Logical Sequence
Even if the writer includes plenty of information to support their point, the writing is only coherent when the information is in a logical order. First, the writer should introduce the main idea, whether for a paragraph, a section, or the entire piece. Then they should present evidence to support the main idea by using transitional language. This shows the reader how the information relates to the main idea and to the sentences around it. The writer should then take time to interpret the information, making sure necessary connections are obvious to the reader. Finally, the writer can summarize the information in a closing section.

Though most writing follows this pattern, it isn't a set rule. Sometimes writers change the order for effect. For example, the writer can begin with a surprising piece of supporting information to grab the reader's attention, and then transition to the main idea. Thus, if a passage doesn't follow the logical order, don't immediately assume it's wrong. However, most writing usually settles into a logical sequence after a nontraditional beginning.

Introductions and Conclusions
Examining the writer's strategies for introductions and conclusions puts the reader in the right mindset to interpret the rest of the text. Look for methods the writer might use for introductions such as:

- Stating the main point immediately, followed by outlining how the rest of the piece supports this claim.

- Establishing important, smaller pieces of the main idea first, and then grouping these points into a case for the main idea.

- Opening with a quotation, anecdote, question, seeming paradox, or other piece of interesting information, and then using it to lead to the main point.

Whatever method the writer chooses, the introduction should make their intention clear, establish their voice as a credible one, and encourage a person to continue reading.

Conclusions tend to follow a similar pattern. In them, the writer restates their main idea a final time, often after summarizing the smaller pieces of that idea. If the introduction uses a quote or anecdote to grab the reader's attention, the conclusion often makes reference to it again. Whatever way the writer chooses to arrange the conclusion, the final restatement of the main idea should be clear and simple for the reader to interpret. Finally, conclusions shouldn't introduce any new information.

Precision

People often think of precision in terms of math, but precise word choice is another key to successful writing. Since language itself is imprecise, it's important for the writer to find the exact word or words to convey the full, intended meaning of a given situation. For example:

> The number of deaths has gone down since seat belt laws started.

There are several problems with this sentence. First, the word *deaths* is too general. From the context, it's assumed that the writer is referring only to deaths caused by car accidents. However, without clarification, the sentence lacks impact and is probably untrue. The phrase "gone down" might be accurate, but a more precise word could provide more information and greater accuracy. Did the numbers show a slow and steady decrease of highway fatalities or a sudden drop? If the latter is true, the writer is missing a chance to make their point more dramatically. Instead of "gone down" they could substitute *plummeted*, *fallen drastically*, or *rapidly diminished* to bring the information to life. Also, the phrase "seat belt laws" is unclear. Does it refer to laws requiring cars to include seat belts or to laws requiring drivers and passengers to use them? Finally, *started* is not a strong verb. Words like *enacted* or *adopted* are more direct and make the content more real. When put together, these changes create a far more powerful sentence:

> The number of highway fatalities has plummeted since laws requiring seat belt usage were enacted.

However, it's important to note that precise word choice can sometimes be taken too far. If the writer of the sentence above takes precision to an extreme, it might result in the following:

The incidence of high-speed, automobile accident related fatalities has decreased 75% and continued to remain at historical lows since the initial set of federal legislations requiring seat belt use were enacted in 1992.

This sentence is extremely precise, but it takes so long to achieve that precision that it suffers from a lack of clarity. Precise writing is about finding the right balance between information and flow. This is also an issue of conciseness (discussed in the next section).

The last thing to consider with precision is a word choice that's not only unclear or uninteresting, but also confusing or misleading. For example:

The number of highway fatalities has become hugely lower since laws requiring seat belt use were enacted.

In this case, the reader might be confused by the word *hugely*. Huge means large, but here the writer uses *hugely* to describe something small. Though most readers can decipher this, doing so disconnects them from the flow of the writing and makes the writer's point less effective.

Conciseness

"Less is more" is a good rule to follow when writing a sentence. Unfortunately, writers often include extra words and phrases that seem necessary at the time, but add nothing to the main idea. This confuses the reader and creates unnecessary repetition. Writing that lacks conciseness is usually guilty of excessive wordiness and redundant phrases. Here's an example containing both of these issues:

> When legislators decided to begin creating legislation making it mandatory for automobile drivers and passengers to make use of seat belts while in cars, a large number of them made those laws for reasons that were political reasons.

There are several empty or "fluff" words here that take up too much space. These can be eliminated while still maintaining the writer's meaning. For example:

- "Decided to begin" could be shortened to "began"
- "Making it mandatory for" could be shortened to "requiring"
- "Make use of" could be shortened to "use"
- "A large number" could be shortened to "many"

In addition, there are several examples of redundancy that can be eliminated:

- "Legislators decided to begin creating legislation" and "made those laws"
- "Automobile drivers and passengers" and "while in cars"
- "Reasons that were political reasons"

These changes are incorporated as follows:

> When legislators began requiring drivers and passengers to use seat belts, many of them did so for political reasons.

There are many general examples of redundant phrases, such as "add an additional," "complete and total," "time schedule," and "transportation vehicle." If asked to identify a redundant phrase on the test, look for words that are close together with the same (or similar) meanings.

Editing Written Work

Revisions

Leaving a few minutes at the end to revise and proofread offers an opportunity for writers to polish things up. Putting one's self in the reader's shoes and focusing on what the essay actually says helps writers identify problems—it's a movement from the mindset of writer to the mindset of editor. The goal is to have a clean, clear copy of the essay. The following areas should be considered when proofreading:

- Sentence fragments
- Awkward sentence structure
- Run-on sentences
- Incorrect word choice

- Grammatical agreement errors
- Spelling errors
- Punctuation errors
- Capitalization errors

Purposes for Writing

No matter the genre or format, all authors are writing to persuade, inform, entertain, or express feelings. Often, these purposes are blended, with one dominating the rest. It's useful to learn to recognize the author's intent.

Persuasive writing is used to persuade or convince readers of something. It often contains two elements: the argument and the counterargument. The argument takes a stance on an issue, while the counterargument pokes holes in the opposition's stance. Authors rely on logic, emotion, and writer credibility to persuade readers to agree with them. If readers are opposed to the stance before reading, they are unlikely to adopt that stance. However, those who are undecided or committed to the same stance are more likely to agree with the author.

Informative writing tries to teach or inform. Workplace manuals, instructor lessons, statistical reports and cookbooks are examples of informative texts. Informative writing is usually based on facts and is often void of emotion and persuasion. Informative texts generally contain statistics, charts, and graphs. Though most informative texts lack a persuasive agenda, readers must examine the text carefully to determine whether one exists within a given passage.

Stories or narratives are designed to entertain. When you go to the movies, you often want to escape for a few hours, not necessarily to think critically. Entertaining writing is designed to delight and engage the reader. However, sometimes this type of writing can be woven into more serious materials, such as persuasive or informative writing to hook the reader before transitioning into a more scholarly discussion.

Emotional writing works to evoke the reader's feelings, such as anger, euphoria, or sadness. The connection between reader and author is an attempt to cause the reader to share the author's intended emotion or tone. Sometimes in order to make a piece more poignant, the author simply wants readers to feel emotion that the author has felt. Other times, the author attempts to persuade or manipulate the reader into adopting his stance. While it's okay to sympathize with the author, be aware of the individual's underlying intent.

Intended Audience

Authors identify an audience for their writing, which is critical in shaping the theme of the work. For example, the audience for J.K. Rowling's *Harry Potter* series would be different than the audience for a biography of George Washington. The audience an author chooses to address is closely tied to the purpose of the work. The choice of an audience also drives the choice of language and level of diction an author uses. Ultimately, the intended audience determines the level to which that subject matter is presented and the complexity of the theme.

Techniques to Convey Meaning

Rhetorical Strategies
Rhetoric refers to an author's use of particular strategies, appeals, and devices to persuade an intended audience. The more effective the use of rhetoric, the more likely the audience will be persuaded.

Determining an Author's Point of View
A *rhetorical strategy*—also referred to as a *rhetorical mode*—is the structural way an author chooses to present his/her argument. Though the terms noted below are similar to the organizational structures noted earlier, these strategies do not imply that the entire text follows the approach. For example, a cause and effect organizational structure is solely that, nothing more. A persuasive text may use cause and effect as a strategy to convey a singular point. Thus, an argument may include several of the strategies as the author strives to convince his or her audience to take action or accept a different point of view. It's important that readers are able to identify an author's thesis and position on the topic in order to be able to identify the careful construction through which the author speaks to the reader. The following are some of the more common rhetorical strategies:

- *Cause and effect*—establishing a logical correlation or causation between two ideas
- *Classification/division*—the grouping of similar items together or division of something into parts
- *Comparison/contrast*—the distinguishing of similarities/differences to expand on an idea
- *Definition*—used to clarify abstract ideas, unfamiliar concepts, or to distinguish one idea from another
- *Description*—use of vivid imagery, active verbs, and clear adjectives to explain ideas
- *Exemplification*—the use of examples to explain an idea
- *Narration*—anecdotes or personal experience to present or expand on a concept
- *Problem/Solution*—presentation of a problem or problems, followed by proposed solution(s)

Rhetorical Strategies and Devices
A *rhetorical device* is the phrasing and presentation of an idea that reinforces and emphasizes a point in an argument. A rhetorical device is often quite memorable. One of the more famous uses of a rhetorical device is in John F. Kennedy's 1961 inaugural address: "Ask not what your country can do for you, ask what you can do for your country." The contrast of ideas presented in the phrasing is an example of the

rhetorical device of antimetatabolee. Some other common examples are provided below, but test takers should be aware that this is not a complete list.

Device	Definition	Example
Allusion	A reference to a famous person, event, or significant literary text as a form of significant comparison	"We are apt to shut our eyes against a painful truth, and listen to the song of that siren till she transforms us into beasts." Patrick Henry
Anaphora	The repetition of the same words at the beginning of successive words, phrases, or clauses, designed to emphasize an idea	"We shall not flag or fail. We shall go on to the end. We shall fight in France, we shall fight on the seas and oceans, we shall fight with growing confidence … we shall fight in the fields and in the streets, we shall fight in the hills. We shall never surrender." Winston Churchill
Understatement	A statement meant to portray a situation as less important than it actually is to create an ironic effect	"The war in the Pacific has not necessarily developed in Japan's favor." Emperor Hirohito, surrendering Japan in World War II
Parallelism	A syntactical similarity in a structure or series of structures used for impact of an idea, making it memorable	"A penny saved is a penny earned." Ben Franklin
Rhetorical question	A question posed that is not answered by the writer though there is a desired response, most often designed to emphasize a point	"Can anyone look at our reduced standing in the world today and say, 'Let's have four more years of this?'" Ronald Reagan

Rhetorical Appeals

In an argument or persuasive text, an author will strive to sway readers to an opinion or conclusion. To be effective, an author must consider his or her intended audience. Although an author may write text for a general audience, he or she will use methods of appeal or persuasion to convince that audience. Aristotle asserted that there were three methods or modes by which a person could be persuaded. These are referred to as *rhetorical appeals*.

The three main types of rhetorical appeals are shown in the following graphic.

Ethos, also referred to as an *ethical appeal*, is an appeal to the audience's perception of the writer as credible (or not), based on their examination of their ethics and who the writer is, his/her experience or incorporation of relevant information, or his/her argument. For example, authors may present testimonials to bolster their arguments. The reader who critically examines the veracity of the testimonials and the credibility of those giving the testimony will be able to determine if the author's use of testimony is valid to his or her argument. In turn, this will help the reader determine if the author's thesis is valid. An author's careful and appropriate use of technical language can create an overall knowledgeable effect and, in turn, act as a convincing vehicle when it comes to credibility. Overuse of technical language, however, may create confusion in readers and obscure an author's overall intent.

Pathos, also referred to as a *pathetic* or *emotional appeal*, is an appeal to the audience's sense of identity, self-interest, or emotions. A critical reader will notice when the author is appealing to pathos through anecdotes and descriptions that elicit an emotion such as anger or pity. Readers should also beware of factual information that uses generalization to appeal to the emotions. While it's tempting to believe an author is the source of truth in his or her text, an author who presents factual information as universally true, consistent throughout time, and common to all groups is using *generalization*. Authors who exclusively use generalizations without specific facts and credible sourcing are attempting to sway readers solely through emotion.

Logos, also referred to as a *logical appeal*, is an appeal to the audience's ability to see and understand the logic in a claim offered by the writer. A critical reader has to be able to evaluate an author's arguments for validity of reasoning and for sufficiency when it comes to argument.

Practice Questions

1. Read the following poem. Which option best expresses the symbolic meaning of the "road" and the overall theme?

> Two roads diverged in a yellow wood,
> And sorry I could not travel both
> And be one traveler, long I stood
> And looked down one as far as I could
> To where it bent in the undergrowth;
> Then took the other, as just as fair,
> And having perhaps the better claim,
> Because it was grassy and wanted wear;
> Though as for that the passing there
> Had worn them really about the same,
> And both that morning equally lay
> In leaves no step had trodden black.
> Oh, I kept the first for another day!
> Yet knowing how way leads on to way,
> I doubted if I should ever come back.
> I shall be telling this with a sigh
> Somewhere ages and ages hence:
> Two roads diverged in a wood, and I—
> I took the one less traveled by,
> And that has made all the difference—Robert Frost, "The Road Not Taken"

    a. A divergent spot where the traveler had to choose the correct path to his destination
    b. A choice between good and evil that the traveler needs to make
    c. The traveler's struggle between his lost love and his future prospects
    d. Life's journey and the choices with which humans are faced

2. Which option best exemplifies an author's use of *alliteration* and *personification*?
    a. Her mood hung about her like a weary cape, very dull from wear.
    b. It shuddered, swayed, shook, and screamed its way into dust under hot flames.
    c. The house was a starch sentry, warning visitors away.
    d. At its shoreline, visitors swore they heard the siren call of the cliffs above.

3. Read the following poem. Which option best depicts the rhyme scheme?

> A slumber did my spirit seal;
> I had no human fears:
> She seemed a thing that could not feel
> The touch of earthly years.—from William Wordsworth, "A Slumber Did My Spirit Seal"

    a. BAC BAC
    b. ABAB
    c. ABBA
    d. AB CD AB

4. Read the following poem. Which option describes its corresponding meter?

> Half a league, half a league
> Half a league onward,
> All in the valley of Death
> Rode the six hundred.
> 'Forward, the Light Brigade!
> Charge for the guns!' he said:
> Into the valley of Death
> Rode the six hundred.—Alfred Lord Tennyson *"The Charge of the Light Brigade"*

    a. Iambic (unstressed/stressed syllables)
    b. Anapest (unstressed/unstressed/stressed syllables)
    c. Spondee (stressed/stressed syllables)
    d. Dactyl (stressed/unstressed/unstressed syllables)

5. This work, published in 1922, was a modernist piece that was banned both in the United States and overseas for meeting the criteria of obscenity. Taking place in a single day (June 16th, 1904), the novel contains eighteen episodes reflecting the activities of character Leopold Bloom in Dublin, Ireland. Originally written as to portray an Odysseus figure for adults, the structure of the work is often viewed as convoluted and chaotic, as its author utilized the stream of consciousness technique. Its literary reception was vastly polarized and remains so to this day, although modern critics tend to hail the novel as addressing the vast panoramic of futility within contemporary history.

The above passage describes which famous literary work?
    a. James Joyce's *Ulysses*
    b. Anne Sexton's poem "45 Mercy Street"
    c. F. Scott Fitzgerald's *Tender is the Night*
    d. George Eliot's *Middlemarch: A Study of Provincial Life*

6. In 1889, Jerome K. Jerome wrote a humorous account of a boating holiday. Originally intended as a chapter in a serious travel guide, the work became a prime example of a comic novel. Read the passage below, noting the word/words in italics. Answer the question that follows.

> I felt rather hurt about this at first; it seemed somehow to be a sort of slight. Why hadn't I got housemaid's knee? Why this invidious reservation? After a while, however, less grasping feelings prevailed. I reflected that I had every other known malady in the pharmacology, and I grew less selfish, and determined to do without housemaid's knee. Gout, in its most malignant stage, it would appear, had seized me without my being aware of it; and *zymosis* I had evidently been suffering with from boyhood. There were no more diseases after *zymosis*, so I concluded there was nothing else the matter with me.—Jerome K. Jerome, *Three Men in a Boat*

Which definition best fits the word *zymosis*?
    a. Discontent
    b. An infectious disease
    c. Poverty
    d. Bad luck

7. Read the following poem. Which option best describes the use of the spider?

> The spider as an artist
> Has never been employed
> Though his surpassing merit
> Is freely certified
> By every broom and Bridget
> Throughout a Christian land.
> Neglected son of genius,
> I take thee by the hand—Emily Dickinson, "Cobwebs"

    a. Idiom
    b. Haiku
    c. ABBA rhyming convention
    d. Simile

8. Which of the following is a pre-reading strategy used to support comprehension?
    a. Skimming the text for content
    b. Summarizing the text effectively
    c. Organizing the main ideas and supporting details
    d. Clarifying unfamiliar ideas in the text

9. Which best describes the *plot* in fiction?
    a. What happens in the story or the storyline
    b. Character development
    c. The time and place of the story
    d. The events in the story that are true

10. Which option best portrays *second person point of view*?
    a. I went down the road, hoping to catch a glimpse of his retreating figure.
    b. You, my dear reader, can understand loss and grief, too.
    c. He left her standing there, alone to face the world.
    d. There's nothing wrong with Margaret.

11. Which option best defines a *fable*?
    a. A melancholy poem lamenting its subject's death
    b. An oral tradition influenced by culture
    c. A story with events that occur in threes and in sevens
    d. A short story with animals, fantastic creatures, or other forces within nature

12. Which of the following describes the organizational pattern of chronological or sequence order?
    a. Text organized by describing a dilemma and a possible solution
    b. Text organized by observing the consequences of an action
    c. Text organized by the timing of events or actions
    d. Text organized by analyzing the relative placement of an object or event

13. Which phrase best completes the definition of a *memoir*?
    a. A historical account of a person's life written by one who has intimate knowledge of the person's life
    b. A historical account of a person's life written by the person himself or herself
    c. A fictional account about a famous person
    d. A nonfictional account about a famous person without factual reference

14. Which of the following is an example of a rhetorical strategy?
    a. Cause and effect
    b. Antimetatabolee
    c. Individual vs. Self
    d. Ad hominem

15. Which poem belongs to the metaphysical literary movement?
    a. Emily Dickinson's "If I Should Die"
    b. Elizabeth Barrett Browning's "A Child Asleep"
    c. Andrew Marvell's "To His Coy Mistress"
    d. Sylvia Plath's "The Bell Jar"

16. Which word serves as the best example of the poetic device, *onomatopoeia*?
    a. Crackle
    b. Eat
    c. Provide
    d. Walking

17. Which term best defines a *sonnet*?
    a. A Japanese love poem
    b. An eight-line stanza or poem
    c. A fourteen-line poem written in iambic pentameter
    d. A ceremonious, lyric poem

18. Which literary school of thought developed out of structuralism in the twentieth century?
    a. Deconstruction
    b. Post-Structuralism
    c. Marxism
    d. Both A and B

19. Which phrase below best defines *inference*?
    a. Reading between the lines
    b. Skimming a text for context clues
    c. Writing notes or questions that need answers during the reading experience
    d. Summarizing the text

20. Which word best defines the prior knowledge a reader brings to the reading?
    a. Meta-cognitive
    b. Foreshadowing
    c. Schema
    d. Prediction

Answer Explanations

1. D: Choice *D* correctly summarizes Frost's theme of life's journey and the choices one makes. While Choice *A* can be seen as an interpretation, it is a literal one and is incorrect. Literal is not symbolic. Choice *B* presents the idea of good and evil as a theme, and the poem does not specify this struggle for the traveler. Choice *C* is a similarly incorrect answer. Love is not the theme.

2. B: Only Choice *B* uses both repetitive beginning sounds (alliteration) and personification—the portrayal of a building as a human crumbling under a fire. Choice *A* is a simile and does not utilize alliteration or the use of consistent consonant sounds for effect. Choice *C* is a metaphor and does not utilize alliteration. Choice *D* describes neither alliteration nor personification.

3. B: The correct answer is ABAB. Choice *A* is not a valid rhyme scheme. Choice *C* would require the second and third lines to rhyme, so it is incorrect. Choice *D* would require the first and fifth lines rhyme, then the second and sixth. This is also incorrect as the passage only contains four lines.

4. D: The correct answer is dactyl. If read with the combination of stressed and unstressed syllables as Tennyson intended and as the poem naturally flows, the reader will stumble upon the stressed/unstressed/unstressed rhythmic, dactyl meter similar to a waltz beat. Choices *A*, *B*, and *C* describe meters that do not follow the dactyl pattern.

5. A: The correct answer is *A* as it is the only option that utilizes stream of consciousness technique in a novel format. Choice *B* is a poem by poet Anne Sexton, not a novel. Although Ms. Sexton's works were often criticized for their intimate content, this answer does not meet the question's criteria. Choices *C* and *D* are both incorrect. Both are novels, but not of the appropriate time period, country, or literary content.

6. B: The correct answer is an infectious disease. By reading context, all other options can be eliminated since the author restates zymosis as disease.

7. D: The correct answer is simile. Choice *A* is incorrect because the poem does not contain an idiom. Choice *B* is incorrect since the poem is not haiku. Choice *C* is incorrect as it does not use the ABBA rhyming convention.

8. A: The correct answer is skimming the text for content. Skimming text for content is an important pre-reading strategy where readers identify important ideas and words without reading every line of the text. Summarizing text effectively, organizing main ideas and supporting details, and clarifying unfamiliar ideas in the text are all reading strategies to be used during or after reading a text.

9. A: The correct answer is "what happens" or the storyline. Choice *B* refers to characters in fiction. Choice *C* defines the setting. Choice *D* is incomplete. It may be partially true, but it isn't always the case. Most fiction is based on the imaginary.

10. B: The correct answer is *B* as the author is speaking directly to the reader and uses the pronoun *you*. Choice *A* uses first person point of view, which uses the pronoun *I*. Choice *C* uses third person point of view which utilizes pronouns such as *he*, *she*, or *we*. Choice *D* is unclear.

11. D: The correct answer is a short story with animals, fantastic creatures, or other forces within nature. Choice *A* defines an elegy. Choice *B* partially alludes to folklore. Choice *C* defines a fairytale.

12. C: The correct answer is text organized by the timing of events or actions. Chronological or sequence order is the organizational pattern that structures text to show the passage of time or movement through steps in a certain order. Choice *A* demonstrates the problem/solution structure. Choice *B* defines the cause/effect pattern. Choice *D* represents the spatial order structure.

13. A: The correct answer is a historical account of a person's life written by one who has intimate knowledge of the person's life. Choice *B* is not applicable since it is the definition of an autobiography. Choice *C* strictly refers to fiction and is not applicable to nonfiction. Choice *D* indicates that a memoir is not based on historical fact. In many instances, it is.

14. A: The correct answer is cause and effect. A writer may use cause and effect as a strategy to illustrate a point in order to convince an audience. Choice *B* is a rhetorical device, not a strategy. Choice *C* refers to a narrative conflict, and Choice *D* is a logical fallacy.

15. C: The correct answer is Andrew Marvell's *"To His Coy Mistress."* Emily Dickinson, Elizabeth Barrett Browning, and Sylvia Plath all belonged to different literary movements and contexts.

16. A: The correct answer is *crackle* as it is the only option that reflects the sound that the action would make. The other options do not.

17. C: The correct answer is a fourteen-line poem written in iambic pentameter. Choice *A* is incorrect as it incorrectly alludes to the haiku form. Choice *B* defines the octave poetic structure. Choice *D* defines what a poetic ode is.

18. D: The correct answer is that both Deconstruction and Post-structuralism developed in response to the Structuralism movement of the twentieth century. Choices *A* and *B* are incomplete answers as they do not complete both literary movements which encapsulate the response to Structuralism. Choice *C* is incorrect as Marxism was a response to the writings of Karl Marx and not in direct response to Structuralism.

19. A: Inferring is reading between the lines. Choice *B* describes the skimming technique. Choice *C* describes a questioning technique readers should employ, and Choice *D* is a simple statement regarding summary. It's an incomplete answer and not applicable to inference.

20. C: The correct answer is schema. Choice *A* is the name of a research-based strategy that asks the reader to decode text passages. Choice *B* is a literary device. Choice *D* is incorrect. It is part of reading instruction strategy, but not entirely applicable to a reader's prior knowledge he or she brings to the experience.

History and Social Science

Indigenous Peoples Before the Arrival of Europeans

During the last Ice Age, large glaciers covered much of North America, trapping seawater and lowering the sea level. This exposed a land bridge between northwest Asia and North America that has been named Beringia. Nomadic peoples from Siberia used the Beringia land bridge to cross into North America. When the Ice Age ended a few thousand years later, the glaciers melted, the sea level rose, and Beringia disappeared beneath the ocean. The nomads who had crossed into North America before the Ice Age ended were searching for prey such as mastodons and wooly mammoths. These nomadic peoples lived in small groups and slowly spread out across North and South America during the next several millennia.

Several thousand years ago, the Neolithic Revolution occurred. This event occurred at different times in different places around the world, but it marked an important turning point in human history. The Neolithic Revolution included the development of agriculture and the domestication of animals. In North America, the primary crops were maize (corn), tomatoes, pumpkins, chilies, potatoes, and beans. There were only a few animals for Native Americans to domesticate, including the dog (in North America) and the llama (in Central America). Dogs were used to guard and hunt, and llamas produced wool and also transported goods.

The development of agriculture and domesticated animals led to a major change in North American societies: instead of small nomadic bands of hunter-gatherers, many native peoples became semi-sedentary. They began to form settlements, create social hierarchies, and develop new religious beliefs. However, many Native Americans remained semi-nomadic and lived in villages for only part of the year. Most Native American villages engaged in long distance trade with other groups. In general, most Native American peoples practiced animist beliefs—in other words, they thought that everything in the natural world had some spiritual power, including plants, animals, and rocks. In most Native American societies, women were responsible for farming while men hunted and fished.

Although most Native Americans continued to live in small villages, some larger settlements eventually developed. In Central America in 1325 A.D., the Aztec built the city of Tenochtitlan, located on the site of present day Mexico City, which was thought to contain more than 200,000 inhabitants. This meant it could have been one of the largest cities in the world before Spanish conquistadors destroyed it in 1521. In North America, Native Americans built the city of Cahokia (near the modern city of St. Louis), which may have had up to 40,000 residents before it was abandoned sometime around 1300. Cahokia also included a large circle of timber posts that may have had been used for astronomical predictions, similar to Stonehenge in Britain.

North and South America were rich in natural resources and also featured a variety of climates and geographies. This led to the development of various Native American societies before European colonists arrived.

The Iroquois and Algonquians were the major tribes in the eastern part of North America. They spoke different languages and frequently fought each other. The vast forests, especially in the Northeast, Midwest, and Southeast, provided wood for building wigwams and longhouses, as well as tools and weapons. Native Americans also used major waterways such as the Ohio and Mississippi Rivers to engage in trade, participate in small- and large-scale fishing activities, and launch raids against each other.

Several different tribes also lived between the Mississippi River and the Rocky Mountains—an area later known as the Great Plains. The Sioux, Comanche, Blackfoot, and Cheyenne were among these more nomadic peoples who hunted buffalo. They lived in teepees that were easy to take apart and rebuild in a new location as the tribe moved across the vast prairies. Native Americans sometimes set fire to the grasslands in order to control vegetation and improve grazing conditions.

The Pueblo people—including the Zuni, Hope, and Acoma tribes—lived in the deserts of the southwest. They used clay bricks to build large apartment complexes called pueblos, digging into the side of cliffs to create shelter. Since the environment was so dry, they had to build complex irrigation systems in order to grow crops.

The Tlingit, Chinook, and Salish people lived on the Pacific coast where they survived by hunting and fishing. Salmon were a staple of their diet and culture, playing an important part in their eating habits as well as their religious beliefs. The tribes developed techniques to create waterproof baskets and woven raincoats due to the wet climate of the Pacific Northwest.

The Aleuts and Inuit lived in the arctic and subarctic regions of North America where they hunted seals and whales. Because of the harsh conditions, they built semi-subterranean shelters that were insulated against the cold.

European Exploration and Settlement of North America

When examining how Europeans explored what would become the United States of America, one must first examine why Europeans came to explore the New World as a whole. In the fifteenth century, tensions increased between the Eastern and Mediterranean nations of Europe and the expanding Ottoman Empire to the east. As war and piracy spread across the Mediterranean, the once-prosperous trade routes across Asia's Silk Road began to decline, and nations across Europe began to explore alternative routes for trade.

Italian explorer Christopher Columbus proposed a westward route. Contrary to popular lore, the main challenge that Columbus faced in finding backers was not proving that the world was round. Much of Europe's educated elite knew that the world was round; the real issue was that they rightly believed that a westward route to Asia, assuming a lack of obstacles, would be too long to be practical. Nevertheless, Columbus set sail in 1492 after obtaining support from Spain and arrived in the West Indies three months later.

Spain launched further expeditions to the new continents and established *New Spain*. The colony consisted not only of Central America and Mexico, but also the American Southwest and Florida. France claimed much of what would become Canada, along with the Mississippi River region and the Midwest. In addition, the Dutch established colonies that covered New Jersey, New York, and Connecticut. Each nation managed its colonies differently, and thus influenced how they would assimilate into the United States. For instance, Spain strove to establish a system of Christian missions throughout its territory, while France focused on trading networks and had limited infrastructure in regions such as the Midwest.

Even in cases of limited colonial growth, the land of America was hardly vacant, because a diverse array of Native American nations and groups were already present. Throughout much of colonial history, European settlers commonly misperceived native peoples as a singular, static entity. In reality, Native Americans had a variety of traditions depending on their history and environment, and their culture continued to change through the course of interactions with European settlers; for instance, tribes such as the Cheyenne and Comanche used horses, which were introduced by white settlers, to become powerful warrior nations. However, a few generalizations can be made: many, but not all, tribes were matrilineal, which gave women a fair degree of power, and land was commonly seen as belonging to everyone. These differences, particularly European settlers' continual focus on land ownership, contributed to increasing prejudice and violence.

Situated on the Atlantic Coast, the Thirteen Colonies that would become the United States of America constituted only a small portion of North America. Even those colonies had significant differences that stemmed from their different origins. For instance, the Virginia colony under John Smith in 1607 started with male bachelors seeking gold, whereas families of Puritans settled Massachusetts. As a result, the Thirteen Colonies—Virginia, Massachusetts, Connecticut, Maryland, New York, New Jersey, Pennsylvania, Delaware, Rhode Island, New Hampshire, Georgia, North Carolina, and South Carolina— had different structures and customs that would each influence the United States.

Competition among several imperial powers in eastern areas of North America led to conflicts that would later bring about the independence of the United States. The Seven Years' War from 1756 to 1763, also known as the French and Indian War, ended with Great Britain claiming France's Canadian territories as well as the Ohio Valley. The same war was costly for all the powers involved, which led to increased taxes on the Thirteen Colonies. In addition, the new lands to the west of the colonies attracted new settlers, and they came into conflict with Native Americans and British troops that were trying to maintain the traditional boundaries. These growing tensions with Great Britain, as well as other issues, eventually led to the American Revolution, which ended with Britain relinquishing its control of the colonies.

Britain continued to hold onto its other colonies, such as Canada and the West Indies, which reflects the continued power of multiple nations across North America, even as the United States began to expand across the continent. Many Americans advocated expansion regardless of the land's current inhabitants, but the results were often mixed. Still, events both abroad and within North America contributed to the growth of the United States. For instance, the rising tumult in France during the French Revolution and the rise of Napoleon led France to sell the Louisiana Purchase, a large chunk of land consisting not only of Louisiana but also much of the Midwest, to the United States in 1803. Meanwhile, as Spanish power declined, Mexico claimed independence in 1821, but the new nation became increasingly vulnerable to foreign pressure. In the Mexican-American War from 1846 to 1848, Mexico surrendered territory to the United States that eventually became California, Nevada, Utah, and New Mexico, as well as parts of Arizona, Colorado, and Wyoming.

Even as the United States sought new inland territory, American interests were also expanding overseas via trade. As early as 1784, the ship *Empress of China* traveled to China to establish trading connections. American interests had international dimensions throughout the nation's history. For instance, during the presidency of Andrew Jackson, the ship *Potomac* was dispatched to the Pacific island of Sumatra in 1832 to avenge the deaths of American sailors. This incident exemplifies how U.S. foreign trade connected with imperial expansion.

This combination of continental and seaward growth adds a deeper layer to American development, because it was not purely focused on western expansion. For example, take the 1849 Gold Rush; a large number of Americans and other immigrants traveled to California by ship and settled western territories before more eastern areas, such as Nevada and Idaho. Therefore, the United States' early history of colonization and expansion is a complex network of diverse cultures.

Causes and Effects of the Revolutionary War

The American Revolution largely occurred as a result of changing values in the Thirteen Colonies that broke from their traditional relationship with England. Early on in the colonization of North America, the colonial social structure tried to mirror the stratified order of Great Britain. In England, the landed elites were seen as intellectually and morally superior to the common man, which led to a paternalistic relationship. This style of governance was similarly applied to the colonial system; government was left to the property-owning upper class, and the colonies as a whole could be seen as a child dutifully serving "Mother England."

However, the colonies' distance from England meant that actual, hereditary aristocrats from Britain only formed a small percentage of the overall population and did not even fill all the positions of power. By the mid-eighteenth century, much of the American upper class consisted of local families who acquired status through business rather than lineage. Despite this, representatives from Britain were appointed to govern the colonies. As a result, a rift began to form between the colonists and British officials.

Tensions began to rise in the aftermath of the French and Indian War of 1754 to 1763. To recover the financial costs of the long conflict, Great Britain drew upon its colonies to provide the desired resources. Since the American colonists did not fully subscribe to the paternal connection, taxation to increase British revenue, such as the Stamp Act of 1765, was met with increasing resistance. Britain sent soldiers to the colonies and enacted the 1765 Quartering Act to require colonists to house the troops. In 1773, the new Tea Act, which created a monopoly, led some colonists to raid a ship and destroy its contents in the Boston Tea Party.

Uncertain about whether they should remain loyal to Britain, representatives from twelve colonies formed the First Continental Congress in 1774 to discuss what they should do next. When Patriot militiamen at Lexington and Concord fought British soldiers in April 1775, the Revolutionary War began. While the rebel forces worked to present the struggle as a united, patriotic effort, the colonies remained divided throughout the war. Thousands of colonists, known as Loyalists or Tories, supported Britain. Even the revolutionaries proved to be significantly fragmented, and many militias only served in their home states. The Continental Congress was also divided over whether to reconcile with Britain or push for full separation. These issues hindered the ability of the revolutionary armies to resist the British, who had superior training and resources at their disposal.

Even so, the Continental Army, under General George Washington, gradually built up a force that utilized Prussian military training and backwoods guerrilla tactics to make up for their limited resources. Although the British forces continued to win significant battles, the Continental Army gradually reduced Britain's will to fight as the years passed. Furthermore, Americans appealed to the rivalry that other European nations had with the British Empire. The support was initially limited to indirect assistance, but aid gradually increased. After the American victory at the Battle of Saratoga in 1777, France and other nations began to actively support the American cause by providing much-needed troops and equipment.

In 1781, the primary British army under General Cornwallis was defeated by an American and French coalition at Virginia, which paved the way for negotiations. The Treaty of Paris in 1783 ended the war, recognized the former colonies' independence from Great Britain, and gave America control over territory between the Appalachian Mountains and Mississippi River. However, the state of the new nation was still uncertain. The new nation's government initially stemmed from the state-based structure of the Continental Congress and was incorporated into the Articles of Confederation in 1777.

The Articles of Confederation emphasized the ideals of the American Revolution, particularly the concept of freedom from unjust government. Unfortunately, the resulting limitations on the national government left most policies—even ones with national ramifications—up to individual states. For instance, states sometimes simply decided to not pay taxes. Many representatives did not see much value in the National Congress and simply did not attend the meetings. Some progress was still made during the period, such as the Northwest Ordinance of 1787, which organized the western territories into new states; nevertheless, the disjointed links in the state-oriented government inhibited significant progress.

Although many citizens felt satisfied with this decentralized system of government, key intellectuals and leaders in America became increasingly disturbed by the lack of unity. An especially potent fear among them was the potential that, despite achieving official independence, other powers could threaten America's autonomy. In 1786, poor farmers in Massachusetts launched an insurrection, known as Shay's Rebellion, which sparked fears of additional uprisings and led to the creation of the *Constitutional Convention* in 1787.

While the convention initially intended to correct issues within the Articles of Confederation, speakers, such as James Madison, compellingly argued for the delegates to devise a new system of government that was more centralized than its predecessor. The Constitution was not fully supported by all citizens, and there was much debate about whether or not to support the new government. Even so, in 1788, the Constitution was ratified. Later additions, such as the Bill of Rights, would help protect individual liberty by giving specific rights to citizens. In 1789, George Washington became the first president of the newly created executive branch of the government, and America entered a new stage of history.

Formation of National Government

America's first system of government was actually laid out in the Articles of Confederation, and not the Constitution. The Articles of Confederation were ratified during the Revolutionary War and went into effect in 1781. The Articles of Confederation created a relatively weak central government and allowed individual states to retain most of the power. Under this system, the national government did not have a president or judiciary. Each state had only one vote in the Confederation Congress and most major decisions required unanimous approval by all thirteen states. Despite this requirement, the Confederation Congress did pass some important legislation, including the Northwest Ordinance, which organized the land west of Appalachian Mountains. The territories eventually became the states of Ohio, Indiana, Michigan, Illinois, Wisconsin, and Minnesota. However, Congress did not have the power to tax and could only request money from the states without any way to enforce its demands. A Revolutionary War veteran named Daniel Shays led an armed insurrection in western Massachusetts in 1787. Although Shay's Rebellion was defeated, it drew attention to the weaknesses of the Articles of Confederation.

The Constitutional Convention met in Philadelphia a few months after the rebellion in order to create a stronger federal government. However, delegates disagreed over how to structure the new system. The Virginia Plan was one proposal that included a bicameral legislature where states were awarded representation based on their population size. This would benefit more populous states at the expense of smaller states. The other main proposal was the New Jersey Plan, which retained many elements of the Articles of Confederation, including a unicameral legislature with one vote per state. This plan would put states on an equal footing regardless of population.

Eventually, delegates agreed to support the Connecticut Compromise (also known as the Great Compromise), which incorporated elements from both the Virginia and New Jersey Plans. Under the new Constitution, Congress would be a bicameral body. In the House of Representatives, states would be allocated seats based on population, but in the Senate each state would have two votes. The Constitution also included a president and judiciary that would each serve to check the power of other branches of government. In addition, Congress had the power to tax and had more enforcement powers.

Slavery was another contentious issue during the Constitutional Convention. Slavery was more common in the Southern states and less common in the North. The Southern states wanted slaves to be counted when calculating representation in Congress but not when it came to assessing taxes. Northern states wanted the opposite and eventually the two sides agreed to the Three-Fifths Compromise where slaves were counted as three-fifths of a person for the purposes of both taxation and representation. The Constitution also included a provision that allowed slave owners to recover slaves who had escaped and permitted the international slave trade to continue until 1808.

Once the Constitution had been drafted, nine of the thirteen states had to ratify it. Vigorous debate erupted over whether or not the Constitution should be approved. Two different political factions emerged. The Federalists supported the Constitution because they felt a stronger central government was necessary in order to promote economic growth and improve national security. Several leading federalists, including Alexander Hamilton, John Jay, and James Madison, published a series of articles urging voters to support the Constitution. However, the Anti-Federalists, including Thomas Jefferson and Patrick Henry, felt that the Constitution took too much power away from the states and gave it to the national government. They also thought there weren't enough protections for individual rights and lobbied for the addition of a Bill of Rights that guaranteed basic liberties. Ultimately, the Constitution was ratified in 1788 and the Bill of Rights was approved a year later.

The Electoral College unanimously elected George Washington as the nation's first president in 1789. Despite this appearance of unity, deep political divisions led to the formation of the nation's first party system. Washington supported the Federalist ideology and appointed several Federalists to his cabinet, including Alexander Hamilton as secretary of the treasury. The Anti-Federalist faction evolved into the Democratic-Republican Party and favored stronger state governments instead of a powerful federal government. As settlers moved into the new Northwest Territories, Washington helped pacify Indians who opposed further expansion. He also successfully put down a rebellion in western Pennsylvania by farmers opposed to a federal tax on whiskey.

A number of different issues divided the Federalists and the Democratic-Republicans, including the French Revolution, which began in 1789. Initially, many Americans supported the French effort to replace their monarchy and create a republican government. However, the French Revolution quickly became more violent, as thousands of suspected opponents of the revolution were executed during the Reign of Terror. The Federalists, including Washington, were horrified by the violence, while Jefferson and the Democratic-Republicans thought the United States should help its former ally. Washington ensured that the country remain officially neutral.

Washington declined to seek a third term and another Federalist, John Adams, became our second president. Adams signed the Alien and Sedition Acts, which made it a criminal offense to criticize the government, and allowed the president to deport aliens suspected of treason. Adams and the Federalists argued that the laws were necessary in order to improve security as Europe became embroiled in a war against the new French republic. Jefferson and the Democratic-Republicans said the laws restricted free speech. Jefferson made the acts an important topic in 1800 when he successfully ran for president.

Jefferson's victory marked a turning point in the political system because the Democratic-Republicans gained more power while the Federalists went into decline. He repealed the Alien and Sedition Acts when he was elected. The Federalists were further weakened when Hamilton was killed in a duel in 1804.

Jefferson accomplished several significant achievements during his presidency, and one of the most important was the Louisiana Purchase in 1803. For $15 million, Jefferson bought French territory west of the Mississippi River that doubled the size of the United States. He then appointed Meriwether Lewis and William Clark to lead an expedition to explore the vast new territory and study its geography, vegetation, and plant life. Clark also brought his African-American slave, York, on the journey. York helped hunt and even saved Clark's life during a flood. The expedition was also aided by Sacagawea, a Shoshone woman, who acted as a guide and interpreter. The explorers also established relations with Native American tribes and set the stage for further western expansion in the 1800s.

Several key Supreme Court decisions were also issued during this time. The case of *Marbury vs. Madison* established the policy of judicial review, which declared that the Supreme Court could rule whether or not an act of Congress was constitutional. The case of *McCullough vs. Maryland* affirmed that Congress had the power to pass laws that were "necessary and proper" in order to carry out its other duties. The case also upheld the supremacy of federal laws over state laws when they came into conflict.

War between the United States and Britain broke out in 1812 because the United States was drawn into a conflict between Britain and France. Britain refused to stop interfering with American ships bound for France and had begun forcibly recruiting American citizens into the British navy. Furthermore, the British still occupied several forts near the Great Lakes and continued to encourage Indians to attack American settlements in the Northwest Territories.

This led to war in 1812, and many Native American leaders allied themselves with the British, including the Shawnee warrior Tecumseh. Tecumseh temporarily united several tribes but his confederacy fell apart when he was killed in battle. This further weakened Native American resistance and facilitated American settlement in the Northwest Territory after the war.

The United States also achieved a victory at the Battle of Lake Erie where several American ships routed a British squadron. However, an American attempt to invade Canada failed, and the British humiliated the nation by invading Washington D.C. and burning down several public buildings, including the White House. The United States did achieve another victory after hostilities had ceased when future president Andrew Jackson repulsed a British attack at New Orleans. The war did not result in any major territorial gains or losses, but it did reaffirm American independence and gave America its national anthem, the "Star Spangled Banner." It also led to the collapse of the Federalist Party, which had opposed the war. The Democratic-Republicans dominated politics for the next decade, which was known as the "Era of Good Feelings," thus marking the end of the first party system.

Origins and Events of the Civil War

Origins of the Civil War

In the early 1800s, political and economic differences between the North and South became more apparent. Politically, a small but vocal group of abolitionists emerged in the North who demanded a complete end to slavery throughout the United States. William Lloyd Garrison edited the abolitionist newspaper *The Liberator* and vehemently denounced the brutality of slavery. His criticism was so vicious that the legislature of Georgia offered a $5,000 bounty to anyone who could capture Garrison and deliver him to state authorities. Other activists participated in the Underground Railroad—a network that helped fugitive slaves escape to the Northern United States or Canada.

Economic differences emerged as the North began to industrialize, especially in the textile industry where factories increased productivity. However, the Southern economy remained largely agricultural and focused on labor-intensive crops such as tobacco and cotton. This meant that slavery remained an essential part of the Southern economy. In addition, the North built more roads, railroads, and canals, while the Southern transportation system lagged behind. The Northern economy was also based on cash, while many Southerners still bartered for goods and services. This led to growing sectional tension between the North and South as their economies began to diverge further apart.

These economic differences led to political tension as well, especially over the debate about the expansion of slavery. This debate became more important as the United States expanded westward into the Louisiana Purchase and acquired more land after the Mexican-American War. Most Northerners were not abolitionists. However, many opposed the expansion of slavery into the western territories because it would limit their economic opportunities. If a territory was open to slavery, it would be more attractive to wealthy slave owners who could afford to buy up the best land. In addition, the presence of slave labor would make it hard for independent farmers, artisans, and craftsman to make a living, because they would have to compete against slaves who did not earn any wages. For their part, Southerners felt it was essential to continue expanding in order to strengthen the southern economy and ensure that the Southern way of life survived. As intensive farming depleted the soil of nutrients, Southern slave owners sought more fertile land in the west.

Both the North and South also feared losing political power as more states were admitted to the nation. For example, neither side wanted to lose influence in the United States senate if the careful balance of free and slave state representation was disrupted. Several compromises were negotiated in Congress, but they only temporarily quieted debate. The first such effort, called the Missouri Compromise, was passed in 1820, and it maintained political parity in the U.S. Senate by admitting Missouri as a slave state and Maine as a free state. The Missouri Compromise banned slavery in the portion of the Louisiana Purchase that was north of the $36^{\circ}30'$ parallel and permitted slavery in the portion south of that line as well as Missouri.

However, the slavery debate erupted again after the acquisition of new territory during the Mexican-American War. The Compromise of 1850 admitted California as a free state and ended the slave trade, but not slavery itself, in Washington D.C., in order to please Northern politicians. In return, Southern politicians were able to pass a stronger fugitive slave law and demanded that New Mexico and Utah be allowed to vote on whether or not slavery would be permitted in their state constitutions. This introduced the idea of popular sovereignty where the residents of each new territory, and not the federal government, could decide whether or not they would become a slave state or a free state. This essentially negated the Missouri Compromise of 1820. The enhanced fugitive slave law also angered many Northerners, because it empowered federal marshals to deputize anyone, even residents of a free state, and force them to help recapture escaped slaves. Anyone who refused would be subject to a $1,000 fine (equivalent to more than $28,000 in 2015).

The debate over slavery erupted again only a few years later when the territories of Kansas and Nebraska were created in 1854. The application of popular sovereignty meant that pro- and anti-slavery settlers flooded into these two territories to ensure that their faction would have a majority when it came time to vote on the state constitution. Tension between pro- and anti-slavery forces in Kansas led to an armed conflict known as "Bleeding Kansas."

John Brown was a militant abolitionist who fought in "Bleeding Kansas" and murdered five pro-slavery settlers there in 1856. He returned to the eastern United States and attacked the federal arsenal at Harper's Ferry, Virginia, in 1859. He hoped to seize the weapons there and launch a slave rebellion, but federal troops killed or captured most of Brown's accomplices and Brown was executed. The attack terrified Southerners and reflected the increasing hostility between North and South.

The sectional differences that emerged in the last several decades culminated in the presidential election of 1860. Abraham Lincoln led the new Republican Party, which opposed slavery on moral and economic grounds. The question of how best to expand slavery into new territories split the Democratic Party into two different factions that each nominated a presidential candidate. A fourth candidate also ran on a platform of preserving the union by trying to ignore the slavery controversy.

Lincoln found little support outside of the North but managed to win the White House since the Democratic Party was divided. Southern states felt threatened by Lincoln's anti-slavery stance and feared he would abolish slavery throughout the country. South Carolina was the first Southern state to secede from the Union and ten more eventually followed. Lincoln declared that the Union could not be dissolved and swore to defend federal installations. The Civil War began when Confederate troops fired on Fort Sumter in Charleston in 1861.

Events of the Civil War
The First Battle of Bull Run (also known as the First Battle of Manassas) in 1861 was the first major infantry engagement of the Civil War. Both the Northern and Southern troops were inexperienced and although they had equal numbers, the Confederates emerged victorious. Many had thought the war would be short, but it continued for another four years.

The Union navy imposed a blockade on the Confederacy and captured the port of New Orleans in 1862. The Union navy was much stronger than the Confederate fleet and prevented the Southern states from selling cotton to foreign countries or buying weapons.

In 1862, Union forces thwarted a Confederate invasion of Maryland at the Battle of Antietam. This engagement was the single bloodiest day of the war and more than 23,000 men on both sides were killed or wounded. Union troops forced the Confederates to retreat, and that gave Lincoln the political capital he needed to issue the Emancipation Proclamation in 1863. This declaration did not abolish slavery, but it did free slaves in Southern territory. It also allowed African Americans to join the Union navy and about 200,000 did so. The 54th Massachusetts Infantry was a famous unit of African American soldiers who led an assault on Fort Wagner in South Carolina in 1863. Although the attack failed, the 54th Massachusetts witnessed African American troops fighting bravely under fire.

The Siege of Vicksburg in 1863 was a major Union victory because they gained control of the Mississippi River and cut the Confederacy in half. This made it difficult the Confederacy to move troops around and communicate with their forces. Grant commanded the Northern forces in the siege and eventually became the Union army's top general.

The Battle of Gettysburg in 1863 marked the turning point of the Civil War. Robert E. Lee led Confederate troops into Pennsylvania, but in three days of heavy fighting, the Union army forced them to retreat. The victory bolstered Northern morale and weakened Southern resolve. Never again would Confederate forces threaten Northern territory.

In 1864, Union general William T. Sherman captured Atlanta and then marched more than 200 miles to Savannah. Along the way, he destroyed anything that could support the Southern war effort, such as railroads and cotton mills. At this point, the Southern economy was beginning to collapse. The North had more manpower than the South and could afford to sustain more casualties. The North also had more industrial capacity to produce weapons and supplies and more railroads to transport men and equipment.

Eventually, Robert E. Lee surrendered to Ulysses S. Grant at Appomattox, Virginia, on April 9, 1865. Five days later, John Wilkes Booth assassinated Lincoln in Washington D.C. Vice President Andrew Johnson, a Democrat, succeeded him and soon came into conflict with Republicans in Congress about how to reintegrate Southern states into the nation. This process was known as Reconstruction and lasted from 1865 to 1877.

Reconstruction

Johnson opposed equal rights for African Americans and pardoned many Confederate leaders. However, many Congressional Republicans wanted to harshly punish Southerners for their attempts to secede from the Union. They were known as Radical Republicans because they also wanted to give former slaves equal rights.

Johnson vetoed bills that were designed to protect the rights of freed slaves, but Congress overrode his vetoes. This led to increasing conflict between Johnson and Congress, which eventually caused Radical Republicans to impeach him. Although Johnson was acquitted in 1868, he had very little power, and Radical Republicans took control of the Reconstruction process.

Republicans passed three important constitutional amendments as part of the Reconstruction process. The 13th amendment was ratified in 1865, and it abolished slavery throughout the country. The 14th Amendment was ratified in 1868 and gave equal rights to all citizens. The 15th Amendment was ratified in 1870 and specifically granted all men the right to vote regardless of race.

Southerners resisted these demands and passed laws that prohibited freed slaves from owning weapons or testifying against whites. They also formed militias and vigilante groups, such as the Ku Klux Klan, in order to intimidate African Americans who tried to vote. Congress sent federal troops into Southern states in order to enforce the law and prevent vigilante violence.

After the much-disputed election of 1876, the Democrats offered to let the Republicans have the White House if they agreed to end Reconstruction. After the Republicans agreed, federal troops were withdrawn and African Americans in the South were subjected to discrimination until the Civil Rights movement of the 1960s. Scholars often consider the Reconstruction era the beginning of Jim Crow and a transition into a new form of "institutionalized racism" that still pervades much of modern U.S. society.

Settlement of the West

<u>Manifest Destiny</u>
The concept of Manifest Destiny emerged during the 1800s and introduced the idea that God wanted Americans to civilize and control the entire continent. This led to conflict when the province of Texas declared its independence from Mexico and asked to be annexed by the United States. President James K. Polk tried to buy Texas, but when Mexico refused, he sent troops into the disputed territory. Mexican troops responding by attacking an American unit, which led to war in 1846.

Manifest Destiny also sparked a desire to expand American influence into Central and South America. Adventurers launched several unsuccessful attempts to invade Nicaragua and Cuba.

Territorial Acquisitions

The United States purchased Alaska from Russia in 1867 for $7.2 million. At the time, the purchase was unpopular with the public, but seal hunting became very profitable and gold was discovered in 1896. Alaska became a state in 1959.

In 1893, American businessmen launched an armed coup, overthrew the queen of Hawaii, and asked Congress to annex Hawaii. The businessmen owned sugar plantations and feared the queen's attempts to enact reform would threaten their political influence. Hawaii became a U.S. territory in 1898 and a state in 1959.

The last phase of American territorial expansion occurred as a result of the Spanish-American War in 1898. New ideas arose in the late 19th century that helped justify further expansion. Some intellectuals applied Charles Darwin's ideas of "survival of the fittest" to the human race and called this new concept Social Darwinism. They used this idea to justify why stronger groups of people colonized and exploited weaker groups. In addition, imperialists also used the idea of the White Man's Burden to justify further expansion. They claimed that Caucasians were obligated to civilize and govern groups thought to be less advanced.

These ideas were used to justify America's new status as a colonial power as a result of the Spanish-American War. Although Spain had once been a powerful empire, it had been in decline. The United States went to war against Spain in 1898 when the American battleship USS Maine exploded in Havana Harbor and killed more than 250 sailors. The U.S. Navy defeated the Spanish fleet in several engagements and then the Army followed up with a victory at San Juan Hill, which included the famous charge by Teddy Roosevelt and the Rough Riders.

The war lasted less than four months and made the United States a world power. The U.S. also acquired several Spanish colonies, including Puerto Rico, Guam, and the Philippines. Guam became an important refueling station for American naval forces in the Pacific and remains a U.S. territory today, along with Puerto Rico. When the United States occupied the Philippines, the Filipino people launched a rebellion in order to obtain their independence. The U.S. Army put down the insurrection, but in doing so, they committed many atrocities against the Filipino people. The Philippines would remain an American territory until 1946.

The Transformation of the U.S. from an Agrarian to an Industrial Economy

After the end of the Civil War, America experienced a period of intense industrialization, immigration, and urbanization, and all three trends were interrelated. The process of industrialization had begun before the Civil War but expanded into more sectors of the economy in the later part of the century. This era is often called the Second Industrial Revolution and included growth in the chemical, petroleum, iron, steel, and telecommunications industries. For example, the Bessemer process made it much easier to produce high quality steel by removing impurities during the smelting process.

The writer Mark Twain called the late 19th century the Gilded Age because the era was also one of extreme social inequality. Some corporations expanded and began to control entire industries. For example, by 1890, the Standard Oil Company produced 88 percent of all the refined oil in the nation. This made a few individuals, such as John D. Rockefeller who owned Standard Oil, extremely wealthy. On the other hand, many workers earned low wages and began to form labor unions, such as the

American Federation of Labor in 1886, in order to demand better working conditions and higher pay. Strikes were one of the most common ways workers could express their dissatisfaction, and the Pullman Strike of 1894 was one of the largest such incidents in the 19th century. Workers went on strike after the Pullman Company, which manufactured railroad cars, cut wages by about 25 percent. More than 125,000 workers around the country walked off the job and attacked workers hired to replace them. Federal troops were sent in to end the strike, and more than eighty workers were killed or wounded during confrontations. The strike was unsuccessful, but Congress passed a law making Labor Day a federal holiday in order to placate union members.

Immigration also played an important part in the economic and social changes that occurred during the late 19th century. Immigration patterns changed during this time and immigrants from Southern and Eastern Europe, such as Italy and Poland, began to surpass the number of arrivals from Northern and Western Europe. The immigrants sought economic opportunity in the United States because wages for unskilled workers were higher than in their home countries. Some Americans resented the influx of immigrants because they spoke different languages and practiced Catholicism. In 1924, Congress passed a law that restricted immigration from Southern and Eastern Europe.

Increased urbanization was the last factor that contributed to the rapid changes of the Gilded Age. Factories were located near cities in order to draw upon a large pool of potential employees. Immigrants flooded into cities in search of work, and new arrivals often settled in the same neighborhoods where their compatriots lived. Between 1860 and 1890, the urbanization rate increased from about 20 percent to 35 percent. Cities struggled to keep up with growing populations, and services such as sanitation and water often lagged behind demand. Immigrants often lived in crowded living conditions that facilitated the spread of diseases.

The Progressive Era and the New Deal

The social inequalities and economic abuses of the Gilded Age did not go unnoticed, and in the 1890s many reformers began to demand change. This period was called the Progressive Era and included activists in both the Democratic and Republican parties. The Progressives wanted to use scientific methods and government regulation to improve society. For example, they advocated the use of initiative, referendum, and recall to make government more responsive to its citizens. Progressives also argued that it was necessary to breakup large monopolies (known as trust busting) in order to promote equal economic competition. In 1911, Rockefeller's Standard Oil was split up into thirty-four different companies in order to promote competition, and the Federal Trade Commission was established in 1914 in order to prevent other monopolies from forming. Many Progressives also supported several constitutional amendments that were ratified in early 20th century, including the 17th amendment, which established the direct election of U.S. Senators in 1913 (previously state legislatures had elected senators). They also favored the Prohibition of alcohol that went into effect with the 18th Amendment in 1919. Progressives also advocated for women's rights and backed the 19th Amendment, which gave women the right to vote in 1920.

Many journalists who supported the reform movement of the Progressives were known as Muckrackers because they helped expose political corruption and social inequality. Upton Sinclair wrote a novel in 1906 called "The Jungle," which exposed poor working conditions and health violations in the Chicago meatpacking industry. His exposé led to the passages of the Pure Food and Drug Act in 1906, which authorized the federal government to inspect the purity of foodstuffs and medicines. Jacob Riis was a photographer who documented the crowded and unhealthy living conditions that many immigrants and poor workers endured.

World War I, from 1914 to 1918, led to a communist revolution in Russia in 1917. Many Americans wanted to prevent political radicals from gaining influence in the United States. A number of strikes and bombings around the country led the federal government to crack down on anarchists, socialists, and communists in an event known as the First Red Scare. In 1919, U.S. Attorney General A. Mitchell Palmer launched a series of raids and arrested resident aliens suspected of belonging to radical groups. About 500 resident aliens were eventually deported.

In 1933, President Franklin D. Roosevelt introduced the New Deal, which was a series of executive orders and laws passed by Congress in response to the Great Depression. The programs focused on relief, recovery, and reform, and were enacted until 1938. The second New Deal from 1935-1938 promoted the Social Security Act, labor unions, and aided tenant farmers and migrant workers who were struggling from the economic devastation of the Great Depression.

Social Developments
With the ratification of the 19th Amendment in 1920, women obtained the right to vote. This achievement was partly due to women's contributions on the home front during World War I. Women served as Army nurses and worked in factories to help produce weapons, ammunition, and equipment. As more women entered the workforce, they became more financially independent and began to socialize without being supervised by a chaperone, as was the norm during the 19th century. Overall, women during this period, known as "New Women," took on a more active role in public life, pursued higher education in greater numbers, and sought more sexual freedom. During the 1920s, women, known as "flappers," began to flaunt social conventions by wearing short skirts, bobbing hair, smoking cigarettes, and driving automobiles. Nevertheless, a "glass ceiling" still remains in place decades after women's suffrage in regards to a gender wage gap.

Millions of African Americans also moved north during and after World War I in search of work in a phenomenon known as the Great Migration. This led to increased racial tension as whites and blacks competed for jobs and housing. This culminated in a wave of race riots that swept across the country in the summer of 1919. In Chicago, conflict broke out between whites and blacks at a segregated beach, which led to five days of violence during which thirty-eight people were killed and more than 500 injured. The impact of the Great Migration can still be seen in contemporary, heavily segregated Rust Belt cities such as Gary, IN and Milwaukee, WI.

The invention of the automobile also contributed to social change. Henry Ford applied the method of assembly line construction and scientific management to the automobile manufacturing industry. This made it much cheaper to manufacture cars and allowed more people to purchase them. Automobiles allowed young men and women to socialize and date without adult supervision. Automobiles also improved transportation, increased mobility, and spawned the first suburbs.

Cultural Developments
Motion picture cameras were invented in the late 19th century, and the film industry experienced significant growth in the early 20th century. Because the first movies were silent, dialogue was displayed on intertitles and a live orchestra usually performed during a screening. "Birth of a Nation," by D.W. Griffith, was one of the first major cinema blockbusters, and it portrayed the Ku Klux Klan in a heroic light. Millions of Americans saw the film, which helped the Klan spread throughout the Northern and Western United States.

The Great Migration also led to cultural changes during the 1920s known as the Harlem Renaissance. The movement was based in the neighborhood of Harlem and led to a rebirth of black literature, art, music, and fashion. Jazz was an important feature of the Harlem Renaissance and challenged musical conventions by emphasizing improvisation and spontaneity. Jazz became very popular with both whites and blacks during the 1920s. Langston Hughes was a poet of the Harlem Renaissance who encouraged his readers to take pride in their black identity.

Economic Developments

The Panic of 1893 was a worldwide economic depression that devastated the American economy. Businesses went bankrupt, banks collapsed, and unemployment rose to approximately 17 percent. The economy began to recover by 1897, and the beginning of World War I boosted the U.S. economy as European nations bought American goods.

In 1918, the United States emerged from World War I as a major economic power because it had helped finance the Allied war effort and produced large amounts of weapons and equipment. The American agricultural sector also prospered because European farms had been devastated by the war. This sent crop prices up, and farmers used the money to buy more land and equipment. Although the 1920s is usually depicted as an era of economic prosperity, agricultural prices fell after World War I, and farmers were unable to pay back their debts.

Stock market speculation increased during the 1920s, and investors borrowed money in order to purchase shares. This did not cause any concern as long as the stock market went up, but it led to disaster when stock prices fell sharply in October 1929 and investors were unable to repay their loans. The stock market crash may have triggered the Great Depression, but it did not cause it. The Great Depression spread around the globe as nations stopped trading with each other. In the United States, families lost their savings when banks failed because there was no federal insurance. The economy went into a downward spiral because as more people lost their jobs, they had little money to spend, which led to further layoffs and more economic contraction. Unemployment peaked at 25 percent between 1932 and 1933.

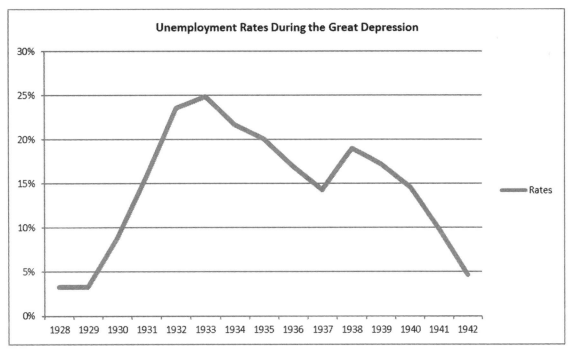

Democratic candidate Franklin D. Roosevelt was elected president in 1932 on his promise to help the economy recover by increasing government spending. After taking office in 1933, Roosevelt introduced a barrage of proposals, called the New Deal, that he hoped would boost employment, stimulate demand, and increase government regulation. Some elements of the New Deal were temporary, such as the Civilian Conservation Corps, which put young men to work improving parks between 1933 and 1942. Other New Deal programs endure to this day, such as the Social Security Administration, which has provided pensions to retirees, temporary payments to unemployed workers, and benefits to handicapped individuals since 1935. In addition, the Securities and Exchange Commission was created in 1934 and continues to regulate stock markets and investment companies. The Wagner Act of 1935 was also an important part of the New Deal because it guaranteed the right of workers to unionize and go on strike. The 21st Amendment was ratified in 1933 and repealed Prohibition, which had been hard to enforce and was unpopular. Roosevelt also hoped it would create jobs and stimulate spending. The New Deal helped reduce unemployment, but the economy did not completely recover until America entered World War II and production increased in order to support the war efforts.

The United States as a World Power

The United States gained prestige and international status after the Spanish-American War of 1898, because the United States defeated Spain and acquired several colonies. American participation in World War I made the United States an economic and financial leader as well. The United States loaned money to Britain and France and supplied weapons and equipment that helped the Triple Entente achieve victory. The United States and USSR emerged from World War II as the only surviving superpowers because so much of the rest of the world had been devastated. This system was described as bipolar because there were two centers of power.

The United States was the leader of the free world during the Cold War and formed military and economic alliances with other nations. With the collapse of the USSR in 1991, the United States was the only surviving world power. This era was a unipolar system because there were no other major powers that could rival the United States.

World War I and II

World War I began in 1914 with the assassination of Franz Ferdinand, the apparent heir of the Austro-Hungarian Empire. A network of secret alliances meant that most European nations were quickly drawn into the conflict, although President Woodrow Wilson initially tried to keep the United States neutral. The war involved two major European alliances: the Triple Entente of Britain, France, and Russia, and the Central Powers, which included Germany and Austria-Hungary. The British implemented a naval blockade that was very successful, and the Germans retaliated by launching submarine attacks. German submarines attacked any ship carrying supplies to the Triple Entente, including the passenger ship RMS Lusitania in 1915. About 1,200 people died, including more than 100 Americans. The Germans temporarily halted their unrestricted submarine campaign, but eventually resumed the attacks in 1917. In addition, in 1917, Germany asked Mexico to attack the United States in a communiqué known as the Zimmerman telegram. These events led the United States to join the Triple Entente in 1917, although significant numbers of American troops did not arrive in Europe until 1918. American reinforcement helped the British and French, who had been fighting continuously since 1914, launch a final offensive that defeated Germany in 1918. American forces suffered about 320,000 casualties. World War I also led to significant changes on the home front as women took on new responsibilities, and thousands of African Americans migrated north in search of work. World War I also led to a communist revolution that transformed Russia into the USSR in 1922.

After Germany was defeated in 1918, Wilson made a proposal known as the Fourteen Points and argued that the best way to resolve the conflict was by promoting free trade and democracy. For instance,

Wilson wanted nations to respect the right to navigate in international waters and create a League of Nations that would resolve future disputes. Some of his suggestions, such as the League of Nations, were adopted, but many were not. In 1919, Germany was forced to sign the Treaty of Versailles, which imposed harsh economic penalties and restricted the German military. Ultimately, the Treaty of Versailles created resentment in Germany that lead to World War II. America emerged as an important player in world affairs after World War I because the American economy had supplied the Triple Entente with arms and equipment and American soldiers helped to achieve victory.

World War II to the Present

In the period between the world wars, fascism became popular in many European countries that were ravaged by the Great Depression. Fascism is a political ideology that advocates for a dictatorship in order to provide stability and unity. Adolf Hitler emerged as a prominent fascist leader in Germany and eventually brought the Nazi party to power in 1933. Germany, Italy, and Japan formed an alliance called the Axis and began to threaten other countries. The League of Nations could not diffuse the conflict. World War II broke out when Germany invaded Poland in 1939. Hitler quickly conquered most of Europe, except for Britain, and attacked the USSR in 1941. The United States sent military equipment and weapons to Britain and the USSR, but did not formally join the war until the Japanese attacked Pearl Harbor on December 7, 1941. Again, women played an important role on the home front by working in factories to build guns, tanks, planes, and ships. African Americans, Native Americans, and Japanese Americans also contributed by fighting on the front lines.

American forces first landed in North Africa where they, along with British and French troops, defeated German and Italian forces in 1942. In 1943, Allied forces invaded Italy, and Soviet troops began to push the German army back out of the USSR. Allied troops landed in France in 1944 and the Soviets began to advance on Germany as well. By May 1945, Hitler had committed suicide and Germany had been defeated.

This also brought about an end to the Holocaust. The Holocaust was a genocide committed by Hitler's Nazi Germany and collaborators that resulted in the deaths of more than 6 million Jews and 5 million Romans, gypsies, Afro-Europeans, disabled citizens, and homosexuals. A network of facilities in Germany and its territories were used to house victims for slave labor and mass murder, among other heinous crimes. The Nuremberg trials were part of the aftermath of the Holocaust, which served to prosecute important members of Nazi Germany leadership.

In the Pacific theater, American naval forces defeated the Japanese fleet in several key engagements, including the battle of Midway in 1942. American troops began recapturing territory in the Pacific as well and eventually pushed the Japanese back to their home islands in 1945. The Japanese refused to surrender until American planes dropped atomic bombs on the cities of Nagasaki and Hiroshima in August 1945.

Because World War II devastated most of Europe, the United States and the USSR emerged as the only superpowers when it ended. However, the erstwhile allies were suspicious of each other, which led to the Cold War.

Individuals Who Shaped United States Foreign Policy
Woodrow Wilson
President Woodrow Wilson declared war on Germany on April 2, 1917. American troops helped defeat the German army in September 1918. Fighting ended in November of that year after Germany signed a

peace agreement. President Woodrow Wilson's plan for peace was the League of Nations, which was adopted as part of the Treaty of Versailles in 1919, but then rejected by the U.S. Senate.

Franklin D. Roosevelt

Democratic candidate Franklin D. Roosevelt was elected president in 1932 on his promise to help the economy recover by increasing government spending. After taking office in 1933, Roosevelt introduced a barrage of proposals, called the New Deal, that he hoped would boost employment, stimulate demand, and increase government regulation. Some elements of the New Deal were temporary, such as the Civilian Conservation Corps, which put young men to work improving parks between 1933 and 1942. Other New Deal programs endure to this day, such as the Social Security Administration, which has provided pensions to retirees, temporary payments to unemployed workers, and benefits to handicapped individuals since 1935. In addition, the Securities and Exchange Commission was created in 1934 and continues to regulate stock markets and investment companies. The Wagner Act of 1935 was also an important part of the New Deal because it guaranteed the right of workers to unionize and go on strike. The 21st Amendment was ratified in 1933 and repealed Prohibition, which had been hard to enforce and was unpopular. Roosevelt also hoped it would create jobs and stimulate spending. The New Deal helped reduce unemployment, but the economy did not completely recover until America entered World War II and production increased in order to support the war efforts.

Events that Shaped United States Foreign Policy

Marshall Plan

After World War II, the United States offered European countries the Marshall Plan—a grant of American subsidies to help Europe and Japan recover economically. The largest recipients were England, France, and West Germany. Aside from sincere humanitarian desires, the Marshall Plan also served the interests of the United States by ensuring that Europe's citizens did not resort to Communism out of desperation. In turn, the Soviet Union developed their own plan, the Molotov Plan, to help their Communist Allies' recovery.

NATO

NATO (North Atlantic Treaty Organization) is an organization of states from North America and Europe, led by the United States. This organization was formed after the end of World War II to counter the Soviet Union and Warsaw Pact's efforts to spread Communism across the world.

Korean War

When Communist North Korea invaded South Korea in June 1950, the U.N. sent a group of troops led by the U.S. to help South Korea. This action led to a three-year conflict that ended in a cease-fire in 1953. Although war was never officially declared and neither side won, the fighting showcased President Truman's hard stance against Communism.

Vietnam War

In 1954, rebels seized control of Vietnam from France. The country was split into two regimes with the northern part under Communist leadership. As the threat of communism continued to loom, the U.S. sent advisors and weapons to South Vietnam beginning in 1955. The U.S. got more directly involved in the 1960s during the presidency of Lyndon B. Johnson, who sent troops in great numbers to help South Vietnam win the fight. Many Americans opposed the war, which caused anti-war protests and unrest. A cease-fire was signed in 1973, and the last U.S. forces pulled out in 1975.

Cuban Missile Crisis

The Cuban Missile Crisis in 1962 was sparked by the failed invasion of Cuba by the U.S. a year earlier. After the invasion, the Soviets placed nuclear missiles aimed at the U.S. in Cuba. However, when U.S. spy planes spotted them, President John F. Kennedy demanded the dismantling and removal of the missile sites, and as a concession agreed to go forward with the planned removal of U.S. missile sites in Turkey. A year later on November 22, 1963, President Kennedy was assassinated in Dallas by Lee Harvey Oswald.

Sputnik I

The Cold War prompted the *space race* between the U.S. and Soviets, each attempting to outdo the other with different space exploration milestones. In 1957, the Russians launched *Sputnik*, the first satellite, into space. This prompted President Eisenhower to establish the National Aeronautics and Space Administration (NASA) in 1958. Although the Soviets were also the first nation to send a human into space in 1961, the U.S. quickly caught up. President Kennedy vowed to land an American on the moon by 1969—a feat that was accomplished by astronaut Neil Armstrong on July 20, 1969.

Gulf War

In 1990, Iraqi dictator Saddam Hussein invaded Kuwait in order to take possession of the tiny country's huge oil fields. A few months later, U.S. President George H.W. Bush launched Operation Desert Storm with a coalition of several Middle Eastern and European countries. This Gulf War started with air bombings and ended in a five-day ground war that drove Hussein out.

Civil Rights and Women's Movements

Although the Declaration of Independence declared "all men are created equal," blacks, women, and other minorities struggled for more than a century to make this dream a reality. The U.S. Constitution legalized slavery, and it was not abolished until the 13th Amendment was ratified in 1865. The 14th Amendment, ratified in 1868, granted African Americans citizenship, and the 15th Amendment, ratified in 1870, explicitly granted them the right to vote. However, white Southerners passed laws, known as the Jim Crow system, that prevented blacks from exercising their rights and, when that failed, they relied on violence and intimidation to oppress African Americans. For example, many Southern states required voters to pass literacy tests and used them to prevent blacks from casting a ballot. Whites were either exempt from the test or were held to much lower standards. Blacks who protested their oppression could be assaulted and even killed with impunity. In the 1896 decision *Plessy vs. Ferguson*, the U.S. Supreme Court ruled that "separate but equal" schools for white and black students were permissible. In reality, black schools were almost always inferior to white schools.

The emergence of the Civil Rights Movement after World War II finally destroyed the Jim Crow system. In the 1954 decision *Brown vs. Board of Education*, the Supreme Court reversed the "separate but equal" doctrine and declared that separate schools were inherently unequal because they stigmatized African American students. In 1957, President Dwight D. Eisenhower used federal troops to force the high school in Little Rock, Arkansas, to integrate and accept nine black students. This encouraged civil rights activists to demand additional reforms. In 1955, Rosa Parks refused to give up her seat on a bus in Montgomery, Alabama, which led to a boycott. Martin Luther King Jr. led the bus boycott and became a national leader in the Civil Rights Movement. In 1960, four students in Greensboro, North Carolina, launched a peaceful sit-in at a segregated lunch counter, which sparked similar protests around the country. White activists from the North went south to help blacks register to vote, and in 1964 three activists were murdered in Mississippi. That same year, King led 250,000 protesters in a march on Washington D.C. where he delivered his famous "I Have a Dream Speech."

Although King advocated for peaceful protests, many other civil rights activists disagreed with him. For example, Malcolm X believed that blacks should use violence to defend themselves. Furthermore, King worked with white activists while Malcom X rejected any cooperation. Malcolm X was assassinated in 1965, and, despite his reputation as a non-violent leader, King was also gunned down in 1968.

Under mounting pressure, Congress passed several important pieces of legislation. The 1964 Civil Rights Act banned discrimination based on race, color, religion, sex, or national origin. The Voting Rights Act of 1965 prohibited the use of poll taxes or literacy tests to prohibit voting. The Civil Rights Act of 1968 banned housing discrimination. In 1967, Carl Stokes became the first black mayor of a major American city, Cleveland. That same year, Thurgood Marshall became the first African American to serve on the Supreme Court. President Gerald Ford declared February to be black history month. In 1989, Colin Powell became the first black chairman of the Joint Chiefs of Staff. Despite these reforms, activists claim institutional racism is still a problem in the 21st century. The Civil Rights movement inspired women, Latinos, and other groups to make similar demands for equal rights.

Women

In 1776, Abigail Adams urged her husband, founding father John Adams, to advocate for women's rights, but it would take more than a century before women could vote. In 1848, activists organized a convention in Seneca Falls, New York, to organize the women's suffrage movement, and their efforts slowly gained momentum. The ratification of the 19th Amendment in 1920 finally gave women the right to vote.

Although women had achieved political equality, they continued to demand reform throughout the 20th century. In the early 1900s, Margaret Sanger provided women with information about birth control, which was illegal at the time. Women entered the industrial workforce in large numbers during World War II, but when the war ended, they were fired so that veterans would have jobs when they came home. Many women were frustrated when told they had to return to their domestic lives. Simone de Beauvoir, a French writer, published her book "The Second Sex" after World War II, and an English translation was published in 1953. It highlighted the unequal treatment of women throughout history and sparked a feminist movement in the United States. In 1963, Betty Friedan published a book, called "The Feminine Mystique," that revealed how frustrated many suburban wives were with the social norms that kept them at home. During the 1960s, women participated in the sexual revolution and exerted more control over their own sexuality. In 1972, Congress passed Title IX, which prohibited sexual discrimination in education and expanded women's sports programs. In the 1970s, women's rights activists also pushed for greater access to birth control, and in 1973 the Supreme Court issued the landmark decision *Roe vs. Wade* which removed many barriers to abortion services. Women also demanded greater protection from domestic abuse and greater access to divorce.

During the 20th century, many American women made notable achievements, including Amelia Earhart, who was the first woman to cross the Atlantic in an airplane in 1928. In 1981, Sandra Day O'Connor became the first woman to serve on the Supreme Court. In 1983, Sally Ride became the first female astronaut. In 1984, Geraldine Ferraro became the first woman to run for vice-president, although she was unsuccessful. However, many activists continue to demand reform in the 21st century. For example, women only account for 20 percent of the U.S. Senate and House of Representatives. Furthermore, women only earn 79 percent of what men in similar jobs are paid. In 1980, President Jimmy Carter declared March to be women's history month.

Hispanics

After World War II, many Hispanics also began to demand greater equality. In 1949, veterans protested a refusal by a Texas town to bury a Mexican American soldier, who died during World War II, in the local cemetery, because only whites could be buried there. Activists called themselves Chicanos, a term that previously was used as a pejorative to describe Mexican Americans. Cesar Chavez was a labor union activist who organized transient Hispanic agricultural workers in an effort to obtain better working conditions in the 1960s and 1970s. Activists encouraged a sense of pride in Chicano identity, especially in arts and literature. In 1968, President Lyndon B. Johnson declared National Hispanic Heritage Month would run from mid-September to mid-October.

In 1959, biochemist Severo Ochoa became the first Hispanic to win a Nobel Prize. Franklin Chang-Diaz became the first Hispanic astronaut in 1986, and he flew a total of seven space shuttle missions. In 1990, Oscar Hijuelos became the first Hispanic American to win the Pulitzer Prize. Sonja Sotomayor became the first Hispanic to serve on the Supreme Court in 2009.

Native Americans

Native Americans suffered centuries of oppression at the hands of European colonists, and later American settlers as they pushed further west. Native Americans resisted attempts to encroach on their lands but were pushed onto smaller and smaller reservations. The Massacre at Wounded Knee in 1890 was the last major conflict between Native Americans and U.S. forces. However, American officials continued to try and force Native Americans to assimilate into white culture.

In 1968, a group of Native Americans formed the American Indian Movement in order to combat racism and demand greater independence. Between 1969 and 1971, a group of Native American activists occupied the federal prison on Alcatraz Island near San Francisco, although it had been closed since 1963. The activists offered to buy back the island for $9.40 in order to draw attention to how the federal government had forced tribes to sell their lands at low prices. Other activists disrupted Thanksgiving Day ceremonies aboard a replica of the Mayflower in Boston in 1970. In 1971, Native American activists also occupied Mount Rushmore, which is located on ground the Native Americans consider sacred. Violence broke out between activists and law enforcement officials in 1973 when Native Americans occupied the town of Wounded Knee, sight of the famous massacre.

In 1970, President Richard Nixon granted Native American tribes more autonomy. In 1978, Congress passed the American Indian Religious Freedom Act, which guaranteed Native Americans' rights to practice their religious ceremonies and visit sacred sites. In 1990, President George H.W. Bush declared November Native American History Month. In 1969, Navarre Scott Momaday became the first Native American to win a Pulitzer Prize for his book "House Made of Dawn." In 2014, Diane Humetewa, a member of the Hopi tribe, became the first Native American woman to serve as a federal judge. However, many Native American communities still suffer from high rates of unemployment, alcoholism, and domestic abuse.

Asian Americans

Asian Americans also faced discrimination throughout American history and in 1882, Congress passed a law banning all Chinese immigrants. During World War II, more than 100,000 Japanese Americans were interned in concentration camps. In 1982, two American autoworkers beat Vincent Chin to death with a baseball bat because his assailants blamed him for the loss of jobs in the automotive manufacturing industry.

In the 1960s, activists demanded that the term "Asian American" replace the word "oriental," because it carried a stigma. Asian Americans also promoted a sense of pride in their cultural identity and successfully pushed for the creation of ethnic studies programs. Ellison Onizuka became the first Asian American astronaut in 1985, although he perished in the space shuttle Challenger disaster. In 1990, President George H.W. Bush declared May Asian Pacific American Heritage Month and Sheryl WuDunn became the first Asian American to win a Pulitzer Prize that same year.

U.S. Leadership in World Affairs from the Collapse of the Soviet Union to Present

The post-World War II era led to a number of social, economic, and technological changes in the United States. The counter-culture phenomenon was one of the most powerful social movements in the latter half of the twentieth century in the U.S. The counter-culture movement challenged social norms and rejected traditional authority figures. The movement began in the 1950s with the beatniks, a group of non-conformist writers and artists who were dissatisfied with society. The beatniks sought inspiration in African and Asian cultures and many eschewed materialism.

Political Developments
President Franklin D. Roosevelt created the New Deal in order to stimulate the economy and improve government regulation. The New Deal also marked an important shift in American politics because the Democratic Party began to favor government intervention while Republicans opposed it. This was a reversal of the parties' previous platforms. The Democratic Party relied on a coalition of labor unions, Catholics, African Americans, and other minorities. The Republican Party included conservatives, evangelicals, and business leaders.

The Great Society was another major government program that the Democratic Party supported. President Lyndon B. Johnson sought to end poverty and improve education. For example, he raised the minimum wage and created programs to provide poor Americans with job training. The Great Society also implemented a number of Civil Rights laws that will be discussed in greater detail later.

The presidential election of 1980 was another watershed moment. Republican nominee Ronald Reagan carried forty-three states, and the Republicans won a majority in the U.S. Senate after twenty-eight years of Democratic control. Reagan presented an optimistic message and broadcasted a television advertisement that proclaimed "It's morning again in America." He promised to restore America's military power, cut government regulations, and reduce taxes. Reagan enjoyed the support of resurgent conservative Christian evangelicals, who wanted to restore morality to American society. They were particularly concerned about issues such as abortion. The Moral Majority, founded by Baptist minister Jerry Falwell in 1979, was one key group that helped Reagan win the election. This coalition helped realign party loyalties, as more liberal Republicans and conservative Democrats shifted their allegiance.

Economic Developments
America emerged as one of the most powerful economies in the world after 1945. The US economy, especially manufacturing, was very prosperous during the 1950s and 1960s. The economy successfully switched from wartime production, and consumer demand was very high. During the Great Depression, few families had disposable income. Although most workers earned good wages during World War II, they had little to spend it on because most goods were rationed. Once production of consumer goods resumed, families used their savings to buy cars, household appliances, and televisions. This was good for the economy, and unemployment remained below 5 percent for most of the 1950s and 1960s. However, during the latter part of the 20th century, the manufacturing base in the North and Midwest began to crumble and the area became known as the Rust Belt. Manufacturing jobs began to move from

the North and Midwest to states in the South and West, known as the Sun Belt, where land was cheap and wages were low.

Purposes of Government

The United States of America's government, as outlined by the Constitution, is designed to serve as a compromise between democracy and preceding monarchical systems. The American Revolution brought independence from Britain and freedom from its aristocratic system of governance. On the other hand, the short-lived Articles of Confederation revealed the significant weaknesses of state-based governance with limited national control. By dividing power between local, state, and federal governments, the United States can uphold its value of individual liberties while, nevertheless, giving a sense of order to the country.

The federal government, which is in charge of laws that affect the entire nation, is split into three main branches: executive, judicial, and legislative. It is important to realize that the three segments of the federal government are intended to stand as equal counterparts to the others, and that none of them are "in charge." The executive branch centers on the president, the vice president, and the cabinet. The president and vice president are elected every four years. Also known as the commander-in-chief, the president is the official head of state and serves as the nation's head diplomat and military leader. The vice president acts as the president of the Senate in the legislative branch, while the president appoints members of the cabinet to lead agencies, including the Treasury and Department of Defense. However, the president can only sign and veto laws and cannot initiate them himself.

Instead, the legislative branch, specifically Congress, proposes and debates laws. Congress is bicameral because it is divided into two separate legislative houses. Each state's representation in the House of Representatives is determined proportionally by population, with the total number of voting seats limited to 435. The Senate, in contrast, has only two members per state and a total of one hundred senators. Members of both houses are intended to represent the interests of the constituents in their home states and to bring their concerns to a national level. Ideas for laws, called bills, are proposed in either chamber and then are voted upon according to the body's rules; should the bill pass the first round of voting, the other legislative chamber must approve it before it can be sent to the president. Congress also has a variety of other powers, such as the rights to declare war, collect taxes, and impeach the president.

The judicial branch, though it cannot pass laws itself, serves to interpret the laws. At the federal level, this is done through several tiers of judicial bodies. At the top, the Supreme Court consists of judges appointed by the president; these judges serve for life, unless they resign from their position or are removed by Congress for improper behavior. The Supreme Court's decisions in trials and other judgments rest on the justices' interpretations of the Constitution and enacted laws. As the Constitution remains fundamental to the American legal system, the Supreme Court's rulings on how laws follow or fail to uphold the Constitution have powerful implications on future rulings. Beneath the Supreme Court, there are a number of other federal judicial bodies—courts of appeals, district courts, and courts of special jurisdiction.

While the federal government manages the nation as a whole, state governments address issues pertaining to their specific territory. In the past, states claimed the right, known as nullification, to refuse to enforce federal laws that they considered unconstitutional. However, conflicts between state and federal authority, particularly in the South in regard to first, slavery, and later, discrimination, have led to increased federal power, and states cannot defy federal laws. Even so, the Tenth Amendment limits federal power to those specifically granted in the Constitution, and the rest of the powers are retained by the states and citizens. Therefore, individual state governments are left in charge of decisions with immediate effects on their citizens, such as state laws and taxes. Like the federal government, state governments consist of executive, judicial, and legislative branches, but the exact configuration of those branches varies between states. For instance, while most states follow the bicameral structure of Congress, Nebraska has only a single legislative chamber. State governments have considerable authority within their states, but they cannot impose their power on other states, nor can they secede from the United States.

Local governments, which include town governments, county boards, library districts, and other agencies, are especially variable in their composition. They often reflect the overall views of their state governments but also have their own values, rules, and structures. Generally, local governments function in a democratic fashion, although the exact form of government depends on its role. Depending on the location within the state, local government may have considerable or minimal authority based on the population and prosperity of the area; some counties may have strong influence in the state, while others may have a limited impact.

Native American tribes are treated as dependent nations that answer to the federal government but may be immune to state jurisdiction. As with local governments, the exact form of governance is left up to the tribes, which ranges from small councils to complex systems of government. Other U.S. territories, including the District of Columbia (site of Washington, D.C.) and acquired islands, such as Guam and Puerto Rico, have representation within Congress, but their legislators cannot vote on bills.

As members of a democracy, U.S. citizens are empowered to elect most government leaders, but the process varies between branch and level of government. Presidential elections at the national scale use the Electoral College system. Rather than electing the president directly, citizens cast their ballots to select electors, who generally vote for a specific candidate, that represent each state in the college. Legislative branches at the federal and state level are also determined by elections, albeit without an Electoral College. In some areas, judges are elected, but in other states judges are appointed by elected officials. It should also be noted that the two-party system was not built into the Constitution but gradually emerged over time.

Functions of Federal, State, and Local Governments in the United States

Constitutional Underpinnings
The role of government is to maintain a society and provide public services through its formal institutions, protect the citizens of the state, and regulate the economic system. To determine how a government should perform these functions and to protect the rights and liberties of the citizens, states enact a *constitution*, a written document that typically establishes the form of government and delegation of powers within the government, delineates limits on government, and defines protected rights, liberties, and privileges.

The many underpinnings, or foundations, upon which the *Constitution* of the United States was founded include:

Articles of Confederation (1781-1789)
The Articles of Confederation established a formal agreement or confederation between the original thirteen states. The Articles of Confederation established a central government composed of a unicameral legislative assembly in which each state was granted a single representative. Passing a bill required votes from nine of the thirteen representatives. Under the Articles of Confederation, the

centralized government, the Continental Congress, was granted very limited powers, rendering it largely ineffective. Those powers included:

- Borrowing money from states or foreign government
- Creating post offices
- Appointing military offices
- Declaring war
- Signing treaties with foreign states

The weak central government established under the Articles of Confederation lacked the power to impose taxes, enforce a draft to staff the new army and navy, regulate trade, or enforce the laws enacted in Congress. As such, the sovereignty remained primarily with the states. Under the Articles, the states reserved the powers to impose taxes upon each other and the citizens of their states, regulate trade within their states, coin and print money, and sign treaties with foreign states. The states also often ignored the laws enacted by the Congress because there was no executive branch to enforce the law.

This imbalance of power between the central government and the states led to crisis within the states, resulting in economic difficulties and violence. The lack of common currency and investment in interstate infrastructure greatly hindered economic growth. In the years 1786 and 1787, farmers in several states staged a series of protests over local tax and debt collection imposed on struggling farms, commonly known as Shay's Rebellion.

Constitutional Convention, 1787
The failures of the Articles of Confederation to effectively govern on a national level directly led to the Constitutional Convention, and those experiences influenced the founders' decision to include a more robust federal government in the United States Constitution. The Constitutional Convention faced several challenges, including disputes over representation between large and small states, tension between the southern and northern states over slavery, differing visions of how power would be delegated within the government, and opposition to ceding states' sovereignty to a national federal government.

New Jersey Plan
Led by William Patterson, the New Jersey Plan called for a unicameral legislature that would grant each state a single vote. It proposed a plural executive power selected by the legislature, which would possess no veto power over the legislature, as well as judges appointed by the executive power for the duration of their lives.

The Virginia Plan
Drafted by James Madison, the Virginia Plan featured a bicameral legislature with two houses. The representatives of the lower house were to be selected by the people, and then the lower house would elect the upper house. The number of representatives of each house would be based upon population or the amount of money contributed to the federal government by each state; thus, large states supported the Virginia Plan. In this plan, the legislature could appoint judges and select a single executive with veto power.

<u>Compromises</u>
Connecticut Compromise
This compromise included aspects of both the New Jersey Plan and Virginia Plan in a bicameral legislature. Representation in the House of Representatives was proportional to a state's population, and in the Senate, states enjoyed equal representation with two senators per state.

Slavery Compromises
Several other compromises were made during the Convention, including the *Three-Fifths Compromise,* which, in an effort to appease both the South states who wanted slaves to be counted as part of the population for the purpose of representation but not counted for the purpose of taxes, and the North, who demanded slaves be counted for taxes but not representation, the framers of the Constitution determined that three-fifths of the slave population of each state would be counted for the purpose of both taxes and representation. In an additional compromise called the *Commerce and Slave Trade Compromise*, Congress agreed not to tax exports from states or ban the trading of slaves for twenty years. This eased Southerners' fears that if the Northern states controlled the federal government, then they could enforce antislavery policies.

Constitution vs. Articles of Confederation
The Constitution addressed the weaknesses of the Articles of Confederation in the following ways:

- Unlike the sovereign states under the Articles of Confederation, the people are now the sovereign, and they bestow sovereignty to both the states and federal government, according to principles of Federalism.

- The Constitution creates a robust central government with many specific and implied powers.

- The Constitution empowers the federal government to levy taxes against the states.

- The Constitution establishes an executive branch of the federal government to enforce the laws; it is led by a president who serves as the commander-in-chief.

- The Constitution establishes a federal judiciary branch with a Supreme Court and lower courts to interpret the laws enacted by the legislative branch.

- The Constitution removes the states' power to coin and print money and establishes a national currency; Congress may regulate interstate and international commerce.

- The Constitution specifies representation in Congress based on population and equal representation for each state in the Senate.

- The Constitution requires a simple majority in both houses to enact laws rather than a vote of at least nine out of thirteen, as specified in the Articles of Confederation. In addition, senators vote separately under the Constitution, while states vote as a single bloc in the Constitution.

- The Constitution requires a two-thirds majority vote in the House of Representatives and a two-thirds majority in the Senate to amend the Constitution, while the Articles of Confederation required a unanimous vote.

Federalism

To strengthen the central government, while still appeasing the individual states who preferred to remain sovereign over their territories, the framers of the Constitution based the new government upon the principles of *Federalism*—a compound government system that divides powers between a central government and various regional governments. The Constitution clearly defined the roles of both the state governments and the new federal government, specifying the limited power of the federal government and reserving all other powers not restricted by the Constitution to the states in the Tenth Amendment to the Constitution, commonly referred to as the Reservation Clause.

The Constitution establishes the specific powers granted to the federal and state governments.

- Delegated powers: the specific powers granted to the federal government by the Constitution
- Implied powers: the unstated powers that can be reasonably inferred from the Constitution
- Inherent powers: the reasonable powers required by the government to manage the nation's affairs and maintain sovereignty
- Reserved powers: the unspecified powers belonging to the state that are not expressly granted to the federal government or denied to the state by the Constitution
- Concurrent powers: the powers shared between the federal and state governments

The Constitution would delegate the following expanded powers to the federal government:

- Coin money
- Declare war
- Establish lower federal courts
- Sign foreign treaties
- Expand the territories of the United States, and admit new states into the union
- Regulate immigration
- Regulate interstate commerce

The following powers were reserved for the states:

- Establish local governments
- Hold elections
- Implement welfare and benefit programs
- Create public school systems
- Establish licensing standards and requirements
- Regulate state corporations
- Regulate commerce within the state

The *concurrent* powers granted to both the federal and state governments in the Constitution include:

- The power to levy taxes
- The power to borrow money
- The power to charter incorporations

Ratifying the Constitution

The framers of the Constitution signed the Constitution on September 17, 1787, but the Articles of Confederation required nine of the thirteen states to ratify the document. Conventions were held in all thirteen states and sparked heated debates between those who supported and those who opposed the new system of government. The Federalists supported the expansion of the federal government, and the anti-Federalists feared that a stronger central government would weaken the states. The anti-Federalists also sought additional protection for civil liberties. The debates between these two parties continued for two years and inspired a series of essays known as the *Federalist Papers* and *Anti-Federalist Papers* authored anonymously by leaders of their respective party.

Notable Federalists and authors of the *Federalist Papers* include:

- Alexander Hamilton: founder of the Federalist Party and advocate for a centralized financial system

- George Washington: commander-in-chief of the Continental Army and future first president of the United States

- James Madison: one of the primary drafters of the Constitution and the future fourth president of the United States

- John Jay: president of the Continental Congress and future first chief justice of the United States

- John Adams: future second president of the United States

Notable anti-Federalists and authors of the *Anti-Federalist Papers* include:

- Thomas Jefferson: primary author of the Declaration of Independence and future third president of the United States

- Patrick Henry: governor of Virginia (1776-1779, 1784-1786)

- Samuel Adams: governor of Massachusetts (1794-1797), lieutenant governor of Massachusetts (1789-1794), and president of the Massachusetts Senate (1782-1785, 1787-1788)

- George Mason: one of only three delegates who did not sign the Constitution at the Constitutional Convention and author of Objections to This Constitution of Government (1787) and the Virginia Declaration of Rights of 1776, which served as the basis for the Bill of Rights

The first state to ratify the Constitution was Delaware in a unanimous vote on December 7, 1787. Several other states followed, and eventually, after ten months, New Hampshire became the ninth state to ratify the Constitution in June 1788. However, some states still remained divided between Federalist and anti-Federalist sentiments and had yet to approve the document, including the two most populous states, Virginia and New York. To reconcile their differing views, the Federalists agreed to include a bill of rights if anti-Federalists supported the new Constitution. Federalist sentiment prevailed, and the remaining states approved the document. On May 29, 1790, the last holdout, Rhode Island, ratified the Constitution by two votes. As promised, the Bill of Rights—the first 10 amendments to the Constitution—was added in 1791, providing expanded civil liberty protection and due process of law.

Three Branches of the U.S. Government

A *political institution* is an organization created by the government to enact and enforce laws, act as a mediator during conflict, create economic policy, establish social systems, and carry out some power.

These institutions maintain a rigid structure of internal rules and oversight, especially if the power is delegated, like agencies under the executive branch.

The Constitution established a federal government divided into three branches: legislative, executive, and judicial.

The Three Branches of the U.S. Government

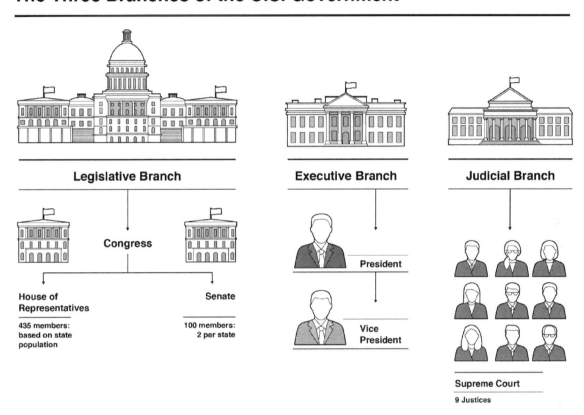

Executive Branch
The executive branch is responsible for enforcing the laws. The executive branch consists of the president, the vice president, the president's cabinet, and federal agencies created by Congress to execute some delegated.

The president of the United States:

- Serves a four-year term and is limited to two terms in office
- Is the chief executive officer of the United States and commander-in-chief of the armed forces
- Is elected by the Electoral College
- Appoints cabinet members, federal judges, and the heads of federal agencies
- Vetoes or signs bills into law
- Handles foreign affairs, including appointing diplomats and negotiating treaties
- Must be thirty-five years old, a natural-born U.S. citizen, and have lived in the United States for at least fourteen years

The vice president:

- Serves four-year terms alongside and at the will of the president
- Acts as president of the Senate
- Assumes the presidency if the president is incapacitated
- Assumes any additional duties assigned by the president

The cabinet members:

- Are appointed by the president
- Act as heads for the fifteen executive departments
- Advise the president in matters relating to their departments and carry out delegated power

Note that the president can only sign and veto laws and cannot initiate them himself. As head of the executive branch, it is the responsibility of the president to execute and enforce the laws passed by the legislative branch.

Although Congress delegates their legislative authority to agencies in an enabling statute, they are located in the executive branch because they are tasked with executing their delegating authority. The president enjoys the power of appointment and removal over all federal agency workers, except those tasked with quasi-legislative or quasi-judicial powers.

Legislative Branch
The legislative branch is responsible for enacting federal laws. This branch possesses the power to declare war, regulate interstate commerce, approve or reject presidential appointments, and investigate the other branches. The legislative branch is *bicameral*, meaning it consists of two houses: the lower house, called the House of Representatives, and the upper house, known as the Senate. Both houses are elected by popular vote.

Members of both houses are intended to represent the interests of the constituents in their home states and to bring their concerns to a national level. Ideas for laws, called bills, are proposed in one chamber and then are voted upon according to the body's rules; should the bill pass the first round of voting, the other legislative chamber must approve it before it can be sent to the president.

The two houses (or chambers) are similar though they differ on some procedures such as how debates on bills take place.

House of Representatives
The House of Representatives is responsible for enacting bills relating to revenue, impeaching federal officers including the president and Supreme Court justices, and electing the president in the case of no candidate reaching a majority in the Electoral College.

In the House of Representatives:

- Each state's representation in the House of Representatives is determined proportionally by population, with the total number of voting seats limited to 435.

- There are six nonvoting members from Washington, D.C., Puerto Rico, American Samoa, Guam, Northern Mariana Islands, and the U.S. Virgin Islands.

- The Speaker of the House is elected by the other representatives and is responsible for presiding over the House. In the event that the president and vice president are unable to fulfill their duties, the Speaker of the House will succeed to the presidency.

- The representatives of the House serve two-year terms.

- The requirements for eligibility in the House include:

    o Must be twenty-five years of age
    o Must have been a U.S. citizen for at least seven years
    o Must be a resident of the state they are representing by the time of the election

Senate

The Senate has the exclusive powers to confirm or reject all presidential appointments, ratify treaties, and try impeachment cases initiated by the House of Representatives.

In the Senate:

- The number of representatives is one hundred, with two representatives from each state.
- The vice president presides over the Senate and breaks the tie, if necessary.
- The representatives serve six-year terms.
- The requirements for eligibility in the Senate include:
    o Must be thirty years of age
    o Must have been a U.S. citizen for the past nine years
    o Must be a resident of the state they are representing at the time of their election

Legislative Process

Although all members of the houses make the final voting, the senators and representatives serve on committees and subcommittees dedicated to specific areas of policy. These committees are responsible for debating the merit of bills, revising bills, and passing or killing bills that are assigned to their committee. If it passes, they then present the bill to the entire Senate or House of Representatives (depending on which they are a part of). In most cases, a bill can be introduced in either the Senate or the House, but a majority vote of both houses is required to approve a new bill before the president may sign the bill into law.

Judicial Branch

The *judicial branch*, though it cannot pass laws itself, is tasked with interpreting the law and ensuring citizens receive due process under the law. The judicial branch consists of the Supreme Court, the highest court in the country, overseeing all federal and state courts. Lower federal courts are the district courts and court of appeals.

The Supreme Court:

- Judges are appointed by the president and confirmed by the Senate.
- Judges serve until retirement, death, or impeachment.
- Judges possess sole power to judge the constitutionality of a law.
- Judges set precedents for lower courts based on their decisions.
- Judges try appeals that have proceeded from the lower district courts.

Checks and Balances

Notice that a system of checks and balances between the branches exists. This is to ensure that no branch oversteps its authority. They include:

- Checks on the Legislative Branch:
  - The president can veto bills passed by Congress.
  - The president can call special sessions of Congress.
  - The judicial branch can rule legislation unconstitutional.
- Checks on the Executive Branch:
  - Congress has the power to override presidential vetoes by a two-thirds majority vote.
  - Congress can impeach or remove a president, and the chief justice of the Supreme Court presides over impeachment proceedings.
  - Congress can refuse to approve presidential appointments or ratify treaties.
- Checks on the Judicial Branch:
  - The president appoints justices to the Supreme Court, as well as district court and court of appeals judges.
  - The president can pardon federal prisoners.
  - The executive branch can refuse to enforce court decisions.
  - Congress can create federal courts below the Supreme Court.
  - Congress can determine the number of Supreme Court justices.
  - Congress can set the salaries of federal judges.
  - Congress can refuse to approve presidential appointments of judges.
  - Congress can impeach and convict federal judges.

The three branches of government operate separately, but they must rely on each other to create, enforce, and interpret the laws of the United States.

Checks and Balances

Executive Branch

Appoint Justices to the Supreme Court and Pardon Federal Prisoners

Override Presidential Vetoes by 2/3 vote and Impeach the President

Preside Over Impeachment Proceedings

Legislative Branch

Judicial Branch

Create Federal Courts Below the Supreme Court and Impeach Federal Judges

Rule Legislation Unconstitutional

The Role of State Government

While the federal government manages the nation as a whole, state governments address issues pertaining to their specific territory. In the past, states claimed the right, known as nullification, to refuse to enforce federal laws that they considered unconstitutional. However, conflicts between state and federal authority, particularly in the South in regard to first, slavery, and later, discrimination, have led to increased federal power, and states cannot defy federal laws. Even so, the Tenth Amendment limits federal power to those powers specifically granted in the Constitution, and the rest of the powers are retained by the states and citizens. Therefore, individual state governments are left in charge of decisions with immediate effects on their citizens, such as state laws and taxes.

In this way, the powers of government are separated both horizontally between the three branches of government (executive, legislative, and judicial) and vertically between the levels of government (federal, state, and local).

Like the federal government, state governments consist of executive, judicial, and legislative branches, but the exact configuration of those branches varies between states. For example, while most states follow the bicameral structure of Congress, Nebraska has only a single legislative chamber. Additionally, requirements to run for office, length of terms, and other details vary from state to state. State governments have considerable authority within their states, but they cannot impose their power on other states.

Separation of Powers

Federal Government Powers	(shared)	State Government Powers
coin money	levy taxes	hold elections
declare war	borrow money	implement welfare and benefit programs
regulate immigration	charter incorporations	establish licensing standards
regulate interstate commerce		regulate state corporations

Local Self-Government in Massachusetts and the United States

Local self-government refers to a system in which citizens of small or large groups (city, state, or country) govern them. They control their own rules and government affairs. The United States has two political parties based on self-government: Republican and Democratic. Each political party has varying opinions on taxes, policies, role of the government, health care, immigration, and gun control. Prior to Republican and Democratic Party formations, Massachusetts created one of the first forms of localized self-government.

Massachusetts played a huge role in the history of local self-governments. In 1620, Pilgrims settled in Plymouth Colony and signed the Mayflower Compact. The Mayflower Compact was one of the first forms of democracy in the United States. The agreement allowed Massachusetts to form a government that established majority vote policies. This very compact was one of the groundbreaking agreements for local self-governments in the United States.

In 1774, the Parliament of Great Britain passed the Massachusetts Government Act. This act basically revoked the power of the elected government in Massachusetts and returned power to Great Britain. Clearly, there was a lot of friction between the leaders of Great Britain and Massachusetts. The British governor, Thomas Gage, remained in Massachusetts to see that Massachusetts' officials no longer ran elections or town meetings. Gage implemented the Intolerable Acts in response to the Massachusetts' revolt best known as the Boston Tea Party. The Massachusetts Government Act and the Intolerable Acts ignited the American War of Independence in 1775. The fight for local self-government mounted once again in Massachusetts.

How Laws are Enacted and Enforced

To enact a new law:

- The bill is introduced to Congress.
- The bill is sent to the appropriate committee for review and revision.
- The approved bill is sent to the Speaker of the House and the majority party leader of the Senate, who places the bill on the calendar for review.
- The houses debate the merits of the bill and recommend amendments.

    o In the House of Representatives, those who wish to debate about a bill are allowed only a few minutes to speak, and amendments to the bill are limited.

    o In the Senate, debates and amendments are unlimited, and those who wish to postpone a vote may do so by filibuster, refusing to stop speaking.

- The approved bill is revised in both houses to ensure identical wording in both bills.
- The revised bill is returned to both houses for final approval.
- The bill is sent to the president, who may

    o Sign the bill into law

    o Veto the bill

    o Take no action, resulting in the bill becoming law if Congress remains in session for ten days or dying if Congress adjourns before ten days have passed

Political Process in the United States

Political Beliefs and Behaviors
Political beliefs are the beliefs held by the citizens of a nation about the government, leaders, policies, and the related political issues of their state. Political beliefs differ among individual citizens, but in America, a strong basis of democracy shapes the political beliefs, behaviors, and attitudes.

Democratic Values
The foundation of democratic values upon which the United States is based include:

- The people are sovereign, and they elect a representative government to exercise that sovereignty.
- The citizens of the nation are equal under the law.
- The peaceful transition of power is valued regardless of election results.
- The private property of individuals cannot be taken by force by the government without due process or fair compensation.
- The civil liberties of the citizens of the state cannot be abridged or violated by the government without due process.
- The government should be accountable to the citizenry.

Political Socialization
American citizens undergo a process of *political socialization* from early childhood to adulthood during which they develop their individual sense of political identity and civic pride. Children learn about politics in the home from an early age, whether from the views, opinions, and facts of family and friends, or through the media to which they are exposed.

In school, they learn about the nation's political history, basic politics, and democratic values, as well as the ideals of patriotism and the processes of government. As they grow older, they join interest groups, labor unions, religious groups, and political organizations that further influence their political beliefs. This socialization shapes not only the political beliefs and values of individual citizens and groups but the political ideals of the nation and public opinion.

Public Opinion
Public opinion is the shared political ideals, opinions, and attitudes of the people of a state regarding the politics, current events, and social issues that influence policy and shape the political atmosphere of a state. Public opinion is the result of political beliefs, socialization, and current events. Political scientists measure public opinion through:

- Distribution of opinion across demographics such as age, race, gender, and religion
- Strength of the opinion
- Stability of the opinion over time

Public opinion refers to the majority opinion in a democratic state. Citizens express public opinion through the interest groups they join, the media they consume and interact with, and the leaders they elect. To measure public opinion, scientists use polls to gather data. Accurate polling requires:

- Random sampling of representative populations
- Unbiased questions
- Clear instructions for how to answer questions
- Controlled procedures such as the use of telephone, mail, Internet, or in-person interviews with an unbiased pollster
- Accurate reporting of the results, including information about methods, inconsistencies, respondents, and possible sources and degree of error

Political Participation

Citizens express their political beliefs and public opinion through participation in politics. The conventional ways citizens can participate in politics in a democratic state include:

- Obeying laws
- Voting in elections
- Running for public office
- Staying interested and informed of current events
- Learning U.S. history
- Attending public hearings to be informed and to express their opinions on issues, especially on the local level
- Forming interest groups to promote their common goals
- Forming political action committees (PACs) that raise money to influence policy decisions
- Petitioning government to create awareness of issues
- Campaigning for a candidate
- Contributing to campaigns
- Using mass media to express political ideas, opinions, and grievances

Electoral Process, Political Parties, Interest Groups, and Mass Media

As members of a Constitutional Republic with certain aspects of a *democracy*, U.S. citizens are empowered to elect most government leaders, but the process varies between branch and level of government. Presidential elections at the national level use the *Electoral College* system. Rather than electing the president directly, citizens cast their ballots to select *electors* that represent each state in the college.

Legislative branches at the federal and state level are also determined by elections. In some areas, judges are elected, but in other states judges are appointed by elected officials. The U.S. has a *two-party system*, meaning that most government control is under two major parties: the Republican Party and the Democratic Party. It should be noted that the two-party system was not designed by the Constitution but gradually emerged over time.

Electoral Process

During the *electoral process*, the citizens of a state decide who will represent them at the local, state, and federal level. Different political officials that citizens elect through popular vote include but are not limited to:

- City mayor
- City council members
- State representative
- State governor
- State senator
- House member
- U.S. Senator
- President

The Constitution grants the states the power to hold their own elections, and the voting process often varies from city to city and state to state.

While a popular vote decides nearly all local and state elections, the president of the United States is elected by the *Electoral College*, rather than by popular vote. Presidential elections occur every four years on the first Tuesday after the first Monday in November.

The electoral process for the president of the United States includes:

Primary Elections and Caucuses
In a presidential election, *nominees* from the two major parties, as well as some third parties, run against each other. To determine who will win the nomination from each party, the states hold *primary elections* or *caucuses*.

During the primary elections, the states vote for who they want to win their party's nomination. In some states, primary elections are closed, meaning voters may only vote for candidates from their registered party, but other states hold *open primaries* in which voters may vote in either party's primary.

Some states hold *caucuses* in which the members of a political party meet in small groups, and the decisions of those groups determine the party's candidate.

Each state holds a number of delegates proportional to its population, and the candidate with the most delegate votes receives the domination. Some states give all of their delegates (*winner-take-all*) to the primary or caucus winner, while some others split the votes more proportionally.

Conventions
The two major parties hold national conventions to determine who will be the nominee to run for president from each party. The *delegates* each candidate won in the primary elections or caucuses are the voters who represent their states at the national conventions. The candidate who wins the most delegate votes is given the nomination. Political parties establish their own internal requirements and procedures for how a nominee is nominated.

Conventions are typically spread across several days, and leaders of the party give speeches, culminating with the candidate accepting the nomination at the end.

Campaigning
Once the nominees are selected from each party, they continue campaigning into the national election. Prior to the mid-1800s, candidates did not actively campaign for themselves, considering it dishonorable to the office, but campaigning is now rampant. Modern campaigning includes, but is not limited to:

- Raising money
- Meeting with citizens and public officials around the country
- Giving speeches
- Issuing policy proposals
- Running internal polls to determine strategy
- Organizing strategic voter outreach in important districts
- Participating in debates organized by a third-party private debate commission
- Advertising on television, through mail, or on the Internet

General Election
On the first Tuesday after the first Monday in November of an election year, every four years, the people cast their votes by secret ballot for president in a *general election*. Voters may vote for any

candidate, regardless of their party affiliation. The outcome of the popular vote does not decide the election; instead, the winner is determined by the Electoral College.

Electoral College

When the people cast their votes for president in the general election, they are casting their votes for the *electors* from the *Electoral College* who will elect the president. In order to win the presidential election, a nominee must win 270 of the 538 electoral votes. The number of electors is equal to the total number of senators and representatives from each state plus three electoral votes for Washington D.C. which does not have any voting members in the legislative branch.

The electors typically vote based on the popular vote from their states. Although the Constitution does not require electors to vote for the popular vote winner, no elector voting against the popular vote has ever changed the outcome of an election. Due to the Electoral College, a nominee may win the popular vote and still lose the election.

For example, let's imagine that there only two states, Wyoming and Nebraska, in a presidential election. Wyoming has three electoral votes and awards them all to the winner of the election by majority vote. Nebraska has five electoral votes and also awards them all to the winner of the election by majority vote. If 500,000 people in Wyoming vote and the Republican candidate wins by a vote of 300,000 to 200,000, the Republican candidate will win the three electoral votes for the state. If the same number of people vote in Nebraska, but the Republican candidate loses the state by a vote of 249,000 to 251,000, the Democratic candidate wins the five electoral votes from that state. This means the Republican candidate will have received 549,000 popular votes but only three electoral votes, while the Democratic candidate will have received 451,000 popular votes but will have won five electoral votes. Thus, the Republican won the popular vote by a considerable margin, but the Democratic candidate will have been awarded more electoral votes, which are the only ones that matter.

	Wyoming	Nebraska	Total # of Votes
Republican Votes	300,000	249,000	**549,000**
Democratic Votes	200,000	251,000	**451,000**
Republican Electoral Votes	3	0	**3**
Democratic Electoral Votes	0	5	**5**

If no one wins the majority of electoral votes in the presidential election, the House of Representatives decides the presidency, as required by the Twelfth Amendment. They may only vote for the top three candidates, and each state delegation votes as a single bloc. Twenty-six votes, a simple majority, are required to elect the president. The House has only elected the president twice, in 1801 and 1825.

Here how many electoral votes each state and the District of Columbia have:

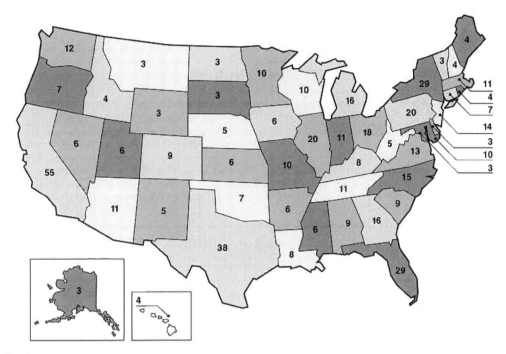

Political Parties

A *political party* is an organized group of voters who share the same political values and support or oppose the same policies. Members of a political party vote for the candidates from their party who they believe share their values and will approve or reject the policies they support or oppose. Political parties often determine the positions party members take on issues of policy, such as the economy, taxation, and social services.

The Founding Fathers of the United States opposed the divisiveness they associated with political parties, and President George Washington railed against the evil of political parties in his Farewell Address. However, the ratification of the Constitution led to the creation of the first two American political parties, the Federalists and the anti-Federalist Democratic-Republican Party. When Andrew Jackson became the fourth president of the United States as a Democrat, his opposition organized under the Whig Party. The Whigs asserted Congress' supremacy over the president and primarily focused on economic concerns, like banking and violations.

Slavery divided the nation and created unrest among the political parties, as members took opposing views and splintered into separate sects of the party or started new parties with members who shared their views. The Whig Party, so divided by the differing views of the members, collapsed. Former Whigs joined or formed the following parties:

- Constitutional Union Party: Devoted itself to a single-issue platform of preserving the Union and recognizing the Constitution as the supreme rule of law. The party did not take a firm issue on slavery, but vigorously opposed secession.

- Democratic Party: Divided into northern and southern factions over slavery, but the Democrats sought to compromise and remain unified.

- Know-Nothing Party: Advocated for an anti-immigration single-party platform, especially immigrants from Catholic countries.

- Republican Party: Formed in response to the Kansas-Nebraska Act, which threatened to extend slavery into new territories, called for the abolition of slavery and argued for a more modernized economy.

Declaration of Independence, Bill of Rights, and the Constitution of the Commonwealth of Massachusetts

Declaration of Independence

The Second Continental Congress met on May 10, 1775 and appointed George Washington as chief of the Continental Army. Although skirmishes began to occur, the Continental Congress made one more attempt to reconcile with the British by sending them the Olive Branch Petition. The petition was refused, and this rejection, combined with a pamphlet written by Thomas Paine in early 1776 called *Common Sense*, pushed the colonists to seek independence in earnest. A committee was chosen to draft a Declaration of Independence, which was written by Thomas Jefferson and approved on July 4, 1776. Another committee was appointed to create an organized government, which was adopted by Congress in November 1777 as the Articles of Confederation. However, this was not approved by all the states until March 1781; therefore, throughout much of the Revolutionary War, there was no official form of government.

The Bill of Rights

The first ten amendments of the Constitution are called the Bill of Rights. They were passed to win over anti-Federalists during the ratification of the Constitution. Anti-Federalists wanted assurances that the federal government would protect certain fundamental civil liberties. The Bill of Rights includes:

- Amendment I: Establishes freedom of religion, speech, and press; the right to assemble in peaceful protest; and the right to petition the government without fear of reprisal

- Amendment II: Establishes the right to bear arms

- Amendment III: Establishes the right to refuse to quarter, or house, soldiers in time of war

- Amendment IV: Establishes protection against unreasonable search and seizure and requires a warrant based on probable cause supported by specific information

- Amendment V: Protects against self-incrimination in criminal trials, except in cases of military court martial; protects against being tried more than once for the same crime, known as double jeopardy; and protects against seizure of private property for public use without compensation

- Amendment VI: Establishes extensive set of rights to protect defendants in a criminal trial—the right to a speedy and timely trial before a judge and impartial jury of peers, the right to be informed of criminal accusations, the right to present and compel witnesses in defense of the accused, the right to confront witnesses against the accused, and the right to assistance of counsel

- Amendment VII: Protects the right to a trial by jury in civil cases exceeding a dollar amount of $20

- Amendment VIII: Protects against cruel and unusual punishment and excessive fines

- Amendment IX: Establishes the existence of additional fundamental rights unnamed in the Constitution; protects those rights that are not enumerated

- Amendment X: Reserves all powers that are not specified to the federal government or prohibited to the states or the people, establishing the principles of separation of powers and Federalism

Constitution of the Commonwealth of Massachusetts

In 1779, John Adams wrote the Constitution of the Commonwealth of Massachusetts. In 1780, voters approved the Constitution of the Commonwealth of Massachusetts, making it one of the first constitutions in the fifty states. This fundamental leading document was one of the first constitutions written and served as an example for the Constitution of the United States. The Constitution of the Commonwealth of Massachusetts is divided into four parts:

- Preamble
- Declaration of Rights (composed of thirty articles)
- Framework of Government
- Articles of Amendment

Briefly review each section of the Constitution of the Commonwealth of Massachusetts below.

Preamble
The Preamble of the Constitution of the Commonwealth of Massachusetts is a humbled introduction to this major piece of history. The last paragraph of the Constitution of the Commonwealth of Massachusetts is similar to the United States Constitution. Both documents were clearly developed for the people, by the people.

Declaration of Rights
The Declaration of Rights is made up of thirty articles, otherwise known as "Part the First." Each article provides rights of those individuals governed in the Commonwealth of Massachusetts. For example, Article XXI reads: "The freedom of deliberation, speech and debate, in either house of the legislature, is so essential to the rights of the people, that it cannot be the foundation of any accusation or prosecution, action or complaint, in any other court or place whatsoever." This article protects the rights of people—innocent until proven guilty.

Framework of Government
The Framework of Government is divided into five chapters, known as "Part the Second." This section of the Constitution of the Commonwealth of Massachusetts formally names the state Massachusetts. It also creates three primary branches of government: executive, bicameral, and legislative. The three branches of government were established to ensure separation between different powers.

Articles of Amendment
Currently, there are 120 Articles of Amendment in the Constitution of the Commonwealth of Massachusetts. In order for an amendment to pass, it needs two-thirds majority votes.

Responsibilities of United States Citizens

Obeying Laws

Citizens living in a democracy have several rights and responsibilities to uphold. The first duty is that they uphold the established laws of the government. In a democracy, a system of nationwide laws is necessary to ensure that there is some degree of order. Therefore, citizens must try to obey the laws and also help enforce them because a law that is inadequately enforced, such as early civil rights laws in the South, is almost useless. Optimally, a democratic society's laws will be accepted and followed by the community as a whole.

However, conflict can occur when an unjust law is passed. For example, much of the civil rights movement centered around Jim Crow laws in the South that supported segregation between black and whites. Yet these practices were encoded in state laws, which created a dilemma for African Americans who wanted equality but also wanted to respect the law. Fortunately, a democracy offers a degree of protection from such laws by creating a system in which government leaders and policies are constantly open to change in accordance with the will of citizens. Citizens can influence the laws that are passed by voting for and electing members of the legislative and executive branches to represent them at the local, state, and national levels.

Voting

In a democratic state, the most common way to participate in politics is by voting for candidates in an election. Voting allows the citizens of a state to influence policy by selecting the candidates who share their views and make policy decisions that best suit their interests, or candidates who they believe are most capable of leading the country. In the United States, all citizens—regardless of gender, race, or religion—are allowed to vote unless they have lost their right to vote through due process, such as felons.

Since the Progressive movement and the increased social activism of the 1890s to the 1920s that sought to eliminate corruption in government, direct participation in politics through voting has increased. Citizens can participate by voting in the following types of elections:

- Direct primaries: Citizens can nominate candidates for public office.

- National, state, and municipal elections: Citizens elect their representatives in government.

- Recall elections: Citizens can petition the government to vote an official out of office before their term ends.

- Referendums: Citizens can vote directly on proposed laws or amendments to the state constitution.

- Voter initiatives: Citizens can petition their local or state government to propose laws that will be approved or rejected by voters.

Running for Public Office

An extension of citizens' voting rights is their ability to run as elected officials. By becoming leaders in the government, citizens can demonstrate their engagement and help determine government policy. The involvement of citizens as a whole in the selection of leaders is vital in a democracy because it helps to prevent the formation of an elite cadre that does not answer to the public. Without the engagement of citizens who run for office, voters are limited in their ability to select candidates that appeal to them.

In this case, voting options would become stagnant, which inhibits the ability of the nation to grow and change over time. As long as citizens are willing to take a stand for their vision of America, America's government will remain dynamic and diverse.

Citizen Interest

These features of a democracy give it the potential to reshape itself continually in response to new developments in society. In order for a democracy to function, it is of the utmost importance that citizens care about the course of politics and be aware of current issues. Apathy among citizens is a constant problem that threatens the endurance of democracies. Citizens should have a desire to take part in the political process, or else they simply accept the status quo and fail to fulfill their role as citizens. Moreover, they must have acute knowledge of the political processes and the issues that they can address as citizens. A fear among the Founding Fathers was the prevalence of mob rule, in which the common people did not take interest in politics except to vote for their patrons; this was the usual course of politics in the colonial era, as the common people left the decisions to the established elites. Without understanding the world around them, citizens may not fully grasp the significance of political actions and thereby fail to make wise decisions in that regard. Therefore, citizens must stay informed about current affairs, ranging from local to national or global matters, so that they can properly address them as voters or elected leaders.

Historical Knowledge

Furthermore, knowledge of the nation's history is essential for healthy citizenship. History continues to have an influence on present political decisions. For example, Supreme Court rulings often take into account previous legal precedents and verdicts, so it is important to know about those past events and how they affect the current processes. It is especially critical that citizens are aware of the context in which laws were established because it helps clarify the purpose of those laws. For example, an understanding of the problems with the Articles of Confederation allows people to comprehend some of the reasons behind the framework of the Constitution. In addition, history as a whole shapes the course of societies and the world; therefore, citizens should draw on this knowledge of the past to realize the full consequences of current actions. Issues such as climate change, conflict in the Middle East, and civil rights struggles are rooted in events and cultural developments that reach back centuries and should be addressed.

Therefore, education is a high priority in democracies because it has the potential to instill generations of citizens with the right mind-set and knowledge required to do their part in shaping the nation. Optimally, education should cover a variety of different subjects, ranging from mathematics to biology, so that individuals can explore whatever paths they wish to take in life. Even so, social studies are especially important because students should understand how democracies function and understand the history of the nation and world. Historical studies should cover national and local events as well because they help provide the basis for the understanding of contemporary politics. Social studies courses should also address the histories of foreign nations because contemporary politics increasingly has global consequences. In addition, history lessons should remain open to multiple perspectives, even those that might criticize a nation's past actions, because citizens should be exposed to diverse perspectives that they can apply as voters and leaders.

Basic Economic Terms

Economics is the study of human behavior in response to the production, consumption, and distribution of assets or wealth. Economics can help individuals or societies make decisions or plans for themselves or communities, dependent upon their needs, wants, and resources. Economics is divided into two subgroups: microeconomics and macroeconomics.

Microeconomics is the study of individual or small group behaviors and patterns in relationship to such things as earning and spending money. It focuses on particular markets within the economy, and looks at single factors that could potentially affect individuals or small groups. For example, the use of coupons in a grocery store can affect an individual's product choice, quantity purchased, and overall savings that a person may later roll into a different purchase. Microeconomics is the study of scarcity, choice, opportunity costs, economics systems, factors of production, supply and demand, market efficiency, the role of government, distribution of income, and product markets.

Macroeconomics examines a much larger scale of the economy. It focuses on how a society or nation's goods, services, spending habits, and other factors affect the people of that entity. It focuses on aggregate factors such as demand and output. For example, if a national company moves its production overseas to save on costs, how will production, labor, and capital be affected? Macroeconomics analyzes all aggregate indicators and the microeconomic factors that influence the economy. Government and corporations use macroeconomic models to help formulate economic policies and strategies.

Microeconomics

Scarcity

People have different needs and wants, and the question arises, are the resources available to supply those needs and wants? Limited resources and high demand create scarcity. When a product is scarce, there is a short supply of it. For example, when the newest version of a cellphone is released, people line up to buy the phone or put their name on a wait list if the phone is not immediately available. The product, the new cellphone, may become a scarce commodity. In turn, because of the scarcity, companies may raise the cost of the commodity, knowing that if it is immediately available, people may pay more for the instant gratification—and vice versa. If a competing company lowers the cost of the phone but has contingencies, such as extended contracts or hidden fees, the buyer will still have the opportunity to purchase the scarce product. Limited resources and extremely high demand create scarcity and, in turn, cause companies to acquire opportunity costs.

Choice and Opportunity Costs

On a large scale, governments and communities have to assess different opportunity costs when it comes to using taxpayers' money. Should the government or community build a new school, repair roads, or allocate funds to local hospitals are all examples of choices taxpayers may have to review at some point in time. How do they decide which choice is the best, since each one has a trade off? By comparing the opportunity cost of each choice, they may decide what they are willing to live without for the sake of gaining something else.

Economic Systems
Economic systems determine what is being produced, who is producing it, who receives the product, and the money generated by the sale of the product. There are two basic types of economic systems: market economies (including free and competitive markets), and planned or command economies.

- Market Economies are characterized by:

    - Privately owned businesses, groups, or individuals providing goods or services based on demand.

    - The types of goods and services provided (supply) are based on that demand.

    - Two types: competitive market and free market.

Competitive Market	Free Market
Due to the large number of both buyers and sellers, there is no way any one seller or buyer can control the market or price.	Voluntary private trades between buyers and sellers determine markets and prices without government intervention or monopolies.

- Planned or Command Economies:

    - In planned or command economies, the government or central authority determines market prices of goods and services.

    - The government or central authority determines what is being produced as well as the quantity of production.

    - Some advantages to command economies include a large number of shared goods such as public services (transportation, schools, or hospitals).

    - Disadvantages of command economies include wastefulness of resources.

Factors of Production
There are four factors of production:

1. Land: both renewable and nonrenewable resources
2. Labor: effort put forth by people to produce goods and services
3. Capital: the tools used to create goods and services
4. Entrepreneurship: persons who combine land, labor, and capital to create new goods and services

The four factors of production are used to create goods and services to make economic profit. All four factors strongly impact one another.

Market Efficiency and the Role of Government (Taxes, Subsidies, and Price Controls)
Market efficiency is directly affected by supply and demand. The government can help the market stay efficient by either stepping in when the market is inefficient and/or providing the means necessary for markets to run properly. For example, society needs two types of infrastructure: physical (bridges, roads, etc.) and institutional (courts, laws, etc.). The government may impose taxes, subsidies, and price

controls to increase revenue, lower prices of goods and services, ensure product availability for the government, and maintain fair prices for goods and services.

The Purpose of Taxes, Subsidies, and Price Controls

Taxes	Subsidies	Price Controls
-Generate government revenue -Discourage purchase or use of "bad" products such as alcohol or cigarettes	-Lower the price of goods and services -Reassure the supply of goods and services -Allow opportunities to compete with overseas vendors	-Act as emergency measures when government intervention is necessary -Set a minimum or maximum price for goods and services

Distribution of Income

Distribution of income refers to how wages are distributed across a society or segments of a society. If everyone made the same amount of money, the distribution of income would be equal. That is not the case in most societies. The wealth of people and companies varies. Income inequality gaps are present in America and many other nations. Taxes provide an option to redistribute income or wealth because they provide revenue to build new infrastructure and provide cash benefits to some of the poorest members in society.

Product Markets

Product markets are marketplaces where goods and services are bought and sold. Product markets provide sellers a place to offer goods and services to consumers, and for consumers to purchase those goods and services. The annual value of goods and services exchanged throughout the year is measured by the Gross Domestic Product (GDP), a monetary measure of goods and services made either quarterly or annually. Department stores, gas stations, grocery stores, and other retail stores are all examples of product markets. However, product markets do not include any raw, scarce, or trade materials.

Theory of the Firm

The behavior of firms is composed of several theories varying between short- and long-term goals. There are four basic firm behaviors: perfect competition, profit maximization, short run, and long run. Each firm follows a pattern, depending on its desired outcome. Theory of the Firm posits that firms, after conducting market research, make decisions that will maximize their profits since they are for-profit entities.

- Perfect competition:
    - In perfect competition, several businesses are selling the same product at the same time.
    - There are so many businesses and consumers that none will directly impact the market.
    - Each business and consumer is aware of the competing businesses and markets.
- Profit maximization:
    - Firms decide the quantity of a product that needs to be produced in order to receive maximum profit gains. Profit is the total amount of revenue made after subtracting costs.
- Short run:
    - A short amount of time where fixed prices cannot be adjusted
    - The quantity of the product depends on the varying amount of labor. Less labor means less product.

- Long run:
    - An amount of time where fixed prices can be adjusted
    - Firms try to maximize production while minimizing labor costs.

Overall, microeconomics operates on a small scale, focusing on how individuals or small groups use and assign resources.

Macroeconomics

Macroeconomics analyzes the economy as a whole. It studies unemployment, interest rates, price levels, and national income, which are all factors that can affect the nation as a whole, and not just individual households. Macroeconomics studies all large factors to determine how, or if, they will affect future trend patterns of production, consumption, and economic growth.

Measures of Economic Performance

It is important to measure economic performance to determine if an economy is growing, stagnant, or deteriorating. To measure the growth and sustainability of an economy, several indicators can be used. Economic indicators provide data that economists can use to determine if there are faulty processes or if some form of intervention is needed.

One of the main indicators to measure economic performance is the growth of the country's Gross Domestic Product (GDP). GDP growth provides important information that can be used to determine fiscal or financial policies. The GDP does not measure income distribution, quality of life, or losses due to natural disasters. For example, if a community lost everything to a hurricane, it would take a long time to rebuild the community and stabilize its economy. That is why there is a need to take into account more balanced performance measures when factoring overall economic performance.

Other indicators used to measure economic performance are unemployment or employment rates, inflation, savings, investments, surpluses and deficits, debt, labor, trade terms, the HDI (Human Development Index), and the HPI (Human Poverty Index).

Unemployment

Unemployment occurs when an individual does not have a job, is actively trying to find employment, and is not getting paid. Official unemployment rates do not factor in the number of people who have stopped looking for work, unlike true unemployment rates that do, causing them to be higher.

There are three types of unemployment: cyclical, frictional, and structural.

Cyclical
The product of a business cycle. This usually occurs during a recession.
Frictional
The difficulty of matching qualified workers for specific jobs. An example would be a person changing careers.
Structural
When a person no longer qualifies for a specific job, or failing out of a retraining course for a job.

Given the nature of a market economy and the fluctuations of the labor market, a 100 percent employment rate is impossible to reach.

Inflation

Inflation is when the cost of goods and services rises over time. Supply, demand, and money reserves all affect inflation. Generally, inflation is measured by the Consumer Price Index (CPI), a tool that tracks price changes of goods and services over time. The CPI measures goods and services such as gasoline, cars, clothing, and food. When the cost of goods and services increase, the quantity of the product may decrease due to lower demand. This decreases the purchasing power of the consumer. Basically, as more money is printed, it holds less and less value in purchasing power. For example, when inflation occurs, consumers in the United States are spending and saving less because the U.S. dollar is worth less, and therefore the consumer cannot buy or save as much money. However, if inflation occurs steadily over time, the people can better plan and prepare for future necessities.

Inflation can vary from year to year, usually never fluctuating more than 2 percent. Central banks try to prevent drastic increases or decreases of inflation to prohibit prices from rising or falling far from the minimum. Inflation can also vary based on different monetary currencies. Although rare, any country's economy may experience hyperinflation (when inflation rates increase to over 50 percent), while other economies may experience deflation (when the cost of goods and services decrease over time). Deflation occurs when the inflation rate drops below zero percent.

Business Cycle

A business cycle is when the Gross Domestic Product (GDP) moves downward and upward over a long-term growth trend. These cycles help determine where the economy currently stands, as well as where the economy could be heading. Business cycles usually occur almost every six years, and have four phases: expansion, peak, contraction, and trough. Here are some characteristics of each phase:

- Expansion:
    - Increased employment rates and economic growth
    - Production and sales increase
    - On a graph, expansion is where the lines climb.
- Peak:
    - Employment rates are at or above full employment and the economy is at maximum productivity.
    - On a graph, the peak is the top of the hill, where expansion has reached its maximum.
- Contraction:
    - When growth starts slowing
    - Unemployment is on the rise.
    - On a graph, contraction is where the graph begins to slide back down or contract.
- Trough:
    - The cycle has hit bottom and is waiting for the next cycle to start again.
    - On a graph, the trough is the bottom of the contraction prior to when it starts to climb back up.

When the economy is expanding or "booming," the business cycle is going from a trough to a peak. When the economy is headed down and toward a recession, the business cycle is going from a peak to a trough.

Four phases of a business cycle:

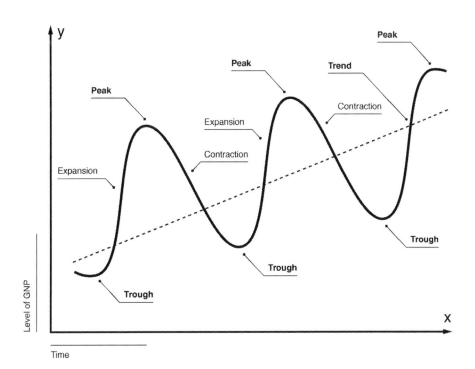

Fiscal Policy

A fiscal policy is when the government is involved in adjusting spending and tax rates to assist the way in which an economy financially functions. Fiscal policies can either increase or decrease tax rates and spending. These policies represent a tricky balancing act, because if the government increases taxes too much, consumer spending and monetary value will decrease. Conversely, if the government lowers taxes, consumers will have more money in their pockets to buy more goods and services, which increases demand and the need for companies to supply those goods and services. Due to the higher demand, suppliers can add jobs to fulfill that demand. While the increase of supply, demand, and jobs are positive for the overall economy, they may result in a devaluation of the dollar and less purchasing power.

Money and Banking

Money is the universal form of currency used throughout goods and services exchanges that holds its value over time. Money provides a convenient way for sellers and consumers to understand the value of their goods and services. As opposed to bartering (when sellers and consumers exchange goods or services as equal trades), money is quick and easy for both buyers and sellers.

There are three main forms of money: commodity, fiat, and bank. Here are characteristics of each form:

- Commodity money: Money as a valuable good, such as precious metals
- Fiat money: The value of the good set by supply and demand rather than the actual value it represents, such as paper money
- Bank money: Money that is credited by a bank to those who deposit it into bank accounts, such as checking and savings accounts or credit

While price levels within the economy set the demand for money, most countries have central banks that supply the actual money. Essentially, banks buy and sell money. Borrowers can take loans and pay back the bank, with interest, providing the bank with extra capital.

A central bank has control over the printing and distribution of money. Central banks serve three main purposes: manage monetary growth to help steer the direction of the economy, be a backup to commercial banks that are suffering, and provide options and alternatives to government taxation.

The Federal Reserve is the central bank of the United States. The Federal Reserve controls banking systems and determines the value of money in the United States. Basically, the Federal Reserve is the bank for banks.

All Western economies have to keep a minimum amount of protected cash called *required reserve*. Once banks meet those minimums, they can then lend or loan the excess to consumers. The required reserves are used within a fractional reserve banking system (fractional because a small portion is kept separate and safe). Not only do banks reserve, manage, and loan money, but they also help form monetary policies.

Monetary Policy
The central bank and other government committees control the amount of money that is made and distributed. The money supply determines monetary policy. Three main features sustain monetary policy:

- Assuring the minimum amount held within banks (bank reserves). When banks are required to hold more money in reserve funds, banks are less willing to lend money to help control inflation.

- Adjusting interest rates. For example, if the value of money is low, companies and consumers buy more (products, employees, stocks) because prices are cheap. Just like an investment, it is risky, but can pay off in the long term.

- The purchase and sales of bonds (otherwise known as open market operations). When buying bonds to increase money and selling bonds to reduce the supply, the central bank helps control the money supply.

In the United States, the Federal Reserve maintains monetary policy. There are two main types of monetary policy: expansionary monetary policy and contractionary monetary policy.

- Expansionary monetary policy:
  - Increases the money supply
  - Lowers unemployment
  - Increases consumer spending
  - Increases private sector borrowing

- o Possibly decreases interest rates to very low levels, even near zero
- o Decreases reserve requirements and federal funds
- Contractionary monetary policy:
  - o Decreases the money supply
  - o Helps control inflation
  - o Possibly increases unemployment due to slowdowns in economic growth
  - o Decreases consumer spending
  - o Decreases loans and/or borrowing

The Federal Reserve uses monetary policy to try to achieve maximum employment and secure inflation rates. Because the Federal Reserve is the "bank of banks," it truly strives to be the last-resort option for distressed banks. This is because once these kinds of institutions begin to rely on the Federal Reserve for help, all parts of the banking industry—such as those dealing with loans, bonds, interest rates, and mortgages—are affected.

Economic Growth
Economic growth is measured by the increase in the Gross National Product (GNP) or Gross Domestic Product (GDP). The increase of goods and services over time indicates positive movement in economic growth. Keep in mind that the quantity of goods and services produced is not necessarily an indicator of economic growth. The value of the goods and services produced matters more than the quantity.

There are many causes of economic growth, which can be short- or long-term. In the short term, if aggregate demand (the total demand for goods and services produced at a given time) increases, then the overall Gross Domestic Product (GDP) increases as well. Not only will the GDP increase, interest rates may decrease. With reduced interest rates, spending and investing will increase. Consumer and government spending will also increase because there will be more disposable income. Real estate prices will rise, and there will be lower income taxes. All of these short-term factors can stimulate economic growth.

In the long term, if aggregate supply (the total supply of goods or services in a given time period) increases, then there is potential for an increase in capital as well. With more working capital, more infrastructure and jobs can be created. With more jobs, there is an increased employment rate, and education and training for jobs will improve. New technologies will be developed, and new raw materials may be discovered. All of these long-term factors can also stimulate economic growth.

Outside of the short- and long-term causes for economic growth, other factors include low inflation and stability. Lower inflation rates encourage more investing versus higher inflation rates that cause instability in the market. Stability encourages businesses to continue investing. If the market is unstable, investors may question the volatility of the market.

Potential Costs of Economic Growth:

- Inflation: When economic growth occurs, inflation tends to be high. If supply cannot keep up with demand, then the inflation rate may be unmanageable.
- Economic booms and recessions: The economy goes through cycles of booms and recessions. This causes inflation to increase and decrease over time, which puts the economy into a continuous cycle of rising and falling.

- Account inefficiencies: When the economy grows, consumers and businesses increase their import spending. The increase of import spending affects the current account and causes a shortage.
- Environmental costs: When the economy is growing, there is an abundance of output, which may result in more pollutants and a reduction in quality of life.
- Inequalities: Growth occurs differently among members of society. While the wealthy may be getting richer, those living in poverty may just be getting on their feet. So while economic growth is happening, it may happen at two very different rates.

While these potential costs could affect economic growth, if the growth is consistent and stable, then growth can occur without severe inflation swings. Also, as technology improves, new ways of production can reduce negative environmental factors as well.

Principles of Capitalism

Capitalism is an economic and political system controlled by private individuals or companies as opposed to states. The ownership and investments of production, distribution, and exchange are privately controlled to make profits. Three important aspects of capitalism are private property, profit, and supply and demand. Review each characteristic of capitalism below.

<u>Characteristics of Capitalism</u>
Private Property
Private property is the ownership of privatized property. In a capitalist economy, ownership of private property is fundamental in terms of value and trade. If an individual or a corporation does not own private property, he or she does not have the power to trade it. As private property values increase, the value of the property is more powerful. Private property owners have the right to trade or exchange property as they please. For example, let's say someone owns a beachfront condo and wants to vacation in the snowy mountains. All snowy mountain private property owners can compete for the vacationer's booking, which in turn decreases prices. If the tables were turned, and someone owning a mountain home wants to vacation in a beachfront condo, beachfront condo owners would also be competing for the booking and, in turn, dropping prices.

Profit
Profit is when someone or something makes money. The difference in cost of goods versus the labor to make the goods could lead to financial gains or revenue. There are three levels of profit:

- Gross Profit: total revenue minus the cost of goods
- Operating Profit: gross profit minus operating expenses
- Net Profit: income left after all expenses are deducted

Supply and Demand
Supply and demand is one of the key concepts to a functioning economy. Supply is the amount of goods or services available to consumers. Demand refers to the amount of goods or services requested by consumers. One affects the other. If consumers need a particular product and there are limited quantities available, the value of the product increases. On the other hand, if there is an abundance of a product, costs may be driven down due to competition. For example, think of the "hot" toy during the holiday season. Oftentimes, it is difficult to find in stores, and people usually turn to the Internet to buy the hot item. Due to the high demand of the desired product, suppliers may raise the price to increase profitability.

Early Human Civilizations

Ancient Greece
Ancient Greece formed from scattered farming communities between 800 BCE and 500 BCE. In this early era of Greece, the polis, or city-state, held all of the political power locally. City-states were self-ruling and self-sufficient. The idea of a self-governing state had an enduring effect on the government of Greece and would result in the demokratia (rule by the people), which would spread and influence the world. As farming villages grew and marketplaces were built, a government with laws, an organized army, and tax collection took shape.

Each city-state was different from one another, but some unifying traits included a common language, a shared belief system, an agriculturally based economy, and rule by several wealthy citizens instead of rule by a king or queen. However, these few aristocratic rulers, known as *oligarchs,* often owned the best and most land, which created tension as the population grew. As a result, many citizens moved to less populated or newly conquered areas. By 800 BCE, there were over 1500 city-states, each with its own rulers and rules. Greek city-states were concentrated on the coast, resulting in greater contact with other civilizations through trade. City-states' governments and culture continued to diverge as time progressed. For example, in the fifth century BCE, Athens became the first direct democracy in the world, and Athenian citizens would vote directly on legislation. Only adult, male, landowning citizens could vote, but it was a remarkable departure from all contemporary forms of government to provide for direct democracy, especially relative to other city-states' oligarchies. Another world-renowned example is Sparta, which based its entire social system and constitution on military training and ability.

The Greek religion was polytheistic. Every city-state had a temple dedicated to a particular god or goddess; however, the whole of ancient Greece believed that Zeus, residing in Mount Olympus, was the most powerful of the gods. The physical presence of the temple, the rituals and festivals that dotted the Greek year, and the widespread belief in the gods controlling every aspect of human life heavily influenced their agricultural economy, government, and interactions with other ancient civilizations.

The ancient Greeks were known for their citizen-soldiers, known as *hoplites.* No ancient civilization could field a professional military due to economic restraints, such as a lack of a banking system and the need for agricultural laborers, but the hoplites were famous in ancient times for their tactics and skill. Hoplites were armed with spears and large shields, and they would fight in a phalanx formation. The Romans would later adopt many of the Greek military principles. Greek city-states fought numerous wars among each other, the largest being the Peloponnesian War, as well as wars against Persia. Fought between 499 BCE and 449 BCE, the Greco-Persian Wars pitted the Greek city-states against the mighty Persian Empire after the latter invaded. Although ancient sources are difficult to authenticate, it is certain that the Persian forces vastly outnumbered the Greeks who historically struggled to unite, even against a common enemy. This conflict included the legendary Battle of Thermopylae where three hundred Spartans, led by the Spartan king Leonidas, held off the elite contingent of the Persian army, the Immortals, for two days. After several setbacks and disastrous turns, the Greeks eventually defeated the Persian fleet at the naval Battle of Mycale and forced the Persians out of Europe. Greek unification did not last beyond this victory, and by 404 BCE, Sparta crushed Athens in the Peloponnesian War. Athens would never again attain its status as the leading city-state.

Roman Empire
Although already one of the world's most powerful civilizations, Rome began to strain under political pressure and domestic unrest in the mid-first century BCE. In 48 BCE, Gaius Julius Caesar seized power over the republic, but his assassination in 44 BCE on the Ides of March threw the republic back into

turmoil. Caesar's great-nephew turned son adopted by will, Octavian, eventually emerged as the sole leader of Rome, and historians define this point as the beginning of the Roman Empire. Octavian would serve as the first emperor under the name Augustus. His rule would be one of the most peaceful and prosperous in Roman history, often referred to as the *Pax Romana* or *Pax Augusta*. Although the Roman Empire did not adhere to the republic's democratic principles and separations of powers, the Roman Empire would be the vehicle that enabled Rome to conquer and administer enormous territory.

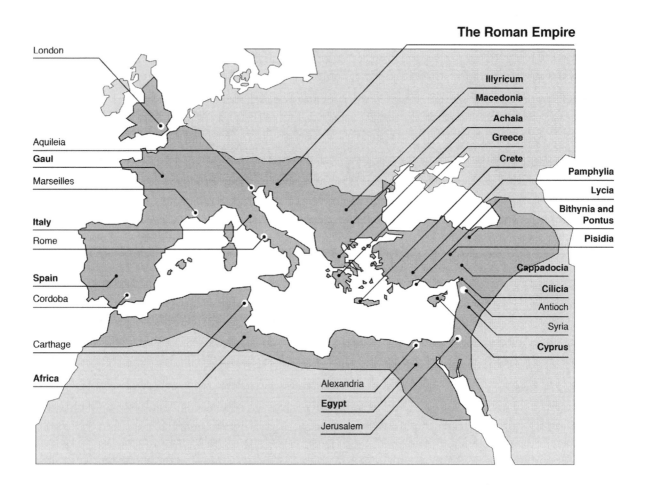

As Rome became an empire, its influence both in the ancient world and in the modern world began to take shape. Rome's ability to absorb and adapt the cultural achievements of Greece and push them on conquered cultures was a key to their success. Rome was highly influenced by Greek culture, religions, ideas, literature, and politics but kept at its roots the Roman ideals of simplicity, honesty, and loyalty. Rome was able to hold together a government that included multiple races, languages, and cultures in peace through the successful use of these ideas. In addition, Rome applied concepts developed by the Persians in the administration and political organization of its territories. By the time Rome became an empire, the government was highly structured with a complex civil service that addressed and administrated localized affairs.

Rome's decline began well before its eventual fall. There are many aspects to Rome's demise, including social, political, moral, religious, and economic. Each took their toll on the strength of the empire, and by 400 A.D., Rome collapsed under public unrest and religious discord, along with the invasion of the Huns of Mongolia and Germanic tribes. Although ultimately defeated, Rome's legacy extends all the way through to the present day. The Roman Republic's democratic elements and robust civil service would be the model for much of the West, especially the United States. That is to say nothing of the advancements in literature, technology, architecture, urban planning, and hygiene across the empire that influenced every future Western civilization.

Persian Empire

The Persian Empire consisted of multiple countries, religions, languages, and races governed by a central government. Cyrus the Great was known for his social and political acumen. He was able to navigate the empire's diversity with his "carrot or stick" approach. Cyrus the Great would offer foreign civilizations some degree of home rule, as long as they paid tribute to Persia and adopted some of its norms, or else the might of the legendary Persian military would crush them. As long as the citizens of Persia paid taxes and were peaceful, they were allowed to keep their own religious customs, local culture, and local economies. It was not until his successors that this political policy began to wan with the onset of multiple rebellions that weakened the centralized government.

The government of Persia delegated power among four governing capitals. Each state had a satrap, or governor. The satrapy government allowed for regional self-governance with a military leader and an official record-keeper that reported to the central government. The empire was also innovative in its road construction and postal systems. By allowing some degree of regional autonomy, Persia was able to rule over an unprecedented territory in ancient history. For example, Babylon even requested to be part of Persia because of its unique policies. The empire's enormity and vast scope influenced world history for centuries. Persian scholars and political philosophers would later influence rulers in the Renaissance and Enlightenment eras.

Maurya Empire

The Maurya Empire established a centralized government to govern its vast territories, and it specialized in tax collection, administration, and the military. It was modeled after the Greek and Persian governments, who, through trade and invasion, had influenced Chandragupta's government layout. Previously, regional chieftains and small armies governed India, which led to continuous skirmishes and wars. Chandragupta cleared out the chieftains and imposed regulated laws and tax reforms. The centralized form of government allowed for a period of peace, scientific advancement, and religious growth.

The centralized government was made up of four provinces organized under one capital. Each emperor had a cabinet of ministers known as a *Mantriparishad,* or Council of Ministers, to help guide him—an idea that is still used in governments across the world. Princes, or Kumaras, likewise oversaw each province, with a council of ministers called the *Mahamatyas.* A civil service was developed to govern many aspects of life and infrastructure, including waterworks, roads, and international trade. The army was expanded into one of the largest in the world at the time. Trade became a major source of revenue as other empires sought spices, food, and cloth from India.

India's three main religions flourished in this period. Hinduism, a blend of multiple beliefs, appeared in the Epic Age and became a central religion. Buddhism appeared as a consequence of the harsh social structure that had left a wide gap in the social and economic freedoms of the people. Chandragupta later accepted Jainism, a religion of total peace and unity with the world. Overall, the Maurya Empire featured a balance of religions that promoted peace as foundational and sought social harmony. The centralized government discouraged the infamous Indian caste system, which organized society by social status and led to discrimination against the lower castes.

Chinese Empire

Between 1000 BCE and 500 A.D., ancient China was unified under three successive dynasties: the Zhou Dynasty, the Qin Dynasty, and the Han Dynasty, in respective chronological order. The Zhou Dynasty was the longest dynasty in Chinese history and began after the fall of the Shang Dynasty. Originally, the Zhou Dynasty had moved away from the Shang Empire, created their own government, and formed alliances with enemies of the Shang. When war eventually broke, the people of Shang, so angered by their own government's foolishness, put up little resistance against the rebellion.

Under the Zhou Dynasty, the kingdom's ruler legitimized their power through the Mandate of Heaven, meaning they believed the rulers of the land were put in place by a higher being that could not be disposed. The Zhou claimed that the Shang Dynasty had forfeited their claim due to their mismanagement of the kingdom. This would be a common theme for dynasty takeovers. A centralized government was established, but the Zhou Dynasty never achieved complete centralized control across the kingdom. The economy was heavily agricultural and organized based on feudalism, an economical system in which a wealthy, landowning class rules the peasant class. These aristocratic rulers retained considerable power and regularly rebelled against the central government.

The Qin Dynasty was the first imperial dynasty, originally organized under Emperor Qin Shi Huangdi. The imperial state had a more centralized government, which limited the aristocratic landowners' power, stabilized the economy, and boosted the army. The Qin Dynasty formed a political structure that allowed China to start seriously building projects like the Great Wall of China. Its form of government would be adopted by many dynasties in China's history. The Qin Dynasty was short-lived and ended when Emperor Qin Shi Huangdi died prematurely, and rebel leaders fought for control of the kingdom. Liu Bang of Han defeated Xiang Yu of Chu at the Battle of Gaixia in 202 BCE, establishing the Han Dynasty.

Like the previous imperial dynasty, power was consolidated under a single emperor who dominated the Han Dynasty's centralized government. Under the emperor, a cabinet of ministers and chosen nobility acted as advisors who retained limited power. The Han dynasty was a golden era of Chinese innovation and technology, all driven by the tremendous growth in commerce and trade. To facilitate commerce, the Han Dynasty issued one of the world's earliest currencies under a money economy. Han coinage would remain the dominant currency from its introduction in 119 BCE until the Tang Dynasty in 618 A.D. A uniform currency was an essential part of the legendary Silk Road, which began under the Han Dynasty.

Major Developments in World History in Western Civilization

Development of Early Western Civilization

There were a number of powerful civilizations during the classical period. Mesopotamia was home to one of the earliest civilizations between the Euphrates and the Tigris rivers in the Near East. The rivers provided water and vegetation for early humans, but they were surrounded by desert. This led to the beginning of irrigation efforts to expand water and agriculture across the region, which resulted in the area being known as the Fertile Crescent.

The organization necessary to initiate canals and other projects led to the formation of cities and hierarchies, which would have considerable influence on the structure of later civilizations. For instance, the new hierarchies established different classes within the societies, such as kings, priests, artisans, and workers. Over time, these city-states expanded to encompass outside territories, and the city of Akkad became the world's first empire in 2350 B.C. In addition, Mesopotamian scribes developed systemized drawings called pictograms, which were the first system of writing in the world; furthermore, the creation of wedge-shaped cuneiform tablets preserved written records for multiple generations.

Later, Mesopotamian kingdoms made further advancements. For instance, Babylon established a sophisticated mathematical system based on numbers from one to sixty; this not only influenced modern concepts, such as the number of minutes in each hour, but also created the framework for math equations and theories. In addition, the Babylonian king Hammurabi established a complex set of laws, known as the Code of Hammurabi, which would set a precedent for future legal systems.

Meanwhile, another major civilization began to form around the Nile River in Africa. The Nile's relatively predictable nature allowed farmers to use the river's water and the silt from floods to grow many crops along its banks, which led to further advancements in irrigation. Egyptian rulers mobilized the kingdom's population for incredible construction projects, including the famous pyramids. Egyptians also improved pictographic writing with their more complex system of hieroglyphs, which allowed for more diverse styles of writing. The advancements in writing can be seen through the Egyptians' complex system of religion, with documents such as the *Book of the Dead* outlining not only systems of worship and pantheons of deities but also a deeper, more philosophical concept of the afterlife.

While civilizations in Egypt and Mesopotamia helped to establish class systems and empires, other forms of government emerged in Greece. Despite common ties between different cities, such as the Olympic Games, each settlement, known as a polis, had its own unique culture. Many of the cities were oligarchies, in which a council of distinguished leaders monopolized the government; others were dictatorships ruled by tyrants. Athens was a notable exception by practicing an early form of democracy in which free, landholding men could participate, but it offered more freedom of thought than other systems.

Taking advantage of their proximity to the Mediterranean Sea, Greek cities sent expeditions to establish colonies abroad that developed their own local traditions. In the process, Greek merchants interacted with Phoenician traders, who had developed an alphabetic writing system built on sounds instead of pictures. This diverse network of exchanges made Greece a vibrant center of art, science, and philosophy. For example, the Greek doctor Hippocrates established a system of ethics for doctors called the Hippocratic Oath, which continues to guide the modern medical profession. Complex forms of literature were created, including the epic poem "The Iliad," and theatrical productions were also developed. Athens in particular sought to spread its vision of democratic freedom throughout the world, which led to the devastating Peloponnesian War between allies of Athens and those of oligarchic Sparta from 431 to 404 B.C.

Alexander the Great helped disseminate Greek culture to new regions, also known as *diffusion*. Alexander was in fact an heir to the throne of Macedon, which was a warrior kingdom to the north of Greece. After finishing his father's work of unifying Greece under Macedonian control, Alexander successfully conquered Mesopotamia, which had been part of the Persian Empire. The spread of Greek institutions throughout the Mediterranean and Near East led to a period of Hellenization, during which various civilizations assimilated Greek culture; this allowed Greek traditions, such as architecture and philosophy, to endure into the present day.

Greek ideas were later assimilated, along with many other concepts, into the Roman Empire. Located west of Greece on the Italian peninsula, the city of Rome gradually conquered its neighbors and expanded its territories abroad; by 44 B.C., Rome had conquered much of Western Europe, northern Africa, and the Near East. Romans were very creative, and they adapted new ideas and innovated new technologies to strengthen their power. For instance, Romans built on the engineering knowledge of Greeks to create arched pathways, known as aqueducts, to transport water for long distances and devise advanced plumbing systems.

One of Rome's greatest legacies was its system of government. Early Rome was a republic, a democratic system in which leaders are elected by the people. Although the process still heavily favored wealthy elites, the republican system was a key inspiration for later institutions such as the United States. Octavian "Augustus" Caesar later made Rome into an empire, and the senate had only a symbolic role in the government. The new imperial system built on the examples of earlier empires to establish a vibrant dynasty that used a sophisticated legal code and a well-trained military to enforce order across vast regions. Even after Rome itself fell to barbarian invaders in fifth century A.D., the eastern half of the empire survived as the Byzantine Empire until 1453 A.D. Furthermore, the Roman Empire's institutions continued to influence and inspire later medieval kingdoms, including the Holy Roman Empire; even rulers in the twentieth century called themselves Kaiser and Tsar, titles which stem from the word "Caesar."

In addition, the Roman Empire was host to the spread of new religious ideas. In the region of Israel, the religion of Judaism presented a new approach to worship via monotheism, which is the belief in the existence of a single deity. An offshoot of Judaism called Christianity spread across the Roman Empire and gained popularity. While Rome initially suppressed the religion, it later backed Christianity and allowed the religious system to endure as a powerful force in medieval times.

Middle Ages

Early Middle Ages

The Middle Ages refers to the period from the fifth century to the fifteenth century, beginning with the fall of the Roman Empire and ending with the Renaissance and Age of Exploration. Sharp population decline, intensely localized governance, frequent invasions, famine, and disease defined the early Middle Ages and explain why it is sometimes referred to as the *Dark Ages*. Manorialism and feudalism were the dominant economic systems of the period. Peasants would rent patches of land to farm on enormous manors of aristocrats, while knights and lower nobles would exchange military service with the aristocracy in exchange for control over a manor. In addition, much of the knowledge gained during the Age of Antiquity was lost during this period.

High Middle Ages

During the High Middle Ages, signs of revival began to emerge. Christians began to see the need to live out the fundamental convictions of Christianity and also saw the need for the clergy to exemplify Christ. After several reforms, religious orders developed, such as the Franciscans and Dominicans. The orders protected the knowledge and texts of the church, becoming a strong intellectual body. As a consequence, there was a revival in learning in the monasteries that trickled out to the cathedrals and then to schools.

Around 570 A.D., the Islamic prophet Muhammad was born in Mecca. Muhammad was a trade merchant who, coming into contact with Christian and Jewish traders, blended their religions with his own religious experience in which he believed that Allah was the one true god. He believed that Allah had called him to preach the Islamic religion. At first, he met with little success, as most Arabs believed in many and differing gods. However, in a few years, he was able to unite the nomadic tribes under Islam.

After Muhammad's death, his successors, known as *caliphs,* developed the religion of Islam into a system of government and spread the faith and government control into the Middle East, North Africa, Spain, and southern France. At one point, the Islamic Empire was larger than the Roman Empire. With invasion, Islam spread the Arabic language and embraced Greek science and Indian mathematics. From 900 A.D. to 1100 A.D., Islam experienced a golden age.

In 1095, European Christians launched military strikes against Muslims in the Holy Land, and the entire series of armed religious conflicts is known as the *Crusades*. During the Crusades, Italy's trade flourished because the movement of people facilitated commerce and communication with the Middle East and Africa. In the High Middle Ages, Italy expanded trade into Europe, and merchants across Europe began to settle in areas with good trade routes. Others who had a trade to sell settled in these areas, forming towns and local governments. The development of commerce would be the impetus for the Renaissance.

Age of Exploration
The traveling merchants, the Crusades, the conquests of foreign lands, and the writings of ancient Greece expanded the known world of Europeans to include Europe, northern Africa, the Middle East, and Asia. Early explorers such as Marco Polo brought back amazing stories and exotic goods from Asia, while ports in the Middle East and around the Mediterranean spread cultures through trade. However, the very existence of America and Australia was unknown to the ancient and medieval world. Likewise, there was very little knowledge of sub-Saharan Africa until the late Renaissance era.

In an effort to find better trade routes to China, explorers discovered unknown lands that would change the world in dramatic fashion. Over a two hundred year period from 1450 to 1650, the great explorers of the age would discover new lands, unknown people, and better trade routes to the silks, spices, precious metals, and other sought-after goods Europe was eager to own.

Portugal and Spain funded the first explorations and, along with Italy, dominated the discovery of new lands and trade routes for the first one hundred years of exploration. In 1488, Portuguese explorer Bartolomeu Dias became the first European to sail around the Cape of Good Hope in South Africa and the first European to sail from the Atlantic Ocean to the Indian Ocean. On a voyage lasting from 1497 to 1499, Vasco da Gama, another Portuguese explorer, followed the route of Dias and became the first European to reach India by sea.

Portuguese explorers' success led to Portugal's dominance over trade with Africa and Asia. In West Africa, the Portuguese traded for slaves, and in east Africa, they captured city-states and opened trading posts. The coastal trading posts were utilized to launch further exploration and trade farther east with China and Japan. During a voyage launched in 1500, Dias went on to reach Brazil after his ship was blown off course to Africa. Brazil would later become Portugal's most lucrative colony due to the sugar plantations farmed by African slaves and indigenous people.

By the 1530s, France, England, the Netherlands, and Scotland were beginning to send explorers on their own expeditions. In 1534, the king of France sent Jacques Cartier to discover a western passage to the Asian markets, and during his voyage in 1534, Cartier became the first European to travel down the Saint Lawrence River and explore Canada, which Cartier named after Iroquois settlements that he encountered. Englishman Francis Drake was the first European to successfully circumnavigate the world, completing the three-year voyage in 1580. Another Englishman, Henry Hudson, was hired by the Dutch East India Company to find a northwest passage to India, and he explored the modern New York metropolitan area in the early seventeenth century. The Dutch would use this knowledge to colonize the area around the Hudson River, including New Amsterdam.

Even more devastating than the loss of their land, contact by Europeans exposed the indigenous people of America to devastating new diseases. Without any type of immunization, mild European diseases decimated the populations of the natives. Often the illness and death of natives made conquering the areas swift, and with it the loss of the culture, traditions, and languages of the native people. However, diseases such as syphilis and cholera were brought back from expeditions, ravaging European countries. The high death toll from disease, coupled with the deaths from native-born slave labor, caused a labor shortage that the Spanish replenished with slaves from their trade deals in West Africa. These slaves were mainly brought to the Caribbean Islands, though they were shipped to other Spanish colonies. The British colonies would later import millions of slaves to the modern-day American South to harvest cotton.

The Italian Renaissance

The Renaissance, meaning *rebirth*, began in the fourteenth century in Italy and spread throughout Europe during the fifteenth century. Its philosophy was humanism, or the study of man and his relationship with the world. It was a time when reason and knowledge were highly valued. The Roman Catholic Church kept pace with Europe's focus on mankind and nature, instead of heaven and heavenly beings. Popes sponsored educational enhancements and were, in some instances, as is the case with Pope Pius II, trained as classical scholars. In the early 1500s, Julius II had masters such as Michelangelo create artistic masterpieces that celebrated humans. Indeed, the arts moved toward a more realistic and proportional style with Italian painters such as Leonardo da Vinci, Raphael, and Titian leading the way.

The literary greats of the age were writing in their own vernacular, or language, instead of Latin. This was one of the greatest leaps forward; it not only built their native language, but it also allowed the Italian people to learn and grow in literacy. This and the advances in printing made the written word more accessible and widely dispersed than ever before. The dissemination of knowledge to larger groups of people would change the world, especially as the Renaissance spread to other European nations.

Renaissance in Northern Europe

The ideas in Italy began to spread northward, allowing the arts to flourish in Germany, such as Albrecht Dürer, and in the Netherlands, like Johannes Vermeer and Rembrandt. England began a long history of great literature with Geoffrey Chaucer's *The Canterbury Tales* and Edmund Spenser's *The Faerie Queene*. The highest literary achievements of the Renaissance came from two English playwrights, Christopher Marlowe and his better-known contemporary, William Shakespeare. But the Renaissance did not stray far from religious themes; instead, they humanized them, as is the case of Italian works of art. It was also an early changing point in Christianity, as theologians like Meister Eckhart, Thomas à Kempis, and Sir Thomas More began to use humanism to question the need for priestly intervention, favoring instead direct worship of God.

The invention of movable type by Johannes Gutenberg in 1439 started a revolution in printing that saw the expansion of books go from approximately 100,000 laboriously hand-copied books in Europe to over 9 million by 1500. The literacy rate in Europe improved vastly, as did the printing of religious writings. News could now travel to distant places, allowing for unprecedented communication both locally and globally. Movable type would be one of the major inventions of the Renaissance, heavily influencing the Reformation and Enlightenment.

The Reformation

In 1517, Martin Luther, a German monk and professor of theology, nailed his famous *Ninety-Five Theses,* or *Disputation on the Power of Indulgences,* to the door of the cathedral in Wittenberg, Germany. Pope Leo X demanded Luther to rescind, but Luther stood his ground, which launched the Protestant Reformation. There were serious problems in the Catholic Church, including clergy accepting simony, or the sale of church offices; pluralism, or having multiple offices; and the violation of vows. In addition, the worldly behavior of the church leaders and the biblical ignorance of the lower clergy prompted Luther to ignite a fire that could not be swept away or cleared up. The Roman Catholic Church could not weather this call for reform like it had done before. This was instead a call to cast off the Catholic faith for Protestantism. Many church denominations were formed under Protestantism, the first being Lutheranism, which gained strength in Germany and Switzerland.

Shortly after, the Roman Catholic Church issued a Counter Reformation in an attempt to quell the spread of Protestantism by addressing some of the complaints. In its initial stages, the Counter Reformation had little effect, and many Germans adopted Lutheranism as its officially recognized religion. By 1555, the Catholic Church recognized Lutheranism under the Peace of Augsburg, which allowed rulers to decide on which religion their kingdom would follow. In Germany there was peace, but civil wars broke out in France and the Netherlands. The Spanish-ruled Netherlands' struggle was as political as it was social, with other countries joining the fight against Catholic Spain.

In the 1600s, the peace in Germany faded as the country allied itself with either the Protestant Union or the Catholic League. The Thirty Years' War broke out in 1618 and became one of the most destructive wars in European history. It was a war of political and religious hostility that would involve Germany, Denmark, France, Austria, Spain, and Sweden, to some degree. Though it ended in 1648 with the Peace of Westphalia, France and Spain would wage war until 1659. The Treaty of Westphalia emphasized national self-determination, which directly led to the development of the nation-state. For the first time in human history, local people controlled the right to build a nation-state with the accompanying legitimacy to control their region. The new states, most of which were carved out of the Holy Roman Empire, were allowed to determine their religion, including Catholicism, Lutheranism, and Calvinism.

The Enlightenment

In the Enlightenment, also known as the *Age of Reason,* that followed the Renaissance, Europe began to move toward a view that men were capable of improving the world, including themselves, through rational thinking. The Enlightenment placed a heavy emphasis on individualism and rationalism. During the Renaissance, scholars looked at the Middle Ages as a lost period and considered their own time as modern and new. The Enlightenment, building on the foundations of humanism, began a prolific era of literature, philosophy, and invention.

By the 1700s, Europe had entered the High Enlightenment Age, where events started to take place as a result of the rational thought promoted by the first half of the age. The idea that everything in the universe could be reasoned and cataloged became a theme that set Diderot to work at the first encyclopedia and inspired Thomas Paine and Thomas Jefferson during the initial political unrest in the American colonies.

In the later years of the Enlightenment, the ideal vision that society could be reborn through reason was tested in the French Revolution of 1789. Instead of becoming a leader in rational thinking and orderly government, the revolution turned into the Reign of Terror that saw the mass execution of French citizens and opened the way for the rise of Napoleon.

American Revolution

The American Revolution occurred as a result of changing values in the Thirteen Colonies that broke from their traditional relationship with England. Early on in the colonization of North America, the colonial social structure tried to mirror the stratified order of Great Britain. In England, the landed elites were seen as intellectually and morally superior to the common man, which led to a paternalistic relationship. This style of governance was similarly applied to the colonial system; government was left to the property-owning upper class, and the colonies as a whole could be seen as a child dutifully serving "Mother England."

However, the colonies' distance from England meant that actual, hereditary aristocrats from Britain only formed a small percentage of the overall population and did not even fill all the positions of power. By the mid-eighteenth century, much of the American upper class consisted of local families who acquired status through business rather than lineage. Despite this, representatives from Britain were appointed to govern the colonies. As a result, a rift began to form between the colonists and British officials.

Uncertain about whether they should remain loyal to Britain, representatives from twelve colonies formed the First Continental Congress in 1774 to discuss what they should do next. When Patriot militiamen at Lexington and Concord fought British soldiers in April 1775, the Revolutionary War began. While the rebel forces worked to present the struggle as a united, patriotic effort, the colonies remained divided throughout the war. Thousands of colonists, known as Loyalists or Tories, supported Britain. Even the revolutionaries proved to be significantly fragmented, and many militias only served in their home states. The Continental Congress was also divided over whether to reconcile with Britain or push for full separation. These issues hindered the ability of the revolutionary armies to resist the British, who had superior training and resources at their disposal.

Even so, the Continental Army, under General George Washington, gradually built up a force that utilized Prussian military training and backwoods guerrilla tactics to make up for their limited resources. Although the British forces continued to win significant battles, the Continental Army gradually reduced Britain's will to fight as the years passed. Furthermore, Americans appealed to the rivalry that other European nations had with the British Empire. The support was initially limited to indirect assistance, but aid gradually increased. After the American victory at the Battle of Saratoga in 1777, France and other nations began to actively support the American cause by providing much-needed troops and equipment.

In 1781, the primary British army under General Cornwallis was defeated by an American and French coalition at Virginia, which paved the way for negotiations. The Treaty of Paris in 1783 ended the war, recognized the former colonies' independence from Great Britain, and gave America control over territory between the Appalachian Mountains and Mississippi River. However, the state of the new nation was still uncertain. The new nation's government initially stemmed from the state-based structure of the Continental Congress and was incorporated into the Articles of Confederation in 1777.

French Revolution

Unlike the United States' revolution against a ruler across the ocean, the French Revolution was an internal fight. In 1789, tension between the lower class (peasants) and middle class (bourgeois) and the extravagant wealthy upper class of France came to a head. The Old Regime, headed by the monarchy, was overthrown, and the Third Estate, made up of the bourgeois class, seized power. The American Revolution, overtaxation, years of bad harvests, drastic income inequality, and the Enlightenment influenced the French Revolution. In August 1789, the National Constituent Assembly, a democratic assembly formed during the French Revolution, passed the Declaration of the Rights of Man and of the Citizen, which defined the natural right of men to be free and equal under the law.

Napoleon

France radically changed the government from a monarchy to a democracy with provisions for civil rights, religious freedoms, and decriminalization of various morality crimes, like same-sex relationships. Two political powers emerged: liberal republicans called *Girondists* and radical revolutionaries, known as *Jacobins*. Conflict between the parties resulted in the Reign of Terror—a period of mass executions— and eventually the rise of Napoleon who set up a nationalist military dictatorship. During the revolution, Napoleon Bonaparte consolidated power after becoming famous for his heroism during the revolutionary wars against Britain, Austria, and other monarchies that sought to retain their right of royal rule. However, by 1804, Napoleon declared himself emperor and remilitarized France, and he conquered most of Europe in a series of global conflicts collectively known as the *Napoleonic Wars,* starting in 1803 and continuing until Napoleon's defeat at the Battle of Waterloo in 1815.

After the chaos sparked by the French Revolution that fanned across Europe during the revolutionary wars, European powers met at the Congress of Vienna in November 1814 to June 1815 to rebalance power and restore old boundaries. The Congress of Vienna carved out new territories, changing the map of Europe. France lost all of its conquered territories, while Prussia, Austria, and Russia expanded their own. With the restoration of a balance of power, Europe enjoyed nearly fifty years of peace.

Latin American Wars of Independence

Fueled by the successful American Revolution, Napoleon's rise to power, and the writings of the Enlightenment, a spirit of revolution swept across the Americas. The French colony in Haiti was the first major revolution occurring in 1791. The Haitian Revolution was the largest slave uprising since the Roman Empire, and it holds a unique place in history because it is the only slave uprising to establish a slave-free nation ruled by nonwhites and former slaves. In 1804, the Haitians achieved independence and became the first independent nation in Latin America. When Napoleon conquered Spain in 1808, Latin American colonies refused to recognize his elder brother, Joseph Bonaparte, as the new Spanish monarch and advocated for their own independence. Known as the *Latin American Wars of Independence,* Venezuela, Colombia, Ecuador, Argentina, Uruguay, Paraguay, Chile, Peru, and Bolivia all achieved independence between 1810 and 1830. In 1824, Mexico declared itself a republic when, after several attempts by the lower classes of Mexico to revolt, the wealthier classes joined and launched a final and successful revolt. When Napoleon overtook Portugal, King John VI fled to Brazil and set up court. Later he left his son Pedro behind to rule. Pedro launched a revolution that saw him crowned emperor.

By the mid-1800s, the revolutions of Latin America ceased, and only a few areas remained under European rule. The U.S. president James Monroe issued the Monroe Doctrine, which stated that the Americas could no longer be colonized. It was an attempt to stop European nations, especially Spain, from colonizing areas or attempting to recapture areas. England's navy contributed to the success of the doctrine, as they were eager to increase trade with the Americas and establish an alliance with the United States.

First World War

The onset of World War I began with the precarious balance of power and the geographic divisions written by the Napoleonic Wars' Vienna Congress.

Austria-Hungary's large empire was diverse in culture and included various peoples of several races, languages, and beliefs. However, minorities in their lands in the Balkans grew tired of foreign control. This was especially true in Bosnia, which was all but under control by the nationalistic secret military society, the Black Hand. This nationalistic sentiment grew until, in 1914, Gavrilo Princip, a Serb patriot and member of the Black Hand, assassinated Archduke Franz Ferdinand, heir presumptive to the throne of Austria-Hungary. In response, Emperor Franz Joseph I of Austria-Hungary declared war on the kingdom of Serbia, officially launching the First World War.

Europe had tied itself into a tangled web of alliances and mutual protection pacts. Germany and Austria-Hungary were allies. Russia promised protection to France and Serbia, and England maintained a tacit support to its past allies throughout the mainland. Each of the Allies soon mobilized to support each other. Germany had already planned for declarations of war, however, and was nervous about fighting a two-border war against both France and Russia, so it developed the Schlieffen Plan—a strategy to quickly demolish French resistance before turning around to fight Russia on the Eastern Front. However, this plan relied on the neutrality of England; after Germany invaded Belgium to attack France, England's declaration of war ensured that a long war would be inevitable.

The Great War lasted from 1914 to 1918 and was the deadliest war in European history until World War II, with approximately 16 million combatants and civilians dying in the conflict. The carnage was largely a result of technological innovation outpacing military tactics. World War I was the first military conflict to deploy millions of soldiers and the first war to involve telephones, tanks, aircrafts, chemical weapons, and heavy artillery. These twentieth-century technological innovations were deployed alongside outdated military tactics, particularly trench warfare. As a result, hundreds of thousands of troops would die during battles without achieving any meaningful strategic gains. Countries were devastated by the loss of the male population and struggled to cope with a depleted workforce, and widows and orphans struggled to regain any degree of normalcy.

Due to the high death tolls, the Allies' need of the financial support, and the anger associated with the war, the Treaty of Versailles harshly punished Germany, who the Allies blamed for the war. The Allies coerced Germany into signing the treaty that was a death sentence to their country's economy. It contained a "guilt clause," which, unlike the Congress of Vienna's terms for the similarly belligerent France, made oppressive demands on Germany. The treaty took German lands, enforced a heavy reparations debt that was impossible to pay, and stripped Germany of its colonies. After suffering enormous losses during the war itself, the Treaty of Versailles ensured that no national recovery would be possible.

In the aftermath, Russia, Italy, and Germany turned to totalitarian governments, and colonies of Europe started to have nationalistic, anticolonial movements. The Russian Revolution of 1917 led to a civil war in which the Bolsheviks, or Communists, took control under the guidance of Communist revolutionary Vladimir Lenin and established the Soviet Union. The Communist government turned into a dictatorship when Stalin emerged as leader in 1924. Stalin ruled with an iron fist and executed all of his political opponents, including the Bolsheviks. Dissatisfaction with the treaty in Italy led to the rise of fascist leader Benito Mussolini. Germany suffered through several small revolutions, splintering political parties, and class division; this, combined with wartime debt and hyperinflation—a result of the Treaty of Versailles—caused many to become desperate, especially during the throes of the Great Depression. Adolf Hitler, a popular leader in the National Socialist German Workers' Party (Nazi Party), organized street violence against Communists. In the 1932 parliamentary elections, the Nazis emerged as the largest party in the *Reichstag* (German Parliament), but the Nazis did not have enough votes to name Hitler as chancellor. The street violence against Communists and Jews continued unabated, and on

January 30, 1933, political pressure led to President von Hindenburg naming Adolf Hitler the chancellor of Germany. Hitler immediately expelled Communists, the second most popular political party, from the *Reichstag*, and coerced the *Reichstag* to pass the Enabling Act of 1933, effectively creating a dictatorship.

Second World War
Nazi Germany had risen to power through the 1920s and 1930s, with Hitler's belief that Germany would only recover its honor if it had a resounding military victory over Europe. Nazi ideology adhered to an extreme nationalism advocating for the superiority of the German people and the necessity of expanding their lands into an empire. Jews, Communists, and other nonconformists were banned from political and social participation.

In 1936, German troops violated the Treaty of Versailles by moving outside Germany's borders, with a remilitarization of the Rhineland. The Rome-Berlin Axis, an alliance between Germany and Italy, was forged in the same year. Germany was the only European power to support Italy's invasion and annexation of Ethiopia, and in exchange, Italy supported Germany's annexation of Austria. In 1936, a civil war broke out in Spain between Spanish nationalist rebels and the government of the Spanish Republic. Mussolini and Hitler supported the Spanish nationalist general Francisco Franco and used the Spanish Civil War as a testing ground for their new alliance. The Allies did not respond to these actions, and when Germany demanded the return of the Sudetenland, a territory in Czechoslovakia, France and Great Britain agreed in hopes of an appeasement despite the protests of the Czech government. Hitler then moved into more areas farther afield, which prompted the Soviet Union to sign a nonaggression pact with Germany. On September 1, 1939, Germany invaded Poland, and on September 3, 1939, France and Great Britain declared war on Germany, jumpstarting the deadliest conflict in world history.

Although less discussed than the Holocaust, the Japanese military committed similar war crimes across Asia, executing between three and ten million Chinese and Koreans, among others, between 1937 and 1945. In one event, the Rape of Nanking, Japanese soldiers captured Nanking and brutally murdered 300,000 civilians. An additional twenty thousand women, children, and elderly were raped during the massacre. Japanese newspapers closely covered a contest between two Japanese officers to see who could kill more people with a sword during the Rape of Nanking. Stalin also committed heinous war crimes during World War II, with estimates ranging from four to ten million deaths as a result of executions and sentences to the Gulag. The United States has also faced criticism for its decision to drop two nuclear bombs on the Japanese cities of Hiroshima and Nagasaki, killing more than 129,000 civilians, leveling both cities, and ending the war. The American government justified the use of nuclear weapons as the only way to avoid a ground invasion of Japan that would have cost more Japanese and American lives than the bombs.

Towns and cities had been leveled, civilian and soldier death tolls were crippling to economies, and countries struggled well into the 1950s to recover economically. It became a breeding ground for Communism, and in China, the end of the war meant a reprisal of the civil war between Mao Zedong's Communists and nationalists that had been interrupted by world war. Another result of the war was a changed map of the world, as countries were divided or newly formed, and the end of most of Britain's colonialism occurred as a result of the empire's economic and military losses. Following the war, Great Britain, France, Portugal, Belgium, Italy, the Netherlands, and Japan had either granted freedom to colonies or lost areas during the war. Many African and Middle Eastern countries would be granted their independence; however, the newly formed countries' borders were drawn according to those of the former colonies, creating ethnic and religious tensions that still exist today.

In an effort to stop a world war from occurring again, the Allies created the United Nations to be a safeguard and upholder of peace. This proved especially important, yet difficult, as the world was divided between a capitalist Western bloc and a Communist Eastern bloc. Germany was divided between the United States and Soviet Union to maintain peace and to better control the reconstruction of Germany; occupation zones were established, with East Germany occupied by the Soviet Union and West Germany occupied by Great Britain, France, and the United States.

Industrialization, Nationalism, Immigration, and Globalization in Modern World History

Industrialization

In the modern world, industrialization is the initial key to modernization and development. For developed nations, the process of industrialization took place centuries ago. England, where the *Industrial Revolution* began, actually began to produce products in factories in the early 1700s. Later, the United States and some nations of Western Europe followed suit, using raw materials brought in from their colonies abroad to make finished products. For example, cotton was spun into fabric on elaborate weaving machines that mass-produced textiles. As a result, nations that perfected the textile process were able to sell their products around the world, which produced enormous profits. Over time, those nations were able to accumulate wealth, improve their nation's infrastructure, and provide more services for their citizens. Similar to the events of the eighteenth and nineteenth centuries, nations throughout the world are undergoing the same process in today's world. China exemplifies this concept. In China, agriculture was once the predominant occupation, and although it is true that agriculture is still a dominant sector of the Chinese economy, millions of Chinese citizens are flocking to major cities like Beijing, Shanghai, and Hangzhou, due to the availability of factory jobs that allow its workers a certain element of *social mobility*, or the ability to rise up out of one's socioeconomic situation.

Nationalism and Imperialism

With most revolutions, nationalism, or the devotion to one's country, plays a central role. The American and French revolutions, along with the revolutions of Latin America, were fought with the desire to improve the prosperity and position of its civilians. After the Napoleonic Wars and the Congress of Vienna, the years of undisturbed peace resulted in a buildup of nationalism. Countries like Italy and Poland resented Austrian and Russian rule as much as they had disliked French occupation. A rise in nationalism in Germany was a constant threat to Austria, as it tried to govern multiple cultures and languages across a wide geographic area. The precarious situation would remain hostile to some degree until the outbreak of World War I. The Industrial Revolution had made the lower and middle classes restless for change and improvements. By 1848, uprisings began to spring up all over Europe, beginning with France. Many who had nationalistic leanings toward a country that was either no longer in existence or had been forced into another country were able to separate from other nations. The Hungarians broke with Vienna, though they were forced back soon after, the Romanians split from papal power, and the Italians threatened rebellion.

The development of imperialism began in the mid-nineteenth century and lasted until the twentieth century, with much of the imperialized world gaining freedom after World Wars I and II. The spread of imperialism that was to follow the revolutions of the eighteenth and nineteenth centuries can be traced, in part, to the idea of nationalism. Some countries believed they were doing a good, and even a moral, thing by conquering and colonizing new territory to spread their culture, traditions, religion, and government. However, a darker side of nationalism—the feeling of superiority and right—caused the takeover of areas and the enforcement of foreign rules and laws.

Globalization

The world economy also became increasingly interconnected during the post-World War II era. This accelerated the process of globalization, which is the integration of ideas and products from different cultures. This benefitted the United States economically because businesses, such as McDonald's and Coca-Cola, found many consumers around the world who were eager to consume American goods. However, the process works both ways, and many aspects of foreign culture, such as Japanese cartoons and animation, have become very popular in the United States. Many critics also point out that globalization has hurt the American economy in recent decades because manufacturing jobs have gone overseas to countries in South America and Asia where wages are low.

Immigration

Immigration has changed the demographics of countries and can have positive and negative effects. Migration and immigration have occurred due to famine, warfare, and lack of economic prospects. Immigration can aid countries struggling to maintain a workforce, and it can also bring in needed medical professionals, scientists, and others with special training. However, immigration also puts strain on developed economies to support migrants who arrive without the necessary education and training to thrive in the advanced economies. Until recently, immigrants were encouraged, or in some cases, forced to assimilate and take on the customs and culture of their new country. For example, in the United States, legislation was passed to force German immigrants to learn English. More recently, developed countries have struggled to assimilate new arrivals to their countries, such as the recent surge of refugees into Europe. Unfortunately, the failure to adequately assimilate immigrants has created greater inequality and prevalence of radical behavior.

Basic Concepts of Geography

Geography helps people better understand the role that location plays in the past, present, and future. Historians make frequent use of maps in their studies to get a clearer picture of how history unfolded. Since the beginning of history, many different groups have fought conflicts that originated from struggles for land or other resources; therefore, knowing the location and borders of different empires and kingdoms helps reveal how they interacted with each other. In addition, environmental factors, such as access to water and the proximity of mountains, often help to shape the course of civilizations. Even single events and battles make more sense with maps that show how the warring sides met and maneuvered.

Furthermore, determining the geography of historical events, in particular geographical change over time, is essential due to the role that physical settings play in the present. Many important geographic landmarks continue to exist in the world, and they are often commemorated for their roles in history. Yet the physical geography has sometimes changed significantly. For instance, the Aswan Dam significantly reshaped the flow of the Nile River, which was the heart of ancient Egyptian society; without knowledge of the past geography, it is difficult to fully understand the civilization's context and how it differs from the present reality.

History also depends on archaeology, the study of human artifacts, for the evidence necessary to make conclusions about cultures. These items are generally buried, which helps preserve the artifacts yet makes it difficult to locate them. Historical geography helps in that regard by ascertaining key sites of human activity that could potentially retain artifacts. These insights help archaeologists discover new aspects of ancient cultures, which in turn strengthen historical arguments. Maps themselves sometimes serve as artifacts in their own right because they help reveal how humans of earlier periods viewed the world.

Along with the historical implications, knowledge of the world's geography remains important for people in the present day. The most immediate use of geography is in navigation. Tools such as Global Positioning Systems have helped improve navigation, but they too represent an approach to geography that demonstrates how it continues to have a fundamental role in human society. Humans have even begun mapping the trajectories of planets and even their individual terrains.

However, beyond the direct uses for navigation, geography is invaluable in comprehending modern cultures and events. Whether through their proximity to other nations or their relation to environmental features, such as forests and deserts, societies remain deeply connected to their geographical settings. Therefore, to fully understand current affairs, such as wars and poverty, people must have a firm grasp on geographic settings. For instance, a study of nations in Africa, many of which continue to suffer from poverty, would require a close examination of geographic factors. The borders of many African countries were arbitrarily determined during the colonial period, and the conflicts of ethnic groups divided by these borders have influenced current struggles. On the environmental end, some nations have been significantly affected by desertification and deforestation, which makes studies of their ecological geography important as well.

Two recent key developments have made geography more important than ever before. The first change is the globalization of culture, economics, and politics. For much of human history, geography was most important at localized scales. Many people spent their entire lives in isolated communities, with intermittent trade between different centers. Geography was still important, but many people did not need to be familiar with anything other than their immediate locations. Today, on the other hand, places around the world are intricately connected to each other. Travel is relatively easy and quick and enables people to venture between different regions like never before. Areas that used to be geographically isolated from each other can now exchange ideas and products on an unprecedented scale.

In addition, due to the multinational relationship of politics, conflicts that would have been geographically isolated in the past can have international ramifications. Latin American revolutions, such as in Nicaragua during the Cold War, were seen as having larger implications in the struggle between American democracy and Soviet communism, which led to foreign interventions and wars that affected multiple countries. Therefore, geography is critical to not only addressing the current effects of globalization but also understanding how global interactions may influence international politics and economics in the future.

The second major factor in geography's role in modern events is the rising importance of environmental policies and climate change. Scientific developments have increasingly revealed how the planet as a whole can be considered a large ecosystem in its own right, with its own strengths and frailties. A change in one part of the environment, such as industrialization in India and China, can have larger consequences for neighboring regions and for the world as a whole. Geographical insights help to show how the world functions and how humans can work to improve their relationship with the natural world.

Moreover, as climate changes become more evident in the world, geography helps illustrate the effects of new environmental phenomena. For instance, scientists have studied the topography of nations to determine how rising sea levels will alter the land via flooding, and local and national governments are using these findings to prepare for the coming changes. Furthermore, the continued scrutiny of the state of the earth's geography reveals how climate change is transforming the planet at this very moment, as regional climates shift and islands vanish under the sea. As a result, geography will continue to have a role in future developments.

Use of Globes, Maps, and Other Resources to Access Geographic Information

Geography is essential in understanding the world as a whole. This requires a study of spatial distribution, which examines how various locations and physical features are arranged in the world. The most common element in geography is the region, which refers to a specific area that is separate from surrounding ones. Regions can be defined based on a variety of factors, including environmental, economic, or political features, and these different kinds of regions can overlap with each other.

It is also important to know the difference between location and place. A location, defined either through its physical position or through its relation to other locations, determines where something is, and this characteristic is static. A place, on the other hand, describes a combination of physical and human elements in relation to each other; the determination of place is therefore changeable depending on the movement of individuals and groups.

Geography is visually conveyed using maps, and a collection of maps is called an atlas. To illustrate some key points about geography, please refer to the map below.

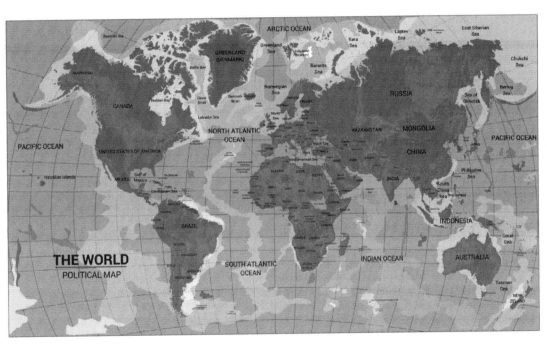

This is a traditional map of the world that displays all of the countries and six of the seven continents. Countries, the most common approach to political regions, can be identified by their labels. The continents are not identified on this map, with the exception of Australia, but they are larger landmasses that encompass most of the countries in their respective areas; the other five visible continents are North America, South America, Europe, Africa, and Asia. The seventh continent, Antarctica, is found at the South Pole and has been omitted from the map.

The absence of Antarctica leads into the issues of distortion, in which geographical features are altered on a map. Some degree of distortion is to be expected with a two-dimensional flat map of the world because the earth is a sphere. A map projection transforms a spherical map of the world into a flattened perspective, but the process generally alters the spatial appearance of landmasses. For instance, Greenland often appears, such as in the map above, larger than it really is.

Furthermore, Antarctica's exclusion from the map is, in fact, a different sort of distortion—that of the mapmakers' biases. Mapmakers determine which features are included on the map and which ones are not. Antarctica, for example, is often missing from maps because, unlike the other continents, it has a limited human population. Moreover, a study of the world reveals that many of the distinctions on maps are human constructions.

Even so, maps can still reveal key features about the world. For instance, the map above has areas that seem almost three-dimensional and jut out. They represent mountains and are an example of topography, which is a method used to display the differing elevations of the terrain. A more detailed topographical map can be viewed below.

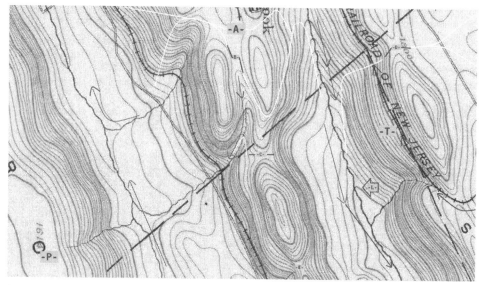

On some colored maps, the oceans, represented in blue between the continents, vary in coloration depending on depth. The differences demonstrate *bathymetry*, which is the study of the ocean floor's depth. Paler areas represent less depth, while darker spots reflect greater depth.

Please also note the many lines running horizontally and vertically along the map. The horizontal lines, known as *parallels,* mark the calculated latitude of those locations and reveal how far north or south these areas are from the equator, which bisects the map vertically. Generally, with exceptions depending on specific environments, climates closer to the equator are warmer because this region receives the most direct sunlight. The equator also serves to split the globe between the Northern and Southern hemispheres.

Longitude, as signified by the vertical lines, determines how far east or west different regions are from each other. The lines of longitude, known as meridians, are also the basis for time zones, which allocate different times to regions depending on their position eastward and westward of the prime meridian. As one travels west between time zones, the given time moves backward accordingly. Conversely, if one travels east, the time moves forward.

There are two particularly significant longitude-associated dividers in this regard. The prime [Greenwich] meridian, as displayed below, is defined as zero degrees in longitude, and thus determines the other lines. The line, in fact, circles the globe north and south, and it therefore divides the world into the

Eastern and Western hemispheres. It is important to not confuse the Greenwich meridian with the International Date Line, which is an invisible line in the Pacific Ocean that was created to represent the change between calendar days. By traveling westward across the International Date Line, a traveler would essentially leap forward a day. For example, a person departing from the United States on Sunday would arrive in Japan on Monday. By traveling eastward across the line, a traveler would go backward a day. For example, a person departing from China on Monday would arrive in Canada on Sunday.

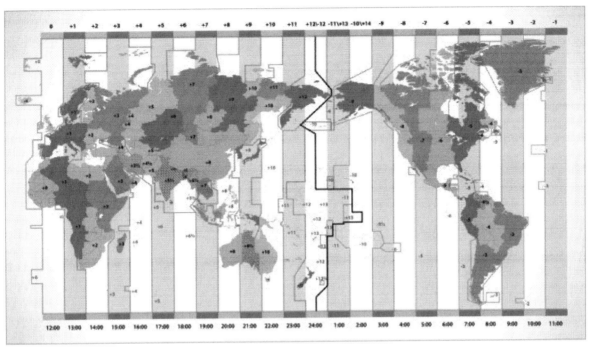

Although world maps are useful in showing the overall arrangement of continents and nations, it is also important at times to look more closely at individual countries because they have unique features that are only visible on more detailed maps.

For example, take the following map of the United States of America. It should be noted that the country is split into multiple states that have their own culture and localized governments. Other countries are often split into various divisions, such as provinces, and while these features are ignored for the sake of clarity on larger maps, they are important when studying specific nations. Individual states can be further subdivided into counties and townships, and they may have their own maps that can be examined for closer analysis.

Global Features

Location is the central theme in understanding spatial concepts. In geography, there are two primary types of locations that people utilize on a daily basis. The first type, *relative location*, is used frequently and involves locating objects by notating their proximity to another, better known object. For example, directions from person to person may relate directly to massive shopping centers, major highways, or well-known intersections. Although relative location is important, in the modern world, it's common to use digital satellite-based technologies, which rely on *GPS* (*Global Positioning System*). To determine *Absolute Location*, or the exact latitudinal and longitudinal position on the globe, GPS uses sensors that interact with satellites orbiting the Earth. *Coordinates* correspond with the positions on a manmade grid system using imaginary lines known as *latitude* (also known as *parallels*) and *longitude* (also known as *meridians*).

In order to understand latitude and longitude, one should think of a simple X and Y-axis. The *equator* serves as the X-axis at zero degrees, and measures distance from north to south. The Y-axis is at zero degrees and is represented by the *Prime Meridian*.

In addition to anchoring the grid system to create the basis for absolute location, these major lines of latitude and longitude also divide the Earth into *hemispheres*. The Equator divides the Earth into the northern and southern hemispheres, while the Prime Meridian establishes the eastern and western hemispheres. Coordinates are always expressed in the following format:

Degrees north or south, degrees east or west, or 40°N, 50°E. Since lines of latitude and longitude are great distance from one another, absolute locations are often found in between two lines. In those cases, degrees are broken down into *minutes* and *seconds*, which are expressed in this manner: (40° 53' 44" N, 50° 22' 65" E).

In addition to the Equator and the Prime Meridian, other major lines of latitude and longitude exist to divide the world into regions relative to the direct rays of the sun. These lines correspond with the Earth's *tilt*, and are responsible for the seasons. For example, the northern hemisphere is tilted directly toward the sun from June 22 to September 23, which creates the summer season in that part of the world. Conversely, the southern hemisphere is tilted away from the direct rays of the sun and experiences winter during those same months.

Place
Both absolute and relative location help humans understand their sense of place. Place is a simple concept that helps to define the characteristics of the world around us. For example, people may create *toponyms* to further define and orient themselves with their sense of place. Toponyms are simply names given to locations to help develop familiarity within a certain location. Although not always the case, toponyms generally utilize geographical features, important people in an area, or even wildlife commonly found in a general location. For example, many cities in the state of Texas are named in honor of military leaders who fought in the Texas Revolution of 1836 (such as Houston and Austin), while other places, such as Mississippi and Alabama, utilize Native American toponyms to define their sense of place.

Regions
In addition to location and place, geographers also divide the world into regions in order to more fully understand differences inherent with the world, its people, and its environment. As mentioned

previously, lines of latitude such as the Equator, the Tropics, and the Arctic and Antarctic Circles already divide the Earth into solar regions relative to the amount of either direct or indirect sunlight that they receive. Although not the same throughout, the middle latitudes generally have a milder climate than areas found within the tropics. Furthermore, tropical locations are usually warmer than places in the middle latitudes, but that is not always the case. For example, the lowest place in the United States—Death Valley, California—is also home to the nation's highest-ever recorded temperature. Likewise, the Andes Mountains in Peru and Ecuador, although found near the Equator, are also home to heavy snow, low temperatures, and dry conditions, due to their elevation.

Formal regions are spatially defined areas that have overarching similarities or some level of *homogeneity* or *uniformity*. Although not exactly alike, a formal region generally has at least one characteristic that is consistent throughout the entire area. For example, the United States could be broken down into one massive formal region due to the fact that in all fifty states, English is the primary language. Of course, English isn't the only language spoken in the United States, but throughout that nation, English is heavily used. As a result, geographers are able to classify the United States as a formal region; but, more specifically, the United States is a *linguistic region*—a place where everyone generally speaks the same language.

Functional regions are similar to formal regions in that they have similar characteristics, but they do not have clear boundaries. The best way to understand these sorts of regions is to consider large cities. Each large city encompasses a large *market area*, whereby people in its vicinity generally travel there to conduct business, go out to eat, or watch a professional sporting event. However, once anyone travels farther away from that *primate city*, they transition to a different, more accessible city for their needs. The functional region, or *area of influence*, for that city, town, or sports team transitions, depending upon the availability of other primate cities. For example, New York City has two primary professional baseball, basketball, and football teams. As a result, its citizens may have affinities for different teams even though they live in the same city. Conversely, a citizen in rural Idaho may cheer for the Seattle Seahawks, even though they live over 500 miles from Seattle, due to the lack of a closer primate city.

Major Physical Features of Massachusetts, the United States, and World Areas

Physical Features of Massachusetts
Massachusetts is the seventh-smallest state in the United States. It is made up of several lakes, rivers, coastlines, reservoirs, valleys, bays, and mountains. Locate some of the following physical features on the Massachusetts state map below:

- Lake Quinsigamond
- Silver Lake
- Connecticut River
- Assabet River
- Charles River
- Neponset River
- Merrimack River
- Cape Cod Canal
- Quabbin Reservoir
- Wachusett Reservoir
- Sudbury Reservoir
- Cobble Mountain Reservoir

- Knightsville Reservoir
- Buzzards Bay
- Cape Cod Bay

Major Landforms, Climates, and Ecosystems

Earth is an incredibly large place filled with a variety of different land and water *ecosystems*. *Marine ecosystems* cover over 75 percent of the Earth's surface and contain over 95 percent of the Earth's water. Marine ecosystems can be broken down into two primary subgroups: *freshwater ecosystems*, which only encompass around 2 percent of the earth's surface; and *ocean ecosystems*, which make up over 70 percent. On land, *terrestrial ecosystems* vary depending on a variety of factors, including latitudinal distance from the equator, elevation, and proximity to mountains or bodies of water. For example, in the high latitudinal regions north of the Arctic Circle and south of the Antarctic Circle, frozen *tundra* dominates. Tundra, which is characterized by low temperatures, short growing seasons, and minimal vegetation, is only found in regions that are far away from the direct rays of the sun.

Physical Features of Massachusetts

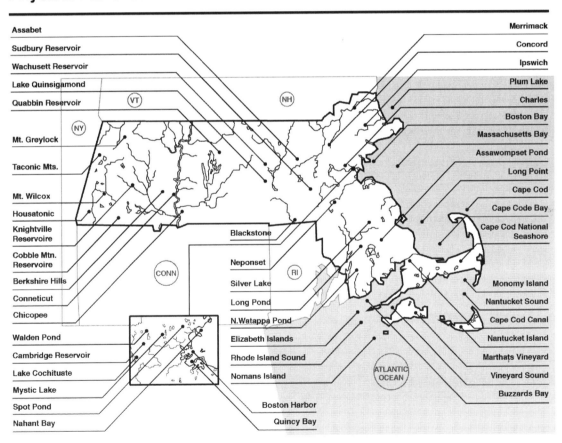

In contrast, *deserts* can be found throughout the globe and are created by different ecological factors. For example, the world's largest desert, the Sahara, is almost entirely within the tropics; however, other deserts like the Gobi in China, the Mojave in the United States, and the Atacama in Chile, are the result of the orographic effect and their close proximity to high mountain ranges such as the Himalayas, the Sierra Nevada, and the Andes, respectively. In the Middle Latitudes, greater varieties of climatological zones are more common due to fluctuations in temperatures relative to the sun's rays, coupled with the particular local topography. In the Continental United States, *temperate deciduous forest* dominates the southeastern portion of the country. However, the Midwestern states such as Nebraska, Kansas, and the Dakotas, are primarily *grasslands*. Additionally, the states of the Rocky Mountains can have decidedly different climates relative to elevation. In Colorado, Denver, also known as the "Mile High City," will often see snowfalls well into late April or early May due to colder temperatures, whereas towns and cities in the eastern part of the state, with much lower elevations, may see their last significant snowfall in March.

In the tropics, which are situated between the Tropics of Cancer and Capricorn, temperatures are generally warmer, due to the direct rays of the sun's persistence. However, like most of the world, the tropics also experience a variety of climatological regions. In Brazil, Southeast Asia, Central America, and even Northern Australia, tropical rainforests are common. These forests, which are known for abundant vegetation, daily rainfall, and a wide variety of animal life, are absolutely essential to the health of the world's ecosystems. For example, the *Amazon Rain Forest* is also referred to as "the lungs of the world," as its billions of trees produce substantial amounts of oxygen and absorb an equivalent amount of carbon dioxide—the substance that many climatologists assert is causing climate change or *global warming*. Unlike temperate deciduous forests whose trees lose their leaves during the fall and winter months, *tropical rain forests* are always lush, green, and warm. In fact, some rainforests are so dense with vegetation that a few indigenous tribes have managed to exist within them without being influenced by any sort of modern technology, virtually maintaining their ancient way of life in the modern era.

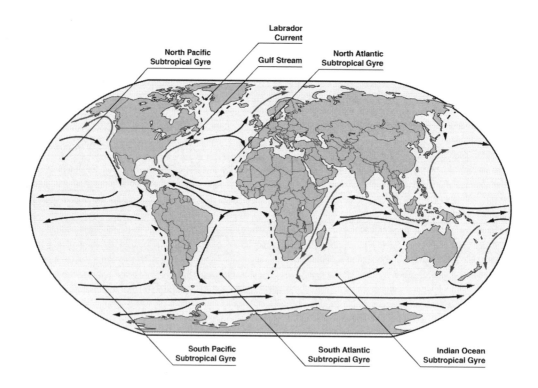

The world's largest ecosystem, the *taiga*, is found primarily in high latitudinal areas, which receive very little of the sun's indirect rays. These forests are generally made up of *coniferous* trees, which do not lose their leaves at any point during the year as *deciduous* trees do. Taigas are cold-climate regions that make up almost 30 percent of the world's land area. These forests dominate the northern regions of Canada, Scandinavia, and Russia, and provide the vast majority of the world's lumber.

Overall, it is important to remember that climates are influenced by five major factors: elevation, latitude, proximity to mountains, ocean currents, and wind patterns. For example, the cold currents off the coast of California provide the West Coast of the United States with pleasant year-round temperatures. Conversely, Western Europe, which is at the nearly the same latitude as most of Canada, is influenced by the warm waters of the *Gulf Stream*, an ocean current that acts as a conveyor belt, moving warm tropical waters to the icy north. In fact, the Gulf Stream's influence is so profound that it even keeps Iceland—an island nation in the far North Atlantic—relatively warm.

Relationship Between Geographic Factors and Historical and Contemporary Developments

Climate Patterns
Weather is defined as the condition of the Earth's atmosphere at a particular time. *Climate* is different; instead of focusing on one particular day, climate is the relative pattern of weather in a place for an extended period of time. For example, the city of Atlanta is in the American South and generally has a humid subtropical climate; however, Atlanta also occasionally experiences snowstorms in the winter months. Despite the occasional snow and sleet storm, over time, geographers, meteorologists, and other Earth scientists have determined the patterns that are indicative to north Georgia, where Atlanta is located. Almost all parts of the world have predictable climate patterns, which are influenced by the surrounding geography.

The Central Coast of California is an example of a place with a predictable climate pattern. Santa Barbara, California, one of the region's larger cities, has almost the same temperature for most of the summer, spring, and fall, with only minimal fluctuation during the winter months. The temperatures there, which average between 75 and 65 degrees Fahrenheit daily regardless as to the time of year, are influenced by a variety of different climatological factors including elevation, location relative to the mountains and ocean, and ocean currents. In the case of Santa Barbara, the city's location on the Pacific Coast and its position near mountains heavily influences its climate. The cold California current, which sweeps down the west coast of the United States, causes the air near the city to be temperate, while the mountains trap cool air over the city and the surrounding area. This pattern, known as the *orographic effect*, or *rain shadow*, also affects temperatures on the leeward side of the mountains by blocking most of the cool air and causing dry conditions to dominate. Temperatures can fluctuate by more than 20 degrees Fahrenheit on opposite sides of the mountain.

Other factors affecting climate include elevation, prevailing winds, vegetation, and latitudinal position on the globe.

Like climate, *natural hazards* also affect human societies. In tropical and subtropical climates, hurricanes and typhoons form over warm water and can have devastating effects. Additionally, tornadoes, which are powerful cyclonic windstorms, also are responsible for widespread destruction in many parts of the United States and in other parts of the world. Like storms, earthquakes, usually caused by shifting plates along faults deep below the Earth's surface, also cause widespread devastation, particularly in nations with a poor or crumbling infrastructure. For example, San Francisco, which experiences earthquakes regularly due to its position near the San Andreas Fault, saw relatively little destruction and deaths (67 total) as a result of the last major earthquake to strike there. However, in 2010, an earthquake of similar magnitude reportedly killed over 200,000 people in the western hemisphere's poorest nation, Haiti.

Although a variety of factors may be responsible for the disparity, modern engineering methods and better building materials most likely helped to minimize destruction in San Francisco. Other natural hazards, such as tsunamis, mudslides, avalanches, forest fires, dust storms, flooding, volcanic eruptions, and blizzards, also affect human societies throughout the world.

Human Migration and Settlement

Migration is governed by two primary causes: *push factors*, which are reasons causing someone to leave an area, and *pull factors*, which are factors luring someone to a particular place. These two factors often work in concert with one another. For example, the United States of America has experienced significant *internal migration* from the industrial states in the Northeast (such as New York, New Jersey, Connecticut) to the Southern and Western states. This massive migration, which continues into the present-day, is due to high rents in the northeast, dreadfully cold winters, and lack of adequate retirement housing, all of which are push factors. These push factors lead to migration to the *Sunbelt*, a term geographers use to describe states with warm climates and less intense winters.

In addition to internal migrations within nations or regions, international migration also takes place between countries, continents, and other regions. The United States has long been the world's leading nation in regard to *immigration*, the process of having people come into a nation's boundaries. Conversely, developing nations that suffer from high levels of poverty, pollution, warfare, and other violence all have significant push factors, which cause people to leave and move elsewhere. This process, known as *emigration*, is when people in a particular area leave in order to seek a better life in a different—usually better—location.

Practice Questions

1. Which of the following correctly lists the Thirteen Colonies?
    a. Connecticut, Delaware, Georgia, Maryland, Massachusetts, New Hampshire, New Jersey, New York, North Carolina, Pennsylvania, Rhode Island, South Carolina, Virginia
    b. Carolina, Connecticut, Delaware, Maryland, Massachusetts, New Hampshire, New Jersey, New York, Ohio, Pennsylvania, Rhode Island, Virginia, West Virginia
    c. Connecticut, Delaware, Georgia, Maine, Massachusetts, New Hampshire, New Jersey, New York, North Carolina, South Carolina, Pennsylvania, Vermont, Virginia
    d. Canada, Connecticut, Delaware, Georgia, Florida, Maryland, Massachusetts, New Hampshire, New York, North Carolina, Rhode Island, South Carolina, Virginia

2. Which of the following was NOT an issue contributing to the American Revolution?
    a. Increased taxes on the colonies
    b. Britain's defeat in the French and Indian War
    c. The stationing of British soldiers in colonists' homes
    d. Changes in class relations

3. The election of a presidential candidate from which party led to the Civil War?
    a. Democrat
    b. Whig
    c. Republican
    d. Federalist

4. Which of the following was NOT an important invention in the twentieth century?
    a. Radio
    b. Telegraph
    c. Television
    d. Computers

5. Which of the following sets comprises a primary cause and effect of the American Revolution?
    a. A cause was the taxation of the colonies, and an effect was the civil rights movement.
    b. A cause was the Declaration of Independence, and an effect was the Constitution.
    c. A cause was the French and Indian War, and an effect was the Bill of Rights.
    d. A cause was the debate over slavery, and an effect was the Seven Years' War.

6. What are the two main parts of the federal legislative branch?
    a. President and vice president
    b. Federal and state
    c. District court and court of appeals
    d. Senate and House of Representatives

7. What was a concern that George Washington warned of in his Farewell Address?
    a. The danger of political parties
    b. To be prepared to intervene in Europe's affairs
    c. The abolition of slavery
    d. To protect states' rights through sectionalism

8. What is NOT a responsibility for citizens of democracy?
    a. To stay aware of current issues and history
    b. To avoid political action
    c. To actively vote in elections
    d. To understand and obey laws

9. Which of the following statements is true?
    a. Times zones are defined by their latitude.
    b. Eastern and Western hemispheres are defined by the prime meridian.
    c. A place is constant, while a location is changeable with the movement of people.
    d. A continent is one of six especially large landmasses in the world.

10. Which of the following statements is true?
    a. Water usage has largely shifted from appropriation to riparian.
    b. Native Americans lived in harmony with nature by never disrupting it.
    c. Cities are fully isolated environments.
    d. Invasive species can have catastrophic impacts on ecosystems.

11. Which of the following are reasons that geography is important to the examination of history?
    I. Historians make use of maps in their studies to get a clear picture of how history unfolded.
    II. Knowing the borders of different lands helps historians learn different cultures' interactions.
    III. Geography is closely linked with the flow of resources, technology, and population in societies.
    IV. Environmental factors, such as access to water and proximity of mountains, help shape the course of civilization.

        a. I, II, and III only
        b. II, III, and IV only
        c. I, II, and IV only
        d. I, III, and IV only

12. Which of the following statements is true?
    a. All Native American tribes are matrilineal.
    b. Japan is struggling to manage its high birthrate.
    c. Shi'a Muslims traditionally follow imams.
    d. Mexico's culture is deeply tied to its Protestant roots.

13. Which of the following advancements was NOT invented by Greek culture?
    a. The alphabet
    b. The Hippocratic Oath
    c. Democratic government
    d. Theater

14. Which of the following was an important development in the twentieth century?
    a. The United States and the Soviet Union officially declared war on each other in the Cold War.
    b. The League of Nations signed the Kyoto Protocol.
    c. World War I ended when the United States defeated Japan.
    d. India violently partitioned into India and Pakistan after the end of colonialism.

15. Which of the following is NOT an example of cross-cultural interactions?
    a. Egyptian and Mayan pyramids
    b. The Spanish language
    c. Styles of sushi
    d. Study of Chinese culture

16. Which of the following is true?
    a. The barter system no longer exists.
    b. Economic resources can be divided into four categories: natural, capital, manufactured, and nonrenewable.
    c. Individuals help to determine the scarcity of items through their choices.
    d. According to the law of supply, as the price of a product increases, the supply of the product will decrease.

17. What is NOT an effect of monopolies?
    a. Promote a diverse variety of independent businesses
    b. Inhibit developments that would be problematic for business
    c. Control the supply of resources
    d. Limit the degree of choice for consumers

18. Which method is NOT a way that governments manage economies in a market system?
    a. Laissez-faire
    b. Mercantilism
    c. Capitalism
    d. Self-interest

19. Which of the following nations did NOT establish colonies in what would become the United States?
    a. Italy
    b. England
    c. France
    d. Spain

Answer Explanations

1. A: Carolina is divided into two separate states—North and South. Maine was part of Nova Scotia and did not become an American territory until the War of 1812. Likewise, Vermont was not one of the original Thirteen Colonies. Canada remained a separate British colony. Finally, Florida was a Spanish territory. Therefore, by process of elimination, *A* is the correct list.

2. B: Britain was not defeated in the French and Indian War, and, in fact, disputes with the colonies over the new territories it won contributed to the growing tensions. All of the other options were key motivations behind the Revolutionary War.

3. C: Abraham Lincoln was elected president as part of the new Republican Party, and his plans to limit and potentially abolish slavery led the southern states to secede from the Union.

4. B: Out of the four inventions mentioned, the first telegraphs were invented in the 1830s, not in the twentieth century. In contrast, the other inventions had considerable influence over the course of the twentieth century.

5. C: The Declaration of Independence occurred during the American Revolution, so it should therefore be considered an effect, not a cause. Similarly, slavery was a cause for the later Civil War, but it was not a primary instigator for the Revolutionary War. Although a single event can have many effects long into the future, it is also important to not overstate the influence of these individual causes; the civil rights movement was only tangentially connected to the War of Independence among many other factors, and therefore it should not be considered a primary effect of it. The French and Indian War (also known as the Seven Years' War) and the Bill of Rights, on the other hand, were respectively a cause and effect from the American Revolution, making Choice *C* the correct answer.

6. D: The president and vice president are part of the executive branch, not the legislative branch. The question focuses specifically on the federal level, so state government should be excluded from consideration. As for the district court and the court of appeals, they are part of the judicial branch. The legislative branch is made up of Congress, which consists of the House of Representatives and the Senate.

7. A: George Washington was a slave owner himself in life, so he did not make abolition a theme in his Farewell Address. On the other hand, he was concerned that sectionalism could potentially destroy the United States, and he warned against it. Furthermore, he believed that Americans should avoid getting involved in European affairs. However, one issue that he felt was especially problematic was the formation of political parties, and he urged against it in his farewell.

8. B: To avoid involvement in political processes such as voting is antithetical to the principles of a democracy. Therefore, the principal responsibility of citizens is the opposite, and they should be steadily engaged in the political processes that determine the course of government.

9. B: Time zones are determined by longitude, not latitude. Locations are defined in absolute terms, while places are in part defined by the population, which is subject to movement. There are seven continents in the world, not six. On the other hand, it is true that the prime meridian determines the border for the Eastern and Western hemispheres.

10. D: Riparian water usage was common in the past, but modern usage has shifted to appropriation. While often practicing sustainable methods, Native Americans used fire, agriculture, and other tools to shape the landscape for their own ends. Due to the importance of trade in providing essential resources to cities, a city is never truly separated from the outside world. However, invasive species are a formidable threat to native environments, making *D* the correct answer.

11. C: I, II, and IV only. Historians make use of maps in their studies to get a clear picture of how history unfolded, knowing the borders of different lands helps historians learn different cultures' interactions, and environmental factors, such as access to water and the proximity of mountains, help determine the course of civilization. The phrase "Geography is closely linked with the flow of resources, technology, and population in societies" is a characteristic of economics.

12. C: While many Native American tribes are matrilineal, not all of them are. Japan is currently coping with an especially low birthrate, not a high one. Mexico's religion, like that of Spain, is primarily Roman Catholic rather than Protestant. On the other hand, Shi'a Islam is based on the view that imams should be honored as Muhammad's chosen heirs to the Caliphate, making *C* correct.

13. A: Although Greeks used the alphabet as the basis for their written language, leading to a diverse array of literature, they learned about the alphabet from Phoenician traders. All the other options, in contrast, were invented in Greece.

14. D: It is important to realize that the Cold War was never an official war and that the United States and the Soviet Union instead funded proxy conflicts. The Kyoto Protocol was signed by members of the United Nations, as the League of Nations was long since defunct. While Japan was a minor participant in World War I, it was not defeated by America until World War II. The correct answer is *D*: India's partition between Hindu India and Islamic Pakistan led to large outbreaks of religious violence.

15. A: Although Egyptian and Mayan civilizations are an interesting subject for comparisons, the two cultures never interacted. The other answers are all examples of interactions between different cultures; a study of Chinese culture, for instance, would require examination of the multiple ethnic groups throughout China.

16. C: Although monetary systems were invented to solve problems with barter systems, it is wrong to assume that barter systems have ceased to exist; bartering remains a common practice throughout the world, albeit less common than money. The four main categories for economic resources are land, labor, capital, and entrepreneurship. The law of supply says that supplies will increase, not decrease, as prices increase. The correct answer is *C,* as scarcity is determined by human choice.

17. A: Rather than competition, a monopoly prevents other businesses from offering a certain product or service to consumers.

18. B: Mercantilism, which is built on the vision of full government control over the economy, is a hallmark of command system economies. Laissez-faire, capitalism, and self-interest, in contrast, are all fundamental concepts behind the market system.

19. A: England, France, and Spain all established North American colonies that would later be absorbed into the United States, but Italy, despite Christopher Columbus' role as an explorer, never established a colony in America.

Science and Technology/Engineering

Basic Characteristics of Living Things

<u>Organism Reproduction</u>
For bacteria, cell reproduction is the same as organism reproduction; binary fission is an asexual process that produces two new cells that are clones of each other because they have identical DNA.

Eukaryotes are more complex than prokaryotes and can go through sexual reproduction. They produce gametes (sex cells). Females make eggs and males make sperm. The process of making gametes is called meiosis, which is similar to mitosis except for the following differences:

- There are two cellular divisions instead of one.

- Four genetically different haploid daughter cells (one set of chromosomes instead of two) are produced instead of two genetically identical diploid daughter cells.

- A process called crossing over (recombination) occurs, which makes the daughter cells genetically different. If chromosomes didn't cross over and rearrange genes, siblings could be identical clones. There would be no genetic variation, which is a critical factor in the evolution of organisms.

In sexual reproduction, a sperm fertilizes an egg and creates the first cell of a new organism, called the zygote. The zygote will go through countless mitotic divisions over time to create the adult organism.

Cell Replication

Cell replication in eukaryotes involves duplicating the genetic material (DNA) and then dividing to yield two daughter cells, which are clones of the parent cell. The cell cycle is a series of stages leading to the growth and division of a cell. The cell cycle helps to replenish damaged or depleted cells. On average, eukaryotic cells go through a complete cell cycle every 24 hours. Some cells such as epithelial, or skin, cells are constantly dividing, while other cells such as mature nerve cells do not divide. Prior to mitosis, cells exist in a nondivisional stage of the cell cycle called interphase. During interphase, the cell begins to prepare for division by duplicating DNA and its cytoplasmic contents. Interphase is divided into three phases: gap 1 (G_1), synthesis (S), and gap 2 (G_2).

<u>DNA Replication</u>
Replication refers to the process during which DNA makes copies of itself. Enzymes govern the major steps of DNA replication.

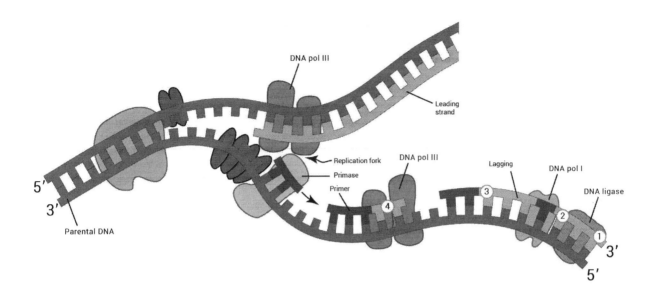

The process begins with the uncoiling of the double helix of DNA. *Helicase*, an enzyme, accomplishes this task by breaking the weak hydrogen bonds uniting base pairs. The uncoiling of DNA gives rise to the replication fork, which has a Y-shape. Each separated strand of DNA will act as a template for the production of a new molecule of DNA. The strand of DNA oriented toward the replication fork is called the *leading strand* and the strand oriented away from the replication fork is named the *lagging strand*.

Replication of the leading strand is continuous. *DNA polymerase*, an enzyme, binds to the leading strand and adds complementary bases. Replication of the lagging strand of DNA on the other hand is discontinuous. DNA polymerase produces discontinuous segments, called *Okazaki fragments*, which are later joined together by another enzyme, *DNA ligase*. To start the DNA synthesis on the lagging strand, the protein *primase* lays down a strip of RNA, called an *RNA primer*, to which the DNA polymerase can bind. As a result, two clones of the original DNA emerge from this process. DNA replication is considered *semiconservative* due to the fact that half of the new molecule is old and the other half is new.

How Organisms Use Energy

When we eat a hamburger, we're eating more than carbohydrates; we're also eating proteins and fats. Plants provide more than just carbohydrates when we eat them; they also are able to use the light energy to make proteins, fats, and, of course, their DNA, because if they didn't have DNA, they'd have no instructions to grow. The following organic compounds and their atoms don't magically appear in organisms—life has to either grab the nutrients from soil or seeds or eat them.

- Carbohydrates, proteins, fats, and DNA/RNA have carbon, hydrogen, and oxygen
- DNA, proteins, and fats also have phosphorous
- DNA and proteins also have nitrogen
- Proteins also can have sulfur

Plants need all of these elements to make food. Where do they get them? Remember that earth's atmosphere is a conglomerate of different gases, including nitrogen. Bacteria in the soil are able to convert that nitrogen into a usable form, and the roots of plants absorb the critical nitrogen. Carbon and oxygen get into the plant via photosynthesis (carbon dioxide), as does the element hydrogen, because plants take in water, which contains hydrogen. Phosphorous and sulfur are absorbed in plants through soil. Since heterotrophs cannot make their own food, they have to eat an autotroph (or eat something that ate an autotroph) in order to obtain these critical elements.

Cycles are a recurring pattern in science, and making food is no exception. When living things die, fungi and bacteria act as decomposers and break down the material. That's actually why dead things and rotten meat smell bad; the decomposers have broken them down so much that gases containing carbon, oxygen, phosphorous, nitrogen, and even smelly sulfur are released. Remember that sulfur is heavy in protein, and eggs are protein-rich. It makes sense that rotten eggs have an unpleasant smell as they release sulfur because they're mostly protein. Once living things decompose, all the elements eventually recycle back to the atmosphere or to the soil, and the atoms are available to construct molecules once again.

Plant Structures, Functions, and Processes

Photosynthesis

Photosynthesis refers to the process used by plants, some algae, and some bacteria to convert sunlight into chemical energy. It combines water and carbon dioxide using light energy to produce the sugar glucose and oxygen. Glucose is converted to adenosine triphosphate (ATP) through cellular respiration. ATP is the molecule that provides energy for all cellular activities and can be thought of as a sort of energy currency.

Photosynthesis is the most prolific process to create useable energy for life on Earth. In plants, photosynthesis takes place in chloroplasts, organelles containing photosynthetic structures and chemicals. *Thylakoids*, the structural units of photosynthesis, are found within chloroplasts and use *chlorophyll*, a green pigment, to harness sunlight in photosynthesis.

Photosynthesis has two types of reactions: light-dependent and light-independent. Light-dependent reactions produce ATP and release oxygen into the atmosphere. Light-independent reactions utilize ATP to produce glucose.

In photosynthesis, solar energy is used to fix carbon dioxide into glucose, oxidizing water to oxygen.

$$6CO_2 + 6H_2O + Energy \rightarrow C_6H_{12}O_6 + 6O_2$$

In aerobic respiration, the opposite happens, and glucose and oxygen are broken down into carbon dioxide and water to liberate energy in the form of ATP.

$$C_6H_{12}O_6 + 6O_2 \rightarrow 6CO_2 + 6H_2O + Energy$$

Heterotrophs are organisms that eat other living things to obtain organic compounds. This is usually simplified as the thought of eating other animals for food to gain energy, as most animals are unable to produce their own food. As a result, heterotrophs are completely dependent on autotrophs and other heterotrophs as food sources. All animals are considered heterotrophs.

Autotrophs are able to fix carbon dioxide into useable organic compounds. Most of them produce their own food by harnessing the power of sunlight and employing photosynthesis. As a result, autotrophs are not dependent on other organisms for sources of carbon. All plants are considered autotrophs.

Cellular Respiration
Cellular respiration is the pathway used by cells to release energy stored in food molecules. It culminates in the production of ATP (adenosine triphosphate), which is the energy currency for all cellular activities.

The two types of cellular respiration are *aerobic* respiration and *anaerobic* respiration. Aerobic respiration requires oxygen while anaerobic respiration does not, but aerobic respiration produces significantly more ATP and is the principal mode of respiration carried out by human cells.

In aerobic respiration, a molecule of glucose is broken down in the cytoplasm into pyruvate during *glycolysis* before further being broken down to a pair of carbon atoms called an *acetyl group*. This acetyl group is ferried by acetyl coenzyme A to the mitochondria where it enters the *Krebs cycle* (also known as the *tricaboxylic acid cycle* and the *TCA cycle*). In the Krebs cycle, the acetyl group is further broken down into carbon dioxide (C2$\rightarrow$CO2)while the energy of its bonds are translated into molecules of NADH (reduced nicotinamide adenine dinucleotide).

These molecules of NADH are the source of electrons and hydrogen ions that are used in the last phase of aerobic respiration to generate ATP so that the energy from the sugar can actually be used. The electrons and hydrogens from the NADH enter the *electron transport chain* (also called the ETC or *oxidative phosphorylation*) where many complicated reactions occur before finally reducing oxygen to water (O2$\rightarrow$H2O).

If no oxygen is available, aerobic respiration can't continue to completion. The cell stops aerobic respiration after the glucose is broken down to pyruvate, and instead converts it to lactate (or lactic acid). This is *fermentation*, and it generates ATP, but it does so only at a much lower rate than aerobic respiration. Because it doesn't use oxygen, fermentation is a type of anaerobic respiration. Many types of bacteria use it as their primary source of energy, but it is also a last defense for human cells when deprived of oxygen for long periods of time.

Systems of the Human Body

Circulatory System
The cardiovascular system includes the heart and blood vessels (capillaries, veins, and arteries). It involves sending nutrients and oxygen to the tissues and transports waste to the organs for disposal.

The heart is central to the circulatory system. It is a hollow, muscular-like pump and its function is to push blood throughout the body. The average heart beats about eighty times per minute. It is composed of four chambers, a right and left ventricle, and a right and left atria. It sits between the lungs on the left of the chest cavity.

Arteries take blood away from the heart. They are thick blood vessels that contract to keep the blood moving throughout the body. In this process, oxygenated blood is pumped into the aorta from the heart.

Veins take blood back to the heart. They are less muscular than arteries and contain valves that stop blood from flowing in the wrong direction. The superior and inferior vena cava are the two largest veins and are located below the heart. Small capillaries connect the veins and arteries. Capillaries deliver oxygen and nutrients to the cells. Additionally, capillaries remove carbon dioxide and other waste products.

Integumentary and Musculoskeletal Systems
The integumentary system is comprised of skin, glands (oil and sweat), nails, and hair.

The skin encompasses the whole body and is the body's largest organ. It consists of three layers: the epidermis, dermis, and subcutaneous tissues. The skin has many functions; it helps the body maintain homeostasis, protects muscle tissue from harmful bacteria and liquids, helps with fluid retention in the body, and it has sensory receptors and motor fibers that are sensitive to touch, temperature, and pain.

The musculoskeletal system is comprised of joints, bones, and connective tissues (cartilage, ligaments, and tendons). This system provides the body with support and stability and gives the body its overall form. As a function of this system, bones store the body's calcium and have bone marrow that generates necessary blood cells. When the body moves, muscle fibers contract and have voluntary and involuntary movements. To function, muscles are dependent upon oxygen and adequate blood supply. Accordingly, the musculoskeletal system works in conjunction with other systems in the body like the respiratory, nervous, and circulatory systems.

Lymphatic System
The lymphatic system is comprised of organs and vessels in the body. This network allows waste, nutrients, and lymph fluid to be distributed between the bloodstream and body tissues.

The lymph system also includes bone marrow, the spleen, thymus, tonsils, and lymph nodes. The lymph nodes filter lymph fluid, where foreign materials, viruses, and bacteria are isolated and combatted by white lymphocytes (white blood cells). As such, the lymph system is a part of the body's overall immune system, which is designed to protect the body against disease. In this process, lymph nodes become enlarged or swollen when the body is infected as it gathers and fights infectious organisms.

Respiratory System
The respiratory system functions to supply the body with oxygen and discard carbon dioxide. This is a complex system that includes the thoracic cage hosting the lungs, the diaphragm, the sternum, twelve pairs of ribs, and twelve thoracic vertebrae. When breathing, the thoracic cage is in motion and is supported by the diaphragm and the pathways for air that connect the lungs, bronchioles, bronchi, trachea, pharynx, mouth, and nose.

While inhaling, air enters the lungs, pressure in the lungs lower, intercostal muscles contract, the diaphragm lowers and contracts, and the sternum and ribs enlarge. While exhaling, the diaphragm and intercostal muscles repose, the sternum and ribs return to its original position of relaxation, air pressure in the lungs enlarge, and air leaves the lungs.

Digestive System
The digestive system functions to digest food, extract and absorb nutrients from food, and rid the body of waste products from what is consumed.

It has two primary parts: the upper digestive tract, which includes the small intestine, stomach, esophagus, and mouth; and the lower digestive tract, which includes the rectum, large intestine, and the digestive tract.

Three phases are associated with digestion: ingestion, digestion, and elimination. The digestive system is a part of a larger system that processes and absorbs nutrients. This includes the nervous system, associated with satiation; the central nervous system, associated with activating digestive fluids; the endocrine system, associated with supplying the body with chemicals to support digestion; and the circulatory system, associated with providing the body with processed nutrients to the body's cells and cleaning up waste products.

The digestion process starts with the mouth and terminates in the small intestine. It begins when food is chewed and saliva is secreted to support the swallowing process. Food passes through the GI tract and is mixed with digestive juices where food molecules are broken down. Accordingly, the body absorbs broken down molecules by the walls of the small intestine and delivers this to the rest of the body via the bloodstream. The waste products from digestion pass through the large intestine and terminate as waste matter.

Central Nervous System
The central nervous system is responsible for the functions of the mind and body. This includes governing mental functions, body movement, and the communication of nerve impulses throughout the body.

It has two parts: the brain and the spinal cord. The brain facilitates thinking, interpreting the phenomenal world, and controls the body's movement. The brain interprets information from our senses. The spinal cord facilitates communication between the body and the brain. If an injury occurs to the spinal cord the brain and body's communication pathway is altered.

There is the autonomic nervous system, which controls the involuntary functions of the body (blood flow, heartbeat, digestion) and the voluntary nervous system, which controls the voluntary functions of the body (sitting, standing, talking). The autonomic nervous system has two parts: the parasympathetic, responsible for gland secretion and muscular activity; and the sympathetic, responsible for sweating, vasoconstriction, and stimulating the heartbeat. The parasympathetic and sympathetic parts of the nervous system function to regulate and balance the entire nervous system.

Urinary System
The urinary system is also called the renal system. It functions to generate, house, and eliminate urine.

Urine is the waste product excreted by the kidneys. The kidneys resemble bean-shaped glands and are located behind the abdominal region of the body. The kidneys function to discard waste, toxins, salts, water, and other elements from the bloodstream. Urine is created in the kidneys when extra water from the blood and waste are filtered. Urine travels through two long tubes called the ureters and fills up the bladder. When the bladder is full, one can urinate through the urethra. This is necessary to eliminate waste in the body.

Endocrine System
The endocrine system is a group of ductless glands that produce hormones derived from the bloodstream and fluids in the tissues. It has a variety of regulatory functions. These functions include the regulation of mood, sleep, reproduction, sexual function, tissue utility, development, growth, and metabolism. The endocrine system is composed of the ovaries in females, testicles in males, adrenal glands, parathyroid glands, the thyroid gland, the pituitary gland, and the pancreas (an endocrine and exocrine gland). The pancreas helps to regulate sugar and aid digestion.

Pituitary, Thyroid, and Parathyroid Glands

The thyroid gland is a part of the endocrine system. It stores iodine and it generates and secretes hormones that control growth and development in a child and key functions of the metabolic process. Also part of the endocrine system is the pituitary gland. This controls lactation in mothers, balances electrolytes in tissues and the blood, regulates the excretion and retention of fluids, and it controls sexual growth and development in children and teens. In addition, the pituitary gland controls and regulates metabolism, stress, excretion, urine, digestion, circulation, breathing, and reproduction. Blood calcium levels, nervous system excitation, phosphorus metabolism, and muscles are controlled by the parathyroid gland secretions.

Reproductive System

For females, external organs of reproduction are the hymen, the vestibule, the clitoris, the labia minora, the labia majora, the mons pubis, the Bartholin's glands, and other glands. The mammary glands of the breast are often considered a part of the reproductive system given their function to produce milk for babies.

Females have internal organs that facilitate reproduction, which include the ovaries, the uterus, the fallopian tubes, and the vagina. Once a month, hormones are activated for ovaries to produce an ovum or egg. In this process, a follicle that has an egg cell is formed. At maturation, the follicle bursts and the egg is released in the process known as ovulation. In this process, the egg travels into the fallopian tube in the direction of the uterus. The endometrium is activated and thickens to generate more blood supply.

Fertilization happens when a sperm travels up the fallopian tube and burrows into an egg. During fertilization, a baby's sex and genes become established. If fertilization does not occur, hormone stimulation is reduced, and the endometrium separates from the uterine wall. The unfertilized egg and blood then exit the body in a process known as menstruation.

For males, the main external reproductive organs are the penis and scrotum. Internal organs associated with reproduction are the testes, epididymides, seminal ducts, seminal vesicles, ejaculatory ducts, and spermatic cords.

Externally, there is the urethra, prostate gland, and other functional glands. Male testes are attached to the scrotum and spermatic cords, which are made up of tissues, blood vessels, and the vas deferens. The testes produce male sperm cells, and hormones and are attached to the vas deferens by an epididymis.

The vas deferens travel through the spermatic cords toward the prostate gland. Ejaculatory ducts are formed when the vas deferens connect to the seminal vesicles. Sperm motility begins when the seminal vesicles and the prostate gland secrete elements into the semen. During this process, semen is released into the urethra and discharged via the ejaculatory ducts.

Human Brain

The human brain is a complex organism. It consists of over 100 billion nerves that communicate through over a trillion synapses (connections).

The brain has five primary parts, which are the medulla oblongata, the pons, the cerebellum, the midbrain, and the cerebrum. The brain also has multiple lobes, which are the frontal lobes, parietal lobes, temporal lobes, and the occipital lobes. A tissue called the meninges surrounds the outer layer of the brain, while the cranium/skull is bone that protects the brain.

The brain functions via specialized and interrelated parts. This includes the cortex (voluntary movements and thinking start here), the brainstem (responsible for sleeping and breathing), the basal ganglia (coordinates messages in the brain), and the cerebellum (controls equilibrium).

The brain has twelve cranial nerves that stem from the brain and are connected to different parts of the body. The twelve cranial nerves are:

- *Olfactory*; controls smell
- *Optic*; controls vision
- *Oculomotor*; controls various eye movements
- *Trochlear*; controls superior oblique eye muscles
- *Trigeminal*; controls various facial functions
- *Abducens*; controls lateral rectus eye muscle
- *Facial*; controls various facial and tongue functions
- *Vestibulocochlear*; controls various ear and hearing functions
- *Glossopharyngeal*; controls taste functions in part of tongue
- *Vagus*; controls gag reflex, soft palate, and vocal cord movements
- *Spinal accessory*; controls trapezius muscles and sternocleidomastoid movements
- *Hypoglossal*; controls tongue movements

Genes and Heredity

All living things are a product of their DNA, specifically portions of their DNA called genes that code for different characteristics.

Learned behavior is not affected by DNA and is not hereditable. Changes in appearance like a woman painting her toenails, a bird whose feathers accidentally fall out due to a tornado, or a person getting a scar are also not heritable. Heritable characteristics are those coded by DNA like eye color, hair color, and height.

A man named Gregor Mendel is considered the father of genetics. He was a monk and a botanist, and through extensive experiments with pea plants, he figured out a great deal about heredity.

Our genetic code comes in pairs. Each chromosome contains many genes, and since we have one chromosome from our mom and one chromosome from our dad, we have two copies of each gene. Genes come in different forms called alleles. The two alleles work together, and when the cell reads them and follows their instructions, the way an organism looks or behaves is called a trait. For some traits, there are only two alleles: a dominant allele and a recessive allele. Even though eye color is a bit more complicated, pretend that brown eyes are dominant over blue eyes, and there are the only two alleles:

- B = Brown eyes
- b = blue eyes

A child inherits these alleles from his parents. There are three possible combinations a child can inherit, dependent on his parents' alleles:

- BB (homozygous dominant)
- Bb (heterozygous)
- bb (homozygous recessive)

The combination of genes above will determine the trait in the offspring. If the child gets any combination with a B, the more powerful allele, his eyes will be brown. Only the bb combination will give the child blue eyes. In this example, the combination of alleles is called a genotype, and the actual eye color the child has is called a phenotype.

Natural Selection and Adaptation

The theory of natural selection is one of the fundamental tenets of evolution. It affects the phenotype, or visible characteristics, of individuals in a species, which ultimately affects the genotype, or genetic makeup, of those same individuals. Charles Darwin was the first to explain the theory of natural selection, and it is described by Herbert Spencer as favoring survival of the fittest. Natural selection encompasses three assumptions:

- A species has heritable traits: All traits have some likelihood of being propagated to offspring.

- The traits of a species vary: Some traits are more advantageous than others.

- Individuals of a species are subject to differing rates of reproduction: Some individuals of a species may not get the opportunity to reproduce while others reproduce frequently.

Over time, certain variations in traits may increase both the survival and reproduction of certain individuals within a species. The desirable heritable traits are passed on from generation to generation. Eventually, the desirable traits will become more common and permeate the entire species. *Natural selection* is one of the processes leading to evolutionary change and is the primary determinant of how a species adapts to its environment.

Adaptation

The theory of *adaptation* is defined as an alteration in a species that causes it to become more well-suited to its environment. It increases the probability of survival, thus increasing the rate of successful reproduction. As a result, an adaptation becomes more common within the population of that species.

For examples, bats use reflected sound waves (echolocation) to prey on insects, and chameleons change colors to blend in with their surroundings to evade detection by its prey and predators. Adaptations are brought about by natural selection.

Adaptive radiation refers to rapid diversification within a species into an array of unique forms. It may occur as a result of changes in a habitat creating new challenges, ecological niches, or natural resources.

Darwin's finches are often thought of as an example of the theory of adaptive radiation. Charles Darwin documented 13 varieties of finches on the Galapagos Islands. Each island in the chain presented a unique and changing environment, which was believed to cause rapid adaptive radiation among the finches. There was also diversity among finches inhabiting the same island. Darwin believed that as a result of natural selection, each variety of finch developed adaptations to fit into its native environment.

A major difference in Darwin's finches had to do with the size and shapes of beaks. The variation in beaks allowed the finches to access different foods and natural resources, which decreased competition and preserved resources. As a result, various finches of the same species were allowed to coexist, thrive, and diversify.

Finches had:

- Short beaks, which were suited for foraging for seeds
- Thin, sharp beaks, which were suited for preying on insects
- Long beaks, which were suited for probing for food inside plants

Darwin believed that the finches on the Galapagos Islands resulted from chance mutations in genes transmitted from generation to generation.

How Organisms Interact with One Another and Their Environment

Life Cycle and Organism Interaction with Habitats

Human development starts when sperm fertilizes an egg to create a zygote, which will develop into an embryo. Pregnant women carry an embryo inside their bodies for nine months before giving birth to a live baby. Human reproduction is a concept best left for an older age, but mentioning that babies come from eggs that grow inside a mom is a concept that can be briefly discussed because all the organisms below develop from external eggs. It will provide a good contrast to emphasize the following life cycles:

Chicken	Hens are female chickens, and they lay about one egg per day. If there is no rooster (male chicken) around to fertilize the egg, the egg never turns into a chick and instead becomes an egg that we can eat. If a rooster is around, he mates with the female chicken and fertilizes the egg. Once the egg is fertilized, the tiny little embryo (future chicken) will start as a white dot adjacent to the yolk and albumen (egg white) and will develop for 21 days. The mother hen sits on her clutch of eggs (several fertilized eggs) to incubate them and keep them warm. She will turn the eggs to make sure the embryo doesn't stick to one side of the shell. The embryo continues to develop, using the egg white and yolk nutrients, and eventually develops an "egg tooth" on its beak that it uses to crack open the egg and hatch. Before it hatches, it even chirps to let the mom know of its imminent arrival!
Frog	Frogs mate similar to the way chickens do, and then lay eggs in a very wet area. Sometimes, the parents abandon the eggs and let them develop on their own. The eggs, like chickens', will hatch around 21 days later. Just like chickens, a frog develops from a yolk, but when it hatches, it continues to use the yolk for nutrients. A chicken hatches and looks like a cute little chick, but a baby frog is actually a tadpole that is barely developed. It can't even swim around right away, although eventually it will develop gills, a mouth, and a tail. After more time, it will develop teeth and tiny legs and continue to change into a fully-grown frog! This type of development is called *metamorphosis*.
Fish	Most fish also lay eggs in the water, but unlike frogs, their swimming sperm externally fertilize the eggs. Like frogs, when fish hatch, they feed on a yolk sac and are called *larvae*. Once the larvae no longer feed on their yolk and can find their own nutrients, they are called fry, which are basically baby fish that grow into adulthood.
Butterfly	Like frogs, butterflies go through a process called *metamorphosis,* where they completely change into a different looking organism. After the process of mating and internal fertilization, the female finds the perfect spot to lay her eggs, usually a spot with lots of leaves. When the babies hatch from the eggs, they are in the larva form, which for butterflies is called a *caterpillar*. The larvae eat and eat and then go through a process like hibernation and form into a *pupa*, or a *cocoon*. When they hatch from the cocoon, the butterflies are in their adult form.
Bugs	After fertilization, other bugs go through incomplete metamorphosis, which involves three states: eggs that hatch, nymphs that look like little adults without wings and molt their exoskeleton over time, and adults.

All of these organisms depend on a proper environment for development, and that environment depends on their form. Frogs need water, caterpillars need leaves, and baby chicks need warmth in order to be born.

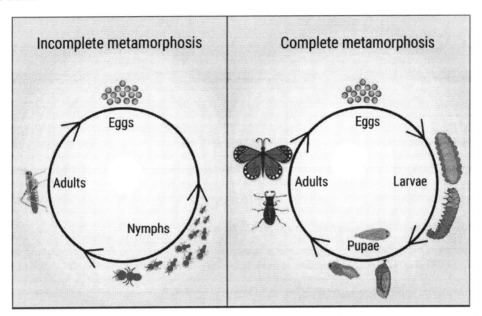

Engaging ways to introduce the life cycle are books like *Rainbow Fish* by Marcus Pfister and *The Very Hungry Caterpillar* by Eric Carle.

Interactions of Organisms and Their Environments
An ecosystem consists of all living (community) and nonliving components (abiotic factors) in an area. *Abiotic factors* include the atmosphere, soil, rocks, and water, which all have a role in sustaining life. The atmosphere provides the necessary gasses, soil contains nutrients for plants, rocks erode and affect topography, and water has many different roles.

An ecosystem not only involves living things interacting with nonliving things, but also involves the community interacting with each other. Food chains depict one type of community interaction, like the one shown here:

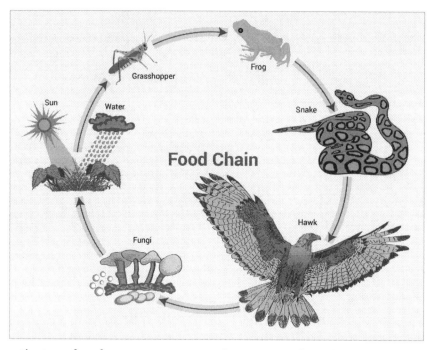

Food chains show the transfer of energy as one organism eats another. They also show an organism's eating habits. Herbivores eat plants and carnivores eat meat. A lion in grassland with no available animal prey will starve to death even though there is lots of grass because lions don't eat grass; that isn't their role in their habitat.

Food webs not only show predator-prey relationships, but they also show another relationship called *competition*.

This food web shows that mice and frogs are competing for grasshoppers. If there is a scarcity of grasshoppers, the mouse and frog populations will decrease.

The final three types of community relationships all fall under the blanket term *symbiosis* and are described in the table below.

	Mutualism	Commensalism	Parasitism
Definition	Both organisms benefit from the relationship	One organism benefits from the relationship	One organism benefits from the relationship, and the other is harmed
Example	Birds and flowers	Whale and barnacle	Dog and flea
Explanation	Birds get nectar. Plants get pollinated.	Barnacle gets a free ride and access to food. Whale doesn't care because the barnacle is just latched on and isn't hurting anything.	Flea sucks dog's blood and gets nutrients. Dog is itchy and gets its blood drained.

The important knowledge for students to retain is:

- Plants need soil and sunlight to survive. This can be demonstrated by growing plants in the classroom.

- Animals in an area can have relationships other than predator-prey.

- Animals have niches in their environment. Some are herbivores (eat plants only), some are carnivores (eat meat only), and some are omnivores like humans (eat both plants and animals).

Inherited Traits, Learned Behaviors, and Organism Survival
Many characteristics are inherited from the DNA obtained from an individual's parents, including skin color, eye shape, hair color, and color-blindness, among others. Learned behavior isn't related to genetics and is a result of training. For example, a dog catching a stick is learned. The overall intelligence of the dog, however, has to do with its genes.

An organism's survival depends on its fitness relative to the environment, and any trait that helps it survive is called an *adaptation*. Whale blubber and shark teeth are examples of adaptations. Blubber keeps whales warm, and a shark's many teeth ensures it's better able to capture prey. Whales don't decide to grow blubber, and sharks don't decide to grow teeth. These characteristics have been inherited from their parents.

Discussion of adaptations can involve showing pictures of various organisms and identifying which of their characteristics would be helpful and why. See below for some ideas for discussion.

Organism	Adaptation to identify	Why it's helpful
Cactus	Spikes	Helps protect from water thieves
Peacock	Feathers	Help scare off predators (look like eyes); also help attract mates
Elephant	Trunk	Helps suck up water
Skunk	Smelly secretions	Helps protect from predators

Composition and Structure of Matter

<u>Atoms</u>
All matter is made of atoms. Atoms are the most basic portion of an element that still retains its properties. All of the elements known to man are catalogued in the periodic table, a chart of elements arranged by increasing atomic number. The atomic number refers to the number of protons in an atom's nucleus. It can be found either in the upper left-hand corner of the box or directly above an element's chemical symbol on the periodic table. For example, the atomic number for hydrogen (H) is 1. The term "atomic mass" refers to the sum of protons and neutrons in an atom's nucleus. The atomic mass can be found beneath an element's abbreviation on the periodic table. For example, the average atomic mass of hydrogen (H) is 1.008. Because protons have a positive charge and neutrons have a neutral charge, an atom's nucleus typically has a positive electrical charge. Electrons orbiting the nucleus have a negative charge. As a result, elements with equal numbers of protons and electrons have no net charge.

States of Matter

There are three fundamental states of matter—liquid, gas, and solid. The molecules in a liquid are not in an orderly arrangement and can move past one another. Weak intermolecular forces contribute to a liquid having an indefinite shape, but definite volume. Lastly, a liquid conforms to the shape of its container, is not easily compressible, and flows quite easily.

The molecules in a gas have a large amount of space between them. A gas will diffuse indefinitely if unconfined, while it will assume the shape and volume of its container if enclosed. In other words, a gas has no definite shape or volume. Lastly, a gas is compressible and flows quite easily.

The molecules in a solid are closely packed together, which restricts their movement. Very strong intermolecular forces contribute to a solid having a definite shape and volume. Furthermore, a solid is not easily compressible and does not flow easily.

Forms of Energy

The different forms of energy are mechanical, electromagnetic, nuclear, chemical, and heat. Mechanical energy is the energy associated with motion, while electromagnetic energy is the energy associated with moving electric charges. Nuclear energy is generated by splitting uranium atoms, a process known as fission, and chemical energy is energy that is released through chemical reactions. Thermal (or heat) energy is the energy from the internal motion of atoms, and it moves from warmer objects to cooler objects.

Energy may be defined as the capacity to do work. It can be transferred between objects, comes in a multitude of forms, and can be converted from one form to another. The Law of Conservation of Energy states that "Energy can neither be created nor be destroyed."

Kinetic Energy and Potential Energy
The two primary forms of energy are kinetic energy and potential energy. Kinetic energy involves the energy of motion. Kinetic energy can be calculated using the following equation:

$KE = 0.5 \times m \times v^2$
KE=kinetic energy; m=mass; v=velocity

Potential energy represents the energy possessed by an object by virtue of its position. Potential energy may be calculated using the following equation:

$PE = m \times g \times h$
PE=potential energy; m=mass; g=acceleration of gravity; h=height

Other Forms of Energy
The following are forms of kinetic energy:

- Radiant energy: This represents electromagnetic energy, which usually travels in waves or particles. Examples of radiant energy include visible light, gamma rays, X-rays, and solar energy.

- Thermal energy: This represents the vibration and movement of molecules and atoms within a substance. It is also known as heat. When an object is heated, its molecules and atoms move and slam into each other faster. Examples of thermal energy include geothermal energy from the Earth, heated swimming pools, baking in an oven, and the warmth of a campfire on a person's skin.

- Sound energy: This represents the movement of energy through a substance such as water or air in waves. Vibrations cause sound energy. Examples of sound energy include a person's voice, clapping, singing, and musical instruments.

- Electrical energy: This utilizes charged particles called electrons moving through a wire. Some examples of electrical energy include lightning, batteries, alternating current (AC), direct current (DC), and static electricity.

- Mechanical energy: This represents the stored energy derived from the movement of objects. The faster an object moves the more energy is stored. Also called motion energy. Examples of mechanical energy include wind, flight of an airplane, electrons orbiting an atom's nucleus, and running.

The following are forms of potential energy:

- Chemical energy: This represents the energy stored in the bonds of molecules and atoms. Chemical energy usually undergoes conversion to thermal energy. Examples of chemical energy include petroleum, coal, and natural gas.

- Elastic energy: This represents the energy stored in an object as its volume or shape is distorted, and is also known as stored mechanical energy. Examples of elastic energy include stretched rubber bands and coiled springs.

- Gravitational energy: This refers to the energy stored as a result of an object's place or position, and increases in height and mass translate to increases in gravitational energy. Examples of gravitational energy include rollercoasters and hydroelectric power.

- Nuclear energy: This refers to the energy stored in an atom's nucleus. Vast amounts of energy can be released through the combination or splitting of nuclei. An example of nuclear energy would be the nucleus of the element uranium.

How Heat Energy is Transferred

Heat can be transferred in three ways: conduction, convection, and radiation. Conduction is heat energy transferred from one substance to another or through a substance by direct contact between molecules. Conduction can take places in solids, liquids, and gases. Objects that transfer heat more efficiently are good conductors of heat, while objects that do no transfer heat efficiently are called insulators. Convection is heat energy transferred through gases and liquids by convection current, while radiation is heat energy transferred through empty space and can take place in gases and liquids.

Motion of Objects

Motion and forces are a critical component of physical science but speed, velocity, and acceleration often get confused. The speed of an object is the rate at which an object moves, while velocity is a speed with a given direction. Finally, acceleration is the rate of change in velocity. For example, the pull of Earth's gravity creates a form of acceleration (gravitational acceleration); it is the acceleration of an object toward Earth.

Velocity is also related to momentum. Momentum depends on the mass and velocity of an object and is given by the following equation:

$$Momentum = mass \times velocity$$

The Law of Conservation of Momentum states that the total momentum of a group of objects stays the same unless outside forces act on the objects; in other words, no momentum is lost, it is just transferred from one object to another.

Acceleration is also related to force. A force causes a change in the speed or direction of an object and is given by the following equation of Newton's Second Law of motion:

$$Force = mass \times acceleration$$

More than one force can act on an object at one time, and the object will move in the direction of the greater force. Newton's Third Law of motion states that forces come in pairs so that for every action, there is an equal and opposite reaction.

Friction can influence the velocity or acceleration of an object. Friction acts in the opposite direction of motion and will cause a moving object to slow down and eventually stop. There are four types of friction: static, sliding, rolling, and fluid friction. Static friction occurs between stationary objects, while sliding friction occurs when solid objects slide over each other. Rolling friction happens when a solid object rolls over another solid object, and fluid friction is friction when an object moves through a fluid or through fluid layers (gas or liquid). This includes the air resistance on an object.

Friction is also related to Newton's First Law of motion. It states that an object at rest stays at rest and an object in motion stays in motion unless acted on by an outside unbalanced force—like friction. Newton's First Law is also called the Law of Inertia, and inertia is the tendency of an object to resist a change in its motion.

Conservation of Energy

There is a fundamental law of thermodynamics (the study of heat and movement) called Conservation of Energy. This law states that energy cannot be created or destroyed, but rather energy is transferred to different forms involved in a process. For instance, a car pushed beginning at one end of a street will not continue down that street forever; it will gradually come to a stop some distance away from where it was originally pushed. This does not mean the energy has disappeared or has been exhausted; it means the energy has been transferred to different mediums surrounding the car. The frictional force from the road on the tires dissipates some of the energy, the air resistance from the movement of the car dissipates some of the energy, the sound from the tires on the road dissipates some of the energy, and the force of gravity pulling on the car dissipates some of the energy. Each value can be calculated in a number of ways including measuring the sound waves from the tires, measuring the temperature change in the tires, measuring the distance moved by the car from start to finish, etc. It is important to understand that many processes factor into such a small situation, but all situations follow the conservation of energy.

As in the earlier example, the rollercoaster at the top of a hill has a measurable amount of potential energy, and when it rolls down the hill, it converts most of that energy into kinetic energy. There are still additional factors like friction and air resistance working on the rollercoaster and dissipating some of the energy, but energy transfers in every situation.

Simple Machines

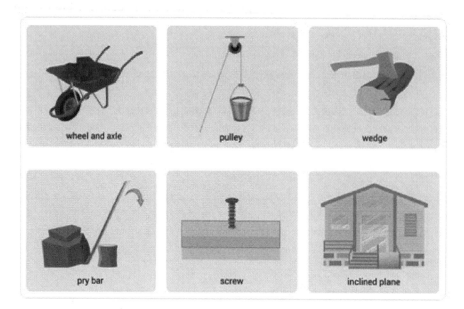

The use of simple machines can help by requiring less force to perform a task with the same result. This is also referred to as mechanical advantage.

Trying to lift a child into the air to pick an apple from a tree would require less force if the child was placed on the end of a teeter-totter and the adult pushed the other end of the teeter-totter down, in order to elevate the child to the same height to pick the apple. In this instance, the teeter-totter is a lever and provides a mechanical advantage to make the job easier.

Solving Practical Problems with Physical Science

Physical science is the study of nonliving forms of science. This natural science tries to explain and predict nature's outcomes based off experimental evidence. Physical science is categorized into four main branches:

- Physics
- Chemistry
- Astronomy
- Earth Science

Review each branch of physical science independently.

Physics
Physics is the study of matter and its motion through space and time. It studies the nature of motion, energy, and force. There are many sub-branches of physics, some of which include astrophysics (study of celestial objects), biophysics (study of biological systems using physics), cryogenics (study of how objects react to low temperatures), mechanics (how objects react to force), and relativity (study of time and space relativity).

To name a few, Newton's three laws of motion—momentum and conservation of energy, the kinetic molecular theory, and basic quantities such as acceleration, force, potential energy, and velocity—are all ways in which physics can solve practical problems. For example, Newton's third law of motion states:

"For every action (force) in nature, there is an equal and opposite reaction." This law demonstrates how things react with momentum and opposite velocity. Think about a trampoline. When someone jumps down, the springs on the trampoline send that person back up into the air.

Chemistry

Chemistry studies what matter is made of. It studies how properties change, combine, or separate. Chemistry is used every day. Ingredient lists, chemical compound reactions, and photosynthesis are just a few examples. There are five sub-branches of chemistry:

- Analytical chemistry: Measures the physical and chemical properties using qualitative and quantitative observations.

- Physical chemistry: Studies how energy and matter affect one another.

- Organic chemistry: Studies compounds with carbon; otherwise know as "The Chemistry of Life."

- Inorganic chemistry: Studies compounds without carbon, such as metals and gases.

- Biochemistry: Studies living organisms and their chemical processes.

Astronomy

Astronomy is one of the oldest natural sciences. It studies the universe as a whole. Astronomy examines celestial objects (such as the stars, planets, moon, asteroids, and galaxies), as well as other non-Earth–related phenomena. It is split into two main sub-branches:

- Observational astronomy: Receives information about astronomical objects and phenomena from observational data.

- Theoretical astronomy: Uses analytical and computer models to describe astronomical objects and phenomena.

Every day there are new astronomical discoveries. Advances in technology have provided astronomers with the ability to observe universal changes in real time.

Earth Science

Earth science is the study of the Earth and its surroundings. It studies how natural environments operate as well as the atmosphere, hydrosphere, lithosphere, and biosphere. Earth science has four main sub-branches:

- Geology: the study of the Earth's structure, materials, and processes

- Meteorology: the study of the Earth's climate and atmosphere

- Oceanography: the study of the Earth's oceans

- Astronomy: the study of the universe

Earth science is a huge part of everyday life. Climate change, pollution, depletion of natural resources, natural disasters, and increased population and waste are just a few of the challenges planet Earth faces. Earth scientists examine ways to improve or decrease the problems at hand and make the public more aware of the importance of caring for the planet they live on.

Forces that Shape the Earth's Surface

Erosion and Weathering

The Earth's surface, like many other things in the broader universe, does not remain the same for long; in fact, it changes from day to day. The Earth's surface is subject to a variety of physical processes that continue to shape its appearance. In each process, water, wind, temperature, or sunlight play a role in continually altering the Earth's surface.

Erosion can be caused by a variety of different stimuli including ice, snow, water, wind, and ocean waves. *Wind erosion* is a specific phenomenon that occurs in generally flat, dry areas with loose topsoil. Over time, the persistent winds can dislodge significant amounts of soil into the air, reshaping the land and wreaking havoc on those who depend on agriculture for their livelihoods. Erosion can also be caused by water and is responsible for changing landscapes as well. For example, the Grand Canyon was carved over thousands of years by the constant movement of the Colorado River. Over time, the river moved millions of tons of soil, cutting a huge gorge in the Earth along the way. In all cases, erosion involves the movement of soil from one place to another. In water erosion, material carried by the water is referred to as *sediment*. With time, some sediment can collect at the mouths of rivers, forming *deltas*, which become small islands of fertile soil. This process of detaching loose soils and transporting them to a different location where they remain for an extended period of time is referred to as *deposition*, and is the end result of the erosion process.

In contrast to erosion, *weathering* does not involve the movement of any outside stimuli. In this physical process, the surface of the Earth is either broken down physically or chemically. *Physical weathering* involves the effects of atmospheric conditions such as water, ice, heat, or pressure. Through the process of weathering over the course of centuries, large rocks can be broken down with the effects of icy conditions. *Chemical weathering* generally occurs in warmer climates and involves organic material that breaks down rocks, minerals, or soil. This process is what scientists believe led to the creation of fossil fuels such as oil, coal, and natural gas.

Volcanism and Plates

Rocks cover the surface of Earth. Igneous rock comes from the molten, hot, liquid magma circulating beneath Earth's surface in the upper mantle. Through vents called volcanoes, magma explodes or seeps onto the Earth's surface. Magma is not uniform; it varies in its elemental composition, gas composition, and thickness or viscosity. There are three main types of volcanoes: shield, cinder, and composite.

Shield volcanoes are the widest because their thin magma flows out of a central crater calmly and quietly, like a gentle fountain. This flowing magma results in layers of solid lava. The slow flow results in a convex hill that spans a wide area.

Like shield volcanoes, *cinder volcanoes* typically have a central crater and thin lava. In contrast to shield volcanoes, they are small, cone-shaped hills with steep sides. They are made of volcanic debris, or cinders. They are often found as secondary volcanoes near shield and composite volcanoes. In cinder volcanoes, the central vent spews lava that shatters into rock and debris and settles around it, resulting in its characteristic cone shape. Cinder volcanoes are surrounded by ashy, loose, magma dust.

Composite volcanoes (also called stratovolcanoes) are the most common and the tallest type of volcano. Their thick magma gets stuck at the vent, and as more and more builds up, the volcano eventually explodes and removes the clog. These eruptions generate loose debris, and once the plug has been violently expelled, the thick lava oozes out like a fountain. These volcanoes are the most dangerous with their extremely violent behavior and huge height. Most volcanoes are located around cracks in Earth's lithosphere.

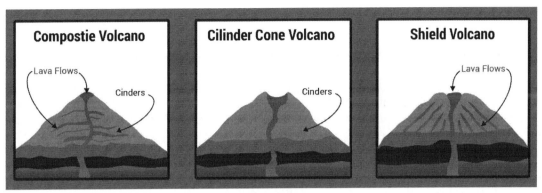

Once magma makes it to the surface, it is called lava. Once it cools, it solidifies into igneous rock. Common examples of igneous rock are obsidian, pumice, and granite. Weathering and erosion result in these rocks becoming soil or sediment and accumulating in layers mostly found in the ocean. These loose sediments settle over time and compress to become a uniform rock in a process called lithification. Examples of sedimentary rock include shale, limestone, and sandstone. As layers are piled atop each other, the bottom rock experiences an intense amount of pressure and transforms into metamorphic rock. Examples of metamorphic rocks are marble and slate. After long periods of time, the metamorphic rock moves closer to the asthenosphere and becomes liquid hot magma. Magma's eventual fate is lava and igneous rock, and the cycle starts anew.

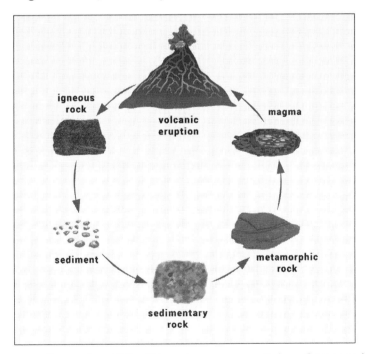

How does magma return to the surface if the lithosphere presses it down? Intense heat from the Earth's core travels to the upper mantle via convection. Convection involves thermal energy (heat) that converts into kinetic energy (movement), resulting in rapidly circulating molecules. Convection moves heat energy through fluids. In a pot of boiling water, the water closest to the burner becomes hot, causing its particles to move faster. Faster-moving molecules have more space between them and become less dense, so they rise. Some will vaporize, and some hit the cool air and slow down, becoming dense and sinking. Likewise, Earth's interior particles undergo convection (the heat source being the nuclear fission from the core), and the rock in the upper mantle will acquire so much kinetic energy that magma will be expelled from underneath Earth to the surface.

There are seven or eight major plates in the lithosphere and several minor plates. These tectonic plates explain the changing topography, or shape, of earth.

There are three types of boundaries between plates: divergent, convergent, and transform. All boundaries can be sites of volcanic activity. A *divergent boundary* occurs when plates separate. Lava fills in the space the plates create and hardens into rock, which creates oceanic crust. In a *convergent boundary*, if one of the plates is in the ocean, that plate is denser due to the weight of water. The dense ocean plate will slip under the land plate, causing a subduction zone where the plate moves underneath. Where plates converge on land, the continental crusts are both lighter with a similar density, and as a result they will buckle together and create mountains.

In *transform boundaries*, adjacent plates sliding past each other create friction and pressure that destroy the edges of the boundary and cause earthquakes. Transform boundaries don't produce magma, as they involve lateral movement.

Just as plates pushing together cause mountains, *canyons* are deep trenches caused by plates moving apart. Weather and erosion from rivers and precipitation run-off also create canyons. *Deltas* form when rivers dump their sediments and water into oceans. They are triangular flat stretches of land that are kind of like a triangular spatula; the handle represents the river and the triangle represents the mouth of a delta.

Sand dunes are another landform caused by wind or waves in combination with the absence of plants to hold sand in place. These are found in sandy areas like the desert or the ocean.

Rock Cycle and Soil Formation

Rocks are solid blocks composed of a combination of minerals. There are three different types of rocks: igneous, sedimentary, and metamorphic.

Igneous rocks are formed from magma in the Earth's mantle or lava that has cooled after volcanic eruptions. *Sedimentary rocks* are little pieces of igneous rocks that break off and then they combine in layers many times at the bottom of oceans. *Metamorphic rocks* are the rocks underneath layers and layers of either sedimentary or igneous rocks that meld together and transform due to the pressure of the layers and the heat radiating upward from the Earth's core.

The differences in the appearances of rocks are called their *physical properties*. Some are shiny and some are dull. Others are hard and don't scratch easily, while still others are soft and can be scratched. They come in a range of colors, and some are even metallic. Many rocks can be found every day in houses. Igneous rocks, like granite, are found on many kitchen countertops, and pumice stones are used in foot care. Metamorphic rock, such as marble, is often found in bathroom countertops. Limestone, a sedimentary rock, is commonly found in cement.

See the example below:

Types of Rocks

Igneous   **Metamorphic**   **Sedimentary**

Granite	Gabbro	Marble	Chlorite Schist	Conglomerate	Shale
Pumice	Basalt	Phyllite	Mica Schist	Limestone	Sandstone
Obsidian		Slate	Quartzite		

To demonstrate the differences between rocks, activities in the classroom could involve taking qualitative data on the rocks while having a theme of the day. For example, igneous rock formation can be demonstrated by making erupting papier-mâché volcanoes. On that day, the class could be full of igneous rocks. Students can use their senses to record properties of the rocks and the proximity and connection to the volcano will help them remember that igneous rocks come from lava.

In order to connect metamorphic rocks to the concept that they are changed due to heat and pressure, metamorphic rocks can be scattered around the room with a stack of books over each one. Students can temporarily remove the "pressure" and examine the look and feel of the rock, recording qualitative data.

Students can investigate sedimentary rocks by digging for buried sedimentary rocks in a sandbox. The physical properties of the rocks can be recorded, and the proximity to the sand communicates that sedimentary rocks are formed by the erosion of subsequent compression of layers of sediment from other rocks. Precipitation and the water cycle results in the weathering and breakdown of rocks. Erosion involves runoff that carries them away to where they pile up into the layers of sediments that form sedimentary rock.

Fossils show Earth's changing history and are trapped in sedimentary rocks. The lower the fossil, the older the organism because it has been buried deeper and deeper over time.

There is an entire field of science called *paleontology* that specifically studies fossils. Fossils can be completely intact organisms, like the mosquito preserved in the sap in the movie *Jurassic Park*. Fossils can also include remnants of an organism left behind, such as bones and teeth. Structures like these have remained intact due to minerals seeping inside and preserving them like the process that occurs in petrified wood. *Trace fossils* like a footprint are also considered fossils even though they aren't actual remains—they are simply evidence that the organism was there.

Trace fossils	Remain	Layer Analysis

Using the sandbox to hunt for fossils will enhance the learning experience. If students also get their hands dirty with soil, the next day, they can compare and contrast soil with sand. While sedimentary rock is the result of erosion and compaction of sediments, soil is the result of weathered rock mixing with decomposing dead organisms to form a loose mix conducive to plant growth. Liquid flows in soil, and air seeps through it as well. Sedimentary rock does not have the same amount of vulnerability to liquids and gases.

Structure of the Earth and Atmosphere

Earth is a complex system of the atmosphere (air), hydrosphere (water), as well as continental land (land). All work together to support the biosphere (life).

The atmosphere is divided into several layers: the troposphere, stratosphere, mesosphere, and thermosphere. The troposphere is at the bottom and is about seven and a half miles thick. Above the troposphere is the 30-mile-thick stratosphere. Above the stratosphere is the mesosphere, a 20-mile layer, followed by the thermosphere, which is more than 300 miles thick.

The troposphere is closest to Earth and has the greatest pressure due to the pull of gravity on its gas particles as well as pressure from the layers above. 78 percent of the atmosphere is made of nitrogen. Surprisingly, the oxygen that we breathe only makes up 21 percent of the gases, and the carbon dioxide critical to insulating Earth makes up less than 1 percent of the atmosphere. There are other trace gases present in the atmosphere, including water vapor.

Although the stratosphere has minimal wind activity, it is critical for supporting the biosphere because it contains the ozone layer, which absorbs the sun's damaging ultra-violet rays and protects living organisms. Due to its low level of air movement, airplanes travel in the stratosphere. The mesosphere contains few gas particles, and the gas levels are so insignificant in the thermosphere that it is considered space.

Visible light is colors reflecting off particles. If all colors reflect, we see white; if no colors reflect, we see black. This means a colored object is reflecting only that color—a red ball reflects red light and absorbs other colors.

Because the thermosphere has so few particles to reflect light rays (photons), it appears black. The troposphere appears blue in the day, and various shades of yellow and orange at sunset due to the

180

angle of the sun hitting particles that refract, or bend, the light. In certain instances, the entire visible spectrum can be seen in the form of rainbows. Rainbows occur when sunlight passes through water droplets and is refracted in many different directions by the water particles.

The hydrosphere, or water-containing portion of the Earth's surface, plays a major role in supporting the biosphere. In the picture below, a single water molecule (molecular formula H_2O) looks like a mouse head. The small ears of the mouse are the two hydrogen atoms connected to the larger oxygen atom in the middle.

Each hydrogen atom has one proton (positively charged, like the plus end of a magnet) in its nucleus (center), while oxygen has eight protons in its center. Hydrogen also has only one electron (negatively charged, like the minus end of a magnet) orbiting around the nucleus. Because hydrogen has only one proton, its electron is pulled more toward the oxygen nucleus (more powerful magnet). This makes hydrogen exist without an electron most of the time, so it is positively charged. On the other hand, oxygen often has two extra electrons (one from each hydrogen), so it is negatively charged. These bonds between the oxygen and hydrogen are called covalent bonds.

This charged situation is what makes water such a versatile substance; it also causes different molecules of water to interact with each other.

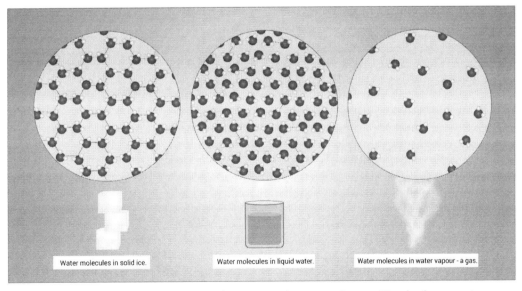

Water molecules in solid ice.   Water molecules in liquid water.   Water molecules in water vapour - a gas.

In a solid form (ice), water lines up in a crystal structure because the positive hydrogen atoms prefer to be next to the negative oxygen atoms that belong to other water molecules. These attractions are represented by the blue lines in the molecular picture of ice above. As heat is added and the ice melts, the water molecules have more kinetic energy and move faster; therefore, they are unable to perfectly arrange in the lattice structure of ice and turn into liquid. If enough heat is added, the water molecules will have so much kinetic energy they vaporize into gas. At this point, there are no bonds holding the water together because the molecules aren't close enough.

Notice how ice in its intricate arrangement has more space between the particles than liquid water, which shows that the ice is less dense than water. This contradicts the scientific fact that solids are denser than liquids. In water's case only, the solid will float due to a lower density! This is significant for the hydrosphere, because if temperatures drop to lower than freezing, frozen water will float to the surface of lakes or oceans and insulate the water underneath so that life can continue in liquid water. If ice was not less dense than liquid water, bodies of water would freeze from the bottom up and aquatic ecosystems would be trapped in a block of ice.

The hydrosphere has two components: seawater and freshwater (less than 5 percent of the hydrosphere). Water covers more than 70 percent of the Earth's surface.

The final piece of the biosphere is the lithosphere, the rocky portion of earth. Geology is the study of solid earth. Earth's surface is composed of elemental chunks called minerals, which are simply crystallized groups of bonded atoms. Minerals that have the same composition but different arrangements are called polymorphs, like graphite and diamonds. All minerals contain physical properties such as luster (shine), color, hardness, density, and boiling point. Their chemical properties, or how they react with other compounds, are also different. Minerals combine to form the rocks that make up Earth.

Earth has distinct layers—a thin, solid outer surface, a dense, solid core, and the majority of its matter between them. It is kind of like an egg: the thin crust is the shell, the inner core is the yolk, and the mantle and outer core that compose the space in between are like the egg white.

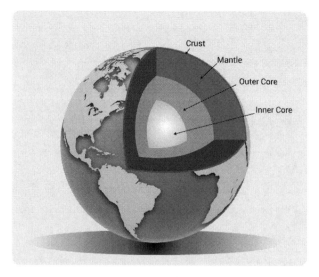

The outer crust of Earth consists of igneous or sedimentary rocks over metamorphic rocks (dense compacted rock underneath). The crust, combined with the upper portion of the mantle, forms the lithosphere, which is broken into several different plates, like puzzle pieces.

Factors that Affect Weather and Climate

Day/Night and Climate Patterns
Day, night, and climate are easy concepts to demonstrate with a globe and a light source. The notion that the Earth spins on a vertical axis is a critical piece, and a model like the one below showing the Sun and Earth's location will explain why the areas that are "day" are light because they face the Sun. The part of the globe that is "night" is simply the part facing away from the Sun.

The climate portion of an early education curriculum can be demonstrated with string and a large ball. If the wall is the Sun, three strings that start from the same point on the wall can be used to demonstrate distances of locations on Earth. One string can be stretched from the wall to the equator (the belt dividing the Earth in half), one from the wall to the North Pole, and one from the wall to the area halfway between. Measuring the string afterwards shows that areas closer to the equator are closer to the Sun, and that fact can easily explain why those areas have hotter climates. It makes sense that beaches like Cancun and Hawaii are hotter because they are close to the equator. Areas farthest away from the Sun (the ones that have the longest string), get less sunlight, so they're really cold (like the North Pole).

Weather Patterns
Weather is different from climate because it varies from day to day and is the result of wind and heat changes. Weather can be mild rain and snow, but it can also be dangerous thunderstorms, hurricanes, tornadoes, and blizzards. Students should be able to recognize simplified concepts of different forms of weather including:

- Rain: water falling from clouds
- Snow: snowflakes falling from clouds
- Thunderstorms: rainstorms with lightning
- Tornadoes: fast-spinning wind that looks like water going down a drain
- Hurricanes: huge storms that start in the ocean with massive winds that can be very destructive
- Blizzards: ferocious snowstorms with very high winds

Another important aspect of weather is that so much of it has to do with precipitation and the water cycle. Most of the phenomena listed above involve rain and snow.

These severe weather conditions can easily be investigated and modeled. There are 2-liter bottle experiments designed to exhibit rain and tornadoes. Hurricanes can also be researched. Hurricanes Alicia in 1983, Katrina and Rita in 2005, and Ike in 2008 are all devastating storms that can not only be used to illustrate the weather phenomenon, but can also be tied to cities and their economies.

Physical Characteristics of Oceans

Oceans cover most of the Earth. There are five oceans on planet Earth: Arctic, Atlantic, Indian, Pacific, and Southern. They are a vital resource for food and energy sources. Oceans have many characteristics, such as salinity (the amount of salt in the water), temperature, currents, and waves. An ocean's characteristics vary from place to place and ocean by ocean. Review the characteristics of oceans on the following page.

Salinity
- Salinity is the amount of salt in water.
- Saltwater is denser than freshwater.

- Saltwater is denser in places with less rain because salt is not evaporated with freshwater.
- Objects are more buoyant in saltier water.

Salinity of the oceans

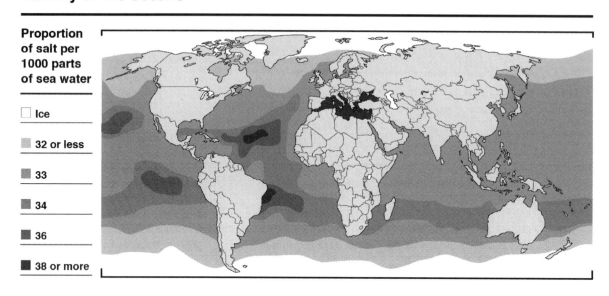

Proportion of salt per 1000 parts of sea water

- ☐ Ice
- 32 or less
- 33
- 34
- 36
- 38 or more

Temperature

Temperature constantly changes with the seasons. Temperature varies on depths of the water. Shallow water tends to be warmer than deep water—otherwise known as *thermocline*.

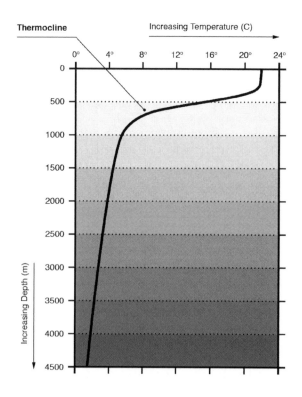

<u>Currents</u>
Seawater continuously moves and changes directions. Currents can influence water temperature. They are generated by forces such as breaking waves, wind energy, and the Coriolis effect. Currents are influenced by the gravitational pull of the moon and the sun.

<u>Waves</u>
Waves are measured by height and length. The top of the wave is called the *crest,* while the lowest point of the wave is called the *trough*. They are mostly created by the wind—the more force in the wind, the larger the wave. There are four types of ocean waves: wind waves, ocean swells, tsunamis, and tidal waves. Once the water reaches the shoreline, waves are referred to as *breaking waves*.

Hydrologic Cycle

The hydrologic cycle is the water cycle. It is the process where water evaporates, travels through the air into the clouds, and then falls from the sky in the form of precipitation (rain or snow), to eventually evaporate again. This continuous cycle is often affected by climate change.

The two largest components of the hydrologic cycle are evaporation and transpiration. Evaporation occurs when water vaporizes into a gas form. Heat is necessary for evaporation to occur. Transpiration is evaporation of water from plant leaves. Water is absorbed through the roots of plants, carried through the stem, and eventually to the leaves. Water is then lost from the leaf's surface by transpiration. Temperature also affects transpiration. The warmer the climate, the quicker water evaporates from plants. Look at the diagrams below demonstrating the process and components of evaporation and transpiration.

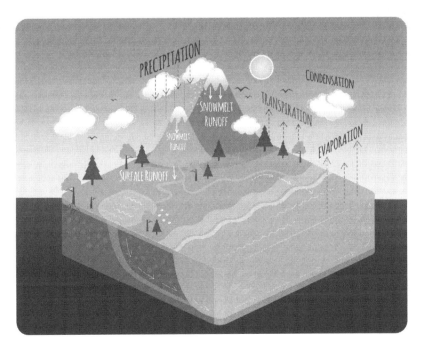

Structure of the Solar System

Earth is part of a solar system that rotates around a star. Our solar system is a miniscule portion of the universe; the Sun is just one star, and there are more stars in the universe than there are grains of sands on Earth. Almost every existing star belongs to a galaxy, clusters of stars, rocks, ice, and space dust.

Between galaxies there is nothing, just darkness. There could be as many as a hundred billion galaxies. There are three main types of galaxies: spiral, elliptical, and irregular.

The majority of galaxies are spiral galaxies, with a large, central galactic bulge, which is a cluster of older stars. They look like a disk with arms circulating stars and gas. Elliptical galaxies have no particular rotation pattern. They can be spherical or extremely elongated and do not have circulating arms. Irregular galaxies have no pattern and can vary significantly in size and shape.

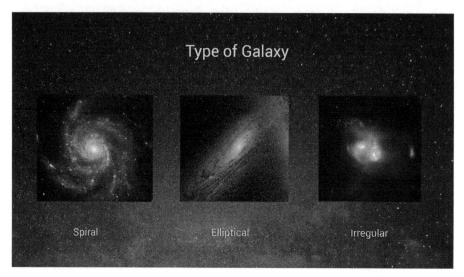

Earth's galaxy, the Milky Way, is a spiral galaxy and contains hundreds of billions of stars.

Pre-stars form from nebulas, clouds of gas and dust that can combine to form two types of small stars: brown and red dwarves. Stars produce enormous amounts energy by combining hydrogen atoms to form helium via nuclear fusion. Brown dwarves don't have enough hydrogen to undergo much fusion and fizzle out. Red dwarves have plenty of gas (hydrogen) to undergo nuclear fusion and mature into white dwarves. When they use all of their fuel (hydrogen), a burst of energy expands the star into a red giant. Red giants eventually condense into a white dwarf, which is a star approaching the end of its life.

Stars that undergo nuclear fusion will run out of gas quickly and burst in violent explosions called supernovas. This burst releases as much energy in a few seconds as the Sun will release in its entire lifetime. The particles from the explosion will condense into the smallest type of star, a neutron star; this will eventually condense into a black hole, which has such a high amount of gravity that not even light energy can escape.

Earth's sun is currently a red dwarf; it is early in its life cycle. As the center of Earth's solar system, the Sun has planets and space debris (rocks and ice) orbiting around it. The various forms of space debris include:

- Comet: made of rock and ice with a tail due to the melting ice

- Asteroid: a large rock orbiting a star. The asteroid belt lies between Mars and Jupiter and separates the smaller rocky planets (Mercury, Venus, Earth, and Mars) from the larger, gassy planets (Jupiter, Saturn, Uranus, and Neptune). Pluto is not considered a planet anymore due to its small size and distance from the Sun.

- Meteoroid: a mini-asteroid with no specific orbiting pattern

- Meteor: a meteoroid that has entered Earth's atmosphere and starts melting due to the warmth provided by our insulating greenhouse gases. These are commonly known as "falling stars."

- Meteorite: a meteor that hasn't completely burned away and lands on Earth. One is believed to have caused the Cretaceous mass extinction.

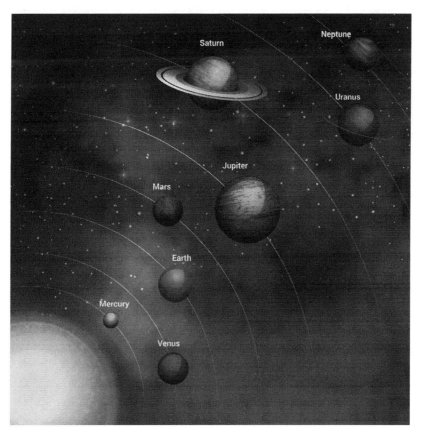

Each planet travels around the Sun in an elliptic orbit. The time it takes for one complete orbit is considered a year. The gravity of the massive Sun keeps the planets rotating, and the farther the planets are from the Sun, the slower they move and the longer their orbits. Earth's journey is little bit over 365 days a year. Because Mercury is so close to the Sun, one year for Mercury is actually only 88 Earth days. The farthest planet, Neptune, has a year that is about 60,255 Earth days long. Planets not only rotate around the Sun, but they also spin like a top. The time it takes for a planet to complete one spin is considered one day. On Earth, one day is about 24 hours. On Jupiter, one day is about nine Earth hours, while a day on Venus is 241 Earth days.

Planets may have natural satellites that rotate around them called moons. Some planets have no moons and some have dozens. In 1969, astronaut Neil Armstrong became the first man to set foot on Earth's only moon.

Relationship Among Objects in the Solar System

To understand seasons and the heating of the planet, refer to this picture:

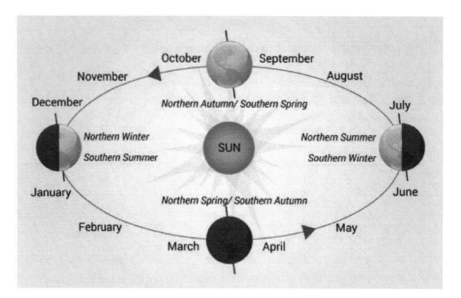

Observing July, these facts are apparent:

- Earth is tilted so that the northern hemisphere is pointing towards the sun. The southern hemisphere is pointed away.

- Because the north is tilted toward the sun, it gets more daylight in July than the southern hemisphere.

These observations explain why in July, the northern hemisphere experiences summer while the southern hemisphere experiences winter.

Notice in December that the opposite is true: the southern hemisphere gets more daylight compared to the northern hemisphere.

In spring and fall, both the north and the south get around the same sun exposure; therefore, those seasons have milder temperatures.

As the earth rotates, the distribution of light slowly changes, which explains why seasons gradually change. In June, the northern hemisphere experiences the summer solstice, the day with the most daylight. As the earth continues to orbit, its days will get shorter and shorter until the winter solstice, the shortest day of the year. Equinoxes occur in the fall and the spring and represent the days when the amount of daylight and darkness are relatively equal.

Just as the earth orbits the sun, the moon orbits the earth. The moon is much closer to earth than the sun. And even though the moon is so close to the earth, the moon contains no life because it lacks water and an atmosphere. Without greenhouse gases to blanket the sun's heat, temperatures on the moon are very low at night.

The moon is visible from the earth because it reflects sunlight at certain points in its orbit. The moon's orbit has a predictable pattern. It has two main phases, waxing and waning. When the moon is waxing, it goes from a new moon to a full moon. Notice that only the left side of the moon is dark during the waxing phase. The waning phase goes from full moon to new moon. Only the right side of the moon is dark when it is waning.

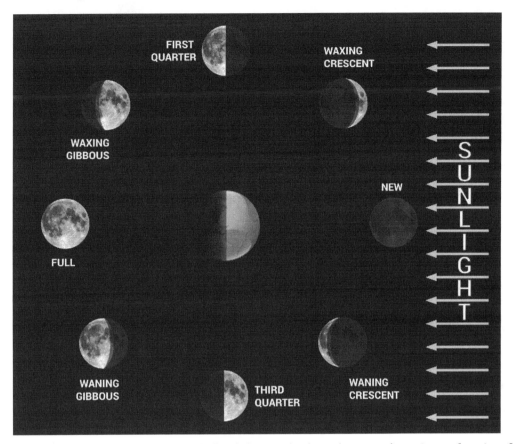

This picture shows that when the moon is behind the earth, then the moon's entire surface is reflected and we see a full moon. When the moon is between the earth and the sun, it is invisible at night, which is called a *new moon*.

Half-moons are visible when the moon and the earth are in a line that is perpendicular to the direction of sunlight. Only half of the moon reflects light to the earth at night, as seen in the figure above.

A moon that looks larger than a half moon is called a *gibbous moon*, and a moon that looks smaller is called a *crescent moon*.

Eclipses occur when the earth, the sun, and the moon are all aligned—the earth blocks the others from seeing each other. If they are perfectly lined up, a total eclipse happens, and if they are only a little lined up, there is a partial eclipse.

There are two types of eclipses: lunar and solar. A lunar eclipse occurs when the earth interrupts the sun's light reflecting off of the full moon. Earth will then cast a shadow on the moon, and particles in earth's atmosphere refract the light so some reaches the surface of the moon, causing the moon to look yellow, brown, or red.

During a new moon, when the moon is between the earth and the sun, the moon will interrupt the sunlight, casting a shadow on earth. This is called a solar eclipse.

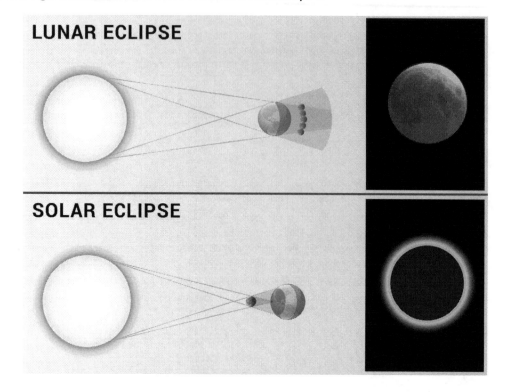

The moon also affects ocean tide due to gravity. Earth is much larger than the moon and has a very significant gravitational force that keeps us on the ground even though it is spinning very quickly. The moon is much smaller than earth, but because it is so close, it has a pulling effect on earth's oceans. When it is closest to earth, it pulls the water more, resulting in high tide. When the moon is farthest from earth, it pulls the ocean less and is called low tide.

Development of Scientific Thinking

Scientific thinking requires skepticism, empiricism, and rationalism of ideas and testable hypotheses. Skepticism constantly questions one's beliefs about theories and conclusions. Empirical evidence is physical evidence that one can see, taste, hear, or smell. Rationalism uses logical reasoning and repeated evidence and testing and helps develop new ideas about the ways things work.

There are seven basic steps to promote scientific thinking:

- Observe: Watch things closely for change.
- Compare: Review the relationship of objects. How are they the same or different?
- Sort and Organize: Group things by traits.
- Predict: Use prior knowledge to form an idea.
- Experiment: Test out the prediction.
- Evaluate: Review the findings of the experiment.
- Apply: Use findings to apply to another subject.

The seven basic steps have been developed over a long period of time. Review the development of scientific thinking from ancient times, the Scientific Revolution, and the seventeenth century.

Ancient Times

In ancient times, scientific thinking was based on authority and observation. Both systems are clearly flawed and not necessarily the best practices used for scientific thinking. Early scientists' theories, including some of Aristotle's, had been proven wrong. People did not rely on the authority of those seen as knowledgeable once data or theories were incorrectly found. On the same note, while authority was unreliable, observations were also not dependable. While observations can be helpful, they cannot be recreated, nor are they consistent.

Scientific Revolution

The Scientific Revolution took place in Europe toward the end of the Renaissance period. Developments in astronomy, biology, mathematics, and physics changed the way scientists thought about science during the early modern period. Two important ideas that changed throughout the Scientific Revolution are:

- "The law of nature" controls the universe and everything in it.
- The law of nature can be understood through observation and reasoning.

There are many fundamental scientists who contributed to the Scientific Revolution. Astronomer Galileo Galilei used telescopic observations to discover the phases of Venus, the Galilean moons (satellites of Jupiter), and sunspots. Due to his substantial impact during the Scientific Revolution, Galileo has been named "the father of science," "the father of observational astronomy," and "the father of the scientific method."

Another key figure of the Scientific Revolution was Sir Isaac Newton. Newton's laws of gravity and motion laid the foundation of today's physics. In 1687, his book *Philosophiae Naturalis Principia Mathematica* (*Mathematical Principles of Natural Philosophy*) was published. Newton's ideas set the groundwork for classical mechanics.

Seventeenth Century

During the seventeenth century, scientific thinking used inductive (keeping an open mind to observe) and deductive (using evidence to support hypotheses) thought processes. The scientific method was created in the seventeenth century. The scientific method provides a process combining hypotheses, observations, experiments, and tests. It is an ongoing process that relies on measurable and empirical data. Look at the diagram below listing the steps of the scientific method:

Importance of Observation and Evidence

Demonstrate knowledge of the basic concepts and processes of scientific experimentation (hypothesis, control, variable, replication of results, collection and communication of scientific information) Scientific questions can be derived from a multitude of sources including observation, experience, or even just wondering how something is made or works. In order to answer these questions, experiments should be designed and conducted to try to achieve a solution. At the end of an experiment, there often is no clear solution and a new experiment must be designed to test the same question. If a sound, logical solution is reached through experimentation, then it must be repeatable, by the experimenter and any other person wishing to test this solution. This entire process is commonly referred to as the scientific method.

A question or situation exists, a hypothesis (or a well-educated guess) is formulated, an experiment is designed to test this guess, a prediction is made as to what the outcome might be based upon research, and a conclusion is formed (either the guess was correct or not). This simple method is repeated over and over, as much as necessary for each question, idea, or proposed investigation.

The importance of having an independent party test a solution is one of the critical parts of scientific inquiry. This ensures an experiment is free from bias, truly repeatable, and documentable to multiple sources. Without this confirmation, people could make erroneous claims and cause disastrous results. There would be no order to the inquiry of science.

In scientific experimentation, safety, respect for living things, and the effect on an environment must be acknowledged and protected, as necessary. There exist universal rules for research in order to preserve these underlying tenets. Most researchers or facilities that demonstrate an adherence to these rules garner the most support from others in the scientific community when accepting ideas.

Major Scientific and Technological Discoveries and Inventions

Research and developments are continuously changing the science and technology fields. New and improved discoveries and inventions constantly appear as science and technology research expands. New information leads to new ideas. Updated information also allows scientists to better existing ideas.

Look at the timeline below listing major scientific and technological discoveries and inventions dating back to the first century. Notice how, as time passed, more discoveries and inventions were made.

Date	Discovery or Invention
1st Century	The Aeolipile: a simple steam turbine
2nd Century	Negative numbers, wheelbarrow, seismometer: an instrument that employs a suspended pendulum or an inverted pendulum
3rd Century	Wood block printing, turbine
4th Century	Fishing reel, oil wells
5th Century	Horse collar
6th Century	Spinning wheel, sulfur matches, toilet paper
7th Century	Porcelain, windmill
8th Century	Mechanical clock
9th Century	Gunpowder, algebra, numeric zero
10th Century	Fireworks, dry docks
11th Century	Ambulance, movable type
12th Century	Mariner's compass
13th Century	Soap, military rocket, eyeglasses
14th Century	Multistage rocket, cannon
15th Century	Rifle, printing press, bookkeeping system
16th Century	Floating dock, revolver
17th Century	Newspaper, gravity, telescope, mechanical calculator, vacuum pump, barometer, friction machine, pendulum clock
18th Century	Piano, commercial steam engine, artificial refrigeration machine, improved steam engine, carbonated water, machine tool, hot-air balloon, steamboat, telegraph, cotton gin, air compressor, smallpox vaccine, paper machine
19th Century	Early battery, morphine, steam locomotive, powered printing press, electricity, electric clock, electric telegraph, bicycle, mechanical computer, friction match, electromagnet, reaping machine, lawn mower, Morse code, fertilizer, reinforced concrete, rechargeable battery, carbon fibers, stainless steel, metal detector, arc welding, machine guns, wind turbine, ballpoint pen, zipper, plastic, periodic table, X-rays

20th Century	Vacuum cleaner, gas turbine, cellophane, television broadcast, tank, silicon, television antenna, electron microscope, programmable computer, DNA, penicillin, polyester, atomic bomb, theory of relativity, ejector seat, HIV/AIDS, quantum theory, atomic clock, nuclear power, hovercraft, hard disc drive, laser, email, pocket calculator, video game console, CD-ROM, cell phone, DVD, USB
Early 21st Century	Facebook, Apple iPod, Apple iPhone, Google Glass, birth control patch, hybrid vehicles, artificial memories, Amazon Kindle, YouTube, teleportation, bionic contact lens, camera pill, artificial liver device, clean water billboard, robotic exoskeleton (ReWalk), artificial pancreas, retinal implants

Cultural Factors that have Promoted or Discouraged Scientific Discovery and Technological Innovation

Over the years, there have been many cultural and historical factors that promote or discourage scientific discoveries and technological innovations. Science has a huge impact on society. Medicine, technology, lifestyles, and social structures are all impacted by scientific discovery and technological innovations. For example, the development of pharmaceutical drugs has not always been an easy road. Drug trials have sometimes failed, leaving lifelong or terminal circumstances for patients. At the same time, drug trials have also found cures and saved many lives.

Historically, there are many factors that have either influenced or discouraged discovery and innovation. Back in the eighteenth century, chemical solutions were often referred to as compounds affecting many chemical reactions. Another historical factor that greatly changed in science was the Copernican Revolution. Nicolaus Copernicus was an early astronomer who proposed the idea that the Earth was stationary and at the center of the universe, whereas now, it is clear that the Earth is one of the many planets orbiting the centralized sun.

Health and Safety Measures Related to Scientific Inquiry

An experiment must be carefully designed to include concerns for safety, use of proper instrumentation for measurement, systematic methods of documentation or data collection, appropriate mathematics for analysis of data and for the interpretation to draw valid conclusions. These conclusions must be explainable and verifiable by an outside source.

Relationships Among Science, Technology, and Engineering

People of all cultures around the world utilize science in order to explore questions and find solutions to problems. The systematic process of designing, conducting, and analyzing experiments is universally known and respected. These processes are time-consuming and require specific knowledge and skills. Therefore, the pursuit of science is its own career path, with many smaller paths for each respective area of study (i.e., life sciences, chemical sciences, physical sciences). Of course, each of those paths splits into even more refined areas and requires much study and dedication. Men and women alike pursue scientific questions; some are driven by pure curiosity and others are compelled by finding a faster, or even a more economical way, of performing a task or producing an object.

Not all ideas, methods, or results are popular or accepted by society. Thus, the pursuit of science is often riddled with controversy. This has been an underlying theme since the early days of astronomical discovery. Copernicus was excommunicated from his religious establishment when he announced the belief that the sun, not the Earth, was the controlling body of the heavens known to humans at the time. Despite his having documented observations and calculations, those opposed to his theory could not be convinced. Copernicus experienced great ridicule and suffering due to his scientific research and assertions. In addition, other scientists have faced adverse scrutiny for their assertions including Galileo, Albert Einstein, and Stephen Hawking. In each case, logical thought, observations, and calculations have been used to demonstrate their ideas, yet opposition to their scientific beliefs still exists.

The possibilities for careers involving science range from conducting research, to the application of science and research (engineering), to academia (teaching). All of these avenues require intensive study and a thorough understanding of the respective branch of science and its components. An important factor of studying and applying science is being able to concisely and accurately communicate knowledge to other people. Many times this is done utilizing mathematics or even through demonstration. The necessity of communicating ideas, research, and results brings people from all nationalities together. This often lends to different cultures finding common ground for research and investigation, and opens lines of communication and cooperation.

Processes of Engineering Design

The engineering design process involves a series of steps to find the solution to a problem. Oftentimes, these steps need to be repeated several times per project. The engineering design process has five common steps:

- Research
- Design and development
- Testing
- Evaluation
- Redesign

Review each step of the engineering design process independently.

Research
Research is how new information is discovered. One must start with a question that he or she is seeking answers to. The systematic form of investigation gathers, analyzes, and studies materials to develop new, or improve existing, ideas. The information used can be old or new as long as it is relevant in growing the desired outcome. There are many types of resources that can be used for research. Sources include the Internet, journal articles, libraries, government documents, and experts.

Design and Development
One of the most important elements of the engineering design process is design and development. A plan must be developed prior to taking action. It is important to have a list of necessary materials to complete the task at hand. The design and development stage should also incorporate diagrams or models into the design plan.

Throughout the design and development phase of the engineering design process, proper consideration of pros and cons must be weighed. Once a problem is identified, is there a probable solution to fix it? *Ideation* is the formation of ideas and concepts. It uses methods such as brainstorming, trigger words, synthetics, and morphological analysis. Once these ideas are in place, it is time to test them.

Testing
Testing provides researchers with the opportunity to see if their ideas work, fail, or need improvements. The ability to test a hypothesis reveals so much more information about the design. While testing, it is important to observe and control variables potentially affecting the outcome. All information should be recorded throughout testing to compare notes once each design test is completed.

Evaluation
Once testing has been completed, the information should be analyzed to see if it supports the intended outcome. The evaluation stage of the engineering design process helps determine the effectiveness of the design. While some aspects may work well, other areas may need to be improved upon. The evaluation process gives researchers the opportunity to see if they need more data or need to adjust specific variables in the design.

Redesign
The redesign process is the final stage in the engineering design process. It takes the information found in the evaluation and uses it to design and implement ideas. The redesign process fixes problems that may have occurred. The ideas are now refined and have evolved over countless tests and evaluations. Once the redesign is completed, it is time to share the results.

Practice Questions

1. Which statement about white blood cells is true?
    a. B cells are responsible for antibody production.
    b. White blood cells are made in the white/yellow cartilage before they enter the bloodstream.
    c. Platelets, a special class of white blood cell, function to clot blood and stop bleeding.
    d. The majority of white blood cells only activate during the age of puberty, which explains why children and the elderly are particularly susceptible to disease.

2. Which locations in the digestive system are sites of chemical digestion?
I. Mouth
II. Stomach
III. Small Intestine

    a. II only
    b. III only
    c. II and III only
    d. I, II, and III

3. What is the theory that certain physical and behavioral survival traits give a species an evolutionary advantage?
    a. Gradualism
    b. Evolutionary advantage
    c. Punctuated equilibrium
    d. Natural selection

4. Which of the following structures is unique to eukaryotic cells?
    a. Cell walls
    b. Nucleuses
    c. Cell membranes
    d. Vacuoles

5. Which is the cellular organelle used for digestion to recycle materials?
    a. The Golgi apparatus
    b. The lysosome
    c. The centrioles
    d. The mitochondria

6. Which of the following leads to diversity in meiotic division but not mitotic division?
    a. Tetrad formation
    b. Disassembly of the mitotic spindle
    c. Extra/fewer chromosomes due to nondisjunction
    d. Fertilization by multiple sperm

7. Why do arteries have valves?
    a. They have valves to maintain high blood pressure so that capillaries diffuse nutrients properly.
    b. Their valves are designed to prevent backflow due to their low blood pressure.
    c. They have valves due to a leftover trait from evolution that, like the appendix, are useless.
    d. They do not have valves, but veins do.

8. If the pressure in the pulmonary artery is increased above normal, which chamber of the heart will be affected first?
    a. The right atrium
    b. The left atrium
    c. The right ventricle
    d. The left ventricle

9. What is the purpose of sodium bicarbonate when released into the lumen of the small intestine?
    a. It works to chemically digest fats in the chyme.
    b. It decreases the pH of the chyme so as to prevent harm to the intestine.
    c. It works to chemically digest proteins in the chyme.
    d. It increases the pH of the chyme so as to prevent harm to the intestine.

10. Which of the following describes a reflex arc?
    a. The storage and recall of memory
    b. The maintenance of visual and auditory acuity
    c. The autoregulation of heart rate and blood pressure
    d. A stimulus and response controlled by the spinal cord

11. Describe the synthesis of the lagging strand of DNA.
    a. DNA polymerases synthesize DNA continuously after initially attaching to a primase.
    b. DNA polymerases synthesize DNA discontinuously in pieces called Okazaki fragments after initially attaching to primases.
    c. DNA polymerases synthesize DNA discontinuously in pieces called Okazaki fragments after initially attaching to RNA primers.
    d. DNA polymerases synthesize DNA discontinuously in pieces called Okazaki fragments which are joined together in the end by a DNA helicase.

12. Which of the following are chief factors that are associated with increased birth and fertility rates?
I. Public education
II. Low infant mortality
III. Low urbanization
IV. Increased cholesterol intake
V. No access to contraception

    a. I and II only
    b. II and V only
    c. I, II, and IV only
    d. III and V only

13. Which of the following characterizes developed countries in Stage 4 of the Demographic Transition Model?
    a. Low birth rate and high immigration rate.
    b. Low birth rate and low mortality rate.
    c. High birth rate and rapidly decreasing death rate.
    d. High birth rate and high emigration rate.

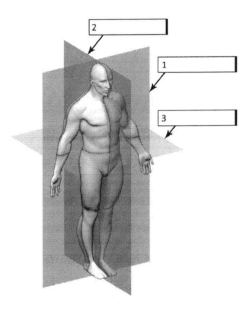

14. Identify the correct sequence of the 3 primary body planes as numbered 1, 2, and 3 in the above image.
   a. Plane 1 is coronal, plane 2 is sagittal, and plane 3 is transverse.
   b. Plane 1 is sagittal, plane 2 is coronal, and plane 3 is medial.
   c. Plane 1 is coronal, plane 2 is sagittal, and plane 3 is medial.
   d. Plane 1 is sagittal, plane 2 is coronal, and plane 3 is transverse.

15. Which of the following is NOT a major function of the respiratory system in humans?
   a. It provides a large surface area for gas exchange of oxygen and carbon dioxide.
   b. It helps regulate the blood's pH.
   c. It helps cushion the heart against jarring motions.
   d. It is responsible for vocalization.

16. Which of the following is NOT a function of the forebrain?
   a. To regulate blood pressure and heart rate
   b. To perceive and interpret emotional responses like fear and anger
   c. To perceive and interpret visual input from the eyes
   d. To integrate voluntary movement

17. What is the major difference between somatic and germline mutations?
   a. Somatic mutations usually benefit the individual while germline mutations usually harm them.
   b. Since germline mutations only affect one cell, they are less noticeable than the rapidly dividing somatic cells.
   c. Somatic mutations are not expressed for several generations, but germline mutations are expressed immediately.
   d. Germline mutations are usually inherited while somatic mutations will affect only the individual.

18. The sun is a major external source of energy. Which of the following is the best demonstration of this?

    a. Flowers tend to bloom in the morning, after dawn.
    b. Large animals like bears do not need to eat food when hibernating.
    c. Deserts can reach scorching temperatures in daylight but subzero temperatures at night.
    d. The tides of the ocean are highly dependent on the movement of the Moon, the celestial body that is highly reflective to sunlight.

19. Find the lowest coefficients that will balance the following combustion equation.

$$\_\_C_2H_{10} + \_\_O_2 \rightarrow \_\_H_2O + \_\_CO_2$$

    a. 1:5:5:2
    b. 4:10:20:8
    c. 2:9:10:4
    d. 2:5:10:4

Answer Explanations

1. A: When activated, B cells create antibodies against specific antigens. White blood cells are generated in yellow bone marrow, not cartilage. Platelets are not a type of white blood cell and are typically cell fragments produced by megakaryocytes. White blood cells are active throughout nearly all of one's life and have not been shown to specially activate or deactivate because of life events like puberty or menopause.

2. D: Mechanical digestion is physical digestion of food and tearing it into smaller pieces using force. This occurs in the stomach and mouth. Chemical digestion involves chemically changing the food and breaking it down into small organic compounds that can be utilized by the cell to build molecules. The salivary glands in the mouth secrete amylase that breaks down starch, which begins chemical digestion. The stomach contains enzymes such as pepsinogen/pepsin and gastric lipase, which chemically digest protein and fats, respectively. The small intestine continues to digest protein using the enzymes trypsin and chymotrypsin. It also digests fats with the help of bile from the liver and lipase from the pancreas. These organs act as exocrine glands because they secrete substances through a duct. Carbohydrates are digested in the small intestine with the help of pancreatic amylase, gut bacterial flora and fauna, and brush border enzymes like lactose. Brush border enzymes are contained in the towel-like microvilli in the small intestine that soak up nutrients.

3. D: The theory that certain physical and behavioral traits give a species an evolutionary advantage is called natural selection. Charles Darwin developed the theory of natural selection that explains the evolutionary process. He postulated that heritable genetic differences could aid an organism's chance of survival in its environment. The organisms with favorable traits pass genes to their offspring, and because they have more reproductive success than those that do not contain the adaptation, the favorable gene spreads throughout the population. Those that do not contain the adaptation often extinguish, thus their genes are not passed on. In this way, nature "selects" for the organisms that have more fitness in their environment. Birds with bright colored feathers and cacti with spines are examples of "fit" organisms.

4. B: The structure exclusively found in eukaryotic cells is the nucleus. Animal, plant, fungi, and protist cells are all eukaryotic. DNA is contained within the nucleus of eukaryotic cells, and they also have membrane-bound organelles that perform complex intracellular metabolic activities. Prokaryotic cells (archae and bacteria) do not have a nucleus or other membrane-bound organelles and are less complex than eukaryotic cells.

5. B: The cell structure responsible for cellular storage, digestion and waste removal is the lysosome. Lysosomes are like recycle bins. They are filled with digestive enzymes that facilitate catabolic reactions to regenerate monomers. The Golgi apparatus is designed to tag, package, and ship out proteins destined for other cells or locations. The centrioles typically play a large role only in cell division when they ratchet the chromosomes from the mitotic plate to the poles of the cell. The mitochondria are involved in energy production and are the powerhouses of the cell.

6. A: Crossing over, or genetic recombination, is the rearrangement of chromosomal sections in tetrads during meiosis, and it results in each gamete having a different combination of alleles than other gametes. The disassembly of the mitotic spindle happens only after telophase and is not related to diversity. While nondisjunction does cause diversity in division and is highly noticeable in gametes formed through meiosis, it can also happen through mitotic division in somatic cells. Although an egg being fertilized by multiple sperm would lead to interesting diversity in the offspring (and possibly fraternal twins), this is not strictly a byproduct of meiotic division.

7. D: Veins have valves, but arteries do not. Valves in veins are designed to prevent backflow, since they are the furthest blood vessels from the pumping action of the heart and steadily increase in volume (which decreases the available pressure). Capillaries diffuse nutrients properly because of their thin walls and high surface area and are not particularly dependent on positive pressure.

8. C: The blood leaves the right ventricle through a semi-lunar valve and goes through the pulmonary artery to the lungs. Any increase in pressure in the artery will eventually affect the contractibility of the right ventricle. Blood enters the right atrium from the superior and inferior venae cava veins, and blood leaves the right atrium through the tricuspid valve to the right ventricle. Blood enters the left atrium from the pulmonary veins carrying oxygenated blood from the lungs. Blood flows from the left atrium to the left ventricle through the mitral valve and leaves the left ventricle through a semi-lunar valve to enter the aorta.

9. D: Sodium bicarbonate, a very effective base, has the chief function to increase the pH of the chyme. Chyme leaving the stomach has a very low pH, due to the high amounts of acid that are used to digest and break down food. If this is not neutralized, the walls of the small intestine will be damaged and may form ulcers. Sodium bicarb is produced by the pancreas and released in response to pyloric stimulation so that it can neutralize the acid. It has little to no digestive effect.

10. D: A reflex arc is a simple nerve pathway involving a stimulus, a synapse, and a response that is controlled by the spinal cord—not the brain. The knee-jerk reflex is an example of a reflex arc. The stimulus is the hammer touching the tendon, reaching the synapse in the spinal cord by an afferent pathway. The response is the resulting muscle contraction reaching the muscle by an efferent pathway. None of the remaining processes is a simple reflex. Memories are processed and stored in the hippocampus in the limbic system. The visual center is located in the occipital lobe, while auditory processing occurs in the temporal lobe. The sympathetic and parasympathetic divisions of the autonomic nervous system control heart and blood pressure.

11. C: The lagging strand of DNA falls behind the leading strand because of its discontinuous synthesis. DNA helicase unzips the DNA helices so that synthesis can take place, and RNA primers are created by the RNA primase for the polymerases to attach to and build from. The lagging strand is synthesizing DNA in a direction that is hard for the polymerase to build, so multiple primers are laid down so that the entire length of DNA can be synthesized simultaneously, piecemeal. These short pieces of DNA being synthesized are known as Okazaki fragments and are joined together by DNA ligase.

12. D: Birth and fertility rates are typically higher in developing countries than in developed countries, and there are a wide variety of reasons for this. Some are rational or obvious, like how access to contraception decreases the number of pregnancies a woman is susceptible to, while others are justifiable, like how high infant mortality would cause women to want to have more children so that more of them make it to adulthood. Other correlations are evident, but not so easily explainable: Public education and urbanization rates are inversely correlated with national birth rates, so that if one goes up, the other goes down. Cholesterol intake has no proven association with birth rates.

13. B: In the Demographic Transition Model, developed countries tend to have low death or mortality rates because of improved healthcare and low birth rates due to access to contraception and myriad other factors. A high birth rate combined with a rapidly decreasing death rate indicates a country that is in the Early Expanding Stage 2 of the DTM, and neither emigration nor immigration plays a major role in any of the DTM stages.

14. A: The three primary body planes are coronal, sagittal, and transverse. The coronal or frontal plane, named for the plane in which a corona or halo might appear in old paintings, divides the body vertically into front and back sections. The sagittal plane, named for the path an arrow might take when shot at the body, divides the body vertically into right and left sections. The transverse plane divides the body horizontally into upper or superior and lower or inferior sections. There is no medial plane, per se. The anatomical direction medial simply references a location close or closer to the center of the body than another location.

15. C: Although the lungs may provide some cushioning for the heart when the body is violently struck, this is not a major function of the respiratory system. Its most notable function is that of gas exchange for oxygen and carbon dioxide, but it also plays a vital role in the regulation of blood pH. The aqueous form of carbon dioxide, carbonic acid, is a major pH buffer of the blood, and the respiratory system directly controls how much carbon dioxide stays and is released from the blood through respiration. The respiratory system also enables vocalization and forms the basis for the mode of speech and language used by most humans.

16. A: The forebrain contains the cerebrum, the thalamus, the hypothalamus, and the limbic system. The limbic system is chiefly responsible for the perception of emotions through the amygdale, while the cerebrum interprets sensory input and generates movement. Specifically, the occipital lobe receives visual input, and the primary motor cortex in the frontal lobe is the controller of voluntary movement. The hindbrain, specifically the medulla oblongata and brain stem, control and regulate blood pressure and heart rate.

17. D: Germline mutations in eggs and sperm are permanent, can be on the chromosomal level, and will be inherited by offspring. Somatic mutations cannot affect eggs and sperm, and therefore are not inherited by offspring. Mutations of either kind are rarely beneficial to the individual, but do not necessarily harm them. Germline cells divide much more rapidly than do somatic cells, and a mutation in a sex cell would promulgate and affect many thousands of its daughter cells.

18. C: Deserts' temperatures are extremely hot in the day and cold at night because of the warming effects of the sun's solar rays, so this is the best example of the sun's energy. Although some flowers do tend to bloom after dawn, this is probably due to day/night cycles regulated by the presence of light rather than intense amounts of energy. Hibernating animals tend to use large repositories of stored nutrients as energy sources rather than relying on the sun's energy, and they may in fact be in caves or hidden underground to shelter them from the sun or weather. The tides are more dependent on the moon due to its gravity rather than any effects its albedo moonlight may have.

19. C: 2:9:10:4. These are the coefficients that follow the law of conservation of matter. The coefficient times the subscript of each element should be the same on both sides of the equation.

Mathematics

Numbers and Operations

Base-10 Numerals, Number Names, and Expanded Form

Numbers used in everyday life are constituted in a base-10 system. Each digit in a number, depending on its location, represents some multiple of 10, or quotient of 10 when dealing with decimals. Each digit to the left of the decimal point represents a higher multiple of 10. Each digit to the right of the decimal point represents a quotient of a higher multiple of 10 for the divisor. For example, consider the number 7,631.42. The digit one represents simply the number one. The digit 3 represents 3×10. The digit 6 represents $6 \times 10 \times 10$ (or 6×100). The digit 7 represents $7 \times 10 \times 10 \times 10$ (or 7×1000). The digit 4 represents $4 \div 10$. The digit 2 represents $(2 \div 10) \div 10$, or $2 \div (10 \times 10)$ or $2 \div 100$.

A number is written in expanded form by expressing it as the sum of the value of each of its digits. The expanded form in the example above, which is written with the highest value first down to the lowest value, is expressed as: $7,000 + 600 + 30 + 1 + .4 + .02$.

When verbally expressing a number, the integer part of the number (the numbers to the left of the decimal point) resembles the expanded form without the addition between values. In the above example, the numbers read "seven thousand six hundred thirty-one." When verbally expressing the decimal portion of a number, the number is read as a whole number, followed by the place value of the furthest digit (non-zero) to the right. In the above example, 0.42 is read "forty-two hundredths." Reading the number 7,631.42 in its entirety is expressed as "seven thousand six hundred thirty-one and forty-two hundredths." The word *and* is used between the integer and decimal parts of the number.

Scientific Notation

Scientific Notation is used to represent numbers that are either very small or very large. For example, the distance to the sun is approximately 150,000,000,000 meters. Instead of writing this number with so many zeros, it can be written in scientific notation as $1.5 * 10^{11}$ meters. The same is true for very small numbers, but the exponent becomes negative. If the mass of a human cell is 0.000000000001 kilograms, that measurement can be easily represented by $1.0 * 10^{-12}$ kilograms. In both situations, scientific notation makes the measurement easier to read and understand. Each number is translated to an expression with one digit in the tens place times an expression corresponding to the zeros.

When two measurements are given and both involve scientific notation, it is important to know how these interact with each other:

- In addition and subtraction, the exponent on the ten must be the same before any operations are performed on the numbers. For example, $(1.3 * 10^4) + (3.0 * 10^3)$ cannot be added until one of the exponents on the ten is changed. The $3.0 * 10^3$ can be changed to $0.3 * 10^4$, then the 1.3 and 0.3 can be added. The answer comes out to be $1.6 * 10^4$.

- For multiplication, the first numbers can be multiplied and then the exponents on the tens can be added. Once an answer is formed, it may have to be converted into scientific notation again depending on the change that occurred.

  - The following is an example of multiplication with scientific notation: $(4.5 * 10^3) * (3.0 * 10^{-5}) = 13.5 * 10^{-2}$. Since this answer is not in scientific notation, the decimal is moved over to the left one unit, and 1 is added to the ten's exponent. This results in the final answer: $1.35 * 10^{-1}$.

- For division, the first numbers are divided, and the exponents on the tens are subtracted. Again, the answer may need to be converted into scientific notation form, depending on the type of changes that occurred during the problem.

- *Order of magnitude* relates to scientific notation and is the total count of powers of 10 in a number. For example, there are 6 orders of magnitude in 1,000,000. If a number is raised by an order of magnitude, it is multiplied times 10. Order of magnitude can be helpful in estimating results using very large or small numbers. An answer should make sense in terms of its order of magnitude.

  - For example, if area is calculated using two dimensions with 6 orders of magnitude, because area involves multiplication, the answer should have around 12 orders of magnitude. Also, answers can be estimated by rounding to the largest place value in each number. For example, 5,493,302 * 2,523,100 can be estimated by 5 * 3 = 15 with 6 orders of magnitude.

Rounding

Rounding numbers changes the given number to a simpler and less accurate number than the exact given number. Rounding allows for easier calculations which estimate the results of using the exact given number. The accuracy of the estimate and ease of use depends on the place value to which the number is rounded. Rounding numbers consists of:

- Determining what place value the number is being rounded to
- Examining the digit to the right of the desired place value to decide whether to round up or keep the digit
- Replacing all digits to the right of the desired place value with zeros

To round 746,311 to the nearest ten thousands, the digit in the ten thousands place should be located first. In this case, this digit is 4 (746,311). Then, the digit to its right is examined. If this digit is 5 or greater, the number will be rounded up by increasing the digit in the desired place by one. If the digit to the right of the place value being rounded is 4 or less, the number will be kept the same. For the given example, the digit being examined is a 6, which means that the number will be rounded up by increasing the digit to the left by one. Therefore, the digit 4 is changed to a 5. Finally, to write the rounded number, any digits to the left of the place value being rounded remain the same and any to its right are replaced with zeros. For the given example, rounding 746,311 to the nearest ten thousand will produce 750,000. To round 746,311 to the nearest hundred, the digit to the right of the three in the hundreds place is examined to determine whether to round up or keep the same number. In this case, that digit is a one, so the number will be kept the same and any digits to its right will be replaced with zeros. The resulting rounded number is 746,300.

Rounding place values to the right of the decimal follows the same procedure, but digits being replaced by zeros can simply be dropped. To round 3.752891 to the nearest thousandth, the desired place value is located (3.752891) and the digit to the right is examined. In this case, the digit 8 indicates that the number will be rounded up, and the 2 in the thousandths place will increase to a 3. Rounding up and replacing the digits to the right of the thousandths place produces 3.753000 which is equivalent to 3.753. Therefore, the zeros are not necessary, and the rounded number should be written as 3.753.

When rounding up, if the digit to be increased is a 9, the digit to its left is increased by 1 and the digit in the desired place value is changed to a zero. For example, the number 1,598 rounded to the nearest ten is 1,600. Another example shows the number 43.72961 rounded to the nearest thousandth is 43.730 or 43.73.

Determining the Reasonableness of Results

When solving math word problems, the solution obtained should make sense within the given scenario. The step of checking the solution will reduce the possibility of a calculation error or a solution that may be *mathematically* correct but not applicable in the real world. Consider the following scenarios:

A problem states that Lisa got 24 out of 32 questions correct on a test and asks to find the percentage of correct answers. To solve the problem, a student divided 32 by 24 to get 1.33, and then multiplied by 100 to get 133 percent. By examining the solution within the context of the problem, the student should recognize that getting all 32 questions correct will produce a perfect score of 100 percent. Therefore, a score of 133 percent with 8 incorrect answers does not make sense, and the calculations should be checked.

A problem states that the maximum weight on a bridge cannot exceed 22,000 pounds. The problem asks to find the maximum number of cars that can be on the bridge at one time if each car weighs 4,000 pounds. To solve this problem, a student divided 22,000 by 4,000 to get an answer of 5.5. By examining the solution within the context of the problem, the student should recognize that although the calculations are mathematically correct, the solution does not make sense. Half of a car on a bridge is not possible, so the student should determine that a maximum of 5 cars can be on the bridge at the same time.

Mental Math Estimation

Once a result is determined to be logical within the context of a given problem, the result should be evaluated by its nearness to the expected answer. This is performed by approximating given values to perform mental math. Numbers should be rounded to the nearest value possible to check the initial results.

Consider the following example: A problem states that a customer is buying a new sound system for their home. The customer purchases a stereo for $435, 2 speakers for $67 each, and the necessary cables for $12. The customer chooses an option that allows him to spread the costs over equal payments for 4 months. How much will the monthly payments be?

After making calculations for the problem, a student determines that the monthly payment will be $145.25. To check the accuracy of the results, the student rounds each cost to the nearest ten (440 + 70 + 70 + 10) and determines that the total is approximately $590. Dividing by 4 months gives an approximate monthly payment of $147.50. Therefore, the student can conclude that the solution of $145.25 is very close to what should be expected.

When rounding, the place-value that is used in rounding can make a difference. Suppose the student had rounded to the nearest hundred for the estimation. The result ($400 + 100 + 100 + 0 = 600$; $600 \div 4 = 150$) will show that the answer is reasonable, but not as close to the actual value as rounding to the nearest ten.

Properties of Rational and Irrational Numbers

All real numbers can be separated into two groups: rational and irrational numbers. *Rational numbers* are any numbers that can be written as a fraction, such as $\frac{1}{3}, \frac{7}{4}$, and -25. Alternatively, *irrational numbers* are those that cannot be written as a fraction, such as numbers with never-ending, non-repeating decimal values. Many irrational numbers result from taking roots, such as $\sqrt{2}$ or $\sqrt{3}$. An irrational number may be written as 34.5684952.... The ellipsis (...) represents the line of numbers after the decimal that does not repeat and is never-ending.

When rational and irrational numbers interact, there are different types of number outcomes. For example, when adding or multiplying two rational numbers, the result is a rational number. No matter what two fractions are added or multiplied together, the result can always be written as a fraction. The following expression shows two rational numbers multiplied together: $\frac{3}{8} * \frac{4}{7} = \frac{12}{56}$. The product of these two fractions is another fraction that can be simplified to $\frac{3}{14}$.

As another interaction, rational numbers added to irrational numbers will always result in irrational numbers. No part of any fraction can be added to a never-ending, non-repeating decimal to make a rational number. The same result is true when multiplying a rational and irrational number. Taking a fractional part of a never-ending, non-repeating decimal will always result in another never-ending, non-repeating decimal. An example of the product of rational and irrational numbers is shown in the following expression: $2 * \sqrt{7}$.

The last type of interaction concerns two irrational numbers, where the sum or product may be rational or irrational depending on the numbers being used. The following expression shows a rational sum from two irrational numbers: $\sqrt{3} + \left(6 - \sqrt{3}\right) = 6$. The product of two irrational numbers can be rational or irrational. A rational result can be seen in the following expression: $\sqrt{2} * \sqrt{8} = \sqrt{2 * 8} = \sqrt{16} = 4$. An irrational result can be seen in the following: $\sqrt{3} * \sqrt{2} = \sqrt{6}$.

Prime and Composite Numbers

Whole numbers are classified as either prime or composite. A prime number can only be divided evenly by itself and one. For example, the number 11 can only be divided evenly by 11 and one; therefore, 11 is a prime number. A helpful way to visualize a prime number is to use concrete objects and try to divide them into equal piles. If dividing 11 coins, the only way to divide them into equal piles is to create 1 pile of 11 coins or to create 11 piles of 1 coin each. Other examples of prime numbers include 2, 3, 5, 7, 13, 17, and 19.

A composite number is any whole number that is not a prime number. A composite number is a number that can be divided evenly by one or more numbers other than itself and one. For example, the number 6 can be divided evenly by 2 and 3. Therefore, 6 is a composite number. If dividing 6 coins into equal piles, the possibilities are 1 pile of 6 coins, 2 piles of 3 coins, 3 piles of 2 coins, or 6 piles of 1 coin. Other examples of composite numbers include 4, 8, 9, 10, 12, 14, 15, 16, 18, and 20.

To determine if a number is a prime or composite number, the number is divided by every whole number greater than one and less than its own value. If it divides evenly by any of these numbers, then the number is composite. If it does not divide evenly by any of these numbers, then the number is prime. For example, when attempting to divide the number 5 by 2, 3, and 4, none of these numbers divide evenly. Therefore, 5 must be a prime number.

Factors and Multiples of Numbers

The factors of a number are all integers that can be multiplied by another integer to produce the given number. For example, 2 is multiplied by 3 to produce 6. Therefore, 2 and 3 are both factors of 6. Similarly, $1 \times 6 = 6$ and $2 \times 3 = 6$, so 1, 2, 3, and 6 are all factors of 6. Another way to explain a factor is to say that a given number divides evenly by each of its factors to produce an integer. For example, 6 does not divide evenly by 5. Therefore, 5 is not a factor of 6.

Multiples of a given number are found by taking that number and multiplying it by any other whole number. For example, 3 is a factor of 6, 9, and 12. Therefore, 6, 9, and 12 are multiples of 3. The multiples of any number are an infinite list. For example, the multiples of 5 are 5, 10, 15, 20, and so on. This list continues without end. A list of multiples is used in finding the least common multiple, or LCM, for fractions when a common denominator is needed. The denominators are written down and their multiples listed until a common number is found in both lists. This common number is the LCM.

Prime factorization breaks down each factor of a whole number until only prime numbers remain. All composite numbers can be factored into prime numbers. For example, the prime factors of 12 are 2, 2, and 3 ($2 \times 2 \times 3 = 12$). To produce the prime factors of a number, the number is factored and any composite numbers are continuously factored until the result is the product of prime factors only. A factor tree, such as the one below, is helpful when exploring this concept.

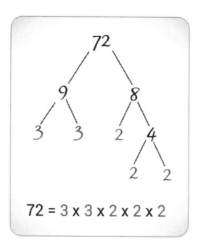

$72 = 3 \times 3 \times 2 \times 2 \times 2$

Functions and Algebra

Expressing Relationships Algebraically

Algebraic expressions are made up of numbers, variables, and combinations of the two, using mathematical operations. Expressions can be rewritten based on their factors. For example, the expression $6x + 4$ can be rewritten as $2(3x + 2)$ because 2 is a factor of both $6x$ and 4. More complex expressions can also be rewritten based on their factors. The expression $x^4 - 16$ can be rewritten as

$(x^2 - 4)(x^2 + 4)$. This is a different type of factoring, where a difference of squares is factored into a sum and difference of the same two terms. With some expressions, the factoring process is simple and only leads to a different way to represent the expression. With others, factoring and rewriting the expression leads to more information about the given problem.

In the following quadratic equation, factoring the binomial leads to finding the zeros of the function: $x^2 - 5x + 6 = y$. This equations factors into $(x - 3)(x - 2) = y$, where 2 and 3 are found to be the zeros of the function when y is set equal to zero. The zeros of any function are the x-values where the graph of the function on the coordinate plane crosses the x-axis.

Factoring an equation is a simple way to rewrite the equation and find the zeros, but factoring is not possible for every quadratic. Completing the square is one way to find zeros when factoring is not an option. The following equation cannot be factored: $x^2 + 10x - 9 = 0$. The first step in this method is to move the constant to the right side of the equation, making it $x^2 + 10x = 9$. Then, the coefficient of x is divided by 2 and squared. This number is then added to both sides of the equation, to make the equation still true. For this example, $\left(\frac{10}{2}\right)^2 = 25$ is added to both sides of the equation to obtain: $x^2 + 10x + 25 = 9 + 25$. This expression simplifies to $x^2 + 10x + 25 = 34$, which can then be factored into $(x + 5)^2 = 34$. Solving for x then involves taking the square root of both sides and subtracting 5. This leads to two zeros of the function: $x = \pm\sqrt{34} - 5$. Depending on the type of answer the question seeks, a calculator may be used to find exact numbers.

Given a quadratic equation in standard form— $ax^2 + bx + c = 0$—the sign of a tells whether the function has a minimum value or a maximum value. If $a > 0$, the graph opens up and has a minimum value. If $a < 0$, the graph opens down and has a maximum value. Depending on the way the quadratic equation is written, multiplication may need to occur before a max/min value is determined.

Exponential expressions can also be rewritten, just as quadratic equations. Properties of exponents must be understood. Multiplying two exponential expressions with the same base involves adding the exponents: $a^m a^n = a^{m+n}$. Dividing two exponential expressions with the same base involves subtracting the exponents: $\frac{a^m}{a^n} = a^{m-n}$. Raising an exponential expression to another exponent includes multiplying the exponents: $(a^m)^n = a^{mn}$. The zero power always gives a value of 1: $a^0 = 1$. Raising either a product or a fraction to a power involves distributing that power: $(ab)^m = a^m b^m$ and $\left(\frac{a}{b}\right)^m = \frac{a^m}{b^m}$. Finally, raising a number to a negative exponent is equivalent to the reciprocal including the positive exponent: $a^{-m} = \frac{1}{a^m}$.

Solving Linear Equations and Inequalities

The sum of a number and 5 is equal to the number times -8. To find this unknown number, a simple equation can be written to represent the problem. Key words such as *sum*, *equal*, and *times* are used to form the following equation with one variable: $n + 5 = -8n$. When solving for n, opposite operations are used. First, n is subtracted from $-8n$ across the equals sign, resulting in $5 = -9n$. Then, -9 is divided on both sides, leaving $n = -\frac{5}{9}$. This solution can be graphed on the number line with a dot as shown below:

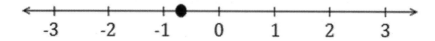

If the problem were changed to say, "The sum of a number and 5 is greater than the number times -8," then an inequality would be used instead of an equation. Using key words again, *greater than* is represented by the symbol >. The inequality $n + 5 > -8n$ can be solved using the same techniques, resulting in $n < -\frac{5}{9}$. The only time solving an inequality differs from solving an equation is when a negative number is either multiplied times or divided by each side of the inequality. The sign must be switched in this case. For this example, the graph of the solution changes to the following graph because the solution represents all real numbers less than $-\frac{5}{9}$. Not included in this solution is $-\frac{5}{9}$ because it is a *less than* symbol, not *equal to*.

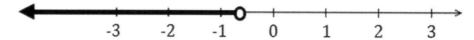

Equations and inequalities in two variables represent a relationship. Jim owns a car wash and charges $40 per car. The rent for the facility is $350 per month. An equation can be written to relate the number of cars Jim cleans to the money he makes per month. Let x represent the number of cars and y represent the profit Jim makes each month from the car wash. The equation $y = 40x - 350$ can be used to show Jim's profit or loss. Since this equation has two variables, the coordinate plane can be used to show the relationship and predict profit or loss for Jim. The following graph shows that Jim must wash at least nine cars to pay the rent, where $x = 9$. Anything nine cars and above yield a profit shown in the value on the y-axis.

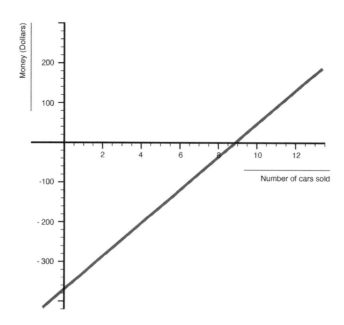

With a single equation in two variables, the solutions are limited only by the situation the equation represents. When two equations or inequalities are used, more constraints are added. For example, in a system of linear equations, there is often—although not always—only one answer. The point of intersection of two lines is the solution. For a system of inequalities, there are infinitely many answers.

The intersection of two solution sets gives the solution set of the system of inequalities. In the following graph, this is the darker shaded region where the shading for the two inequalities overlaps. Any set of x and y found in that region satisfies both inequalities. The line with the positive slope is solid, meaning the values on that line are included in the solution. The with the negative line is dotted, so the coordinates on that line are not included.

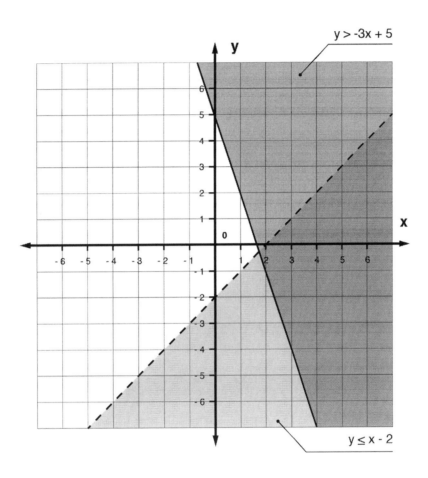

Formulas with two variables are equations used to represent a specific relationship. For example, the formula $d = rt$ represents the relationship between distance, rate, and time. If Bob travels at a rate of 35 miles per hour on his road trip from Westminster to Seneca, the formula $d = 35t$ can be used to represent his distance traveled in a specific length of time. Formulas can also be used to show different roles of the variables, transformed without any given numbers. Solving for r, the formula becomes $\frac{d}{t} = r$. The t is moved over by division so that *rate* is a function of distance and time.

Algebraic Manipulations

Consider real numbers $a, b,$ and c. In algebra, the properties of equality state that if $a = b$, then $a + c = b + c, a - c = b - c, ac = bc,$ and $\frac{a}{c} = \frac{b}{c}$ if $c \neq 0$. These properties consist of the basic techniques that allow for algebraic equations to be solved. The order of operations clarifies the order in which mathematical operations must be performed. When grouping symbols such as parentheses and brackets are present within a mathematical expression, the expression within those symbols must be calculated first. Secondly, any exponents must be evaluated. Then, multiplication and division are performed in order from left to right. Finally, addition and subtraction are performed from left to right. The order of operations can be remembered by the mnemonic device PEMDAS, which stands for Parenthesis, Exponents, Multiplication and Division, and Addition and Subtraction. An expression in which order of operations must be used is $3(5^2 + 8) - 5 \cdot 2 = 3(25 + 8) - 5 \cdot 2 = 3(33) - 5 \cdot 2 = 99 - 10 = 89$.

Three important number properties exist in algebraic manipulations. Both addition and multiplication are associative, which means that grouping within this operation doesn't change the result. The property states that $(a + b) + c = a + (b + c)$ and $(a \cdot b) \cdot c = a \cdot (bc)$. Addition and multiplication are both commutative, which means order doesn't matter. Specifically, $a + b = b + a$ and $a \cdot b = b \cdot a$. Finally, the distributive property defines multiplication over addition. It states that $a \cdot (b + c) = (a \cdot b) + (a \cdot c)$. Order doesn't matter when adding or multiplying. However, order matters when subtracting and dividing.

Together, these properties allow for both algebraic equations to be solved. Consider the equation $3(x + 2) = 5x - 4$. The distributive property can be used first to rewrite as $3x + 6 = 5x - 4$. Then, properties of equality allow 4 to be added to both sides and $3x$ to be subtracted from both sides, resulting in $10 = 2x$. Finally, divide both sides by 5 to obtain the solution, $x = 5$.

Word Problems in Algebra

Fractions appear in everyday situations. They can be simple fractions or appear in the form of ratios, proportions, and percentages. A ratio compares two different quantities. For example, in a classroom of 30 students, if there are 13 girls and 17 boys, the ratio of girls to boys is 13 to 17. This expression can also be written as $\frac{13}{17}$ or 13:17. The order matters when formulating ratios. For the same scenario, the ratio of boys to girls is 17 to 13, which is equivalent to $\frac{17}{13}$ or 17:13. A proportion is an equation involving two ratios, for example: $\frac{a}{b} = \frac{c}{d}$ or a:b = c:d. Usually, in a ratio, one of the quantities is unknown, and cross-multiplication can be used to solve for that unknown quantity. Consider $\frac{2}{5} = \frac{x}{50}$, where x is unknown. Cross-multiplication results in $100 = 5x$, which is solved as $x = 20$.

Percentages are defined as parts per hundred. They are ratios in which the second term is 100. For example, 65% is 65:100 or $\frac{65}{100}$.

Word problems can contain fractions, ratios, proportions, and percentages. Consider the following example. Let's say you have 4.5 cups of spaghetti in the refrigerator and want to serve it to 4 people in equal amounts—how many cups would each person get? To solve this problem, convert the 4.5 cups a mixed number and then divide by 4. Dividing by 4 is the same as multiplying times 1/4. Therefore, the answer is $\frac{9}{2} \cdot \frac{1}{4} = \frac{9}{8}$ of a cup. $\frac{9}{8}$ is an improper fraction, and can be written as the mixed number $1\frac{1}{8}$ to represent 1 and $\frac{1}{8}$ cups of spaghetti.

Here's a word problem that uses ratios and proportions: If 14 out of 200 parts are defective, how many would you expect to be defective out of 500 parts? The following proportion would be solved with x as the unknown quantity: $\frac{14}{200} = \frac{x}{500}$. Cross-multiplying results in $200x = 7,000$ which is solved to obtain $x = 35$. Therefore, one would expect 35 parts to be defective.

Finally, here's an example of a word problem with a percent: 40% of a baseball pitcher's pitches are strikes. If he throws 500 pitches, how many should be strikes? To solve this problem, the percent would be changed into its decimal form and then multiplied times 500 to obtain the result. Therefore, he will throw $.40 \cdot 500 = 200$ strikes out of 500 total pitches.

Algebraic Expressions that Represent Real-World Situations

When given a real-world problem to be solved, the first step is to understand the unknown quantity. A variable, usually x, is used to represent that unknown quantity. If there's more than one unknown quantity, either another variable is needed or, if such a relationship exists, the other quantities can be defined as a mathematical expression in terms of x.

Once the variables are defined, algebraic expressions or equations need to be formed to represent the real-world scenario. The key is to recognize vocabulary that can be translated into mathematical operations. Words and phrases that represent addition are *sum, add, plus, total, increase, more, more than, combined,* and *in all*. Words that represent subtraction are *difference, less, less than, subtract, decrease, reduce, fewer,* and *remain*. Words and phrases that represent multiplication are *product, multiply, times, part of, twice,* and *triple*. Finally, words and phrases that represent division are *quotient, divide, split, each, per, equal parts, average,* and *shared*. Together, a combination of operations and variables form a mathematical expression. The expression can also be turned into an equation if it's set equal to a quantity or another expression. Expressions are evaluated to find the unknown quantity, and equations are solved to find the unknown quantity.

Consider the following scenario: Two consecutive integers exist such that the sum of the second and 4 less than twice the first equals 501. If x is the first integer, the second unknown quantity can be defined in terms of x. The second integer is defined to be $x + 1$ because they are consecutive integers. The problem can be translated into the following equation: $(x + 1) + (2x - 4) = 501$. Solving the equation for x results in $3x - 3 = 501$. Therefore, $x = 168$ and the next consecutive integer is 169.

Functions

A *function* is defined as a relationship between inputs and outputs where there is only one output value for a given input. As an example, the following function is in function notation: $f(x) = 3x - 4$. The $f(x)$ represents the output value for an input of x. If $x = 2$, the equation becomes $f(2) = 3(2) - 4 = 6 - 4 = 2$. The input of 2 yields an output of 2, forming the ordered pair $(2, 2)$. The following set of ordered pairs corresponds to the given function: $(2, 2), (0, -4), (-2, -10)$. The set of all possible inputs of a function is its *domain*, and all possible outputs is called the *range*. By definition, each member of the domain is paired with only one member of the range.

Functions can also be defined recursively. In this form, they are not defined explicitly in terms of variables. Instead, they are defined using previously-evaluated function outputs, starting with either $f(0)$ or $f(1)$. An example of a recursively-defined function is $f(1) = 2, f(n) = 2f(n - 1) + 2n, n > 1$. The domain of this function is the set of all integers.

Domain and Range
The domain and range of a function can be found visually by its plot on the coordinate plane. In the function $f(x) = x^2 - 3$, for example, the domain is all real numbers because the parabola stretches as far left and as far right as it can go, with no restrictions. This means that any input value from the real number system will yield an answer in the real number system. For the range, the inequality $y \geq -3$ would be used to describe the possible output values because the parabola has a minimum at $y = -3$.

This means there will not be any real output values less than −3 because -3 is the lowest value it reaches on the y-axis.

These same answers for domain and range can be found by observing a table. The table below shows that from input values $x = -1$ to $x = 1$, the output results in a minimum of -3. On each side of $x = 0$, the numbers increase, showing that the range is all real numbers greater than or equal to -3.

x (domain/input)	y (range/output)
-2	1
-1	-2
0	-3
-1	-2
2	1

Function Behavior

Different types of functions behave in different ways. A function is defined to be increasing over a subset of its domain if for all $x_1 \geq x_2$ in that interval, $f(x_1) \geq f(x_2)$. Also, a function is decreasing over an interval if for all $x_1 \geq x_2$ in that interval, $f(x_1) \leq f(x_2)$. A point in which a function changes from increasing to decreasing can also be labeled as the *maximum value* of a function if it is the largest point the graph reaches on the y-axis. A point in which a function changes from decreasing to increasing can be labeled as the minimum value of a function if it is the smallest point the graph reaches on the y-axis. Maximum values are also known as *extreme values*. The graph of a continuous function does not have any breaks or jumps in the graph. This description is not true of all functions. A radical function, for example, $f(x) = \sqrt{x}$, has a restriction for the domain and range because there are no real negative inputs or outputs for this function. The domain can be stated as $x \geq 0$, and the range is $y \geq 0$.

A piecewise-defined function also has a different appearance on the graph. In the following function, there are three equations defined over different intervals. It is a function because there is only one y-value for each x-value, passing the Vertical Line Test. The domain is all real numbers less than or equal to 6. The range is all real numbers greater than zero. From left to right, the graph decreases to zero, then increases to almost 4, and then jumps to 6. From input values greater than 2, the input decreases just below 8 to 4, and then stops.

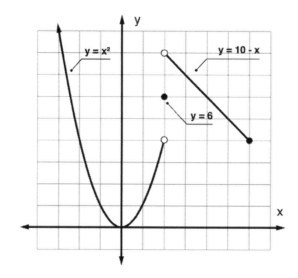

214

Logarithmic and exponential functions also have different behavior than other functions. These two types of functions are inverses of each other. The *inverse* of a function can be found by switching the place of x and y, and solving for y. When this is done for the exponential equation, $y = 2^x$, the function $y = \log_2 x$ is found. The general form of a *logarithmic function* is $y = \log_b x$, which says b raised to the y power equals x.

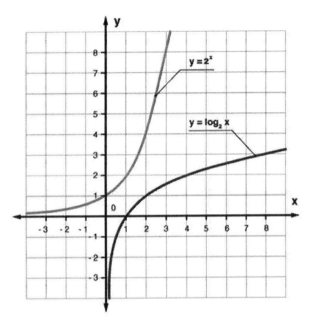

The thick black line on the graph above represents the logarithmic function $y = \log_2 x$. This curve passes through the point $(1, 0)$, just as all log functions do, because any value $b^0 = 1$. The graph of this logarithmic function starts very close to zero, but does not touch the y-axis. The output value will never be zero by the definition of logarithms. The thinner gray line seen above represents the exponential function $y = 2^x$. The behavior of this function is opposite the logarithmic function because the graph of an inverse function is the graph of the original function flipped over the line $y = x$. The curve passes through the point $(0, 1)$ because any number raised to the zero power is one. This curve also gets very close to the x-axis but never touches it because an exponential expression never has an output of zero. The x-axis on this graph is called a horizontal asymptote. An *asymptote* is a line that represents a boundary for a function. It shows a value that the function will get close to, but never reach.

Functions can also be described as being even, odd, or neither. If $f(-x) = f(x)$, the function is even. For example, the function $f(x) = x^2 - 2$ is even. Plugging in $x = 2$ yields an output of $y = 2$. After changing the input to $x = -2$, the output is still $y = 2$. The output is the same for opposite inputs. Another way to observe an even function is by the symmetry of the graph. If the graph is symmetrical about the axis, then the function is even. If the graph is symmetric about the origin, then the function is odd. Algebraically, if $f(-x) = -f(x)$, the function is odd.

Also, a function can be described as periodic if it repeats itself in regular intervals. Common periodic functions are trigonometric functions. For example, $y = \sin x$ is a periodic function with period 2π because it repeats itself every 2π units along the x-axis.

Building a Function
Functions can be built out of the context of a situation. For example, the relationship between the money paid for a gym membership and the months that someone has been a member can be described

through a function. If the one-time membership fee is $40 and the monthly fee is $30, then the function can be written $f(x) = 30x + 40$. The x-value represents the number of months the person has been part of the gym, while the output is the total money paid for the membership. The table below shows this relationship. It is a representation of the function because the initial cost is $40 and the cost increases each month by $30.

x (months)	y (money paid to gym)
0	40
1	70
2	100
3	130

Functions can also be built from existing functions. For example, a given function $f(x)$ can be transformed by adding a constant, multiplying by a constant, or changing the input value by a constant. The new function $g(x) = f(x) + k$ represents a vertical shift of the original function. In $f(x) = 3x - 2$, a vertical shift 4 units up would be $g(x) = 3x - 2 + 4 = 3x + 2$. Multiplying the function times a constant k represents a vertical stretch, based on whether the constant is greater than or less than 1. The function $g(x) = kf(x) = 4(3x - 2) = 12x - 8$ represents a stretch. Changing the input x by a constant forms the function $g(x) = f(x + k) = 3(x + 4) - 2 = 3x + 12 - 2 = 3x + 10$, and this represents a horizontal shift to the left 4 units. If $(x - 4)$ was plugged into the function, it would represent a vertical shift.

A composition function can also be formed by plugging one function into another. In function notation, this is written $(f \circ g)(x) = f(g(x))$. For two functions $f(x) = x^2$ and $g(x) = x - 3$, the composition function becomes $f(g(x)) = (x - 3)^2 = x^2 - 6x + 9$. The composition of functions can also be used to verify if two functions are inverses of each other. Given the two functions $f(x) = 2x + 5$ and $g(x) = \frac{x-5}{2}$, the composition function can be found $(f \circ g)(x)$. Solving this equation yields $f(g(x)) = 2\left(\frac{x-5}{2}\right) + 5 = x - 5 + 5 = x$. It also is true that $g(f(x)) = x$. Since the composition of these two functions gives a simplified answer of x, this verifies that $f(x)$ and $g(x)$ are inverse functions. The domain of $f(g(x))$ is the set of all x-values in the domain of $g(x)$ such that $g(x)$ is in the domain of $f(x)$. Basically, both $f(g(x))$ and $g(x)$ have to be defined.

To build an inverse of a function, $f(x)$ needs to be replaced with y, and the x and y values need to be switched. Then, the equation can be solved for y. For example, given the equation $y = e^{2x}$, the inverse can be found by rewriting the equation $x = e^{2y}$. The natural logarithm of both sides is taken down, and the exponent is brought down to form the equation $\ln(x) = \ln(e) 2y$. $\ln(e)=1$, which yields the equation $\ln(x) = 2y$. Dividing both sides by 2 yields the inverse equation $\frac{\ln(x)}{2} = y = f^{-1}(x)$.

The domain of an inverse function is the range of the original function, and the range of an inverse function is the domain of the original function. Therefore, an ordered pair (x, y) on either a graph or a table corresponding to $f(x)$ means that the ordered pair (y, x) exists on the graph of $f^{-1}(x)$. Basically, if $f(x) = y$, then $f^{-1}(y) = x$. For a function to have an inverse, it must be one-to-one. That means it must pass the *Horizontal Line Test*, and if any horizontal line passes through the graph of the function twice, a function is not one-to-one. The domain of a function that is not one-to-one can be restricted to an interval in which the function is one-to-one, to be able to define an inverse function.

Functions can also be formed from combinations of existing functions. Given $f(x)$ and $g(x)$, $f+g, f-g, fg$, and $\frac{f}{g}$ can be built. The domains of $f+g, f-g$, and fg are the intersection of the domains of f and g. The domain of $\frac{f}{g}$ is the same set, excluding those values that make $g(x)=0$. For example, if $f(x)=2x+3$ and $g(x)=x+1$, $then\ \frac{f}{g}=\frac{2x+3}{x+1}$, and its domain is all real numbers except -1.

<u>Trigonometric Functions</u>

Trigonometric functions are also used to describe behavior in mathematics. *Trigonometry* is the relationship between the angles and sides of a triangle. *Trigonometric functions* include sine, cosine, tangent, secant, cosecant, and cotangent. The functions are defined through ratios in a right triangle. SOHCAHTOA is a common acronym used to remember these ratios, which are defined by the relationships of the sides and angles relative to the right angle. Sine is opposite over hypotenuse, cosine is adjacent over hypotenuse, and tangent is opposite over adjacent. These ratios are the reciprocals of secant, cosecant, and cotangent, respectively. Angles can be measured in degrees or radians.

Here is a diagram of SOHCAHTOA:

SOH $\sin\theta = \frac{\text{opposite}}{\text{hypotenuse}}$

CAH $\cos\theta = \frac{\text{adjacent}}{\text{hypotenuse}}$

TOA $\tan\theta = \frac{\text{opposite}}{\text{adjacent}}$

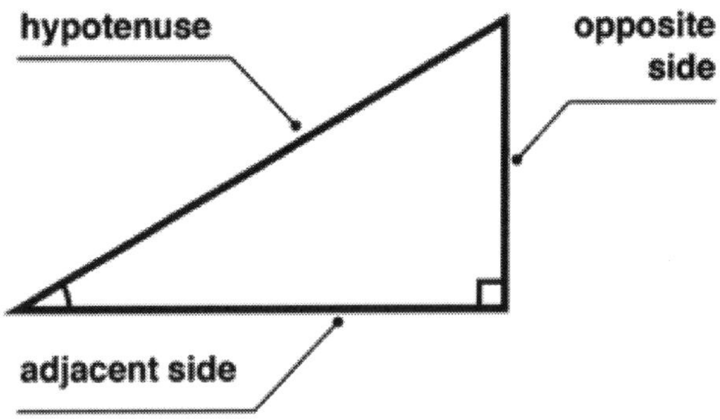

A *radian* is equal to the angle that subtends the arc with the same length as the radius of the circle. It is another unit for measuring angles, in addition to degrees. The unit circle is used to describe different radian measurements and the trigonometric ratios for special angles. The circle has a center at the origin, $(0,0)$, and a radius of 1, which can be seen below. The points where the circle crosses an axis are labeled.

The circle begins on the right-hand side of the x-axis at 0 radians. Since the circumference of a circle is $2\pi r$ and the radius $r=1$, the circumference is 2π. Zero and 2π are labeled as radian measurements at the point $(1,0)$ on the graph. The radian measures around the rest of the circle are labeled also in relation to π; π is at the point $(-1,0)$, also known as 180 degrees. Since these two measurements are equal, $\pi = 180$ degrees written as a ratio can be used to convert degrees to radians or vice versa. For example, to convert 30 degrees to radians, $30\text{ degrees} * \frac{\pi}{180\text{ degrees}}$ can be used to obtain $\frac{1}{6}\pi$ or $\frac{\pi}{6}$. This radian measure is a point the unit circle

The coordinates labeled on the unit circle are found based on two common right triangles. The ratios formed in the coordinates can be found using these triangles. Each of these triangles can be inserted into the circle to correspond 30, 45, and 60 degrees or $\frac{\pi}{6}, \frac{\pi}{4}$, and $\frac{\pi}{3}$ radians.

By letting the hypotenuse length of these triangles equal 1, these triangles can be placed inside the unit circle. These coordinates can be used to find the trigonometric ratio for any of the radian measurements on the circle.

Given any (x, y) on the unit circle, $\sin(\theta) = y$, $\cos(\theta) = x$, and $\tan(\theta) = \frac{y}{x}$. The value θ is the angle that spans the arc around the unit circle. For example, finding $\sin(\frac{\pi}{4})$ means finding the y-value corresponding to the angle $\theta = \frac{\pi}{4}$. The answer is $\frac{\sqrt{2}}{2}$. Finding $\cos(\frac{\pi}{3})$ means finding the x-value corresponding to the angle $\theta = \frac{\pi}{3}$. The answer is $\frac{1}{2}$ or 0.5. Both angles lie in the first quadrant of the unit circle. Trigonometric ratios can also be calculated for radian measures past $\frac{\pi}{2}$, or 90 degrees. Since the same special angles can be moved around the circle, the results only differ with a change in sign. This can be seen at two points labeled in the second and third quadrant.

Trigonometric functions are periodic. Both sine and cosine have period 2π. For each input angle value, the output value follows around the unit circle. Once it reaches the starting point, it continues around and around the circle. It is true that $\sin(0) = \sin(2\pi) = \sin(4\pi)$, etc., and $\cos(0) = \cos(2\pi) = \cos(4\pi)$. Tangent has period π, and its output values repeat themselves every half of the unit circle. The domain of sine and cosine are all real numbers, and the domain of tangent is all real numbers, except the points where cosine equals zero. It is also true that $\sin(-x) = -\sin x$, $\cos(-x) = \cos(x)$, and $\tan(-x) = -\tan(x)$, so sine and tangent are odd functions, while cosine is an even function. Sine and tangent are symmetric with respect the origin, and cosine is symmetric with respect to the y-axis.

The graph of trigonometric functions can be used to model different situations. General forms are $y = a \sin b(x - h) + k$, and $y = a \cos b (x - h) + k$. The variable a represents the amplitude, which shows the maximum and minimum value of the function. The b is used to find the period by using the ratio $\frac{2\pi}{b}$, h is the horizontal shift, and k is the vertical shift. The equation $y = \sin(x)$ is shown on the following graph with the thick black line. The stretched graph of $y = 2 \sin(x)$ is shown in solid black, and the shrunken graph $y = \frac{1}{2} \sin(x)$ is shown with the dotted line.

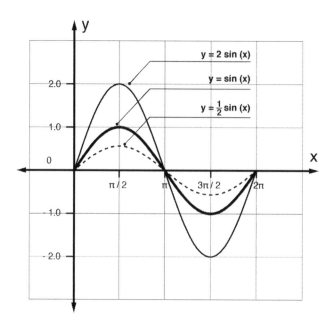

218

Trigonometric functions are used to find unknown ratios for a given angle measure. The inverse of these trig functions is used to find the unknown angle, given a ratio. For example, the expression $\arccos\left(\frac{1}{2}\right)$ means finding the value of x for $\sin(x) = \frac{1}{2}$. Since $\sin(\theta) = \frac{y}{1}$ on the unit circle, the angle whose y-value is $\frac{1}{2}$ is $\frac{\pi}{6}$. The inverse of any of the trigonometric functions can be used to find a missing angle measurement. Values not found on the unit circle can be found using the trigonometric functions on the calculator, making sure its mode is set to degrees or radians.

In order for the inverse to exist, the function must be one-to-one over its domain. There cannot be two input values connected to the same output. For example, the following graphs show the functions $y = \cos(x)$ and $y = \arccos(x)$. In order to have an inverse, the domain of cosine is restricted from 0 to π. Therefore, the range of its inverse function is $[0, \pi]$.

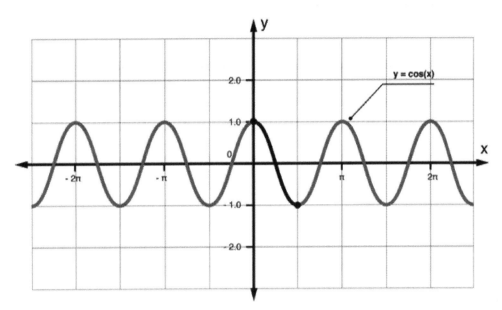

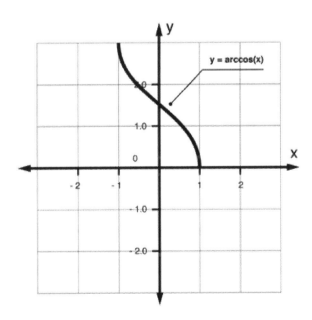

Inverses of trigonometric functions can be used to solve real-world problems. For example, there are many situations where the lengths of a perceived triangle can be found, but the angles are unknown. Consider a problem where the height of a flag (25 feet) and the distance on the ground to the flag is given (42 feet). The unknown, x, is the angle. To find this angle, the equation $\tan x = \frac{42}{25}$ is used. To solve for x, the inverse function can be used to turn the equation into $\tan^{-1}\frac{42}{25} = x$. Using the calculator, in degree mode, the answer is found to be $x = 59.2$ degrees

Trigonometric Identities
From the unit circle, the trigonometric ratios were found for the special right triangle with a hypotenuse of 1.

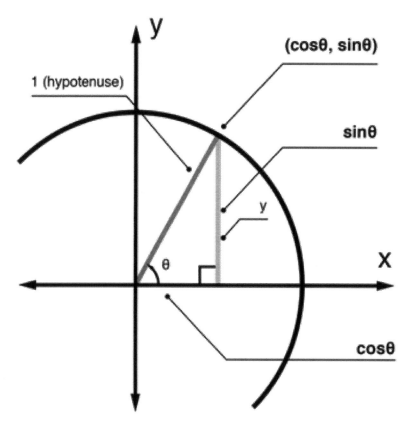

From this triangle, the following Pythagorean identities are formed: $\sin^2\theta + \cos^2\theta = 1$, $\tan^2\theta + 1 = \sec^2\theta$, and $1 + \cot^2\theta = \csc^2\theta$. The second two identities are formed by manipulating the first identity. Since identities are statements that are true for any value of the variable, then they may be used to manipulate equations. For example, a problem may ask for simplification of the expression $\cos^2 x + \cos^2 x \tan^2 x$. Using the fact that $\tan(x) = \frac{\sin x}{\cos x}$, $\frac{\sin^2 x}{\cos^2 x}$ can then be substituted in for $\tan^2 x$, making the expression $\cos^2 x + \cos^2 x \frac{\sin^2 x}{\cos^2 x}$. Then the two $\cos^2 x$ terms on top and bottom cancel each other out, simplifying the expression to $\cos^2 x + \sin^2 x$. By the first Pythagorean identity stated above, the expression can be turned into $\cos^2 x + \sin^2 x = 1$.

Another set of trigonometric identities are the double-angle formulas:

$$\sin 2\alpha = 2 \sin \alpha \; \cos \alpha$$

$$\cos 2\alpha = \begin{cases} \cos^2\alpha - \sin^2\alpha \\ 2\cos^2\alpha - 1 \\ 1 - 2\sin^2\alpha \end{cases}$$

Using these formulas, the following identity can be proved: $\sin 2x = \frac{2\tan x}{1+\tan^2 x}$. By using one of the Pythagorean identities, the denominator can be rewritten as $1 + \tan^2 x = \sec^2 x$. By knowing the reciprocals of the trigonometric identities, the secant term can be rewritten to form the equation $\sin 2x = \frac{2\tan x}{1} * \cos^2 x$. Replacing $\tan(x)$, the equation becomes $\sin 2x = \frac{2\sin x}{\cos x} * \cos^2 x$, where the $\cos x$ can cancel out. The new equation is $\sin 2x = 2 \sin x * \cos x$. This final equation is one of the double-angle formulas.

Other trigonometric identities such as half-angle formulas, sum and difference formulas, and difference of angles formulas can be used to prove and rewrite trigonometric equations. Depending on the given equation or expression, the correct identities need to be chosen to write equivalent statements.

The graph of sine is equal to the graph of cosine, shifted $\frac{\pi}{2}$ units. Therefore, the function $y = \sin x$ is equal to $y = \cos(\frac{\pi}{2} - x)$. Within functions, adding a constant to the independent variable shifts the graph either left or right. By shifting the cosine graph, the curve lies on top of the sine function. By transforming the function, the two equations give the same output for any given input.

Functions of Two Variables
The graph of a function of one variable can be represented in the xy-plane and is known as a *curve*. When a function has two variables, the function is graphed in three-dimensional space, and the graph is known as a *surface*. The graph is the set of all ordered triples (x, y, z) that satisfy the function. Within three-dimensional space, there is a third axis known as the z-axis.

Solving Trigonometric Functions
Solving trigonometric functions can be done with a knowledge of the unit circle and the trigonometric identities. It requires the use of opposite operations combined with trigonometric ratios for special triangles. For example, the problem may require solving the equation $2\cos^2 x - \sqrt{3}\cos x = 0$ for the values of x between 0 and 180 degrees. The first step is to factor out the $\cos x$ term, resulting in $\cos x (2\cos x - \sqrt{3}) = 0$. By the factoring method of solving, each factor can be set equal to zero: $\cos x = 0$ and $(2\cos x - \sqrt{3}) = 0$. The second equation can be solved to yield the following equation: $\cos x = \frac{\sqrt{3}}{2}$. Now that the value of x is found, the trigonometric ratios can be used to find the solutions of $x = 30$ and 90 degrees.

Solving trigonometric functions requires the use of algebra to isolate the variable and a knowledge of trigonometric ratios to find the value of the variable. The unit circle can be used to find answers for special triangles. Beyond those triangles, a calculator can be used to solve for variables within the trigonometric functions.

Solving Logarithmic and Exponential Functions
To solve an equation involving exponential expressions, the goal is to isolate the exponential expression. Once this process is completed, the logarithm—with the base equaling the base of the exponent of both sides—needs to be taken to get an expression for the variable. If the base is e, the natural log of both sides needs to be taken.

To solve an equation with logarithms, the given equation needs to be written in exponential form, using the fact that $\log_b y = x$ means $b^x = y$, and then solved for the given variable. Lastly, properties of logarithms can be used to simplify more than one logarithmic expression into one.

Patterns

Solving problems involving number patterns is a key part of mathematics. Recurring themes and rules appear in many forms in mathematics. Pictorial patterns also exist in mathematics when repetition is seen in visual scenarios. Pattern blocks are a great way to introduce pictorial representations into the classroom.

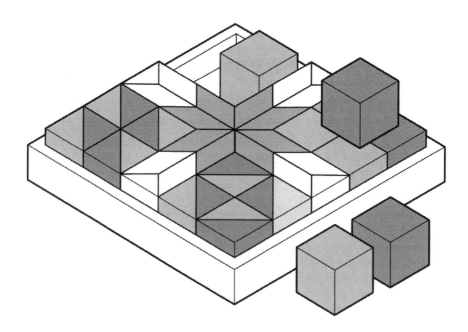

Geometric shapes can be compared, counted, sorted, and described to obtain a sense of pattern. The same is true for numbers and other quantities.

The ability to recognize patterns is a key step in understanding algebra. For example, properties involving real numbers are identified through patterns before the property is introduced. Consider the commutative property of addition, which states that order doesn't matter. Before the property is defined, students will have already realized that changing the order of addition of two numbers doesn't change the result. The same idea is true for multiplication. When learning the multiplication table, its shown that order doesn't matter. For example, both 2 · 3 and 3 · 2 equal 6. Sequences can also use the idea of patterns. The next element in a set of numbers or geometric shapes can be selected based on identifying a pattern in the original set. For example, consider the numbers 1, 4, 9, 16. The next number in the set is 25 because the original four values consist of squares of 1, 2, 3, and 4. Therefore, the next number in the set is the square of 5.

<u>Number Patterns</u>
Given a sequence of numbers, a mathematical rule can be defined that represents the numbers if a pattern exists within the set. For example, consider the sequence of numbers 1, 4, 9, 16, 25, etc. This set of numbers represents the positive integers squared, and an explicitly defined sequence that represents this set is $f_n = n^2$. An important mathematical concept is recognizing patterns in sequences and translating the patterns into an explicit formula. Once the pattern is recognized and the formula is defined, the sequence can be extended easily. For example, the next three numbers in the sequence are 36, 49, and 64.

Direct and Inverse Relationships

A direct relationship occurs between two quantities when one of the quantities is increased and the other also increases—or if one quantity decreases as the other also decreases. If one quantity is multiplied by a constant, the other is increased by that same amount. If a quantity is doubled, the other quantity is also doubled. Tables, graphs, and algebraic expressions are comprised of ordered pairs representing two variables. If each variable increases simultaneously, there is a direct relationship. Algebraically, this scenario can be represented as $y = kx$, where x and y are the variables and k is the proportionality constant. Therefore, they vary linearly. The graph is a straight line with x- and y-intercept (0,0), and in function notation it's of the form $f(x) = kx$.

An inverse relationship exists if the opposite occurs: When one quantity increases, the other decreases. Algebraically, this scenario is represented as $y = \frac{k}{x}$.

Direct and inverse relationships occur frequently in real-world situations. Consider a circle, its radius, and its circumference. The formula for circumference is $C = 2\pi r$, where r is the radius. As the radius of a circle increases, the circumference also increases. Also, if the radius decreases, the circumference decreases. Therefore, there's a direct relationship between the circumference and the radius. Secondly, consider speed and travel time. The faster one drives, the quicker one gets to a destination. If speed is doubled, the amount of time it takes to reach the destination is cut in half. Therefore, there's an inverse relationship between speed and travel time.

Qualitative Graphs

Qualitative graphs can represent functions that exist in the real world. They show the essential content of the real-world situation, but don't need to contain numerical values. The horizontal axis represents the independent variable, and the vertical axis represents the dependent variable. The graph might highlight whether there's a direct or inverse relationship, whether the dependent variable increases or decreases as the independent variable increases or decreases, whether the dependent variable remains constant at any point, or if the graph is periodic in nature, meaning it repeats over a specific time. Because the graph doesn't need to contain numbers, the axes don't need tick marks representing numerical values.

Here are various qualitative graphs representing the distance someone is from home (the dependent variable) plotted against time (the independent variable):

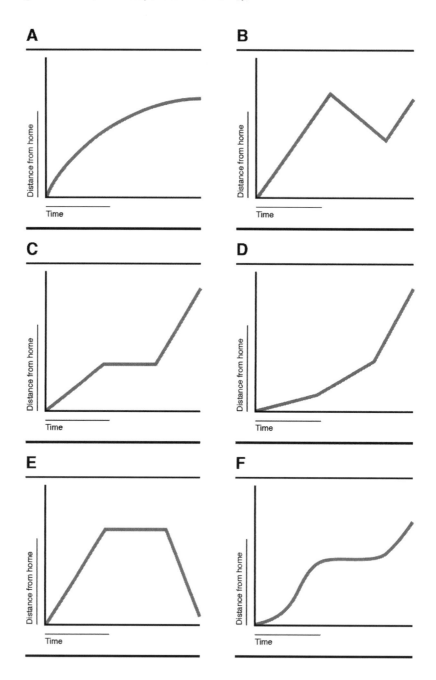

Notice that no numerical values are shown, and, therefore, no ordered pairs are plotted. However, qualitative information can be obtained because each graph starts at the origin, so each scenario begins with the person at home. If we assume that the person is walking, graph A plots the scenario when she is starting to slow down as time increases. Graph B plots a scenario when she walked away from home, then headed back home before eventually traveling away from home again. The horizontal lines in graph C and E represent time periods in which she remained still. Any straight line represents periods in which her speed is constant, and a curve represents periods in which speed varies.

Functional Relationships

A relation is composed of any set of ordered pairs. The set of all first components, or inputs, is the domain of the relation, and the set of all second components, or outputs, is the range of the relation. If every member of the domain corresponds to only one member of the range, the domain is a function. Functions appear in many forms. A table of ordered pairs can represent a function. Here is an example:

x	f(x)
-8	-2
-1	-1
0	0
1	1
8	2

Each row represents an ordered pair. The left column is the domain of the function, and the right column is the range of the function. The $f(x)$ values can be thought of as the y −values.

Secondly, a graph can represent a function. In the x-y plane, plotted ordered pairs represent a function if they pass the vertical line test. If any vertical line drawn through the graph intersects it in more than one location, then the graph is not the graph of a function. Here's an example of the vertical line test for graphing functions:

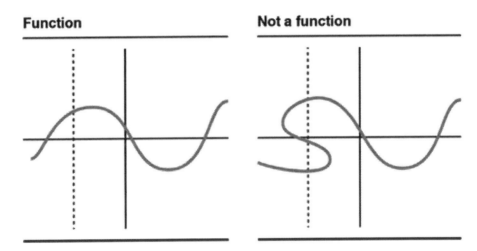

Algebraic expressions can also represent functions. Functions are usually given in the form of equations. Consider the equation $y = x^2 + 5$. The variable x represents the input of the function and is called the independent variable because it can be any member of the domain. The variable y represents the output of the function and is called the dependent variable because its value depends on the value of the independent variable. Every value of x gives only one y value in a function. The output variable can also be represented as $f(x)$ and in this case, and the function would be written as $f(x) = x^2 + 5$. The domain of this function is all real numbers, or $\mathbb{R}$. With an input of 3, the output is found by plugging in 3 for x to obtain $f(3) = 3^2 + 5 = 14$. Together, these two values make up the ordered pair (3, 14).

A verbal statement can also be a representation of a function. Consider the real-world scenario of a machine with an input and an output. It could be a function if each input has only one output. For example, consider days and U.S. presidents. Each day corresponds to only one president in office.

However, a set of years and U.S. presidents doesn't form a function because there are years in which two presidents have been in office.

Formula and Graph of a Linear Function

A linear function is the form $f(x) = mx + b$ where m represents slope and b represents the ordered pair $(0, b)$, which is the y-intercept. The graph of a linear function is a straight line, and it can have a positive slope, a negative slope, no slope, or an undefined slope. Here are examples of the four different slopes:

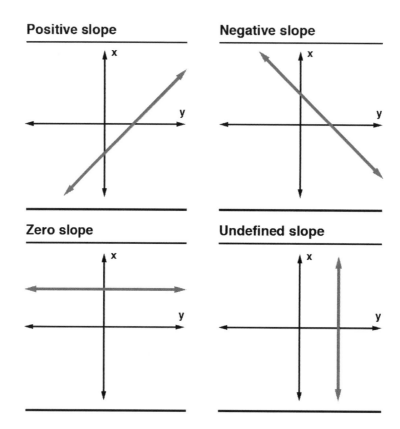

A specific function can be graphed by creating a table of ordered pairs or by using the slope and y-intercept to plot points. In either case, two ordered pairs are necessary to form the line, and a third ordered pair exists as a checking mechanism. In the linear function $f(x) = x + 1$, three ordered pairs can be found by plugging in x-values to obtain y-values. A table of three such ordered pairs is below:

x	y
-1	0
0	1
2	3

Each point can be plotted in the xy-plane and then connected with a straight line to obtain the graph of the function. An alternate method would using the definition of slope as rise over run. Starting at the y-intercept, the next point to the right is obtained by increasing one unit in the positive x-direction and one unit in the positive y-direction. The next two ordered pairs to the right of (0,1) are (1,2) and (2,3). Here is the graph of the function:

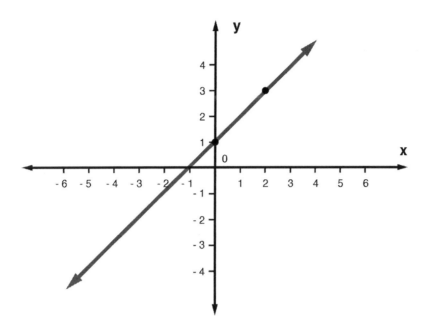

Linear and Nonlinear Functions

<u>Common Functions</u>
Three common functions used to model different relationships between quantities are linear, quadratic, and exponential functions. Linear functions are the simplest of the three, and the independent variable x has an exponent of 1. Written in the most common form, $y = mx + b$, the coefficient of x tells how fast the function grows at a constant rate, and the b-value tells the starting point. A quadratic function has an exponent of 2 on the independent variable x. Standard form for this type of function is $y = ax^2 + bx + c$, and the graph is a parabola. These type functions grow at a changing rate. An exponential function has an independent variable in the exponent $y = ab^x$. The graph of these types of functions is described as *growth* or *decay*, based on whether the base, b, is greater than or less than 1. These functions are different from quadratic functions because the base stays constant. A common base is base *e*.

The three tables below show specific values for three types of functions. The third column in each table shows the change in the y-values for each interval. The first table shows a constant change of 2 for each equal interval, which matches the slope in the equation $y = 2x$. The second table shows an increasing change, but it also has a pattern. The increase is changing by 2 more each time, so the change is quadratic. The third table shows the change as factors of the base, 2. It shows a continuing pattern of factors of the base.

y = 2x		
x	y	Δy
1	2	
2	4	2
3	6	2
4	8	2
5	10	2

y = x²		
x	y	Δy
1	1	
2	4	3
3	9	5
4	16	7
5	25	9

y = 2ˣ		
x	y	Δy
1	2	
2	4	2
3	8	4
4	16	8
5	32	16

Given a table of values, the type of function can be determined by observing the change in y over equal intervals. For example, the tables below model two functions. The changes in interval for the x-values is 1 for both tables. For the first table, the y-values increase by 5 for each interval. Since the change is constant, the situation can be described as a linear function. The equation would be $y = 5x + 3$. For the second table, the change for y is 5, 20, 100, and 500, respectively. The increases are multiples of 5, meaning the situation can be modeled by an exponential function. The equation $y = 5^x + 3$ models this situation.

x	y
0	3
1	8
2	13
3	18
4	23

x	y
0	3
1	8
2	28
3	128
4	628

Quadratic equations can be used to model real-world area problems. For example, a farmer may have a rectangular field that he needs to sow with seed. The field has length $x + 8$ and width $2x$. The formula for area should be used: $A = lw$. Therefore, $A = (x + 8) * 2x = 2x^2 + 16x$. The possible values for the length and width can be shown in a table, with input x and output A. If the equation was graphed, the possible area values can be seen on the y-axis for given x-values.

Exponential growth and decay can be found in real-world situations. For example, if a piece of notebook paper is folded 25 times, the thickness of the paper can be found. To model this situation, a table can be used. The initial point is one-fold, which yields a thickness of 2 papers. For the second fold, the thickness is 4. Since the thickness doubles each time, the table below shows the thickness for the next few folds. Notice the thickness changes by the same factor each time. Since this change for a constant interval of folds is a factor of 2, the function is exponential. The equation for this is $y = 2^x$. For twenty-five folds, the thickness would be 33,554,432 papers.

x (folds)	y (paper thickness)
0	1
1	2
2	4
3	8
4	16
5	32

One exponential formula that is commonly used is the *interest formula*: $A = Pe^{rt}$. In this formula, interest is compounded continuously. A is the value of the investment after the time, t, in years. P is the initial amount of the investment, r is the interest rate, and e is the constant equal to approximately 2.718. Given an initial amount of $200 and a time of 3 years, if interest is compounded continuously at a rate of 6%, the total investment value can be found by plugging each value into the formula. The invested value at the end is $239.44. In more complex problems, the final investment may be given, and the rate may be the unknown. In this case, the formula becomes $239.44 = 200e^{r3}$. Solving for r requires isolating the exponential expression on one side by dividing by 200, yielding the equation $1.20 = e^{r3}$. Taking the natural log of both sides results in $\ln(1.2) = r3$. Using a calculator to evaluate the logarithmic expression, $r = 0.06 = 6\%$.

When working with logarithms and exponential expressions, it is important to remember the relationship between the two. In general, the logarithmic form is $y = \log_b x$ for an exponential form $b^y = x$. Logarithms and exponential functions are inverses of each other.

Linear Equation that Represents a Graph

The following three functions model a linear, quadratic, and exponential function respectively: $y = 2x$, $y = x^2$, and $y = 2^x$. Their graphs are shown below. The first graph, modeling the linear function, shows that the growth is constant over each interval. With a horizontal change of 1, the vertical change is 2. It models a constant positive growth. The second graph shows the quadratic function, which is a curve that is symmetric across the y-axis. The growth is not constant, but the change is mirrored over the axis. The last graph models the exponential function, where the horizontal change of 1 yields a vertical change that increases more and more. The exponential graph gets very close to the x-axis, but never touches it, meaning there is an asymptote there. The y-value can never be zero because the base of 2 can never be raised to an input value that yields an output of zero.

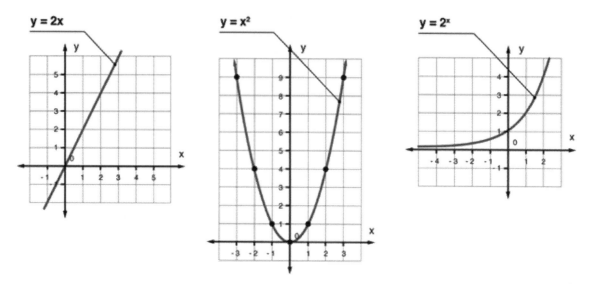

y = 2x   y = x²   y = 2ˣ

Proportions, Constant Rates, and Linear Functions

A rate is a ratio in which two terms are in different units. When rates are expressed as a quantity of one, they are considered unit rates. To determine a unit rate, the first quantity is divided by the second. Knowing a unit rate makes calculations easier than simply having a rate. For example, suppose a 3 pound bag of onions costs $1.77. To calculate the price of 5 pounds of onions, a proportion could show: $\frac{3}{1.77} = \frac{5}{x}$. However, by knowing the unit rate, the value of pounds of onions is multiplied by the unit price. The unit price is calculated: $\$1.77/3lb = \$0.59/lb$. Multiplying the weight of the onions by the unit price yields: $5lb \times \frac{\$0.59}{lb} = \$2.95$. The *lb.* units cancel out.

Similar to unit-rate problems, unit conversions appear in real-world scenarios including cooking, measurement, construction, and currency. Given the conversion rate, unit conversions are written as a fraction (ratio) and multiplied by a quantity in one unit to convert it to the corresponding unit. To determine how many minutes are in $3\frac{1}{2}$ hours, the conversion rate of 60 minutes to 1 hour is written as $\frac{60\ min}{1h}$. Multiplying the quantity by the conversion rate results in $3\frac{1}{2}h \times \frac{60\ min}{1h} = 210\ min$. (The *h* unit is canceled.) To convert a quantity in minutes to hours, the fraction for the conversion rate is flipped to cancel the *min* unit. To convert 195 minutes to hours, $195min \times \frac{1h}{60\ min}$ is multiplied. The result is $\frac{195h}{60}$ which reduces to $3\frac{1}{4}h$.

Converting units may require more than one multiplication. The key is to set up conversion rates so that units cancel each other out and the desired unit is left. To convert 3.25 yards to inches, given that 1yd = 3ft and 12in = 1ft, the calculation is performed by multiplying $3.25\ yd \times \frac{3ft}{1yd} \times \frac{12in}{1ft}$. The *yd* and *ft* units will cancel, resulting in 117in.

<u>Using Proportional Relationships</u>
A proportion is a statement consisting of two equal ratios. Proportions will typically give three of four quantities and require solving for the missing value. The key to solving proportions is to set them up properly. Consider the following: 7 gallons of gas costs $14.70. How many gallons can you get for $20?

The information is written as equal ratios with a variable representing the missing quantity $\left(\frac{gallons}{cost} = \frac{gallons}{cost}\right)$: $\frac{7}{14.70} = \frac{x}{20}$. To solve for x, the proportion is cross-multiplied. This means the numerator of the first ratio is multiplied by the denominator of the second, and vice versa. The resulting products are shown equal to each other. Cross-multiplying results in $(7)(20) = (14.7)(x)$. By solving the equation for x (see the algebra content), the answer is that 9.5 gallons of gas may be purchased for $20.

Percent problems can also be solved by setting up proportions. Examples of common percent problems are:

    a. What is 15% of 25?
    b. What percent of 45 is 3?
    c. 5 is $\frac{1}{2}$% of what number?

Setting up the proper proportion is made easier by following the format: $\frac{is}{of} = \frac{percent}{100}$. A variable is used to represent the missing value. The proportions for each of the three examples are set up as follows:

    a. $\frac{x}{25} = \frac{15}{100}$
    b. $\frac{3}{45} = \frac{x}{100}$
    c. $\frac{5}{x} = \frac{\frac{1}{2}}{100}$

By cross-multiplying and solving the resulting equation for the variable, the missing values are determined to be:

    a. 3.75
    b. $6.\bar{6}$%
    c. 1,000

Linear Equations and Inequalities

Linear equations and linear inequalities are both comparisons of two algebraic expressions. However, unlike equations in which the expressions are equal, linear inequalities compare expressions that may be unequal. Linear equations typically have one value for the variable that makes the statement true. Linear inequalities generally have an infinite number of values that make the statement true.

When solving a linear equation, the desired result requires determining a numerical value for the unknown variable. If given a linear equation involving addition, subtraction, multiplication, or division, working backwards isolates the variable. Addition and subtraction are inverse operations, as are multiplication and division. Therefore, they can be used to cancel each other out.

The first steps to solving linear equations are distributing, if necessary, and combining any like terms on the same side of the equation. Sides of an equation are separated by an *equal* sign. Next, the equation is manipulated to show the variable on one side. Whatever is done to one side of the equation must be done to the other side of the equation to remain equal. Inverse operations are then used to isolate the variable and undo the order of operations backwards. Addition and subtraction are undone, then multiplication and division are undone.

For example, solve $4(t-2) + 2t - 4 = 2(9 - 2t)$

Distributing: $4t - 8 + 2t - 4 = 18 - 4t$

Combining like terms: $6t - 12 = 18 - 4t$

Adding $4t$ to each side to move the variable: $10t - 12 = 18$

Adding 12 to each side to isolate the variable: $10t = 30$

Dividing each side by 10 to isolate the variable: $t = 3$

The answer can be checked by substituting the value for the variable into the original equation, ensuring that both sides calculate to be equal.

Linear inequalities express the relationship between unequal values. More specifically, they describe in what way the values are unequal. A value can be greater than (>), less than (<), greater than or equal to (≥), or less than or equal to (≤) another value. $5x + 40 > 65$ is read as *five times a number added to forty is greater than sixty-five.*

When solving a linear inequality, the solution is the set of all numbers that make the statement true. The inequality $x + 2 \geq 6$ has a solution set of 4 and every number greater than 4 (4.01; 5; 12; 107; etc.). Adding 2 to 4 or any number greater than 4 results in a value that is greater than or equal to 6. Therefore, $x \geq 4$ is the solution set.

To algebraically solve a linear inequality, follow the same steps as those for solving a linear equation. The inequality symbol stays the same for all operations *except* when multiplying or dividing by a negative number. If multiplying or dividing by a negative number while solving an inequality, the relationship reverses (the sign flips). In other words, > switches to < and vice versa. Multiplying or dividing by a positive number does not change the relationship, so the sign stays the same. An example is shown below.

Solve $-2x - 8 \leq 22$

Add 8 to both sides: $-2x \leq 30$

Divide both sides by -2: $x \geq -15$

Solutions of a linear equation or a linear inequality are the values of the variable that make a statement true. In the case of a linear equation, the solution set (list of all possible solutions) typically consists of a single numerical value. To find the solution, the equation is solved by isolating the variable. For example, solving the equation $3x - 7 = -13$ produces the solution $x = -2$. The only value for x which produces a true statement is -2. This can be checked by substituting -2 into the original equation to check that both sides are equal. In this case, $3(-2) - 7 = -13 \rightarrow -13 = -13$; therefore, -2 is a solution.

Although linear equations generally have one solution, this is not always the case. If there is no value for the variable that makes the statement true, there is no solution to the equation. Consider the equation $x + 3 = x - 1$. There is no value for x in which adding 3 to the value produces the same result as subtracting one from the value. Conversely, if any value for the variable makes a true statement, the equation has an infinite number of solutions. Consider the equation $3x + 6 = 3(x + 2)$. Any number substituted for x will result in a true statement (both sides of the equation are equal).

By manipulating equations like the two above, the variable of the equation will cancel out completely. If the remaining constants express a true statement (ex. $6 = 6$), then all real numbers are solutions to the equation. If the constants left express a false statement (ex. $3 = -1$), then no solution exists for the equation.

Solving a linear inequality requires all values that make the statement true to be determined. For example, solving $3x - 7 \geq -13$ produces the solution $x \geq -2$. This means that -2 and any number greater than -2 produces a true statement. Solution sets for linear inequalities will often be displayed using a number line. If a value is included in the set ($\geq$ or $\leq$), a shaded dot is placed on that value and an arrow extending in the direction of the solutions. For a variable > or $\geq$ a number, the arrow will point right on a number line, the direction where the numbers increase. If a variable is < or $\leq$ a number, the arrow will point left on a number line, which is the direction where the numbers decrease. If the value is not included in the set (> or <), an open (unshaded) circle on that value is used with an arrow in the appropriate direction.

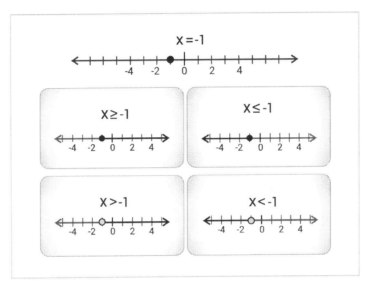

Similar to linear equations, a linear inequality may have a solution set consisting of all real numbers, or can contain no solution. When solved algebraically, a linear inequality in which the variable cancels out and results in a true statement (ex. $7 \geq 2$) has a solution set of all real numbers. A linear inequality in which the variable cancels out and results in a false statement (ex. $7 \leq 2$) has no solution.

Linear Equation that Best Models a Real-World Situation

Linear relationships describe the way two quantities change with respect to each other. The relationship is defined as linear because a line is produced if all the sets of corresponding values are graphed on a coordinate grid. When expressing the linear relationship as an equation, the equation is often written in the form $y = mx + b$ (slope-intercept form) where m and b are numerical values and x and y are variables (for example, $y = 5x + 10$). Given a linear equation and the value of either variable (x or y), the value of the other variable can be determined.

Suppose a teacher is grading a test containing 20 questions with 5 points given for each correct answer, adding a curve of 10 points to each test. This linear relationship can be expressed as the equation $y = 5x + 10$ where x represents the number of correct answers and y represents the test score. To determine the score of a test with a given number of correct answers, the number of correct answers is substituted into the equation for x and evaluated. For example, for 10 correct answers, 10 is substituted for x: $y = 5(10) + 10 \rightarrow y = 60$. Therefore, 10 correct answers will result in a score of 60. The number of correct answers needed to obtain a certain score can also be determined. To determine the number of correct answers needed to score a 90, 90 is substituted for y in the equation (y represents the test score) and solved: $90 = 5x + 10 \rightarrow 80 = 5x \rightarrow 16 = x$. Therefore, 16 correct answers are needed to score a 90.

Linear relationships may be represented by a table of 2 corresponding values. Certain tables may determine the relationship between the values and predict other corresponding sets. Consider the table below, which displays the money in a checking account that charges a monthly fee:

Month	0	1	2	3	4
Balance	$210	$195	$180	$165	$150

An examination of the values reveals that the account loses $15 every month (the month increases by one and the balance decreases by 15). This information can be used to predict future values. To determine what the value will be in month 6, the pattern can be continued, and it can be concluded that the balance will be $120. To determine which month the balance will be $0, $210 is divided by $15 (since the balance decreases $15 every month), resulting in month 14.

Similar to a table, a graph can display corresponding values of a linear relationship.

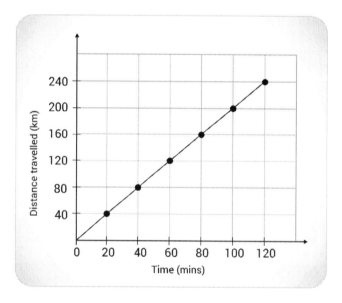

The graph above represents the relationship between distance traveled and time. To find the distance traveled in 80 minutes, the mark for 80 minutes is located at the bottom of the graph. By following this mark directly up on the graph, the corresponding point for 90 minutes is directly across from the 150 kilometer mark. This information indicates that the distance travelled in 80 minutes is 160 kilometers. To predict information not displayed on the graph, the way in which the variables change with respect to one another is determined. In this case, distance increases by 40 kilometers as time increases by 20 minutes. This information can be used to continue the data in the graph or convert the values to a table.

Geometry and Measurement

Calculating Measurement

The length of an object can be measured using standard tools such as rulers, yard sticks, meter sticks, and measuring tapes. The following image depicts a yardstick:

Choosing the right tool to perform the measurement requires determining whether United States customary units or metric units are desired, and having a grasp of the approximate length of each unit and the approximate length of each tool. The measurement can still be performed by trial and error without the knowledge of the approximate size of the tool.

For example, to determine the length of a room in feet, a United States customary unit, various tools can be used for this task. These include a ruler (typically 12 inches/1 foot long), a yardstick (3 feet/1 yard long), or a tape measure displaying feet (typically either 25 feet or 50 feet). Because the length of a room is much larger than the length of a ruler or a yardstick, a tape measure should be used to perform the measurement.

When the correct measuring tool is selected, the measurement is performed by first placing the tool directly above or below the object (if making a horizontal measurement) or directly next to the object (if making a vertical measurement). The next step is aligning the tool so that one end of the object is at the mark for zero units, then recording the unit of the mark at the other end of the object. To give the length of a paperclip in metric units, a ruler displaying centimeters is aligned with one end of the paper clip to the mark for zero centimeters.

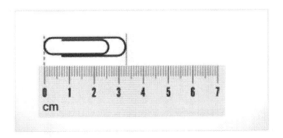

Directly down from the other end of the paperclip is the mark that measures its length. In this case, that mark is two small dashes past the 3 centimeter mark. Each small dash is 1 millimeter (or .1 centimeters). Therefore, the length of the paper clip is 3.2 centimeters.

To compare the lengths of objects, each length must be expressed in the same unit. If possible, the objects should be measured with the same tool or with tools utilizing the same units. For example, a ruler and a yardstick can both measure length in inches. If the lengths of the objects are expressed in different units, these different units must be converted to the same unit before comparing them. If two lengths are expressed in the same unit, the lengths may be compared by subtracting the smaller value from the larger value. For example, suppose the lengths of two gardens are to be compared. Garden A has a length of 4 feet, and garden B has a length of 2 yards. 2 yards is converted to 6 feet so that the measurements have similar units. Then, the smaller length (4 feet) is subtracted from the larger length (6ft): 6ft − 4ft = 2ft. Therefore, garden B is 2 feet larger than garden A.

Unit Conversions

When working with different systems of measurement, conversion from one unit to another may be necessary. The conversion rate must be known to convert units. One method for converting units is to write and solve a proportion. The arrangement of values in a proportion is extremely important. Suppose that a problem requires converting 20 fluid ounces to cups. To do so, a proportion can be written using the conversion rate of 8fl oz = 1c with x representing the missing value. The proportion can be written in any of the following ways:

$$\frac{1}{8} = \frac{x}{20}\left(\frac{c\ for\ conversion}{fl\ oz\ for\ conversion} = \frac{unknown\ c}{fl\ oz\ given}\right); \frac{8}{1} = \frac{20}{x}\left(\frac{fl\ oz\ for\ conversion}{c\ for\ conversion} = \frac{fl\ oz\ given}{unknown\ c}\right)$$

$$\frac{1}{x} = \frac{8}{20}\left(\frac{c\ for\ conversion}{unknown\ c} = \frac{fl\ oz\ for\ conversion}{fl\ oz\ given}\right); \frac{x}{1} = \frac{20}{8}\left(\frac{unknown\ c}{c\ for\ conversion} = \frac{fl\ oz\ given}{fl\ oz\ for\ conversion}\right)$$

To solve a proportion, the ratios are cross-multiplied and the resulting equation is solved. When cross-multiplying, all four proportions above will produce the same equation: $(8)(x) = (20)(1) \rightarrow 8x = 20$. Dividing by 8 to isolate the variable x, the result is $x = 2.5$. The variable x represented the unknown number of cups. Therefore, the conclusion is that 20 fluid ounces converts (is equal) to 2.5 cups.

Sometimes converting units requires writing and solving more than one proportion. Suppose an exam question asks to determine how many hours are in 2 weeks. Without knowing the conversion rate between hours and weeks, this can be determined knowing the conversion rates between weeks and days, and between days and hours. First, weeks are converted to days, then days are converted to hours. To convert from weeks to days, the following proportion can be written:

$$\frac{7}{1} = \frac{x}{2}\left(\frac{days\ conversion}{weeks\ conversion} = \frac{days\ unknown}{weeks\ given}\right)$$

Cross-multiplying produces: $(7)(2) = (x)(1) \rightarrow 14 = x$. Therefore, 2 weeks is equal to 14 days. Next, a proportion is written to convert 14 days to hours: $\frac{24}{1} = \frac{x}{14}\left(\frac{conversion\ hours}{conversion\ days} = \frac{unknown\ hours}{given\ days}\right)$. Cross-multiplying produces: $(24)(14) = (x)(1) \rightarrow 336 = x$. Therefore, the answer is that there are 336 hours in 2 weeks.

Calculating Lengths, Perimeters, Areas, Volumes, and Surface Areas of Geometric Shapes and Figures

<u>Circumference and Volume</u>
The *circumference* of a circle is found by calculating the perimeter of the shape. The ratio of the circumference to the diameter of the circle is π, so the formula for circumference is $C = \pi d = 2\pi r$. To visualize this, one can imagine that a circle is a pie divided into an equal number of slices. The slices can be aligned to form a parallelogram with a height equal to the radius r, and a base equal to half of the circumference of the circle πr. Plugging these expressions into the formula for area of a parallelogram results in $A = bh = \pi r^2$. The *volume* of a cylinder is then found by adding a third dimension onto the circle. Volume of a cylinder is calculated by multiplying the area of the base (which is a circle) by the height of the cylinder. Doing so results in the equation $V = \pi r^2 h$. Next, consider the volume of a rectangular box $= lwh$, where l is length, w is width, and h is height. This can be simplified into $V = Ah$, where A is the area of the base. The *volume* of a pyramid with the same dimensions is $1/3$ of this

quantity because it fills up 1/3 of the space. Therefore, the volume of a pyramid is $V = \frac{1}{3} Ah$. In a similar fashion, the volume of a cone is $\frac{1}{3}$ of the volume of a cylinder. Therefore, the formula for the volume of a cylinder is $\frac{1}{3} \pi r^2 h$.

Perimeter and Area

Both the perimeter and area formulas are applicable in real-world scenarios. Knowing the *perimeter* is useful when the length of a shape's outline is needed. For example, to build a fence around a yard, the yard's perimeter must be calculated so enough materials are purchased to complete the fence. The *area* is necessary anytime the surface of a shape is needed. For example, when constructing a garden, the area of the garden region is needed so enough dirt can be purchased to fill it. Many times, it's necessary to break up the given shape into shapes with known perimeter and area formulas (such as triangles and rectangles) and add the individual perimeters or areas together to determine the desired quantity.

Surface Area and Volume

Many real-world objects are a combination of prisms, cylinders, pyramids, and spheres. *Surface area* problems relate to quantifying the outside area of such a three-dimensional object, and *volume* problems involve quantifying how much the three-dimensional object can hold. For example, when calculating how much paint is needed to paint an entire house, surface area is used. Conversely, when calculating how much water a cylindrical tank can hold, volume is used. The surface area of a *prism* is the sum of all the areas, which simplifies into $SA = 2A + Bh$ where A is the area of the base, B is the perimeter of the base, and h is the height of the prism. The volume of the same prism is $V = Ah$. The surface area of a *cylinder* is the sum of the areas of both ends and the side, which is $SA = 2\pi rh + 2\pi r^2$. The surface area of a *pyramid* is calculated by adding known area formulas. It is equal to the area of the base (which is rectangular) plus the area of the four triangles that form the sides. The surface area of a *cone* is equal to the area of the base plus the area of the top, which is $SA = \pi r^2 + \pi \pi r \sqrt{h^2 + r^2}$. Finally, the surface area of a sphere is $SA = 4\pi r^2$ and its volume is $V = \frac{4}{3}\pi r^3$.

Effects of Changes to Dimensions on Area and Volume

Similar polygons are figures that are the same shape but different sizes. Likewise, similar solids are different sizes but are the same shape. In both cases, corresponding angles in the same positions for both figures are congruent (equal), and corresponding sides are proportional in length. For example, the triangles below are similar. The following pairs of corresponding angles are congruent: $\angle A$ and $\angle D$; $\angle B$ and $\angle E$; $\angle C$ and $\angle F$. The corresponding sides are proportional: $\frac{AB}{DE} = \frac{6}{3} = 2, \frac{BC}{EF} = \frac{9}{4.5} = 2, \frac{CA}{FD} = \frac{10}{5} = 2$. In other words, triangle ABC is the same shape but twice as large as triangle DEF.

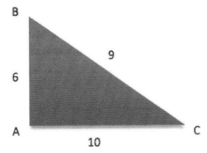
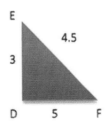

An example of similar triangular pyramids is shown below.

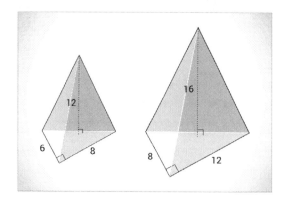

Given the nature of two- and three-dimensional measurements, changing dimensions by a given scale (multiplier) does not change the area of volume by the same scale. Consider a rectangle with a length of 5 centimeters and a width of 4 centimeters. The area of the rectangle is $20cm^2$. Doubling the dimensions of the rectangle (multiplying by a scale factor of 2) to 10 centimeters and 8 centimeters *does not* double the area to $40cm^2$. Area is a two-dimensional measurement (measured in square units). Therefore, the dimensions are multiplied by a scale that is squared (raised to the second power) to determine the scale of the corresponding areas. For the previous example, the length and width are multiplied by 2. Therefore, the area is multiplied by 2^2, or 4. The area of a 5cm × 4cm rectangle is $20cm^2$. The area of a 10cm × 8cm rectangle is $80cm^2$.

Volume is a three-dimensional measurement, which is measured in cubic units. Therefore, the scale between dimensions of similar solids is cubed (raised to the third power) to determine the scale between their volumes. Consider similar right rectangular prisms: one with a length of 8 inches, a width of 24 inches, and a height of 16 inches; the second with a length of 4 inches, a width of 12 inches, and a height of 8 inches. The first prism, multiplied by a scalar of $\frac{1}{2}$, produces the measurement of the second prism. The volume of the first prism, multiplied by $(\frac{1}{2})^3$, which equals $\frac{1}{8}$, produces the volume of the second prism. The volume of the first prism is 8in × 24in × 16in which equals $3,072in^3$. The volume of the second prism is 4in × 12in × 8in which equals $384in^3$ ($3,072in^3 \times \frac{1}{8} = 384in^3$).

The rules for squaring the scalar for area and cubing the scalar for volume only hold true for similar figures. In other words, if only one dimension is changed (changing the width of a rectangle but not the length) or dimensions are changed at different rates (the length of a prism is doubled and its height is tripled) the figures are not similar (same shape). Therefore, the rules above do not apply.

Measurement Problems in Real-World Situations

Measurement problems appear often in the real world, so it's important to understand their setup and solution. Problems related to time can involve calculating how longs events take, which can help answer when events will occur. Real numbers must be converted to hours, minutes, seconds, etc. For example, 100 minutes equals one hour and 40 minutes or 100 seconds equals 1 minute and 40 seconds. Let's say it takes a baker 15 minutes to bake a dozen cookies. If he starts baking at noon, we could determine what time he will be done baking 6 dozen cookies: $6 \cdot 15 = 90$. Therefore, he will be done at 1:30 pm, which is 90 minutes after noon.

Temperature problems usually involve determining the temperature of a substance at a given time. The units of temperature can be degrees Fahrenheit or Celsius, and the units of time can be seconds, minutes, hours, etc. A function can be given that defines temperature as a function of time. To determine the temperature at a given time, plug the time into the independent variable to obtain the dependent variable temperature.

Problems involving rates involve a ratio calculation like 45 miles per hour or fifteen dollars per hour. Use a proportion to determine how many can haircuts can be completed in 6 hours if 3 haircuts can be completed in 2 hours. The proportion $\frac{3}{2} = \frac{x}{6}$ is used to find that $18 = 2x$, and therefore $x = 9$. Therefore, 9 haircuts can be completed in six hours.

Rate of change problems involve calculating a ratio of a quantity per a unit of time. This calculation is the same as using the slope formula on two ordered pairs. Consider the following problem that involves time, temperature, and average rate of change: Last Tuesday, the temperature at 9:00 am was 49 degrees Fahrenheit, and at noon, the temperature was 61 degrees Fahrenheit. What was the average rate of change? The average rate of change is the change in temperature divided by the change in time: $\frac{61-49}{12-9} = \frac{12}{3} = 4$ degrees per hour. Average rates of change are found by determining the averages of multiple rates of change calculations. For example, temperature differentials from more three-hour time periods could be given to calculate an average.

Polygons and Solids

A polygon is a closed two-dimensional figure consisting of three or more sides. Polygons can be either convex or concave. A polygon that has interior angles all measuring less than 180° is convex. A concave polygon has one or more interior angles measuring greater than 180°.

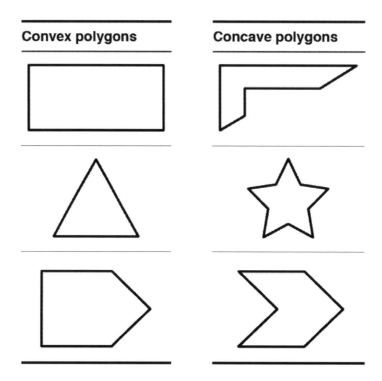

Polygons can be classified by the number of sides (also equal to the number of angles) they have. The following are the names of polygons with a given number of sides or angles:

# of sides	3	4	5	6	7	8	9	10
Name of polygon	Triangle	Quadrilateral	Pentagon	Hexagon	Septagon (or heptagon)	Octagon	Nonagon	Decagon

Equiangular polygons are polygons in which the measure of every interior angle is the same. The sides of equilateral polygons are always the same length. If a polygon is both equiangular and equilateral, the polygon is defined as a regular polygon.

Triangles can be further classified by their sides and angles. A triangle with its largest angle measuring 90° is a right triangle. A triangle with the largest angle less than 90° is an acute triangle. A triangle with the largest angle greater than 90° is an obtuse triangle.

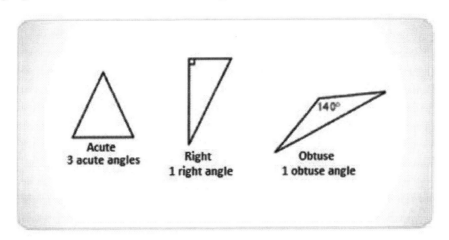

A triangle with three equal sides and three equal angles is an equilateral triangle.

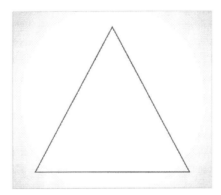

A triangle consisting of two equal sides and two equal angles is an isosceles triangle.

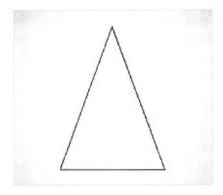

A triangle with no equal sides or angles is a scalene triangle.

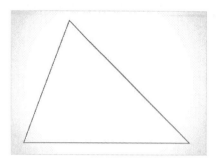

Quadrilaterals can be further classified according to their sides and angles. A quadrilateral with exactly one pair of parallel sides is called a trapezoid. A quadrilateral that shows both pairs of opposite sides parallel is a parallelogram. Parallelograms include rhombuses, rectangles, and squares. A rhombus has four equal sides. A rectangle has four equal angles (90° each). A square has four 90° angles and four equal sides. Therefore, a square is both a rhombus and a rectangle.

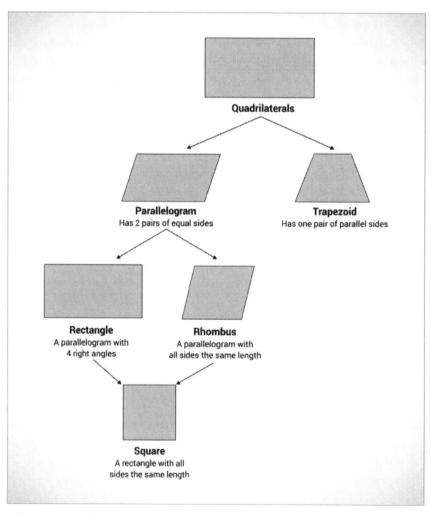

A solid is a three-dimensional figure that encloses a part of space. Solids consisting of all flat surfaces that are polygons are called polyhedrons. The two-dimensional surfaces that make up a polyhedron are called faces. Types of polyhedrons include prisms and pyramids. A prism consists of two parallel faces that are congruent (or the same shape and same size), and lateral faces going around (which are parallelograms). A prism is further classified by the shape of its base, as shown below:

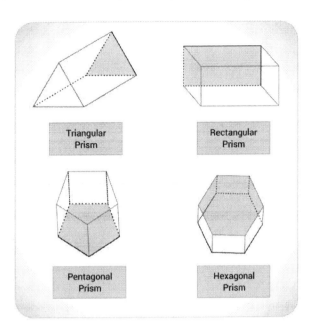

A pyramid consists of lateral faces (triangles) that meet at a common point called the vertex and one other face that is a polygon, called the base. A pyramid can be further classified by the shape of its base, as shown below.

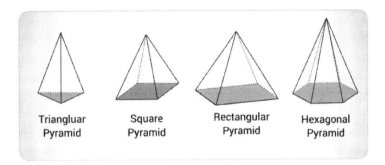

A tetrahedron is another name for a triangular pyramid. All the faces of a tetrahedron are triangles.

Solids that are not polyhedrons include spheres, cylinders, and cones. A sphere is the set of all points a given distance from a given center point. A sphere is commonly thought of as a three-dimensional circle. A cylinder consists of two parallel, congruent (same size) circles and a lateral curved surface. A cone consists of a circle as its base and a lateral curved surface that narrows to a point called the vertex.

Similar polygons are the same shape but different sizes. More specifically, their corresponding angle measures are congruent (or equal) and the length of their sides is proportional. For example, all sides of one polygon may be double the length of the sides of another. Likewise, similar solids are the same shape but different sizes. Any corresponding faces or bases of similar solids are the same polygons that are proportional by a consistent value.

Area and Perimeter of Polygons

The perimeter of a polygon is the distance around the outside of the two-dimensional figure. Perimeter is a one-dimensional measurement and is therefore expressed in linear units such as centimeters (*cm*), feet (*ft*), and miles (*mi*). The perimeter (*P*) of a figure can be calculated by adding together each of the sides.

Properties of certain polygons allow that the perimeter may be obtained by using formulas. A rectangle consists of two sides called the length (*l*), which have equal measures, and two sides called the width (*w*), which have equal measures. Therefore, the perimeter (*P*) of a rectangle can be expressed as $P = l + l + w + w$. This can be simplified to produce the following formula to find the perimeter of a rectangle: $P = 2l + 2w$ or $P = 2(l + w)$.

A regular polygon is one in which all sides have equal length and all interior angles have equal measures, such as a square and an equilateral triangle. To find the perimeter of a regular polygon, the length of one side is multiplied by the number of sides. For example, to find the perimeter of an equilateral triangle with a side of length of 4 feet, 4 feet is multiplied by 3 (number of sides of a triangle). The perimeter of a regular octagon (8 sides) with a side of length of $\frac{1}{2}$cm is $\frac{1}{2}cm \times 8 = 4cm$.

The area of a polygon is the number of square units needed to cover the interior region of the figure. Area is a two-dimensional measurement. Therefore, area is expressed in square units, such as square centimeters (cm^2), square feet (ft^2), or square miles (mi^2). The previous section of this unit covered the topic of finding the area of rectangles and triangles. To find the area (*A*) of a parallelogram, the length of the base (*b*) is multiplied by the length of the height (*h*) $\rightarrow A = b \times h$. Similar to triangles, the height of the parallelogram is measured from one base to the other at a 90° angle (or perpendicular).

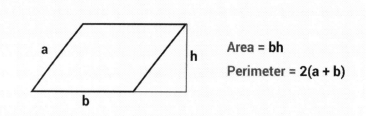

Area = bh

Perimeter = 2(a + b)

The area of a trapezoid can be calculated using the formula: $A = \frac{1}{2} \times (b_1 + b_2)h$, where *h* is the height and b_1 and b_2 are the parallel bases of the trapezoid.

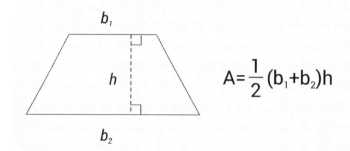

$$A = \frac{1}{2}(b_1 + b_2)h$$

The area of a regular polygon can be determined by using its perimeter and the length of the apothem. The apothem is a line from the center of the regular polygon to any of its sides at a right angle. (Note that the perimeter of a regular polygon can be determined given the length of only one side.) The formula for the area (A) of a regular polygon is $A = \frac{1}{2} \times a \times P$, where a is the length of the apothem and P is the perimeter of the figure. Consider the following regular pentagon:

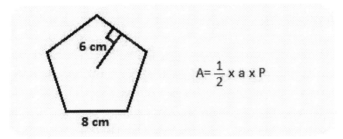

To find the area, the perimeter (P) is calculated first: $8cm \times 5 \rightarrow P = 40cm$. Then the perimeter and the apothem are used to find the area (A): $A = \frac{1}{2} \times a \times P \rightarrow A = \frac{1}{2} \times (6cm) \times (40cm) \rightarrow A = 120cm^2$. Note that the unit is $cm^2 \rightarrow cm \times cm = cm^2$.

The area of irregular polygons is found by decomposing, or breaking apart, the figure into smaller shapes. When the area of the smaller shapes is determined, the area of the smaller shapes will produce the area of the original figure when added together. Consider the example below:

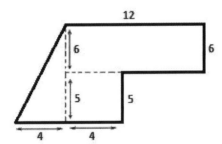

The irregular polygon is decomposed into two rectangles and a triangle. The area of the large rectangles ($A = l \times w \rightarrow A = 12 \times 6$) is 72 square units. The area of the small rectangle is 20 square units ($A = 4 \times 5$). The area of the triangle ($A = \frac{1}{2} \times b \times h \rightarrow A = \frac{1}{2} \times 4 \times 11$) is 22 square units. The sum of the areas of these figures produces the total area of the original polygon: $A = 72 + 20 + 22 \rightarrow A = 114$ square units.

Three-Dimensional Figures

Three-dimensional shapes can be classified by the number and type of faces or the number of edges and vertices. A face is defined as a flat surface that forms a portion of the boundary of a shape. For example, a cube has six equal faces, and each face is a square. Many known two-dimensional shapes like squares, rectangles, and triangles exist as faces within three-dimensional objects. Edges are defined as the intersection of faces and are either straight lines or curves, and their endpoints are known as vertices or corners. Here's an example of a cube with a face, edge, and vertex labeled:

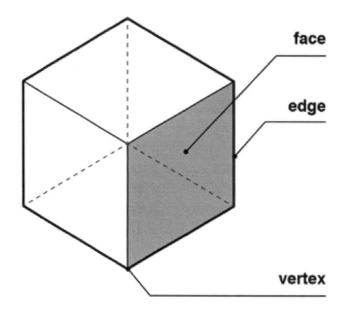

In general, a polyhedron is a three-dimensional figure composed of faces, edges, and vertices. (The plural form of polyhedron is polyhedra.) Polyhedra are classified further by the number of faces, edges, and vertices. A prism is composed of two congruent polygons, called bases, which are connected by parallelograms, called lateral faces. A cube is a prism in which all faces are squares. For rectangular prisms, all six faces are rectangles. A triangular prism has two bases that are triangles and three additional faces that are squares or rectangles. Other types of prisms are pentagonal, hexagonal, and octagonal. They are classified based on their base.

Another type of a polyhedron is a pyramid. A pyramid has one base that's a polygon, and the lateral faces are triangles that meet at a single vertex. Like prisms, they are classified by the shape of the base. For example, a triangular pyramid has a triangle base, and a square pyramid has a square base.

Cones, cylinders, and spheres are also three-dimensional shapes discussed often in mathematics. A sphere consists of one face and no vertices. A cone has one vertex and two faces, and a cylinder has three faces and no vertices.

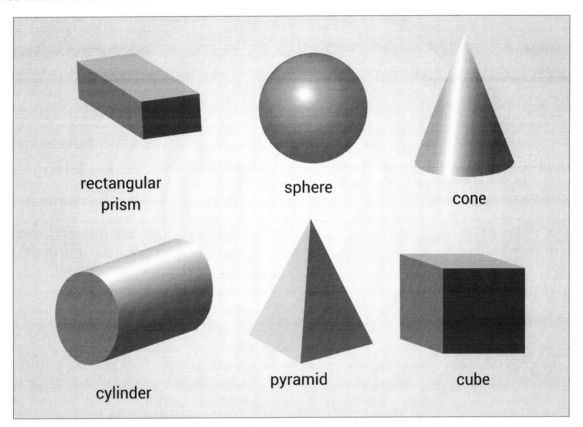

Congruence and Similarity in Terms of Transformations

<u>Rigid Motion</u>
A *rigid motion* is a transformation that preserves distance and length. Every line segment in the resulting image is congruent to the corresponding line segment in the pre-image. Congruence between two figures means a series of transformations (or a rigid motion) can be defined that maps one of the figures onto the other. Basically, two figures are congruent if they have the same shape and size.

Dilation

A shape is dilated, or a *dilation* occurs, when each side of the original image is multiplied by a given scale factor. If the scale factor is less than 1 and greater than 0, the dilation contracts the shape, and the resulting shape is smaller. If the scale factor equals 1, the resulting shape is the same size, and the dilation is a rigid motion. Finally, if the scale factor is greater than 1, the resulting shape is larger and the dilation expands the shape. The *center of dilation* is the point where the distance from it to any point on the new shape equals the scale factor times the distance from the center to the corresponding point in the pre-image. Dilation isn't an isometric transformation because distance isn't preserved. However, angle measure, parallel lines, and points on a line all remain unchanged. The following figure is an example of translation, rotation, dilation, and reflection:

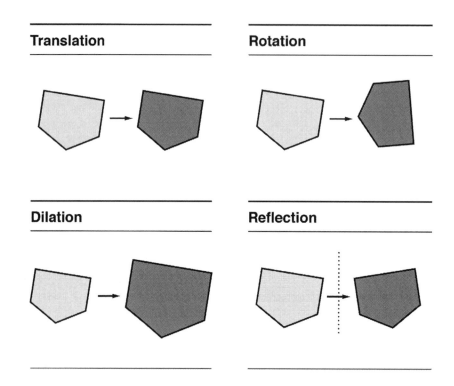

Determining Congruence

Two figures are congruent if there is a rigid motion that can map one figure onto the other. Therefore, all pairs of sides and angles within the image and pre-image must be congruent. For example, in triangles, each pair of the three sides and three angles must be congruent. Similarly, in two four-sided figures, each pair of the four sides and four angles must be congruent.

Similarity

Two figures are *similar* if there is a combination of translations, reflections, rotations, and dilations, which maps one figure onto the other. The difference between congruence and similarity is that dilation can be used in similarity. Therefore, side lengths between each shape can differ. However, angle measure must be preserved within this definition. If two polygons differ in size so that the lengths of corresponding line segments differ by the same factor, but corresponding angles have the same measurement, they are similar.

Triangle Congruence

There are five theorems to show that triangles are congruent when it's unknown whether each pair of angles and sides are congruent. Each theorem is a shortcut that involves different combinations of sides and angles that must be true for the two triangles to be congruent. For example, *side-side-side (SSS)* states that if all sides are equal, the triangles are congruent. *Side-angle-side (SAS)* states that if two pairs of sides are equal and the included angles are congruent, then the triangles are congruent. Similarly, *angle-side-angle (ASA)* states that if two pairs of angles are congruent and the included side lengths are equal, the triangles are similar. *Angle-angle-side (AAS)* states that two triangles are congruent if they have two pairs of congruent angles and a pair of corresponding equal side lengths that aren't included. Finally, *hypotenuse-leg (HL)* states that if two right triangles have equal hypotenuses and an equal pair of shorter sides, then the triangles are congruent. An important item to note is that angle-angle-angle *(AAA)* is not enough information to have congruence. It's important to understand why these rules work by using rigid motions to show congruence between the triangles with the given properties. For example, three reflections are needed to show why *SAS* follows from the definition of congruence.

Similarity for Two Triangles

If two angles of one triangle are congruent with two angles of a second triangle, the triangles are similar. This is because, within any triangle, the sum of the angle measurements is 180 degrees. Therefore, if two are congruent, the third angle must also be congruent because their measurements are equal. Three congruent pairs of angles mean that the triangles are similar.

Proving Congruence and Similarity

The criteria needed to prove triangles are congruent involves both angle and side congruence. Both pairs of related angles and sides need to be of the same measurement to use congruence in a proof. The criteria to prove similarity in triangles involves proportionality of side lengths. Angles must be congruent in similar triangles; however, corresponding side lengths only need to be a constant multiple of each other. Once similarity is established, it can be used in proofs as well. Relationships in geometric figures other than triangles can be proven using triangle congruence and similarity. If a similar or congruent triangle can be found within another type of geometric figure, their criteria can be used to prove a relationship about a given formula. For instance, a rectangle can be broken up into two congruent triangles.

Visualizing Relationships Between Two-Dimensional and Three-Dimensional Objects

Cross Sections and Rotations

Two-dimensional objects are formed when three-dimensional objects are "sliced" in various ways. For example, any cross section of a sphere is a circle. Some three-dimensional objects have different cross sections depending on how the object is sliced. For example, the cross section of a cylinder can be a circle or a rectangle, and the cross section of a pyramid can be a square or a triangle. In addition, three-dimensional objects can be formed by rotating two-dimensional objects. Certain rotations can relate the two-dimensional cross sections back to the original three-dimensional objects. The objects must be rotated around an imaginary line known as the *rotation axis*. For example, a right triangle can be rotated around one of its legs to form a cone. A sphere can be formed by rotating a semicircle around a line segment formed from its diameter. Finally, rotating a square around one of its sides forms a cylinder.

Simplifying Three-Dimensional Objects

Three-dimensional objects can be simplified into related two-dimensional shapes to solve problems. This simplification can make problem-solving a much easier experience. An isometric representation of a three-dimensional object can be completed so that important properties (e.g., shape, relationships of faces and surfaces) are noted. Edges and vertices can be translated into two-dimensional objects as well. For example, below is a three-dimensional object that's been partitioned into two-dimensional representations of its faces:

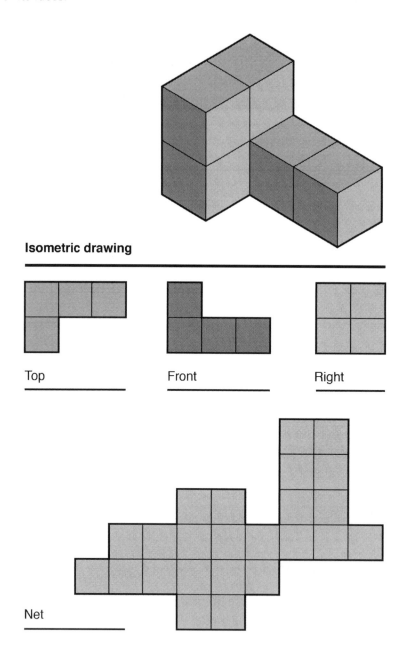

Isometric drawing

Top   Front   Right

Net

The net represents the sum of the three different faces. Depending on the problem, using a smaller portion of the given shape may be helpful, by simplifying the steps necessary to solve.

Connections Between Algebra and Geometry

Coordinate Systems

Coordinate geometry is the intersection of algebra and geometry. Within this system, the points in a geometric shape are defined using ordered pairs. In the two-dimensional coordinate system, an x- and y-axis form the xy-plane. The x-axis is a horizontal scale, and the y-axis is a vertical scale. The ordered pair where the axes cross is known as the origin. To the right of the origin, the x-values are positive, and to the left of the origin, the x-values are negative. Y-values above the origin are positive, and y-values below the origin are negative. The axes split the plane up into four quadrants and the first quadrant is where both x and y values are positive.

Two-dimensional geometric shapes can be placed inside the xy-plane. For example, the following is a circle centered at the ordered pair (1,0) with radius 3.

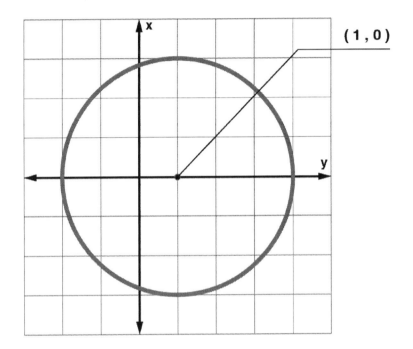

Each point on the circle corresponds to an ordered pair (x,y). Many geometrical shapes can be represented by algebraic equations, and this circle has equation $(x-1)^2 + y^2 = 9$. Ordered pairs that exist on the circle can be found by plugging in either x-values from -2 to 4 or y-values from -3 to 3 and solving for the other variable. Once a geometric shape is inserted into a coordinate system, the distance between two points $(x_1, y_1), (x_2, y_2)$ on the shape can be determined using the two-dimensional distance formula $d = \sqrt{(x_2 - x_1)^2 + (y_2 - y_1)^2}$.

If a third axis, known as the z-axis, is added to the xy-plane, three-dimensional space can be represented. Each axis is perpendicular to the other two, and all three axes intersect at the origin. Each point in the plane is an ordered triple (x,y,z). Three-dimensional geometric shapes can be placed into three-dimensional space. For example, the following is a graph of a cube in the coordinate system. Notice that each vertex corresponds to a different ordered triple.

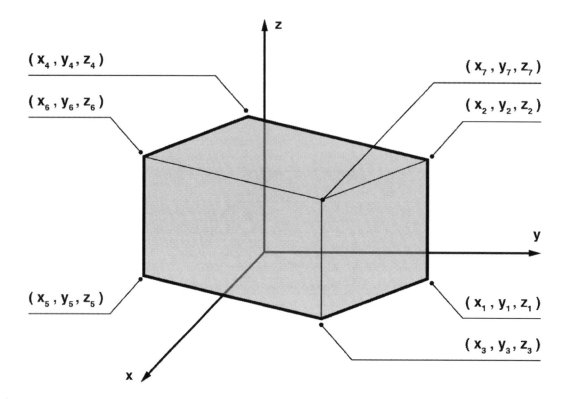

The Pythagorean Theorem

The *Pythagorean theorem* is an important relationship between the three sides of a right triangle. It states that the square of the side opposite the right triangle, known as the *hypotenuse* (denoted as c^2), is equal to the sum of the squares of the other two sides ($a^2 + b^2$). Thus, $a^2 + b^2 = c^2$.

Both the trigonometric functions and the Pythagorean theorem can be used in problems that involve finding either a missing side or a missing angle of a right triangle. To do so, one must look to see what sides and angles are given and select the correct relationship that will help find the missing value. These relationships can also be used to solve application problems involving right triangles. Often, it's helpful to draw a figure to represent the problem to see what's missing.

Statistics and Probability

Measures of Central Tendency and Range

The center of a set of data (statistical values) can be represented by its mean, median, or mode. These are sometimes referred to as measures of central tendency. The mean is the average of the data set. The mean can be calculated by adding the data values and dividing by the sample size (the number of data points). Suppose a student has test scores of 93, 84, 88, 72, 91, and 77. To find the mean, or average, the scores are added and the sum is divided by 6 because there are 6 test scores:

$$\frac{93 + 84 + 88 + 72 + 91 + 77}{6} = \frac{505}{6} = 84.17$$

Given the mean of a data set and the sum of the data points, the sample size can be determined by dividing the sum by the mean. Suppose you are told that Kate averaged 12 points per game and scored a total of 156 points for the season. The number of games that she played (the sample size or the number of data points) can be determined by dividing the total points (sum of data points) by her average (mean of data points): $\frac{156}{12} = 13$. Therefore, Kate played in 13 games this season.

If given the mean of a data set and the sample size, the sum of the data points can be determined by multiplying the mean and sample size. Suppose you are told that Tom worked 6 days last week for an average of 5.5 hours per day. The total number of hours worked for the week (sum of data points) can be determined by multiplying his daily average (mean of data points) by the number of days worked (sample size): $5.5 \times 6 = 33$. Therefore, Tom worked a total of 33 hours last week.

The median of a data set is the value of the data point in the middle when the sample is arranged in numerical order. To find the median of a data set, the values are written in order from least to greatest. The lowest and highest values are simultaneously eliminated, repeating until the value in the middle remains. Suppose the salaries of math teachers are: $35,000; $38,500; $41,000; $42,000; $42,000; $44,500; $49,000. The values are listed from least to greatest to find the median. The lowest and highest values are eliminated until only the middle value remains. Repeating this step three times reveals a median salary of $42,000. If the sample set has an even number of data points, two values will remain after all others are eliminated. In this case, the mean of the two middle values is the median. Consider the following data set: 7, 9, 10, 13, 14, 14. Eliminating the lowest and highest values twice leaves two values, 10 and 13, in the middle. The mean of these values $\left(\frac{10+13}{2}\right)$ is the median. Therefore, the set has a median of 11.5.

The mode of a data set is the value that appears most often. A data set may have a single mode, multiple modes, or no mode. If different values repeat equally as often, multiple modes exist. If no value repeats, no mode exists. Consider the following data sets:

- A: 7, 9, 10, 13, 14, 14
- B: 37, 44, 33, 37, 49, 44, 51, 34, 37, 33, 44
- C: 173, 154, 151, 168, 155

Set A has a mode of 14. Set B has modes of 37 and 44. Set C has no mode.

The range of a data set is the difference between the highest and the lowest values in the set. The range can be considered the span of the data set. To determine the range, the smallest value in the set is subtracted from the largest value. The ranges for the data sets A, B, and C above are calculated as follows: A: $14 - 7 = 7$; B: $51 - 33 = 18$; C: $173 - 151 = 22$.

Best Description of a Set of Data
Measures of central tendency, namely mean, median, and mode, describe characteristics of a set of data. Specifically, they are intended to represent a *typical* value in the set by identifying a central position of the set. Depending on the characteristics of a specific set of data, different measures of central tendency are more indicative of a typical value in the set.

When a data set is grouped closely together with a relatively small range and the data is spread out somewhat evenly, the mean is an effective indicator of a typical value in the set. Consider the following data set representing the height of sixth grade boys in inches: 61 inches, 54 inches, 58 inches, 63 inches, 58 inches. The mean of the set is 58.8 inches. The data set is grouped closely (the range is only 9 inches) and the values are spread relatively evenly (three values below the mean and two values above the mean). Therefore, the mean value of 58.8 inches is an effective measure of central tendency in this case.

When a data set contains a small number of values either extremely large or extremely small when compared to the other values, the mean is not an effective measure of central tendency. Consider the following data set representing annual incomes of homeowners on a given street: $71,000; $74,000; $75,000; $77,000; $340,000. The mean of this set is $127,400. This figure does not indicate a typical value in the set, which contains four out of five values between $71,000 and $77,000. The median is a much more effective measure of central tendency for data sets such as these. Finding the middle value diminishes the influence of outliers, or numbers that may appear out of place, like the $340,000 annual income. The median for this set is $75,000 which is much more typical of a value in the set.

The mode of a data set is a useful measure of central tendency for categorical data when each piece of data is an option from a category. Consider a survey of 31 commuters asking how they get to work with results summarized below.

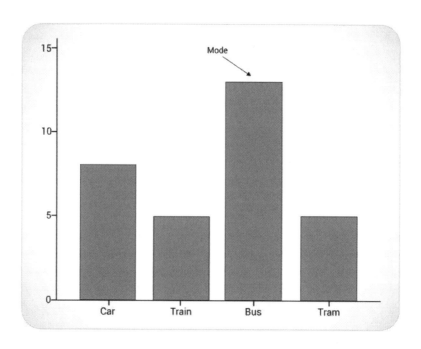

The mode for this set represents the value, or option, of the data that repeats most often. This indicates that the bus is the most popular method of transportation for the commuters.

Effects of Changes in Data

Changing all values of a data set in a consistent way produces predictable changes in the measures of the center and range of the set. A linear transformation changes the original value into the new value by either adding a given number to each value, multiplying each value by a given number, or both. Adding (or subtracting) a given value to each data point will increase (or decrease) the mean, median, and any modes by the same value. However, the range will remain the same due to the way that range is calculated. Multiplying (or dividing) a given value by each data point will increase (or decrease) the mean, median, and any modes, and the range by the same factor.

Consider the following data set, call it set P, representing the price of different cases of soda at a grocery store: $4.25, $4.40, $4.75, $4.95, $4.95, $5.15. The mean of set P is $4.74. The median is $4.85. The mode of the set is $4.95. The range is $0.90. Suppose the state passes a new tax of $0.25 on every case of soda sold. The new data set, set T, is calculated by adding $0.25 to each data point from set P. Therefore, set T consists of the following values: $4.50, $4.65, $5.00, $5.20, $5.20, $5.40. The mean of set T is $4.99. The median is $5.10. The mode of the set is $5.20. The range is $.90. The mean, median and mode of set T is equal to $0.25 added to the mean, median, and mode of set P. The range stays the same.

Now suppose, due to inflation, the store raises the cost of every item by 10 percent. Raising costs by 10 percent is calculated by multiplying each value by 1.1. The new data set, set I, is calculated by multiplying each data point from set T by 1.1. Therefore, set I consists of the following values: $4.95, $5.12, $5.50, $5.72, $5.72, $5.94. The mean of set I is $5.49. The median is $5.61. The mode of the set is $5.72. The range is $0.99. The mean, median, mode, and range of set I is equal to 1.1 multiplied by the mean, median, mode, and range of set T because each increased by a factor of 10 percent.

Describing a Set of Data

A set of data can be described in terms of its center, spread, shape and any unusual features. The center of a data set can be measured by its mean, median, or mode. Measures of central tendency are covered in the *Measures of Center and Range* section. The spread of a data set refers to how far the data points are from the center (mean or median). The spread can be measured by the range or the quartiles and interquartile range. A data set with data points clustered around the center will have a small spread. A data set covering a wide range will have a large spread.

When a data set is displayed as a histogram or frequency distribution plot, the shape indicates if a sample is normally distributed, symmetrical, or has measures of skewness or kurtosis. When graphed, a data set with a normal distribution will resemble a bell curve.

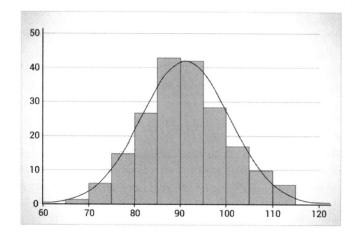

If the data set is symmetrical, each half of the graph when divided at the center is a mirror image of the other. If the graph has fewer data points to the right, the data is skewed right. If it has fewer data points to the left, the data is skewed left.

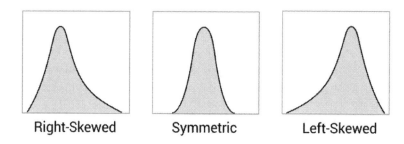

Right-Skewed   Symmetric   Left-Skewed

Kurtosis is a measure of whether the data is heavy-tailed with a high number of outliers, or light-tailed with a low number of outliers.

A description of a data set should include any unusual features such as gaps or outliers. A gap is a span within the range of the data set containing no data points. An outlier is a data point with a value either extremely large or extremely small when compared to the other values in the set.

Interpreting Displays of Data

A set of data can be visually displayed in various forms allowing for quick identification of characteristics of the set. Histograms, such as the one shown below, display the number of data points (vertical axis) that fall into given intervals (horizontal axis) across the range of the set. The histogram below displays the heights of black cherry trees in a certain city park. Each rectangle represents the number of trees with heights between a given five-point span. For example, the furthest bar to the right indicates that two trees are between 85 and 90 feet. Histograms can describe the center, spread, shape, and any unusual characteristics of a data set.

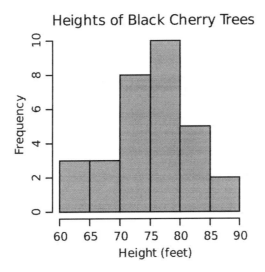

A box plot, also called a box-and-whisker plot, divides the data points into four groups and displays the five number summary for the set, as well as any outliers. The five number summary consists of:

- The lower extreme: the lowest value that is not an outlier
- The higher extreme: the highest value that is not an outlier
- The median of the set: also referred to as the second quartile or Q_2
- The first quartile or Q_1: the median of values below Q_2
- The third quartile or Q_3: the median of values above Q_2

Calculating each of these values is covered in the next section, *Graphical Representation of Data*.

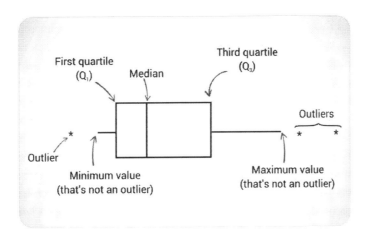

Suppose the box plot displays IQ scores for 12th grade students at a given school. The five number summary of the data consists of: lower extreme (67); upper extreme (127); Q_2 or median (100); Q_1 (91); Q_3 (108); and outliers (135 and 140). Although all data points are not known from the plot, the points are divided into four quartiles each, including 25% of the data points. Therefore, 25% of students scored between 67 and 91, 25% scored between 91 and 100, 25% scored between 100 and 108, and 25% scored between 108 and 127. These percentages include the normal values for the set and exclude the outliers. This information is useful when comparing a given score with the rest of the scores in the set.

A scatter plot is a mathematical diagram that visually displays the relationship or connection between two variables. The independent variable is placed on the *x*-axis, or horizontal axis, and the dependent variable is placed on the *y*-axis, or vertical axis. When visually examining the points on the graph, if the points model a linear relationship, or a line of best-fit can be drawn through the points with the points relatively close on either side, then a correlation exists. If the line of best-fit has a positive slope (rises from left to right), then the variables have a positive correlation. If the line of best-fit has a negative slope (falls from left to right), then the variables have a negative correlation. If a line of best-fit cannot be drawn, then no correlation exists. A positive or negative correlation can be categorized as strong or weak, depending on how closely the points are graphed around the line of best-fit.

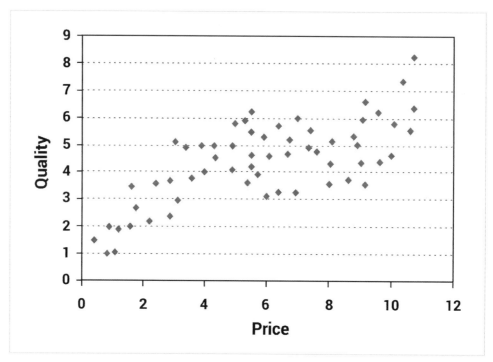

Graphical Representation of Data

Various graphs can be used to visually represent a given set of data. Each type of graph requires a different method of arranging data points and different calculations of the data. Examples of histograms, box plots, and scatter plots are discussed in the previous section *Interpreting Displays of Data*. To construct a histogram, the range of the data points is divided into equal intervals. The frequency for each interval is then determined, which reveals how many points fall into each interval. A graph is constructed with the vertical axis representing the frequency and the horizontal axis representing the intervals. The lower value of each interval should be labeled along the horizontal axis. Finally, for each interval, a bar is drawn from the lower value of each interval to the lower value of the next interval with a height equal to the frequency of the interval. Because of the intervals, histograms do not have any gaps between bars along the horizontal axis.

To construct a box (or box-and-whisker) plot, the five number summary for the data set is calculated as follows: the second quartile (Q_2) is the median of the set. The first quartile (Q_1) is the median of the values below Q_2. The third quartile (Q_3) is the median of the values above Q_2. The upper extreme is the highest value in the data set if it is not an outlier (greater than 1.5 times the interquartile range $Q_3 - Q_1$). The lower extreme is the least value in the data set if it is not an outlier (more than 1.5 times lower than the interquartile range). To construct the box-and-whisker plot, each value is plotted on a number line, along with any outliers. The *box* consists of Q_1 and Q_3 as its *top* and *bottom* and Q_2 as the dividing line inside the box. The *whiskers* extend from the lower extreme to Q_1 and from Q_3 to the upper extreme.

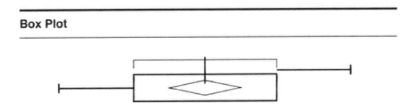

Box Plot

A scatter plot displays the relationship between two variables. Values for the independent variable, typically denoted by *x*, are paired with values for the dependent variable, typically denoted by *y*. Each set of corresponding values are written as an ordered pair (*x, y*). To construct the graph, a coordinate grid is labeled with the *x*-axis representing the independent variable and the *y*-axis representing the dependent variable. Each ordered pair is graphed.

Like a scatter plot, a line graph compares variables that change continuously, typically over time. Paired data values (ordered pair) are plotted on a coordinate grid with the *x*- and *y*-axis representing the variables. A line is drawn from each point to the next, going from left to right. The line graph below displays cell phone use for given years (two variables) for men, women, and both sexes (three data sets).

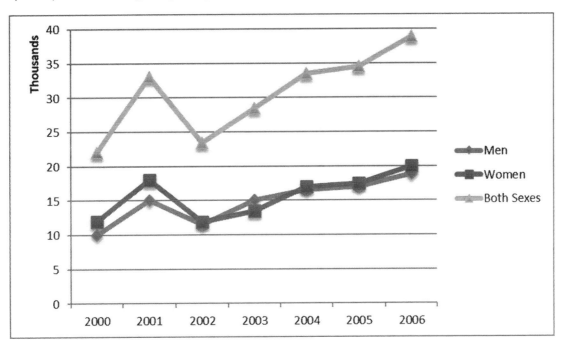

A line plot, also called dot plot, displays the frequency of data (numerical values) on a number line. To construct a line plot, a number line is used that includes all unique data values. It is marked with x's or dots above the value the number of times that the value occurs in the data set.

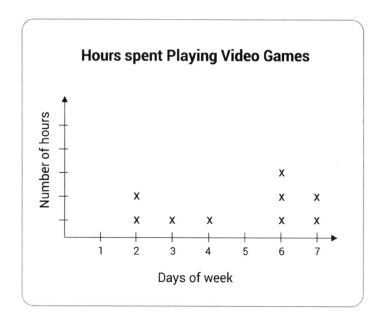

A *bar graph* is a diagram in which the quantity of items within a specific classification is represented by the height of a rectangle. Each type of classification is represented by a rectangle of equal width. Here is an example of a bar graph:

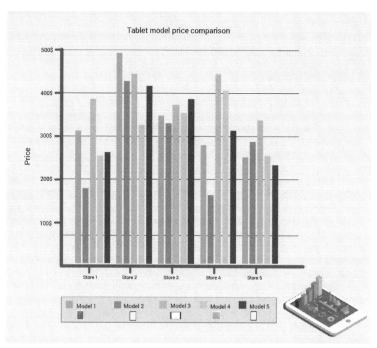

A circle graph, also called a pie chart, shows categorical data with each category representing a percentage of the whole data set. To make a circle graph, the percent of the data set for each category must be determined. To do so, the frequency of the category is divided by the total number of data points and converted to a percent. For example, if 80 people were asked what their favorite sport is and

20 responded basketball, basketball makes up 25% of the data ($\frac{20}{80}$ =.25=25%). Each category in a data set is represented by a *slice* of the circle proportionate to its percentage of the whole.

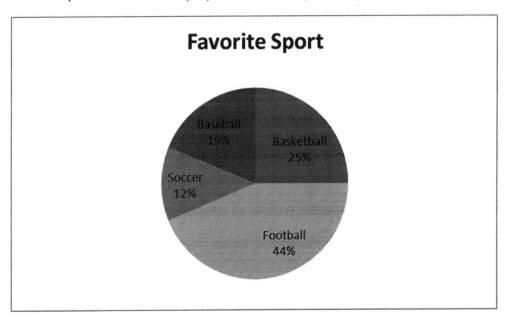

Choice of Graphs to Display Data

Choosing the appropriate graph to display a data set depends on what type of data is included in the set and what information must be displayed. Histograms and box plots can be used for data sets consisting of individual values across a wide range. Examples include test scores and incomes. Histograms and box plots will indicate the center, spread, range, and outliers of a data set. A histogram will show the shape of the data set, while a box plot will divide the set into quartiles (25% increments), allowing for comparison between a given value and the entire set.

Scatter plots and line graphs can be used to display data consisting of two variables. Examples include height and weight, or distance and time. A correlation between the variables is determined by examining the points on the graph. Line graphs are used if each value for one variable pairs with a distinct value for the other variable. Line graphs show relationships between variables.

Line plots, bar graphs, and circle graphs are all used to display categorical data, such as surveys. Line plots and bar graphs both indicate the frequency of each category within the data set. A line plot is used when the categories consist of numerical values. For example, the number of hours of TV watched by individuals is displayed on a line plot. A bar graph is used when the categories consists of words. For example, the favorite ice cream of individuals is displayed with a bar graph. A circle graph can be used to display either type of categorical data. However, unlike line plots and bar graphs, a circle graph does not indicate the frequency of each category. Instead, the circle graph represents each category as its percentage of the whole data set.

Probabilities of Simple and Compound Events and of Independent and Dependent Events

Simple and Compound Events
A *simple event* consists of only one outcome. The most popular simple event is flipping a coin, which results in either heads or tails. A *compound event* results in more than one outcome and consists of

more than one simple event. An example of a compound event is flipping a coin while tossing a die. The result is either heads or tails on the coin and a number from one to six on the die. The probability of a simple event is calculated by dividing the number of possible outcomes by the total number of outcomes. Therefore, the probability of obtaining heads on a coin is $^1/_2$, and the probability of rolling a 6 on a die is $^1/_6$. The probability of compound events is calculated using the basic idea of the probability of simple events. If the two events are independent, the probability of one outcome is equal to the product of the probabilities of each simple event. For example, the probability of obtaining heads on a coin and rolling a 6 is equal to $^1/_2 \times ^1/_6 = ^1/_{12}$. The probability of either A or B occurring is equal to the sum of the probabilities minus the probability that both A and B will occur. Therefore, the probability of obtaining either heads on a coin or rolling a 6 on a die is $^1/_2 + ^1/_6 - ^1/_{12} = ^7/_{12}$. The two events aren't mutually exclusive because they can happen at the same time. If two events are mutually exclusive, and the probability of both events occurring at the same time is zero, the probability of event A or B occurring equals the sum of both probabilities. An example of calculating the probability of two mutually exclusive events is determining the probability of pulling a king or a queen from a deck of cards. The two events cannot occur at the same time.

Measuring Probabilities with Two-Way Frequency Tables

When measuring event probabilities, two-way frequency tables can be used to report the raw data and then used to calculate probabilities. If the frequency tables are translated into relative frequency tables, the probabilities presented in the table can be plugged directly into the formulas for conditional probabilities. By plugging in the correct frequencies, the data from the table can be used to determine if events are independent or dependent.

Differing Probabilities

The probability that event A occurs differs from the probability that event A occurs given B. When working within a given model, it's important to note the difference. $P(A|B)$ is determined using the formula $P(A|B) = \frac{P(A \text{ and } B)}{P(B)}$ and represents the total number of A's outcomes left that could occur after B occurs. $P(A)$ can be calculated without any regard for B. For example, the probability of a student finding a parking spot on a busy campus is different once class is in session.

The Addition Rule

The probability of event A or B occurring isn't equal to the sum of each individual probability. The probability that both events can occur at the same time must be subtracted from this total. This idea is shown in the *addition rule*: $P(A \text{ or } B) = P(A) + P(B) - P(A \text{ and } B)$. The addition rule is another way to determine the probability of compound events that aren't mutually exclusive. If the events are mutually exclusive, the probability of both A and B occurring at the same time is 0.

Uniform and Non-Uniform Probability Models

A *uniform probability model* is one where each outcome has an equal chance of occurring, such as the probabilities of rolling each side of a die. A *non-uniform probability model* is one where each outcome has an unequal chance of occurring. In a uniform probability model, the conditional probability formulas for $P(B|A)$ and $P(A|B)$ can be multiplied by their respective denominators to obtain two formulas for $P(A \text{ and } B)$. Therefore, the multiplication rule is derived as $P(A \text{ and } B) = P(A)P(B|A) = P(B)P(A|B)$. In a model, if the probability of either individual event is known and the corresponding conditional probability is known, the multiplication rule allows the probability of the joint occurrence of A and B to be calculated.

In statistics, a *binomial experiment* is an experiment that has the following properties. The experiment consists of n repeated trial that can each have only one of two outcomes. It can be either a success or a failure. The probability of success, p, is the same in every trial. Each trial is also independent of all other trials. An example of a binomial experiment is rolling a die 10 times with the goal of rolling a 5. Rolling a 5 is a success while any other value is a failure. In this experiment, the probability of rolling a 5 is $\frac{1}{6}$. In any binomial experiment, x is the number of resulting successes, n is the number of trials, p is the probability of success in each trial, and $q = 1 - p$ is the probability of failure within each trial. The probability of obtaining x successes within n trials is:

$$P(X = x) = \frac{n!}{x!\,(n - x)!} p^x (1 - p)^{n-x}$$

With the following being the *binomial coefficient*:

$$\binom{n}{x} = \frac{n!}{x!\,(n - x)!}$$

Within this calculation, $n!$ is n factorial that's defined as:

$$n \cdot (n - 1) \cdot (n - 2) \dots 1$$

Let's look at the probability of obtaining 2 rolls of a 5 out of the 10 rolls.

Start with $P(X = 2)$, where 2 is the number of successes. Then fill in the rest of the formula with what is known, n=10, x=2, p=1/6, q=5/6:

$$P(X = 2) = \left(\frac{10!}{2!\,(10 - 2)!}\right) \left(\frac{1}{6}\right)^2 \left(1 - \frac{1}{6}\right)^{10-2}$$

Which simplifies to:

$$P(X = 2) = \left(\frac{10!}{2!\,8!}\right) \left(\frac{1}{6}\right)^2 \left(\frac{5}{6}\right)^8$$

Then solve to get:

$$P(X = 2) = \left(\frac{3628800}{80640}\right) (.0277)(.2325) = .2898$$

Conditional Probability

<u>Sample Subsets</u>
A sample can be broken up into subsets that are smaller parts of the whole. For example, consider a sample population of females. The sample can be divided into smaller subsets based on the characteristics of each female. There can be a group of females with brown hair and a group of females that wear glasses. There also can be a group of females that have brown hair *and* wear glasses. This "and" relates to the *intersection* of the two separate groups of brunettes and those with glasses. Every female in that intersection group has both characteristics. Similarly, there also can be a group of females that either have brown hair *or* wear glasses. The "or" relates to the union of the two separate groups of brunettes and glasses. Every female in this group has at least one of the characteristics. Finally, the

group of females who do not wear glasses can be discussed. This "not" relates to the *complement* of the glass-wearing group. No one in the complement has glasses. *Venn diagrams* are useful in highlighting these ideas. When discussing statistical experiments, this idea can also relate to events instead of characteristics.

Verifying Independent Events

Two events aren't always independent. For examples, females with glasses and brown hair aren't independent characteristics. There definitely can be overlap because females with brown hair can wear glasses. Also, two events that exist at the same time don't have to have a relationship. For example, even if all females in a given sample are wearing glasses, the characteristics aren't related. In this case, the probability of a brunette wearing glasses is equal to the probability of a female being a brunette multiplied by the probability of a female wearing glasses. This mathematical test of $P(A \cap B) = P(A)P(B)$ verifies that two events are independent.

Conditional Probability

Conditional probability is the probability that event A will happen given that event B has already occurred. An example of this is calculating the probability that a person will eat dessert once they have eaten dinner. This is different than calculating the probability of a person just eating dessert. The formula for the conditional probability of event A occurring given B is $P(A|B) = \frac{P(A \text{ and } B)}{P(B)}$, and it's defined to be the probability of both A and B occurring divided by the probability of event B occurring. If A and B are independent, then the probability of both A and B occurring is equal to $P(A)P(B)$, so $P(A|B)$ reduces to just $P(A)$. This means that A and B have no relationship, and the probability of A occurring is the same as the conditional probability of A occurring given B. Similarly, $P(B|A) = \frac{P(B \text{ and } A)}{P(A)} = P(B)$ if A and B are independent.

Independent Versus Related Events

To summarize, conditional probability is the probability that an event occurs given that another event has happened. If the two events are related, the probability that the second event will occur changes if the other event has happened. However, if the two events aren't related and are therefore independent, the first event to occur won't impact the probability of the second event occurring.

Difference Between Experimentally and Theoretically Determined Probabilities in Real-World Situations

Graphical Displays

Graphical displays are used to visually represent probability distributions in statistical experiments. Specific displays representing probability distributions illustrate the probability of each event. Histograms are typically used to represent probability distributions, and the actual probability can be thought of as $P(x)$, where x is the independent variable.

Expected Value

The *expected value* of a random variable represents the mean value in either a large sample size or after a large number of trials. According to the law of large numbers, after a large number of trials, the actual mean (and that of the probability distribution) is approximately equal to the expected value. The expected value is a weighted average and is calculated as $E(X) = \sum x_i p_i$, where x_i represents the value of each outcome and p_i represents the probability of each outcome. If all probabilities are equal, the expected value is:

$$E(X) = \frac{x_1 + x_2 + \cdots + x_n}{n}$$

Expected value is often called the *mean of the random variable* and is also a measure of central tendency.

Calculating Theoretical Probabilities

Given a statistical experiment, a theoretical probability distribution can be calculated if the theoretical probabilities are known. The theoretical probabilities are plugged into the formula for both the binomial probability and the expected value. An example of this is any scenario involving rolls of a die or flips of a coin. The theoretical probabilities are known without any observed experiments. Another example of this is finding the theoretical probability distribution for the number of correct answers obtained by guessing a specific number of multiple choice questions on a class exam.

Determining Unknown Probabilities

Empirical data is defined as real data. If real data is known, approximations concerning samples and populations can be obtained by working backwards. This scenario is the case where theoretical probabilities are unknown, and experimental data must be used to make decisions. The sample data (including actual probabilities) must be plugged into the formulas for both binomial probability and the expected value. The actual probabilities are obtained using observation and can be seen in a probability distribution. An example of this scenario is determining a probability distribution for the number of televisions per household in the United States, and determining the expected number of televisions per household as well.

Weighing Outcomes

Calculating if it's worth it to play a game or make a decision is a critical part of probability theory. Expected values can be calculated in terms of payoff values, and deciding whether to make a decision or play a game can be done based on the actual expected value. Applying this theory to gambling and card games is fairly typical. The payoff values in these instances are the actual monetary totals.

Fairness

Fairness can be used when making decisions given different scenarios. For example, a game of chance can be deemed fair if every outcome has an equal probability of occurring. Also, a decision or choice can be labeled as fair if each possible option has an equal probability of being chosen. Using basic probability knowledge allows one to make decisions based on fairness. Fairness helps determine if an event's outcome is truly random and no bias is involved in the results. Random number generators are a good way to ensure fairness. An example of an event that isn't fair is the rolling of a weighted die.

Combinations and Permutations

There are many counting techniques that can help solve problems involving counting possibilities. For example, the *Addition Principle* states that if there are m choices from Group 1 and n choices from Group 2, then $n + m$ is the total number of choices possible from Groups 1 and 2. For this to be true, the groups can't have any choices in common. The *Multiplication Principle* states that if Process 1 can be completed n ways and Process 2 can be completed m ways, the total number of ways to complete both Process 1 and Process 2 is $n \times m$. For this rule to be used, both processes must be independent of each other. Counting techniques also involve permutations. A *permutation* is an arrangement of elements in a set for which order must be considered. For example, if three letters from the alphabet are chosen, ABC and BAC are two different permutations. The multiplication rule can be used to determine the total number of possibilities. If each letter can't be selected twice, the total number of possibilities is $26 \times 25 \times 24 = 15{,}600$. A formula can also be used to calculate this total. In general, the notation $P(n, r)$ represents the number of ways to arrange r objects from a set of n and, the formula is:

$$P(n, r) = \frac{n!}{(n-r)!}$$

In the previous example, $P(26, 3) = \frac{26!}{23!} = 15{,}600$. Contrasting permutations, a *combination* is an arrangement of elements in which order doesn't matter. In this case, ABC and BAC are the same combination. In the previous scenario, there are six permutations that represent each single combination. Therefore, the total number of possible combinations is $15{,}600 \div 6 = 2{,}600$. In general, $C(n, r)$ represents the total number of combinations of n items selected r at a time where order doesn't matter, and the formula is:

$$C(n, r) = \frac{n!}{(n-r)! \; r!}$$

Therefore, the following relationship exists between permutations and combinations:

$$C(n, r) = \frac{P(n, r)}{n!} = \frac{P(n, r)}{P(r, r)}$$

Practice Questions

1. Which of the following is equivalent to the value of the digit 3 in the number 792.134?

    a. 3×10

    b. 3×100

    c. $\dfrac{3}{10}$

    d. $\dfrac{3}{100}$

2. How will the following number be written in standard form: $(1 \times 10^4) + (3 \times 10^3) + (7 \times 10^1) + (8 \times 10^0)$

    a. 137

    b. 13,078

    c. 1,378

    d. 8,731

3. How will the number 847.89632 be written if rounded to the nearest hundredth?

    a. 847.90

    b. 900

    c. 847.89

    d. 847.896

4. What is the value of the sum of $\dfrac{1}{3}$ and $\dfrac{2}{5}$?

    a. $\dfrac{3}{8}$

    b. $\dfrac{11}{15}$

    c. $\dfrac{11}{30}$

    d. $\dfrac{4}{5}$

5. What is the value of the expression: $7^2 - 3 \times (4 + 2) + 15 \div 5$?

    a. 12.2

    b. 40.2

    c. 34

    d. 58.2

6. How will $\dfrac{4}{5}$ be written as a percent?

    a. 40%

    b. 125%

    c. 90%

    d. 80%

7. If Danny takes 48 minutes to walk 3 miles, how long should it take him to walk 5 miles maintaining the same speed?

    a. 32 min

    b. 64 min

    c. 80 min

    d. 96 min

8. What are all the factors of 12?

    a. 12, 24, 36

    b. 1, 2, 4, 6, 12

    c. 12, 24, 36, 48

    d. 1, 2, 3, 4, 6, 12

9. A construction company is building a new housing development with the property of each house measuring 30 feet wide. If the length of the street is zoned off at 345 feet, how many houses can be built on the street?

    a. 11

    b. 115

    c. 11.5

    d. 12

10. How will the following algebraic expression be simplified: $(5x^2 - 3x + 4) - (2x^2 - 7)$?

    a. x^5

    b. $3x^2 - 3x + 11$

    c. $3x^2 - 3x - 3$

    d. $x - 3$

11. Kassidy drove for 3 hours at a speed of 60 miles per hour. Using the distance formula, $d = r \times t$ ($distance = rate \times time$), how far did Kassidy travel?

    a. 20 miles

    b. 180 miles

    c. 65 miles

    d. 120 miles

12. If $-3(x + 4) \geq x + 8$, what is the value of x?

    a. $x = 4$

    b. $x \geq 2$

    c. $x \geq -5$

    d. $x \leq -5$

13. Karen gets paid a weekly salary and a commission for every sale that she makes. The table below shows the number of sales and her pay for different weeks.

Sales	2	7	4	8
Pay	$380	$580	$460	$620

Which of the following equations represents Karen's weekly pay?

    a. $y = 90x + 200$
    b. $y = 90x - 200$
    c. $y = 40x + 300$
    d. $y = 40x - 300$

14. Which inequality represents the values displayed on the number line?

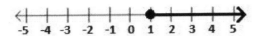

    a. $x < 1$
    b. $x \leq 1$
    c. $x > 1$
    d. $x \geq 1$

15. What is the 42nd item in the pattern: ▲ ○○□ ▲ ○○□ ▲ ...?

    a. ○
    b. ▲
    c. □
    d. None of the above

16. Which of the following statements is true about the two lines below?

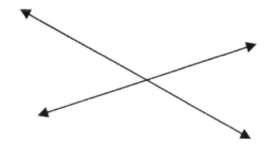

    a. The two lines are parallel but not perpendicular.
    b. The two lines are perpendicular but not parallel.
    c. The two lines are both parallel and perpendicular.
    d. The two lines are neither parallel nor perpendicular.

17. Which of the following figures is not a polygon?

    a. Decagon
    b. Cone
    c. Triangle
    d. Rhombus

18. What is the area of the regular hexagon shown below?

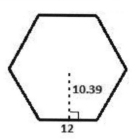

a. 72
b. 124.68
c. 374.04
d. 748.08

19. The area of a given rectangle is 24 centimeters. If the measure of each side is multiplied by 3, what is the area of the new figure?

a. 48cm
b. 72cm
c. 216cm
d. 13,824cm

20. What are the coordinates of the point plotted on the grid?

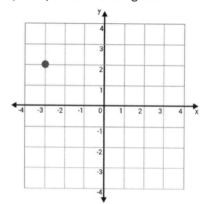

a. (-3, 2)
b. (2, -3)
c. (-3, -2)
d. (2, 3)

21. The perimeter of a 6-sided polygon is 56 cm. The length of three sides is 9 cm each. The length of two other sides is 8 cm each. What is the length of the missing side?

a. 11 cm
b. 12 cm
c. 13 cm
d. 10 cm

22. Katie works at a clothing company and sold 192 shirts over the weekend. $1/3$ of the shirts that were sold were patterned, and the rest were solid. Which mathematical expression would calculate the number of solid shirts Katie sold over the weekend?

a. $192 \times \frac{1}{3}$

b. $192 \div \frac{1}{3}$

c. $192 \times (1 - \frac{1}{3})$

d. $192 \div 3$

23. Which measure for the center of a small sample set is most affected by outliers?
   a. Mean
   b. Median
   c. Mode
   d. None of the above

24. Given the value of a given stock at monthly intervals, which graph should be used to best represent the trend of the stock?
   a. Box plot
   b. Line plot
   c. Line graph
   d. Circle graph

25. What is the probability of randomly picking the winner and runner-up from a race of 4 horses and distinguishing which is the winner?

a. $\frac{1}{4}$

b. $\frac{1}{2}$

c. $\frac{1}{16}$

d. $\frac{1}{12}$

26. In the following expression, which operation should be completed first? $5 \times 6 + 4 \div 2 - 1$.
   a. Multiplication
   b. Addition
   c. Division
   d. Subtraction

27. Which of the following is the definition of a prime number?
   a. A number that factors only into itself and one
   b. A number greater than zero that factors only into itself and one
   c. A number less than 10
   d. A number divisible by 10

28. Determine the next number in the following series: 1, 3, 6, 10, 15, 21, …
    a. 26
    b. 27
    c. 28
    d. 29

29. What of the following is the correct order of operations?
    a. Parentheses, Exponents, Multiplication, Division, Addition, Subtraction
    b. Exponents, Parentheses, Multiplication, Division, Addition, Subtraction
    c. Parentheses, Exponents, Addition, Multiplication, Division, Subtraction
    d. Parentheses, Exponents, Division, Addition, Subtraction, Multiplication

30. The perimeter of a 6-sided polygon is 56 cm. The length of three of the sides are 9 cm each. The length of two other sides are 8 cm each. What is the length of the missing side?
    a. 11 cm
    b. 12 cm
    c. 13 cm
    d. 10 cm

31. Which of the following is a mixed number?
    a. $16\frac{1}{2}$

    b. 16

    c. $\frac{16}{3}$

    d. $\frac{1}{4}$

32. If you were showing your friend how to round 245.2678 to the nearest thousandth, which place value would be used to decide whether to round up or round down?
    a. Ten-thousandth
    b. Thousandth
    c. Hundredth
    d. Thousand

33. Carey bought 184 pounds of fertilizer to use on her lawn. Each segment of her lawn required $12\frac{1}{2}$ pounds of fertilizer to do a sufficient job. If asked to determine how many segments could be fertilized with the amount purchased, what operation would be necessary to solve this problem?
    a. Multiplication
    b. Division
    c. Addition
    d. Subtraction

34. It is necessary to line up decimal places within the given numbers before performing which of the following operations?
    a. Multiplication
    b. Division
    c. Subtraction
    d. Fractions

35. Which of the following expressions best exemplifies the additive and subtractive identity?
    a. $5 + 2 - 0 = 5 + 2 + 0$
    b. $6 + x = 6 - 6$
    c. $9 - 9 = 0$
    d. $8 + 2 = 10$

36. What is an equivalent measurement for 1.3 cm?
    a. 0.13 m
    b. 0.013 m
    c. 0.13 mm
    d. 0.013 mm

37. Katie works at a clothing company and sold 192 shirts over the weekend. $\frac{1}{3}$ of the shirts that were sold were patterned, and the rest were solid. Which mathematical expression would calculate the number of solid shirts Katie sold over the weekend?
    a. $192 \times \frac{1}{3}$
    b. $192 \div \frac{1}{3}$
    c. $192 \times (1 - \frac{1}{3})$
    d. $192 \div 3$

38. Which four-sided shape is always a rectangle?
    a. Rhombus
    b. Square
    c. Parallelogram
    d. Quadrilateral

39. A rectangle was formed out of pipe cleaner. Its length was $\frac{1}{2}$ ft, and its width was $\frac{11}{2}$ inches. What is its area in square inches?
    a. $\frac{11}{4}$ inch^2
    b. $\frac{11}{2}$ inch^2
    c. 22 inch^2
    d. 33 inch^2

40. How will $\frac{4}{5}$ be written as a percent?
    a. 40 percent
    b. 125 percent
    c. 90 percent
    d. 80 percent

41. If Danny takes 48 minutes to walk 3 miles, how long should it take him to walk 5 miles maintaining the same speed?

    a. 32 min

    b. 64 min

    c. 80 min

    d. 96 min

42. Which of the following represents one hundred eighty-two million, thirty-six thousand, four hundred twenty-one and three hundred fifty-six thousandths?

    a. 182,036,421.356

    b. 182,036,421.0356

    c. 182,000,036,421.0356

    d. 182,000,036,421.356

43. A solution needs 5 ml of saline for every 8 ml of medicine given. How much saline is needed for 45 ml of medicine?

    a. $\frac{225}{8}$ ml

    b. 72 ml

    c. 28 m

    d. $\frac{45}{8}$ ml

44. What unit of volume is used to describe the following 3-dimensional shape?

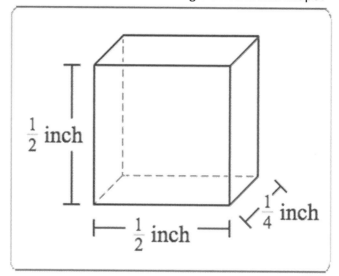

    a. Square inches

    b. Inches

    c. Cubic inches

    d. Squares

45. Which common denominator would be used in order to evaluate $\frac{2}{3} + \frac{4}{5}$?

    a. 15

    b. 3

    c. 5

    d. 10

Answer Explanations

1. D: $\frac{3}{100}$. Each digit to the left of the decimal point represents a higher multiple of 10 and each digit to the right of the decimal point represents a quotient of a higher multiple of 10 for the divisor. The first digit to the right of the decimal point is equal to the value $\div$ 10. The second digit to the right of the decimal point is equal to the value $\div$ (10×10), or the value $\div$ 100.

2. B: 13,078. The power of 10 by which a digit is multiplied corresponds with the number of zeros following the digit when expressing its value in standard form. Therefore, $(1 \times 10^4) + (3 \times 10^3) + (7 \times 10^1) + (8 \times 10^0) = 10,000 + 3,000 + 70 + 8 = 13,078$.

3. A: 847.90. The hundredth place value is located two digits to the right of the decimal point (the digit 9). The digit to the right of the place value is examined to decide whether to round up or keep the digit. In this case, the digit 6 is 5 or greater so the hundredth place is rounded up. When rounding up, if the digit to be increased is a 9, the digit to its left is increased by one and the digit in the desired place value is made a zero. Therefore, the number is rounded to 847.90.

4. B: $\frac{11}{15}$. Fractions must have like denominators to be added. The least common multiple of the denominators 3 and 5 is found. The LCM is 15, so both fractions should be changed to equivalent fractions with a denominator of 15. To determine the numerator of the new fraction, the old numerator is multiplied by the same number by which the old denominator is multiplied to obtain the new denominator. For the fraction $\frac{1}{3}$, 3 multiplied by 5 will produce 15. Therefore, the numerator is multiplied by 5 to produce the new numerator $\left(\frac{1 \times 5}{3 \times 5} = \frac{5}{15}\right)$. For the fraction $\frac{2}{5}$, multiplying both the numerator and denominator by 3 produces $\frac{6}{15}$. When fractions have like denominators, they are added by adding the numerators and keeping the denominator the same: $\frac{5}{15} + \frac{6}{15} = \frac{11}{15}$.

5. C: 34. When performing calculations consisting of more than one operation, the order of operations should be followed: *Parenthesis, Exponents, Multiplication/Division, Addition/Subtraction*. Parenthesis: $7^2 - 3 \times (4 + 2) + 15 \div 5 = 7^2 - 3 \times (6) + 15 \div 5$. Exponents: $7^2 - 3 \times 6 + 15 \div 5 = 49 - 3 \times 6 + 15 \div 5$. Multiplication/Division (from left to right): $49 - 3 \times 6 + 15 \div 5 = 49 - 18 + 3$. Addition/Subtraction (from left to right): $49 - 18 + 3 = 34$.

6. D: 80%. To convert a fraction to a percent, the fraction is first converted to a decimal. To do so, the numerator is divided by the denominator: $4 \div 5 = 0.8$. To convert a decimal to a percent, the number is multiplied by 100: $0.8 \times 100 = 80\%$.

7. C: 80 min. To solve the problem, a proportion is written consisting of ratios comparing distance and time. One way to set up the proportion is: $\frac{3}{48} = \frac{5}{x} \left(\frac{distance}{time} = \frac{distance}{time}\right)$ where x represents the unknown value of time. To solve a proportion, the ratios are cross-multiplied: $(3)(x) = (5)(48) \rightarrow 3x = 240$. The equation is solved by isolating the variable, or dividing by 3 on both sides, to produce $x = 80$.

8. D: 1, 2, 3, 4, 6, 12. A given number divides evenly by each of its factors to produce an integer (no decimals). The number 5, 7, 8, 9, 10, 11 (and their opposites) do not divide evenly into 12. Therefore, these numbers are not factors.

9. A: 11. To determine the number of houses that can fit on the street, the length of the street is divided by the width of each house: $345 \div 30 = 11.5$. Although the mathematical calculation of 11.5 is correct, this answer is not reasonable. Half of a house cannot be built, so the company will need to either build 11 or 12 houses. Since the width of 12 houses (360 feet) will extend past the length of the street, only 11 houses can be built.

10. B: $3x^2 - 3x + 11$. By distributing the implied one in front of the first set of parentheses and the -1 in front of the second set of parentheses, the parenthesis can be eliminated: $1(5x^2 - 3x + 4) - 1(2x^2 - 7) = 5x^2 - 3x + 4 - 2x^2 + 7$. Next, like terms (same variables with same exponents) are combined by adding the coefficients and keeping the variables and their powers the same: $5x^2 - 3x + 4 - 2x^2 + 7 = 3x^2 - 3x + 11$.

11. B: 180 miles. The rate, 60 miles per hour, and time, 3 hours, are given for the scenario. To determine the distance traveled, the given values for the rate (r) and time (t) are substituted into the distance formula and evaluated: $d = r \times t \rightarrow d = (60mi/h) \times (3h) \rightarrow d = 180mi$.

12. D: $x \leq -5$. When solving a linear equation or inequality:

Distribution is performed if necessary: $-3(x + 4) \rightarrow -3x - 12 \geq x + 8$. This means that any like terms on the same side of the equation/inequality are combined.

The equation/inequality is manipulated to get the variable on one side. In this case, subtracting x from both sides produces $-4x - 12 \geq 8$.

The variable is isolated using inverse operations to undo addition/subtraction. Adding 12 to both sides produces $-4x \geq 20$.

The variable is isolated using inverse operations to undo multiplication/division. Remember if dividing by a negative number, the relationship of the inequality reverses, so the sign is flipped. In this case, dividing by -4 on both sides produces $x \leq -5$.

13. C: $y = 40x + 300$. In this scenario, the variables are the number of sales and Karen's weekly pay. The weekly pay depends on the number of sales. Therefore, weekly pay is the dependent variable (y) and the number of sales is the independent variable (x). Each pair of values from the table can be written as an ordered pair (x, y): (2,380), (7,580), (4,460), (8,620). The ordered pairs can be substituted into the equations to see which creates true statements (both sides equal) for each pair. Even if one ordered pair produces equal values for a given equation, the other three ordered pairs must be checked. The only equation which is true for all four ordered pairs is $y = 40x + 300$:

$$380 = 40(2) + 300 \rightarrow 380 = 380$$

$$580 = 40(7) + 300 \rightarrow 580 = 580$$

$$460 = 40(4) + 300 \rightarrow 460 = 460$$

$$620 = 40(8) + 300 \rightarrow 620 = 620$$

14. D: $x \geq 1$. The closed dot on one indicates that the value is included in the set. The arrow pointing right indicates that numbers greater than one (numbers get larger to the right) are included in the set. Therefore, the set includes numbers greater than or equal to one, which can be written as $x \geq 1$.

15. A: o. The core of the pattern consists of 4 items: ▲oo□. Therefore, the core repeats in multiples of 4, with the pattern starting over on the next step. The closest multiple of 4 to 42 is 40. Step 40 is the end of the core (□), so step 41 will start the core over (▲) and step 42 is o.

16. D: The two lines are neither parallel nor perpendicular. Parallel lines will never intersect or meet. Therefore, the lines are not parallel. Perpendicular lines intersect to form a right angle (90°). Although the lines intersect, they do not form a right angle, which is usually indicated with a box at the intersection point. Therefore, the lines are not perpendicular.

17. B: Cone. A polygon is a closed two-dimensional figure consisting of three or more sides. A decagon is a polygon with 10 sides. A triangle is a polygon with three sides. A rhombus is a polygon with 4 sides. A cone is a three-dimensional figure and is classified as a solid.

18. C: 374.04. The formula for finding the area of a regular polygon is $A = \frac{1}{2} \times a \times P$ where a is the length of the apothem (from the center to any side at a right angle) and P is the perimeter of the figure. The apothem a is given as 10.39 and the perimeter can be found by multiplying the length of one side by the number of sides (since the polygon is regular): $P = 12 \times 6 \rightarrow P = 72$. To find the area, substitute the values for a and P into the formula $A = \frac{1}{2} \times a \times P \rightarrow A = \frac{1}{2} \times (10.39) \times (72) \rightarrow A = 374.04$.

19. C: 216cm. Because area is a two-dimensional measurement, the dimensions are multiplied by a scale that is squared to determine the scale of the corresponding areas. The dimensions of the rectangle are multiplied by a scale of 3. Therefore, the area is multiplied by a scale of 3^2 (which is equal to 9): $24cm \times 9 = 216cm$.

20. A: (-3, 2). The coordinates of a point are written as an ordered pair (x, y). To determine the x-coordinate, a line is traced directly above or below the point until reaching the x-axis. This step notes the value on the x-axis. In this case, the x-coordinate is -3. To determine the y-coordinate, a line is traced directly to the right or left of the point until reaching the y-axis, which notes the value on the y-axis. In this case, the y-coordinate is 2. Therefore, the ordered pair is written (-3, 2).

21. C: Perimeter is found by calculating the sum of all sides of the polygon. $9 + 9 + 9 + 8 + 8 + s = 56$, where s is the missing side length. Therefore, 43 plus the missing side length is equal to 56. The missing side length is 13 cm.

22. C: $\frac{1}{3}$ of the shirts sold were patterned. Therefore, $1 - \frac{1}{3} = \frac{2}{3}$ of the shirts sold were solid. Anytime "of" a quantity appears in a word problem, multiplication should be used. Therefore, $192 \times \frac{2}{3} = \frac{192 \times 2}{3} = \frac{384}{3} = 128$ solid shirts were sold. The entire expression is $192 \times \left(1 - \frac{1}{3}\right)$.

23. A: Mean. An outlier is a data value that is either far above or far below the majority of values in a sample set. The mean is the average of all the values in the set. In a small sample set, a very high or very low number could drastically change the average of the data points. Outliers will have no more of an effect on the median (the middle value when arranged from lowest to highest) than any other value above or below the median. If the same outlier does not repeat, outliers will have no effect on the mode (value that repeats most often).

24. C: Line graph. The scenario involves data consisting of two variables, month, and stock value. Box plots display data consisting of values for one variable. Therefore, a box plot is not an appropriate choice. Both line plots and circle graphs are used to display frequencies within categorical data. Neither can be used for the given scenario. Line graphs display two numerical variables on a coordinate grid and show trends among the variables.

25. D: $\frac{1}{12}$. The probability of picking the winner of the race is $\frac{1}{4}\left(\frac{number\ of\ favorable\ outcomes}{number\ of\ total\ outcomes}\right)$. Assuming the winner was picked on the first selection, three horses remain from which to choose the runner-up (these are dependent events). Therefore, the probability of picking the runner-up is $\frac{1}{3}$. To determine the probability of multiple events, the probability of each event is multiplied: $\frac{1}{4} \times \frac{1}{3} = \frac{1}{12}$.

26. A: Using the order of operations, multiplication and division are computed first from left to right. Multiplication is on the left; therefore, the teacher should perform multiplication first.

27. B: A number is prime because its only factors are itself and one. Positive numbers (greater than zero) can be prime numbers.

28. C: Each number in the sequence is adding one more than the difference between the previous two. For example, $10 - 6 = 4, 4 + 1 = 5$. Therefore, the next number after 10 is $10 + 5 = 15$. Going forward, $21 - 15 = 6, 6 + 1 = 7$. The next number is $21 + 7 = 28$. Therefore, the difference between numbers is the set of whole numbers starting at 2: 2, 3, 4, 5, 6, 7, ...

29. A: Order of operations follows PEMDAS—Parentheses, Exponents, Multiplication and Division from left to right, and Addition and Subtraction from left to right.

30. C: Perimeter is found by calculating the sum of all sides of the polygon. $9 + 9 + 9 + 8 + 8 + s = 56$, where s is the missing side length. Therefore, 43 plus the missing side length is equal to 56. The missing side length is 13 cm.

31. A: $16\frac{1}{2}$. A mixed number contains both a whole number and either a fraction or a decimal. Therefore, the mixed number is $16\frac{1}{2}$.

32. A: The place value to the right of the thousandth place, which would be the ten-thousandth place, is what gets utilized. The value in the thousandth place is 7. The number in the place value to its right is greater than 4, so the 7 gets bumped up to 8. Everything to its right turns to a zero, to get 245.2680. The zero is dropped because it is part of the decimal.

33. B: This is a division problem because the original amount needs to be split up into equal amounts. The mixed number $12\frac{1}{2}$ should be converted to an improper fraction first. $12\frac{1}{2} = (12 \times 2) + \frac{1}{2} = \frac{23}{2}$. Carey needs to determine how many times $\frac{23}{2}$ goes into 184. This is a division problem: $184 \div \frac{23}{2} = ?$ The fraction can be flipped, and the problem turns into the multiplication: $184 \times \frac{2}{23} = \frac{368}{23}$. This improper fraction can be simplified into 16 because $368 \div 23 = 16$. The answer is 16 lawn segments.

34. C: Numbers should be lined up by decimal places before subtraction is performed. This is because subtraction is performed within each place value. The other operations, such as multiplication, division, and exponents (which is a form of multiplication), involve ignoring the decimal places at first and then including them at the end.

35. A: The additive and subtractive identity is zero. When added or subtracted to any number, zero does not change the original number.

36. B: 100 cm is equal to 1 m. 1.3 divided by 100 is 0.013. Therefore, 1.3 cm is equal to 0.013 mm. Because 1 cm is equal to 10 mm, 1.3 cm is equal to 13 mm.

37. C: $\frac{1}{3}$ of the shirts sold were patterned. Therefore, $1 - \frac{1}{3} = \frac{2}{3}$ of the shirts sold were solid. Anytime "of" a quantity appears in a word problem, multiplication needs to be used. Therefore, $192 \times \frac{2}{3} = 192 \times \frac{2}{3} = \frac{384}{3} = 128$ solid shirts were sold. The entire expression is $192 \times \left(1 - \frac{1}{3}\right)$.

38. B: A rectangle is a specific type of parallelogram. It has 4 right angles. A square is a rhombus that has 4 right angles. Therefore, a square is always a rectangle because it has two sets of parallel lines and 4 right angles.

39. D: Area = length x width. The answer must be in square inches, so all values must be converted to inches. $\frac{1}{2}$ ft is equal to 6 inches. Therefore, the area of the rectangle is equal to $6 \times \frac{11}{2} = \frac{66}{2} = 33$ square inches.

40. D: 80 percent. To convert a fraction to a percent, the fraction is first converted to a decimal. To do so, the numerator is divided by the denominator: $4 \div 5 = 0.8$. To convert a decimal to a percent, the number is multiplied by 100: $0.8 \times 10 = 80\%$.

41. C: 80 min. To solve the problem, a proportion is written consisting of ratios comparing distance and time. One way to set up the proportion is: $\frac{3}{48} = \frac{5}{x} \left(\frac{distance}{time} = \frac{distance}{time}\right)$ where x represents the unknown value of time. To solve a proportion, the ratios are cross-multiplied: $(3)(x) = (5)(48) \rightarrow 3x = 240$. The equation is solved by isolating the variable, or dividing by 3 on both sides, to produce $x = 80$.

42. A: 182 is in the millions, 36 is in the thousands, 421 is in the hundreds, and 356 is the decimal.

43. A: Every 8 ml of medicine requires 5 ml. The 45 ml first needs to be split into portions of 8 ml. This results in $\frac{45}{8}$ portions. Each portion requires 5 ml. Therefore, $\frac{45}{8} \times 5 = 45 \times \frac{5}{8} = \frac{225}{8}$ ml is necessary.

44. C: Volume of this 3-dimensional figure is calculated using length x width x height. Each measure of length is in inches. Therefore, the answer would be labeled in cubic inches.

45. A: A common denominator must be found. The least common denominator is 15 because it has both 5 and 3 as factors. The fractions must be rewritten using 15 as the denominator.

Integration of Knowledge and Understanding

In mathematics open-response questions, depending on the problem, there could be one correct answer or multiple answers. Students are expected to justify all steps taken to obtain the solution and explain their work as thoroughly as possible. The answer should be organized in a clear and concise manner and meet the given word or page count. Therefore, students must spend time reading and understanding the problem before attempting any work. However, it's important to consider how much time is given for the problem before starting. In other words, work efficiently but not too slowly. The solution process and answer should use the correct mathematical operations, formulas, equations, etc. needed to solve the problem, but the work should also demonstrate a high level of knowledge and understanding of the material.

For example, if the question is to solve an equation for a given variable, an incorrect approach would be to write down the answer. A better approach would be to list every step and name every property needed for each step. This way, each step is justified. Also, checking the answer in the end does not hurt if possible. Also, if graphing or visuals apply to the problem, make sure to include them. If the problem gives excess information, explain why it isn't used. Make sure all answers are labeled with the correct units. For example, if the answer is 6 pounds, 6 would not suffice. Make sure there's enough time to read the entire solution after solving the problem, as this is important step! Make final edits that seem appropriate, and try to fix all math errors as well as spelling and punctuation errors. The people that review and grade the responses are math teachers, so make sure everything makes mathematical sense and is legible. Finally, always consider if your answer makes sense regarding the scale being used. For example, in a statistics problem, if the final answer was to list the number of people necessary to conduct a study, and the math led to a result of over a million people, something might be off. Go back and check the calculations.

Open-Response Item Assignment

Your car is running out of gas, and you pull up an app on your phone to see the gas stations with the cheapest gas within 3 miles. Gas station number 1 sells gas at $2.29 per gallon and is 2.2 miles away. Gas station number 2 sells gas at $2.24 per gallon and is 2.25 miles away. You want to fill up your tank, and you'll need 14 gallons to do so. Which gas station should you go to? How much will you save by going to one gas station versus the other?

Photo Credits

Dear MTEL General Curriculum Test Taker,

We would like to start by thanking you for purchasing this study guide for your MTEL General Curriculum exam. We hope that we exceeded your expectations.

Our goal in creating this study guide was to cover all of the topics that you will see on the test. We also strove to make our practice questions as similar as possible to what you will encounter on test day. With that being said, if you found something that you feel was not up to your standards, please send us an email and let us know.

We have study guides in a wide variety of fields. If you're interested in one, try searching for it on Amazon or send us an email.

Thanks Again and Happy Testing!
Product Development Team
info@studyguideteam.com

Interested in buying more than 10 copies of our product? Contact us about bulk discounts:

bulkorders@studyguideteam.com

FREE Test Taking Tips DVD Offer

To help us better serve you, we have developed a Test Taking Tips DVD that we would like to give you for FREE. **This DVD covers world-class test taking tips that you can use to be even more successful when you are taking your test.**

All that we ask is that you email us your feedback about your study guide. Please let us know what you thought about it – whether that is good, bad or indifferent.

To get your **FREE Test Taking Tips DVD**, email freedvd@studyguideteam.com with "FREE DVD" in the subject line and the following information in the body of the email:

a. The title of your study guide.

b. Your product rating on a scale of 1-5, with 5 being the highest rating.

c. Your feedback about the study guide. What did you think of it?

d. Your full name and shipping address to send your free DVD.

If you have any questions or concerns, please don't hesitate to contact us at freedvd@studyguideteam.com.

Thanks again!